# ZaFTIG

## The Zappa Family Trust Issues Guide

## By Edward Komara with Scott Parker

ZaFTIG: The Zappa Family Trust Issues Guide

By Edward Komara with Scott Parker

SPB Publishing
Waterbury, Connecticut, USA
Copyright © 2015 by Edward Komara and Scott Parker. All rights reserved.
The white zone is for loading and unloading only.
http://spbpublishing.webs.com

Dedication:

For Gail Zappa, Dweezil Zappa, and Scott Parker

Table of Contents

Introduction by Edward Komara                                                9

THEN OR US by Edward Komara                                                 12

FRANK ZAPPA'S HIGHLY AMBIENT DIGITAL DOMAINS
FZ's original compact disc masters: Why he did what he did. By Scott Parker    17

FRANK ZAPPA ON COMPACT DISC: A TIMELINE. By Scott Parker                    32

Catalogue (1-97)

    1. Freak Out! (1966)                                41
    2. Absolutely Free (1967)                           44
    3. Lumpy Gravy (1968)                               46
    4. We're Only In It For The Money (1968)            49
    5. Cruising With Ruben & The Jets (1968)            52
    6. Uncle Meat (1969)                                54
    7. Mothermania (1969)                               57
    8. Hot Rats (1969)                                  59
    9. Burnt Weeny Sandwich (1970)                      61
    10. Weasels Ripped My Flesh (1970)                  63
    11. Chunga's Revenge (1970)                         65
    12. Fillmore East—June 1971 (1971)                  67
    13. Frank Zappa's 200 Motels (1971)                 69
    14. Just Another Band From L.A. (1972)              72
    15. Waka/Jawaka (1972)                              74
    16. The Grand Wazoo (1972)                          76
    17. Over-Nite Sensation (1973)                      78
    18. Apostrophe (') (1974)                           80
    19. Roxy & Elsewhere (1974)                         82
    20. One Size Fits All (1975)                        84
    21. Bongo Fury (1975)                               86
    22. Zoot Allures (1976)                             88
    23. Zappa In New York (1978)                        90
    24. Studio Tan (1978)                               92
    25. Sleep Dirt (1979)                               94
    26. Sheik Yerbouti (1979)                           96
    27. Orchestral Favorites (1979)                     98
    28. Joe's Garage Act I (1979)                       100
    29. Joe's Garage Acts II & III (1979)                102
    30. Tinsel Town Rebellion (1981)                    104

| | |
|---|---|
| 31. Shut Up 'N Play Yer Guitar (1981) | 107 |
| 32. Shut Up 'N Play Yer Guitar Some More (1981) | 110 |
| 33. Return Of The Son Of Shut Up 'N Play Yer Guitar (1981) | 113 |
| 34. You Are What You Is (1981) | 115 |
| 35. Ship Arriving Too Late To Save A Drowning Witch (1982) | 118 |
| 36. The Man From Utopia (1983) | 120 |
| 37. Baby Snakes (1983) | 122 |
| 38. London Symphony Orchestra Vol. I (1983) | 124 |
| 39. Boulez conducts Zappa: The Perfect Stranger (1984) | 126 |
| 40. Them Or Us (1984) | 128 |
| 41. Thing-Fish (1984) | 130 |
| 42. Francesco Zappa (1984) | 133 |
| 43. The Old Masters Box One (1985) | 135 |
| 44. Frank Zappa Meets The Mothers Of Prevention (1985) | 136 |
| 45. Does Humor Belong In Music? (1986) | 138 |
| 46. The Old Masters Box Two (1986) | 140 |
| 47. Jazz From Hell (1986) | 142 |
| 48. London Symphony Orchestra Vol. II (1987) | 144 |
| 49. The Old Masters Box Three (1987) | 146 |
| 50. Guitar (1988) | 147 |
| 51. You Can't Do That On Stage Anymore Vol. 1 (1988) | 151 |
| 52. You Can't Do That On Stage Anymore Vol. 2 (1988) | 155 |
| 53. Broadway The Hard Way (1988) | 157 |
| 54. You Can't Do That On Stage Anymore Vol. 3 (1989) | 160 |
| 55. The Best Band You Never Heard In Your Life (1991) | 163 |
| 56. You Can't Do That On Stage Anymore Vol. 4 (1991) | 166 |
| 57. Make A Jazz Noise Here (1991) | 171 |
| 58. You Can't Do That On Stage Anymore Vol. 5 (1992) | 174 |
| 59. You Can't Do That On Stage Anymore Vol. 6 (1992) | 178 |
| 60. Playground Psychotics (1992) | 184 |
| 61. Ahead Of Their Time (1993) | 188 |
| 62. The Yellow Shark (1993) | 190 |
| 63. Civilization Phaze III (1994) | 192 |
| 64. The Lost Episodes (1996) | 195 |
| 65. Läther (1996) | 198 |
| 66. Frank Zappa Plays The Music Of Frank Zappa, a memorial tribute (1996) | 201 |
| 67. Have I Offended Someone? (1997) | 203 |
| 68. Mystery Disc (1998) | 206 |
| 69. Everything Is Healing Nicely (1999) | 210 |
| 70. FZ:OZ (2002) | 212 |
| 71. Halloween (2003) | 214 |
| 72. Joe's Corsage (2004) | 216 |
| 73. Joe's Domage (2004) | 218 |
| 74. QuAUDIOPHILIAc (2004) | 220 |
| 75. Joe's XMASage (2005) | 222 |
| 76. Imaginary Diseases (2006) | 224 |

| | |
|---|---|
| 77. The MOFO Project/Object (2006) | 226 |
| 78. The MOFO Project/Object (fazedooh) (2006) | 231 |
| 79. Trance-Fusion (2006) | 234 |
| 80. Buffalo (2007) | 237 |
| 81. The Dub Room Special! (2007) | 239 |
| 82. Wazoo (2007) | 241 |
| 83. One Shot Deal (2008) | 243 |
| 84. Joe's Menage (2008) | 246 |
| 85. The Lumpy Money Project/Object (2009) | 248 |
| 86. Philly '76 (2009) | 253 |
| 87. Greasy Love Songs (2010) | 255 |
| 88. "Congress Shall Make No Law . . . " (2010) | 257 |
| 89. Hammersmith Odeon (2010) | 259 |
| 90. Feeding The Monkies At Ma Maison (2011) | 261 |
| 91. Carnegie Hall (2011) | 262 |
| 92. Road Tapes, Venue #1 (2012) | 265 |
| 93. Understanding America (2012) | 267 |
| 94. Finer Moments (2012) | 269 |
| 95. Baby Snakes—The Compleat Soundtrack (2012) | 271 |
| 96. Road Tapes, Venue #2 (2013) | 274 |
| 97. A Token Of His Extreme Soundtrack (2013) | 276 |
| 98. Joe's Camouflage (2014) | 278 |
| 99. Roxy By Proxy (2014) | 280 |
| 100. Dance Me This (2015) | 282 |
| | |
| Name Index | 284 |
| Title and First Line Index | 292 |
| Transcription and Score Index | 339 |
| Chronological Index | 345 |
| About the Authors | 360 |

The Scott Parker Recordings of Frank Zappa series (to date):

Volume 1: Hungry Freaks, Daddy (1959-1969)

Volume 2: Strictly Genteel (1970-1971)

Volume 3: Blessed Relief (1972-1973)

Volume 4: The Hook (1973-1974)

Volume 5: The Return of Rondo Hatton (1974-1975)

The Zappa Supplement One: A Box of History and the Mud Shark Saga

Production credits:

Book ('em, Danno) design and most everything else by SP
Cover concept and photograph by EK
Proofreading by SP and EK
SPB logo "Bunny and Dog" by Kayleigh Parker

# ZaFTIG Introduction

## By Edward Komara

You may wonder about the title "ZaFTIG." I thought of it while compiling the information for this guide: for the "ZAppa Family Trust" CDs of Frank Zappa's music. Jumbling some letters in my mind, I thought of "ZaFTIG" as an acronym for "ZAppa Family Trust Issues (or, Index) Guide." The word is Yiddish and Middle German for "juicy," "succulent," and "pleasantly plump." A fitting title for this ro-bust Zappa guide!

In 2012, the Zappa Family Trust (ZFT) announced its re-acquisition and reissue of the first 63 albums that previously were licensed to Rykodisc. Meanwhile, Scott Parker had published five volumes of his Zappa discography, with another five or six volumes likely to come. To be sure, for the great majority of the albums released during Zappa's lifetime, the only visual change for listeners for the new reissues is the ZFT serial number. But for record collectors and discographers, the appearance of these serial numbers would call for an overhaul of the Zappa discographies to reflect current availability. The online discographers including the ZFT, Zappa Patio, and globalia.net have updated themselves accordingly. But what for print discographers? As one who has collected Parker's Zappa series, I would rather see him treat the rest of the Zappa legacy, than stop to revise the five volumes published to date.

There are three purposes of ZaFTIG:

1. To present a discography of the new Zappa Family Trust CDs and downloads.

2. To offer a means of identifying the songs and tracks that are often played without announcement on the internet station Zappa Radio (and on regular radio, too).

3. To serve as an overall index to the Zappa commercial albums as described in the Scott Parker series. Come the day when his series is complete, a second edition of ZaFTIG will be prepared.


This guide consists of a catalogue with indexes. The catalogue covers the 100 releases prepared through June 2015 by Frank Zappa and, since his death, the Zappa family. The order of album presentation follows the retail CD discography on the ZFT website Zappa.com. Each album entry provides details for original release date, participating musicians, song titles (composers other than Zappa where appropriate), initial announcements and first song lyrics, song durations, serial numbers for the basic releases on original labels, Rykodisc reissues, and current ZFT issues (for other domestic issues and their foreign equivalents, see the Parker book series), notated transcriptions and scores, and notes where need be about track deletions from or additions to the original LP/CD issues.

Additional comments for each recording are provided:

HERE'S THE DEAL: the historical importance and/or musical achievement of the recording.

RATINGS: from 5 stars (most accomplished) to 1 (worst). No recordings were given 1 or 2 stars, because as a guide to Zappa's music, we have to find something of musical worth, aesthetic value, or folklore. In a unique split rating, *Thing-Fish* did receive 2 and half stars and 5 stars to reflect the extreme reactions of Zappa fans to what is arguably for some people his most offensive and confrontational work. 3 or 3 and a half stars may be assigned to flawed albums that nonetheless introduced good songs to the Zappa repertory, or to CDs that are historical in nature. 4 stars means excellent, and 5 means exemplary.

DOWNLOAD THESE: Individual songs to listen to first.

Because ZaFTIG covers the ZFT CD issues, it does not describe the following recordings:

- The three Beat the Boots collections of live recordings made originally without Zappa's authorization

- audience recordings of concerts shared among Zappa fans

- commercial recordings released on 45-rpm singles before March 1966 ("Cucamonga era")

- ZFT download-only releases, such as the AAAFNRAA collections, with the exception of the "Compleat" soundtrack to the film *Baby Snakes* (ZFT no. 95)

- Video-only performances and edits

- Commercial recordings with Zappa as musician, participant, or producer not among those issued on CD by the Zappa Family Trust.

Concert recordings with transcriptions of Zappa's comments to the audiences are included in the Parker Zappa discography series.

Two of the indexes are for musicians and participants, and for titles and first lines. The Name Index will help one quickly identify recordings that have a Mother who lives in one's hometown. The Title/First Name Index will help listeners identify songs they heard off-hand and see on which albums they are available. A third index, for published transcriptions and authorized rental scores, is provided to help users match their sheet music with the proper recording.

The Chronological Index is something new and admittedly risk-taking in the field of Zappa discography. Since 1967, when Zappa incorporated an early-1960s Cucamonga-era track ("Grunion Run") into "Nasal Calliope Retentive Music" on *We're Only In It For The Money* (catalogue entry no. 4), recorded performances from the past have been bundled into collage-like compositions. I wondered what sort of historical or biographical survey emerges when the source recordings are rearranged in chronological order? The Chronological Index was drawn up to facilitate such surveys. Certainly, Zappa's evolution and growth as a composer will be suggested. But also, some concerts, at least in part, may be reconstructed from the various official Zappa releases (which offer superior sound, in contrast to the often grainy, even coarse-sounding audience recordings). Many of my observations as a cataloger are made in the essay that follows. But I should say that dating historical performances was not one of Zappa's high priorities -- his correction of dates for *You Can't Do That On Stage Anymore* volume 1 in the booklet for YCDTOSA volume 2 is his tacit admission of that. To obtain many dates of concert recordings made and used by Zappa, I have had to use several collector/researcher sites, especially the globalia.net website Information Is Not Knowledge (which offers its own useful chronology of its listings). Their efforts have been made mostly from their own private collections of concert audience recordings, documents, and ephemera. Yet few if any of these intrepid collectors/researchers have had opportunities to check their data to the documents and tapes maintained by the Zappa family. Therefore, the Chronological Index is approximate, but it may also shine some light.

Acknowledgements

Most of the compilation was done during the winter and spring of 2013, when I was on sabbatical co-writing with Greg Johnson the book *100 Books Every Blues Fan Must Own* (Lanham, MD: Rowman and Littlefield, 2014). At the end of each writing day, I opened a beer and catalogued a Zappa album.

I thank Scott Parker for providing this opportunity to prepare and publish this guide. He encouraged me to dream big while I was planning the project. Initially we thought this guide would serve the same function as those cheesy little sales booklets that Rykodisc inserted in each Zappa CD jewel case during the 1990s. The way ZaFTIG turned out, the only possible CD release it could accompany is if the Zappa Family Trust ever reissued the three Old Masters boxes. At the very least, the book you are now reading is a compatible bookend to Scott's Zappa book series. Scott provided the Differences remarks to all of the entries, and the What The Deal Is and Ratings to the first 37 albums.

I would like to give a special acknowledgement to Román García Albertos for his globalia.net website Information Is Not Knowledge <http://globalia.net/donlope/fz/index.html> (accessed 12 June 2015). If Scott has worked closely with the Zappateers for his series, then I have relied at least as much on Albertos' website for the lyrics transcriptions and the sources of chord progressions, in order to save time in compiling the catalogue. Every Zappa listener -- whether a Po-Jama Person or a serious collector -- should get to know that site and the Zappa Patio website, too <http://www.lukpac.org/~handmade/patio/> (accessed 12 June 2015).

Finally, my book dedication to Gail Zappa and Dweezil Zappa is sincere. Since Frank Zappa's death in 1993, they have succeeded admirably in providing Frank Zappa's music in the best possible sound through CD reissues and live performances. They have also supported Scott's ongoing Zappa discography. The rest of us should follow their example.

# Then Or Us: An Essay on Zappa's Legacy

## By Edward Komara

I never met Frank Zappa, and I didn't have an opportunity to attend his concerts. So, I have to call myself an armchair scholar of his music. Or to invoke the *One Size Fits All* album, I am a "sofa" scholar. Even so, for the last 30 years, I have enjoyed listening to his music. While compiling the information for ZaFTIG, I acquired some insights about Zappa's legacy of music.

I would like to begin with a few perceptions that Zappa fans had Back Then (1984) compared to Now (2015):

1. NOW: Zappa is respected. BACK THEN: Zappa was not that much respected by the general public, or considered respectable.

2. NOW: Zappa is the sole playlist for his family's Zappa Radio internet station. BACK THEN: "Valley Girl" was the sole Zappa song played on most broadcast radio stations.

3. NOW: Every one of Zappa's 100 albums is currently available. BACK THEN: Nearly every album he made through 1980 was unavailable.

4. NOW: *The Best Band You Never Heard In Your Life* (1990) is regarded by many fans as the last great Zappa album. BACK THEN: *The Grand Wazoo* (1972) was regarded by many fans as the last great Zappa album.


For me, the fourth comparison is interesting because it indicates a schism among Zappa fans that Zappa himself did not intend to cultivate. The man himself took a unified view of his creations, and since the mid-1970s he implored his fans to do the same. Here is his famous description of his "Project/Object" from his *Real Frank Zappa Book* (p.139):

"Project/Object is a term I have used to describe the overall concept of my work in various mediums. Each project (in whatever realm), or interview connected to it, is part of a larger object, for which there is no 'technical name.'

"Think of the connecting material in the Project/Object this way: A novelist invents a character. If the character is a good one, he takes on a life of his own. Why should he get to go to only one party? He could pop up anytime in a future novel.

"Or: Rembrandt got his 'look' by mixing just a little brown into every other color -- he didn't do 'red' unless it had brown in it. The brown itself wasn't especially fascinating, but the result of its obsessive inclusion was that 'look.'

"In the case of the Project/Object, you may find a little poodle over here, a little blow job over there, etc., etc. I am not obsessed by poodles or blow jobs, however; these words (and others of equal insignificance), along with pictorial images and melodic themes, recur throughout the albums, interviews, films, videos (and this book) for no other reason than to unify the 'collection.'"

But Zappa knew his older fans didn't share his unified view of all of his music, as he admitted in 1992 to interviewer Don Menn:

Menn: Do you have a sense of your audience today being the same as your original one?

Zappa: You mean, are the people who buy my records the ones who started buying them in 1964-'65?

Menn: Yeah, the Mothers of Invention crowd.

Zappa: No. I definitely know that it's not, even just referring to the letters that we receive, which are from all age groups. There's little or no communication from anybody that would fit the profile of an early MOI fanatic. There are a few of them still out there, but basically all they liked was early stuff. And that's all they bought. That was it.

(from *Zappa!* [special issue published by *Guitar Player* and *Keyboard* magazines], fall 1992, p.30)


What was the difference between these two kinds of fans? Age, obviously. In 1992, the MOI-era fan was in his late 40s or early 50s, whereas newer fans who came along after the 1982 success of "Valley Girl" were likely to be in their mid-20s. So there was a certain amount of fogeyism to be found among the older fans.

But another difference -- and this one is critical towards understanding the Project/Object -- is that the older fans had received each Zappa album one at a time, and so developed a historical sense about the albums. By contrast, the younger fans, whenever each one discovered Zappa, found a ready pile of albums that could be played in any random order. So the older fans had a good sense of "project,' and the younger ones a sense of "object." What does it take for the "project" fans to acquire a sense of object, and for the "object" fans to acquire a sense of project?

First, three observations should be made, two of them obvious. One is the style of Zappa's music through 1972 is considerably different from his style from 1973 and after. In all of the Mothers of Invention albums, the Flo-and-Eddie era albums, and the solo efforts from *Lumpy Gravy* through *The Grand Wazoo*, one hears a mixture of other composers' styles that doesn't quite blend. Zappa was adept at imitating the music of Igor Stravinsky, George Antheil, Anton Webern, Edgard Varese, Krzysztof Penderecki, John Cage, Sun Ra, Motown writers, doo-wop, bubble-gum pop, lounge music, and 1920s dance music. But an identifiable Zappa style didn't emerge just yet. But upon the creation of *Over-Nite Sensation* in 1973, the molten Zappa music begins to flow, and his influences become much less noticeable. Quite how Zappa developed his personal music so as to generate those initial songs like "Camarillo Brillo" and "Dinah-Moe Humm" has eluded every attempt to explain, even by those musicians close to the man at the time. Every fan who discovered Zappa after 1973 has accepted his post-1972 music without complaint. Those who had collected each album since *Freak Out!* (1966) thought *Over-Nite*

*Sensation* as a sell-out, as a betrayal by Zappa. Which explains why many older fans think of *The Grand Wazoo* (1972) as the last great Zappa album.

Another observation is Zappa's growing reliance during his career on live concert recordings to present new music on his records. Any casual reader of this ZaFTIG will see a gradual change from albums recorded in the recording studio to CDs of new Zappa compositions recorded during live concerts. Until soundboards came into use for rock concerts around 1969, on-location recording of rock concerts was difficult to do, because of the near-impossibility of isolating on the recording tape individual instruments. That Zappa's recordings from his winter 1969 tours with the original Mothers of Invention come out sounding as good as they do in the *You Can't Do That On Stage Anymore* series is miraculous. All of the music on the MGM-Verve Mothers of Invention albums (1966-1968) were recorded in recording studios. The first Zappa albums to combine live and studio recordings in presentations of new music were *Uncle Meat* (1969), *Burnt Weeny Sandwich* (1969) and *Weasels Ripped My Flesh* (1970), on which it was easy to distinguish the studio tracks from the live ones. Live commercial recordings of Zappa's bands through 1980 were often clearly titled as such: *Fillmore East - June 1971*, *Roxy and Elsewhere* and *Zappa in New York*, for example. *Them or Us* (1984) may be the first to combine studio and live recordings with few aural differences between them. For an older generation accustomed to double-live rock albums like, heh, Peter Frampton's *Frampton Comes Alive* (1976), Zappa's increasing use of live recordings to present his latest music, instead of raw renditions of past "greatest hits," is a trifle dis-concert-ing. In hindsight of his dissolution of his last touring band in 1988 and of his 1993 death, if Zappa had waited to finish a tour to record his new material, it is arguable that we would have had four or five fewer albums of his new compositions on CD. Because of his increasing practice of using recordings from live concerts, his few all-studio albums from the 1980s merit renewed attention, especially *You Are What You Is* (1980), *Ship Arriving Too Late To Save A Drowning Witch* (1981), *Thing-Fish* (1984), and *Frank Zappa Meets The Mothers of Prevention* (1985).

A third observation is that the old-fashioned way of recording music was either live in one take, or sequentially by recording a new musical layer while listening to the existing tape, but Zappa's new-fashioned way was taking two existing performances and mashing them together. The old-fashioned way is how studio recordings have always been made. Zappa called his new-fashioned way "xenochrony," and he defined it as a "result of two musicians, who were never in the same room at the same time, playing at two different rates in two different moods for two different purposes, when blended together, yielding a third result which is musical and synchronizes in a strange way." For xenochrony to be convincing, the sound sources would have be absolutely clear and have no tape hiss or extraneous background noise. Some analysts have detected some examples of xenochrony on Zappa's albums as early as *Lumpy Gravy* and *We're Only In It For The Money* (both 1967). Examples of this technique – which Zappa would continue to toy with for the remainder of his life – include the track "Rubber Shirt" from the 1979 album *Sheik Yerbouti*, and every guitar solo heard across all three "acts" of the 1979 album *Joe's Garage*, apart from the transcendent "Watermelon In Easter Hay".

Another "mashup" technique that Zappa regularly employed was the cross-editing of different live concert tapes together to achieve a single, perfect performance. When soundboards and multi-microphone setups came into wide use for concerts, and when individual instruments on a live tape could be isolated, Zappa began assembling completed master tracks from various performances recorded live on a stage instead of in a studio. With this technique, Zappa utilized each separate performance as a "take," the best part or parts of which which could be edited to the best part or parts of other live "takes" in order to create a master devoid of the flaws that inevitably creep in during live performances (or, as Zappa described them, the "human element"). In order to increase the ease of achieving perfection by assembling a track from a selection of live concert tapes, Zappa would have to make sure that his touring bands (particularly those of the 1980s) were performing a given composition with the least variation of tempo from night to night. That need for consistency results in performances that may seem clinical and cool to the older Mothers of Invention fans, who in the 1960s had often heard Zappa and his band members performing in the full heat of improvisation. The CD releases of music by the 1988 touring band, especially *Broadway The Hard Way* (no. 53), *The Best Band You Never Heard In Your Life* (no.55), and *Make A Jazz Noise Here* (no. 57) were arguably the finest results of Zappa's obsessive cross-editing, as detailed in the multiple recording dates and locations in the ZaFTIG entries (courtesy of the Information Is Not Knowledge website acknowledged in the introduction).

The Project approach may be described as historical, chronological, and sequential. The older fans of Zappa are quite likely to be Project-oriented, collecting the records (whether LP or CD) for ownership, and noting which songs appear for the first times on which albums. Many fans of this type are more likely to prefer the original version of "Brown Shoes Don't Make It" on *Absolutely Free* (1966) to the live 1980 concert recording released on *Tinsel Town Rebellion* (1981). Also, when listening to the album *Thing-Fish*, they bothered as much by the re-use of previously released songs like "No Not Now" as they are by the corrosive dramatic content. In sum, the "Project" takes very much a timely approach, with each album occupying what older fans deem its proper place in the Zappa legacy.

I admit to having been a former Project person. Two reasons for having been one is partly due to my historical frame of mind (I am a scholar of music history), and partly due to my collecting of Zappa's music since 1987, when he had released 48 albums, about 30 of which were out-of-print. Early on, I had sought the Mothers of Invention era albums (1966-1970) which were hard to find. Once I found them, I made cassette tape copies to play. These early albums were most of the Zappa that I had initially, so I came to know them very well. Later, on a tip from a college friend, I bought an impressive collection of Zappa LPs from 1966 through 1980. I relied on those for many years. The more I increased my familiarity of his music, the more I did so chronologically. As for the CDs, I purchased those only sparingly to fill gaps among the few albums I lacked. Had I become a Zappa fan in 1995, when the albums he made during his lifetime were reissued at once by Rykodisc, perhaps I could have been more likely to acquire all of the CDs, then listen to them in random order without much thought as to which music came first.

Such randomness is an indication of the Object approach. It may be said to be nonhistorical and hence postmodern in attitude. The recent fans of Zappa are less concerned with owning the records and more with having access to the music. Such access may be through digital downloads or the Zappa Radio internet service. The Object person may be less likely than a Project person to listen through a whole album from start to finish. Rather, they may jump from one era to another, perhaps a song from the 1988 tour, then one from 1975, to one from *Joe's Garage* or *Sheik Yerbouti*. What Object people may lack in consideration of albums as context, they stand to gain in making new and wide connections in Zappa's legacy. So when listening to

*Thing-Fish*, they may not be aware of the re-use of previously released songs, or be bothered such instances were pointed out to them. For their part, the "Object" takes the Zappa oeuvre as one large static timeless pile of music, with each track serving merely as a stepping stone or lead-in to the next Zappa song to be played.

So, in order to handle the project as object, the Zappa listener should stop preferring the earliest versions of a song as the best versions. On the other hand, perhaps the most helpful way for new Zappa fans to appreciate the object as project is to recognize that every song has an album context, because Zappa released very few songs as singles. Once this balance is attained, the listener is in a good position to derive the most enjoyment from Zappa's music -- even those that seem the most derivative to the Project people.

# FRANK ZAPPA'S HIGHLY AMBIENT DIGITAL DOMAINS

**FZ's original compact disc masters: Why he did what he did.**

By Scott Parker (with thanks to Joe Travers)

In a 1983 proposal, Frank Zappa put forth the concept of a medium which would deliver music digitally to consumers. At the time, vinyl ruled the music delivery landscape, and for all the benefits that this medium had to offer (which, viewed from a contemporary perspective, include large cover art and liner notes and a track layout – including the division of tracks into "sides" – carefully designed by the artist), it also had a number of drawbacks germaine to the medium. This included the possibility of poorly-pressed vinyl, and the fact that the album would in any case wear after a number of plays, introducing pops, clicks and other sonic issues which would clutter the sonic landscape and detract from the listening experience. The proposal that FZ came up with was relatively simple in concept – a service which would digitally deliver music to the great buying public via a fiberoptic telephone line. The music would then be archived by the consumer onto a digital tape recorder, Beta Hi-Fi tape or, with the use of a digital-to-analog converter, standard cassette tape. The proposal was the prototype for modern digital downloading, but was not acted upon at the time.

By the time FZ had drafted this proposal however, a more immediately feasible solution to the problems inherent in the vinyl medium had been unveiled. This was the compact disc, a 4.75" aluminum disc which would allow up to 74 minutes of music to be stored digitally, for playback on a specially designed machine which would read the digital information with a laser. This format immediately gained traction as it instantly eliminated the issue of pops and clicks interfering with the listening experience and allowed larger amounts of music to be heard in one go without having to flip over the record halfway through. The first commercially released compact disc, Billy Joel's 1978 album *52nd Street*, was issued in 1982 by CBS Records.

Frank Zappa was, to put it very mildly, something of an audiophile. It is not overstating the point to suggest that his life revolved around achieving the ultimate in sound quality for his vast album catalog. He was frequently appalled at the limitation of the vinyl medium, particularly where it came to his earliest releases on the Verve label, where he felt that the gobs of compression added during the mastering removed the carefully-plotted dynamics from the recordings. Consequently, when the opportunity to issue his albums in the new CD format came along, Frank jumped at it.

However – and somewhat inevitably – FZ could not release his albums on CD in the "as is" state in which they had been presented on vinyl. The reasons for this were varied and complex. One pressing issue was the fact that some of the original master tapes were damaged, due either to poor storage, analog tape formulations which degraded over time or both. Some original master tapes were already unusable due to these issues and would require careful rebuilding before they could be issued on CD.

Another issue was FZ's constant drive to re-invent his own work. Over the years, concert audiences were regularly treated to radically different arrangements of classic Zappa material, tailored specifically for the band lineup FZ working with at the time. So it should come as absolutely no surprise that when the time came for FZ to prepare his back catalog for CD release, he chose to, in some cases, substantially rework them.

But why? The logic is relatively simple – FZ's intention was to create CD masters that were different enough from the original vinyl albums to give fans who already owned the albums a reason to buy them again on CD. He therefore worked under the assumption that the original mixes of those albums were already available on vinyl for anyone who would want to hear them. While it may appear that FZ was exploiting his fans financially by forcing them to buy product they already had by making it slightly different, it would seem more likely that he felt he was improving the albums substantially by reworking them. There is no doubt that, by the time the final CD masters of the albums he would work on were completed before his death in 1993, he considered the CD versions to be the definitive representations of those albums.

The first Frank Zappa CD to see release came in mid-1985, when EMI issued *Boulez Conducts Zappa – The Perfect Stranger*, an album of FZ's "serious" musical pieces that he had released on vinyl the previous year. The nature of the work made it an ideal candidate for CD release, and indeed it was a wonderful listening experience, taken from the the digital master tape used for the vinyl LP. This was followed in January 1986 by *Does Humor Belong In Music?*, the first Frank Zappa album created specifically for the CD format. At nearly 62 minutes, FZ was able to do something with this album that previously he had only dreamed about – creating an extended listening experience, with each song segueing into the next without breaks. Despite the relative newness of the technology, the CD was successful (despite the fact that it was not issued in the US at the time, another first for a Zappa album).

By mid-1985, FZ was busy at his U.M.R.K. home studio preparing his back catalog titles for compact disc release. In February of 1986 he signed a deal with the new American independent, CD-only label, Rykodisc. The parameters of the contract stipulated that he would deliver 24 titles to Ryko within a 3-year time period. In August 1986, the first batch of Zappa titles was issued by Ryko. This batch included *The Grand Wazoo*, *London Symphony Orchestra* and two "two-fer" sets featuring two albums on a single disc, *We're Only In It For The Money/Lumpy Gravy* and *Apostrophe (')/Over-Nite Sensation*. In September 1986, a second batch appeared including *Frank Zappa Meets The Mothers Of Prevention*, *Thing-Fish* and *Shut Up 'N Play Yer Guitar*. For these releases, FZ generally reworked or altered the original vinyl presentations of the albums, with an eye toward creating a "different" or "alternate" product that would make the original vinyl albums largely obsolete and make the CDs desirable even to those who had bought the titles previously on vinyl. For *The Grand Wazoo*, *We're Only In It For The Money*, *Lumpy Gravy*, *Apostrophe (')* and *Over-Nite Sensation*, FZ used the same versions found in the 1985/1986 *Old Masters* box sets. These were subjected to alterations both major (new bass and drum overdubs on *We're Only In It For The Money*) and minor (the application of digital reverb to several of the albums). While both *Over-Nite Sensation* and *Them Or Us* used the standard vinyl LP mixes, the discs themselves suffered from poor mastering which resulted in a quiet, almost lifeless sound and feel. In considering the generally poor (compared to modern audiophile standards) mastering of these earliest Zappa CDs, it is important to remember that the technology was still in its relative infancy at this point, and that much had yet to be learned where it came to taking full advantage of the CD format and its increased dynamic range and sonic capabilities.

Compounding these limitations was the fact that FZ would often sprinkle a generous amount of digital reverb onto the tracks, a procedure which covered up flaws in the master tapes (which had deteriorated over time) and which also gave the more "dry"-sounding albums some added life (in FZ's view).

*The Grand Wazoo* was treated to some digital reverb and given a poor mastering treatment, evidenced by a distinct lack of high end. *Lumpy Gravy* managed to cut out two notes of bass guitar, but was otherwise faithful to the original vinyl LP (if again rather poorly mastered). *London Symphony Orchestra* was a new construction designed to take advantage of the CD's increased running time. For this release, FZ dropped "Pedro's Dowry" and "Envelopes" while adding "Bogus Pomp," an extended piece consisting predominantly of themes taken from FZ's 1970/1971 project *200 Motels*. All of these tracks were given a fresh mix and slathered with digital reverb. *Shut Up 'N Play Yer Guitar* presented the original three albums in that series in full across 2 CDs, but again suffered from poor mastering. *Thing-Fish* was reworked with the end of each vinyl LP side replaced by crossfades; FZ also used an alternate take of one track. Finally, the recent *Frank Zappa Meets The Mothers Of Prevention* album featured all of the tracks present on the US-only vinyl LP and it added two of the three tracks that had appeared on the European-only version of the album.

The next Zappa album to see release on CD was *Jazz From Hell*, a new studio album which had been issued on vinyl on November 15, 1986. Ryko issued the CD version in February 1987, and this time it matched the content of the vinyl LP exactly (apart from a miniscule cut-off of the very first beat of the opening track "Night School" which would be corrected on subsequent issues of this title). From here, all went quiet on the digital front for a while as FZ began making plans for what would would become his Broadway The Hard Way tour, which would kick off the following year. In the midst of tour rehearsals, five catalog titles were issued by Ryko in the fall of 1987. The first of these, issued in September, was the 1979 *Joe's Garage* album, which combined all three "acts" released on two separate vinyl released onto two CDs. Apart from the re-titling of a couple of tracks, there were no major changes made to the musical content by FZ. The next batch of Ryko reissues, released in October 1987, included the first FZ/Mothers Of Invention album *Freak Out!*, which featured digital remixes on some tracks and EQ/digital reverb applied to the remainder of the album. *Cruising With Ruben & The Jets* utilized the overdubbed master (new bass and drums) that had originally seen issue in the 1985 *Old Masters* Box One vinyl set. However, whereas that set featured a version of the closing track "Stuff Up The Cracks" that was devoid of overdubs (as the original multitrack tape could not be found at the time), the CD has this track remixed (though still not overdubbed), with saxophone parts not heard previously.

The 1969 album *Uncle Meat* was issued as an expanded 2-CD set, owing primarily to the fact that the original 2-LP's worth of material, which ran to nearly 76 minutes, would not have fitted onto a single CD at that time (maximum running time being 74 minutes in that era of CD mastering; it would eventually expand to as much as 80 minutes). To fill out the second CD, rather than dig through his archives for unreleased material from the original album sessions, FZ included 46 minutes of bonus material in the form of audio excerpts from his recently-completed *Uncle Meat* movie, which had largely been filmed in 1970. The album itself was again subjected to digital EQ and reverb. A single track, "Mr. Green Genes," was remixed and lost much of its previously-prominent organ track. There was a practical reason for these digital enhancements, as the original edit master for the album was damaged. Instead of attempting to fix this by patching in bits from a safety copy, FZ drowned the damaged sections in varying amounts of digital reverb. This smoke-and-mirrors technique was employed by FZ in the creation of several of these early digital issues, primarily to disguise problems with the analog master tapes.

The last of the October 1987 CD reissues was the much-loved *Hot Rats* album, originally released in 1969. This was a thorough remix from the original multitrack tapes, with beautifully increased clarity and an extended version of "The Gumbo Variations." Unlike many of FZ's CD remixes, this one was indeed quite warmly received by fans and was an example of what could be done for these catalog titles in the CD format.

Since the Ryko titles were easily available in America only at the time, FZ's European distributors EMI released several titles on CD late in the year. Two of these were "two-fer" CDs, one containing *Jazz From Hell* coupled with *Frank Zappa Meets The Mothers Of Prevention* and the other featuring *Ship Arriving Too Late To Save A Drowning Witch* coupled with *The Man From Utopia*. The remaining titles included *You Are What You Is*, *Sheik Yerbouti*, *Tinsel Town Rebellion*, *Joe's Garage Acts I, II & III*, *Shut Up 'N Play Yer Guitar* and *Thing-Fish*. These titles were not approved by FZ, and were sourced from the stereo sub-masters used for each album's respective vinyl releases (apart from *The Man From Utopia*, which includes a version of "Moggio" that was remixed by FZ).

May 1988 saw the release of two new Zappa titles, both issued by Ryko. *You Can't Do That On Stage Anymore* Vol. 1 was the first installment in what proved to be a massive set of live performances spanning the entirety of FZ's career as a live act from 1966 through 1988. Each volume would be a packed-to-the-rafters 2-CD set, with most of these zig-zagging back and forth through eras and band lineups in order to give the impression that all of these musicians are somehow performing at the same imaginary show. This first volume contained material recorded from 1969 through 1984. The second new FZ release was *Guitar*, a 2-CD follow-up to the popular 1981 *Shut Up 'N Play Yer Guitar* albums containing a number of Zappa guitar solos recorded from 1979 through 1984 (this last title was also released on vinyl in an edited form, with several tracks missing). *You Can't Do That On Stage Anymore* Vol. 2 – *The Helsinki Concert* was released on October 25, 1988, another double CD set containing a complete concert as performed in Helsinki, Finland in 1974.

On November 22, 1988, FZ released his 1983 vinyl picture disc soundtrack to his 1979 film *Baby Snakes* on CD for the first time. This was released on FZ's own Barking Pumpkin label, under a new distribution deal with Capitol Records. This release was the same (albeit without the break between "sides" necessitated by vinyl) as the second pressing of the vinyl release (the earliest vinyl pressings featured a different mix). January 1989 saw the release of three more Zappa catalog titles through Rykodisc. *Absolutely Free*, *Waka/Jawaka* and *One Size Fits All* were all given the standard FZ digital reverb treatment, while FZ added bonus material to *Absolutely Free* in the form of both sides of a 1967 Mothers Of Invention single, "Big Leg Emma" and "Why Don'tcha Do Me Right?" May 1989 would see the release of FZ's October 1988 vinyl release *Broadway The Hard Way* on CD, in an expanded form. This release contained performances culled from FZ's final "rock" tour in 1988. The original 1988 vinyl release of this album would be the last FZ would issue initially in the vinyl format; all new releases would now be on CD only. This was accompanied in the same month by the first CD issue of 1975's *Bongo*

*Fury* album; this one featured yet more digital reverb, odd EQ and stereo processing which gave it a rather poor sound quality. November 1989 saw the *Stage* series reach the halfway point with the release of *You Can't Do That On Stage Anymore* Vol. 3, a double-disc set featuring performances spanning the years 1971 through 1984.

The next massive release of Zappa back-catalog items came in May 1990. Previous catalog title remasters had generally been treated to some sort of digital tweaking by FZ; this procedure reached its apex with this batch of eight titles. While some of the albums, namely *Chunga's Revenge, Just Another Band From LA, Zoot Allures* and *Tinsel Town Rebellion*, did not add or remove material as compared to the original vinyl releases, other titles featured major changes – often to the detriment of the album as a whole. The exception to this was the 1970 *Weasels Ripped My Flesh* album, which included an extended version of the opening track "Didja Get Any Onya?" including material from a previously unreleased song, "Kung Fu," recorded in 1969. On the negative side, the *Fillmore East – June 1971* album was edited to remove "Willie The Pimp, Part Two" which gave FZ the ability to present the album in a single non-stop sequence without the side break that including that track would necessitate (as the two "Willie The Pimp" solos heard on the original album were not taken from a single, continuous performance).

The popular 1979 album *Sheik Yerbouti* was reedited to excise a portion of the track "I'm So Cute," allegedly to enable FZ to fit the entire album onto a single CD (although EMI had previously issued this album in unedited form on a single disc). Similarly, the 1981 album *You Are What You Is* removed the guitar solo from the track "Dumb All Over," allegedly because FZ no longer liked it. Making things worse, all of the titles were run through various digital effects, including adding gain, compression, stereo expansion (which contained a noise gate that constantly went on and off depending on the loudness of the material being processed), EQ and reverb. In this case of all eight of these titles, this "re-tweezing" was spectacularly heavy-handed on the part of engineer Bob Stone and FZ himself, resulting in dropouts and an overall poor sound to the albums. These May 1990 CD releases have come to be known as the "bad batch," and resulted in collectors going back to their old vinyl albums in order to hear the music as it was originally intended to be heard.

After an 18-month wait (during which FZ was diagnosed with inoperable prostate cancer and began a lengthy battle with that disease), new material finally made its way to the public in April 1991. *The Best Band You Never Heard In Your Life* was a double-CD set, issued through FZ's Barking Pumpkin label, of material from the 1988 Broadway The Hard Way tour. It was joined in June 1991 by two more double-CD sets: *Make A Jazz Noise Here* featured more material from the 1988 tour, while *You Can't Do That On Stage Anymore* Vol. 4 (issued by Ryko) continued that series with live material spanning the years 1969 through 1988.

It would be another year before the next batch of reissues would hit the market. June 1991 brought us, in the first release of a "catalog" CD title through Barking Pumpkin, the 1992 album *Ship Arriving Too Late To Save A Drowning Witch*. In this case, the CD version matched the vinyl exactly and even included a nifty new photo of FZ and his daughter Moon on the back insert.

September 24, 1991 was the street date for the first CD issues of three of the so-called "ugly albums" – *Studio Tan*, *Sleep Dirt* and *Orchestral Favorites* – that had been assembled by FZ in 1977 to satisfy his contract with Warner Brothers. The albums were delivered to the label at that time without artwork or liner notes, and were issued by Warners in 1978 and 1979 with artwork by artist Gary Panter. FZ encouraged fans not to purchase these albums, hoping that the majority of the material could be issued in a box set he had prepared (also in 1977) titled *Läther*. FZ eventually accepted these titles as part of his core catalog, and issued them on CD through Barking Pumpkin (FZ having fallen out with the Ryko label, initially over the use of an non-retouched photo of FZ used in their *Sheik Yerbouti* artwork) complete with their "ugly" artwork.

The heavy-handed tweaking evident in the last batch of CD reissues was absent here, although the material was certainly worked over. *Studio Tan* featured a remix of "The Adventures Of Greggery Peccary" while *Orchestral Favorites* had EQ work done to it and also had its stereo channels reversed. *Sleep Dirt* was almost a different album – several of the previously-instrumental tracks ("Flambay," "Spider Of Destiny," "Time Is Money") were given new vocal overdubs by Thana Harris (wife of onetime Zappa keyboardist-vocalist Bob Harris). In addition, small sections of "Flambay" and "Spider Of Destiny" were edited out (the second Barking Pumpkin pressing of this CD went even further, with Chester Thompson's drum work on "Regyptian Strut" replaced by a Chad Wackerman overdub).

A month later in October 1991, the "ugly album" reissues were completed with the release, again through Barking Pumpkin, of *Zappa In New York*. This album was also radically changed, expanded to 2 CDs (the original double LP would have fit onto a single disc) with lots of new material added and a fresh mix applied to all of the tracks. Again, this was an example of how this catalog material should always have been handled. This release was accompanied by the last of the original Mothers Of Invention albums to be issued on CD, 1970's *Burnt Weeny Sandwich*. This reissued the musical content of the vinyl LP, though with digital reverb added and using a second-generation copy of the master tape which featured a glitch (owing to a splice held together with sticky tape) at the start of "Little House I Used To Live In."

A few more catalog titles dribbled out to the public in 1992, all under the auspices of Zappa's Barking Pumpkin label. February brought the long-awaited release of the 1974 classic *Roxy & Elsewhere*, containing the complete double album on a single CD. This was released at the same time in Europe via the Zappa Records label (as had a number of back-catalog CDs over the previous two years), though unlike the Zappa Records issue, the second pressing of the Barking Pumpkin disc replaced the original vinyl mix of "Cheepnis" with a newly-created remix (for no stated reason). The rest of the disc retained the original vinyl mix (as had the first Barking Pumpkin pressing and the Zappa Records issue), and sounded great to boot.

April 1992 saw the release of the 1984 *Francesco Zappa* album (containing compositions written by Italian composer Francesco Zappa in the 18th Century, "performed" by FZ's Synclavier), and the same month brought a reissue of *Boulez Conducts Zappa – The Perfect Stranger*, which had been the first Zappa CD ever issued back in 1985. This new edition featured a fresh remix of the entire album, and actually sounded far superior to the original 1985 EMI CD master. The remainder of 1992's release schedule was devoted to new albums. The fifth and sixth installments of the *You Can't Do That On Stage Anymore* series were issued as double-disc sets in July; the former featured a disc from the original 1960s-era Mothers Of Invention, while the latter spanned 1970 through 1988 to give us a collection of FZ's more "controversial" material. These two titles were both issued through Rykodisc, the final Zappa albums issued under the original deal with that company. November 1992 gave fans another new release with *Playground Psychotics*, an album of material from the 1970-1971 "Vaudeville" incarnation of The Mothers, issued by Barking Pumpkin.

The final CD release of old catalog material to be issued during FZ's lifetime was the 1983 album *The Man From Utopia*, which had been released on CD several years previously by EMI. Issued by Barking Pumpkin in January 1993, this new version was remixed and expanded, including a new bonus track in the form of "Luigi & The Wise Guys." With the back catalog now issued to FZ's satisfaction (barring the 1969 *Mothermania* compilation, which he apparently saw no need to reissue in the digital domain), the remainder of 1993 was devoted to the release of two much-anticipated new albums, both again released by Barking Pumpkin Records. The first, *Ahead Of Their Time*, was an album featuring performances of the original Mothers Of Invention, live on stage at the Royal Festival Hall in London in October 1968. On November 2, 1993, Frank Zappa released what was to be the final album issued during his lifetime, *The Yellow Shark*. This album contained material performed in Germany by the classical group Ensemble Modern during a brief tour there in 1992; these would be Frank Zappa's final live performances (although his presence extended to a bit of conducting only; he would not play guitar at these shows). The album was an unexpected hit, reaching an astonishing #2 on Billboard magazine's Top Classical Crossover chart. This long-overdue success no doubt gave Frank Zappa a measure of satisfaction in the final weeks of his life; he finally succumbed to cancer on December 4, 1993.

By the time of FZ's passing, the basics of a deal had already been worked out that would reissue the Zappa back catalog on CD once again. Although rumors of a deal with Rhino Records (who had distributed FZ's two Beat The Boots box sets of bootleg material in 1991 and 1992 and who had also distributed *The Yellow Shark*) were rife for a while, the deal eventually went to Rykodisc, who acquired the rights to the catalog for what was said to be a sum of money large enough that the company had to restructure itself in order to facilitate payment to the Zappa Family Trust, the entity (headed by FZ's wife Gail) set up to protect the interests of the Composer in terms of copyright and other issues, as well as being responsible for the issuing of new archival projects. The first of these projects to be issued, in December 1994, was *Civilization Phaze III*, an album of serious music pieces (performed by FZ's Synclavier and Ensemble Modern) that FZ considered to be his definitive statement as a composer, and which he was working on right up to the final months of his life. This was the first album to be issued by a revamped Barking Pumpkin label, available exclusively by mail order.

May 1995 saw the release of a massive number of FZ back catalog CD reissues, These consisted of "FZ-approved masters"; that is, masters that FZ found acceptable to reissue, as health issues meant that little additional work was done to the material. On the plus side, the artwork for the reissue series was much upgraded. On the downside, many of the issues that had plagued the first run of CDs (primarily those issued via Ryko in the 1980s) were left uncorrected. 1995 Zappa CD masters that remained essentially unchanged from their earlier pressings include *Freak Out!*, *Absolutely Free, Cruising With Ruben & The Jets, Uncle Meat, Hot Rats, Burnt Weeny Sandwich, Weasels Ripped My Flesh, Chunga's Revenge, Fillmore East – June 1971, Just Another Band From LA, Waka/Jawaka, Roxy & Elsewhere* (same as second Barking Pumpkin pressing, including "Cheepnis" remix), *One Size Fits All, Bongo Fury, Zoot Allures, Zappa In New York, Studio Tan, Sleep Dirt, Sheik Yerbouti, Joe's Garage Acts I, II & III, Tinsel Town Rebellion, You Are What You Is, Ship Arriving Too Late To Save A Drowning Witch, The Man From Utopia, Baby Snakes, Boulez Conducts Zappa: The Perfect Stranger* (this one uses the 1992 remix), *Them Or Us, Francesco Zappa, Jazz From Hell, Guitar,* all six volumes of the *You Can't Do That On Stage Anymore* series, *Broadway The Hard Way, Make A Jazz Noise Here, Playground Psychotics, Ahead Of Their Time* and *The Yellow Shark*.

There were, however, some improvements made to select titles. *The Grand Wazoo* had been reissued by Zappa Records in Europe in 1990, and featured greater clarity than the 1986 Ryko disc. This master was used for the 1995 reissue. *Thing-Fish* had also been reissued by Zappa Records in 1990, and featured a number of alternate mixes/edits of tracks ("Prologue," "Galoot Up-Date," "You Are What You Is," "Harry-As-A-Boy," "He's So Gay," "The White Boy Troubles," "Wistful With A Fist-Full") that were carried over to the 1995 master. *We're Only In It For The Money* was separated from *Lumpy Gravy* and issued as two separate discs. For the former, FZ bowed to fan demand and issued the original 1968 mix of the album in a form identical to the original vinyl presentation. *Lumpy Gravy* benefitted from a new-and-improved master with far superior sound quality (even if the mix briefly lapsed into mono at one point), and was now broken up into a number of individual "tracks" by FZ.

*Over-Nite Sensation* and *Apostrophe (')* were similarly issued as two separate discs for the first time. Both had EQ work applied to them and also had their volumes increased compared to the 1986 Ryko CD; *Apostrophe (')* matched the version that Zappa Records had issued in Europe in 1990 (described on that issue as a "U.M.R.K. Remix") and had less digital reverb as well. *Shut Up 'N Play Yer Guitar* was issued as a box set with 3 CDs, in a format similar to the 1982 vinyl box set. This was a noticeable upgrade soundwise from the previous 2-CD issue, and matched the original vinyl apart from a segue inserted between "Why Johnny Can't Read" and "Stucco Homes." *The London Symphony Orchestra* album was issued as a greatly-expanded 2-CD set containing all of the material from the two vinyl albums issued from these sessions, all with a fresh digital remix.

*Them Or Us* featured an extended version of the title track, but also suffered from audio issues similar to those of the infamous 1990 "bad batch" of Ryko-issued CDs. *Frank Zappa Meets The Mothers Of Prevention* was expanded to include all of the material from the US and European vinyl versions of that album. Finally, *Does Humor Belong In Music?* was finally given its first release in the US, complete with a superior digital remix and excellent new artwork by longtime Zappa artist Cal Schenkel. Similarly, *The Best Band You Never Heard In Your Life* had new Schenkel artwork, after a dispute arose with the photographer who took the photo on the original CD cover.

Under the terms of the new deal with Ryko, that label got to release a few new (or new to CD) projects as well. To promote the spring 1995 CD issues, a "best of" compilation titled *Strictly Commercial* was released in August, containing a few rarities (such as the single edits of "Don't Eat The Yellow Snow," "Joe's Garage," and "Montana") which varied depending on the country of issue. The first album of "new" music issued by Ryko appeared in February 1996 with the release of *The Lost Episodes*, an album of outtakes and historically-interesting material (spanning the years 1959 through 1980) assembled by FZ. September 1996 saw the long-awaited release of the *Läther* album, which FZ had originally hoped to issue in 1977 but was prevented from doing so by his ongoing legal troubles with Warner Brothers. Issued as a 3-CD set, this included the complete project plus a few bonus selections assembled by engineer Spencer Chrislu from tapes found in the Zappa Vault by Joe Travers. One of these bonus tracks, a second version of "Regyptian Strut," was remixed by Chrislu. Another new album was released by Barking Pumpkin (mail order only) on October 31, 1996. This was *Frank Zappa Plays The Music Of Frank Zappa – A Memorial Tribute*, an album of guitar solos (some previously unissued) compiled by FZ's eldest son, musician/all around good guy Dweezil Zappa.

In April 1997, Ryko released *Have I Offended Someone?*, an album of FZ's more controversial songs compiled by the Composer himself, most of which had been remixed (as well as including an unreleased live version of "Dumb All Over"). The final "new" Rykodisc release of a Frank Zappa album landed in stores with the September 1998 release of *Mystery Disc*, a single CD containing both of the *Mystery Disc* compilations originally issued with the 1985/1986 *Old Masters* vinyl box sets. Around this time, Ryko was given new masters of the *Tinsel Town Rebellion* and *You Are What You Is* albums to issue, which had been re-transferred by Spencer Chrislu and featured not only far superior sound quality, but also an extended (though still not complete) version of "Dumb All Over" on the latter album. Ryko also issued "Au20 Gold Disc" CDs of *Apostrophe (')* and *One Size Fits All*, which were essentially flat transfers of the original vinyl mixes. All subsequent issues of "new" Frank Zappa material would be released by the Zappa Family Trust itself, via mail order through its Barking Pumpkin, Zappa Records and Vaulternative Records labels.

## THE 2012 ZFT/UNIVERSAL CD REMASTER PROJECT
**A look inside the restoration of Frank Zappa's catalog**

For the next 14 years following the release of Ryko's issue of *Mystery Disc*, the majority of Frank Zappa's catalog remained available through Rykodisc, and no attempts were made after 1998 to fix or improve that company's collection of issue-prone CD masters. This was due in part to a breakdown in relations between Ryko and the Zappa Family Trust over various problems which had been festering since as far back as 1989 (when FZ was upset by Ryko's usage of an unretouched cover photo in their initial CD issue of *Sheik Yerbouti*). The post-1995 Ryko titles received wide distribution, but were not treated to any significant promotion and without the company doing anything to increase their profile (the only folks doing anything in that regard were the ZFT themselves, keeping FZ's legacy alive through new archive CD releases and through the Zappa Plays Zappa tribute band, which began touring in 2006 with Dweezil Zappa at the helm).

The *coup de grace* blow was dealt in 2006, when Ryko was bought out by FZ's old nemesis Warner Brothers, with whom FZ was embroiled in lengthy and energy-draining high-profile lawsuits for several years beginning in 1977. This final indignity spurred Gail Zappa into action, and the next several years were spent laying the groundwork for the ZFT to regain the rights to the Zappa masters that were now owned by Warner Brothers. Surprisingly, this process seems to have gone fairly smoothly and by 2011 the rights to all the catalog titles issued by Ryko were in the hands of the ZFT.

There were two major objectives in reissuing the Zappa catalog for the 21st Century. The first was to ensure that the titles had decent distribution on the retail level, thus making them once again easily available to consumers. The second objective – and a major factor in the minds of most Zappa fans and collectors – was to restore the titles, as much as possible, to a perfect or near-perfect reproduction of their original, pre-digital forms. In other words, most of the imperfections and "issues" with the catalog as it had originally been prepared for CD issue by Frank Zappa would be addressed. The first objective was achieved by placing the catalog with the major-label behemoth Universal Music Group for the purposes of distribution. The second objective would require a great deal of work, the effort being spearheaded by Zappa family Vaultmeister Joe Travers.

The 2012 CD masters would utilize Direct Stream Digital technology, a system that digitally recreates audible signals for the Super Audio CD (or SACD) format. This system archives the material on the analog master tapes onto a digital format in as perfect a manner as possible. To this end, an audiophile rig was brought in (donated for the project by Gus Skinas of the Super Audio Center group) and the master tapes were transferred over a period of about two months.

The process of transferring the tapes was not without complications. While the majority of the tapes played without issues, a few tapes were damaged (owing to poor storage conditions) or fragile, largely owing to the deteriorating condition of the tape stock used to record the original masters. This tapes had to be baked, a process in which damaged master tapes are heated in an oven, allowing the deteriorating tape stock to hold together long enough to be transferred to digital, before a decent transfer could be accomplished. As would be expected in such an endeavor, much "fun" was had attempting to cobble together the definitive version of a given title, which would sometimes require the transfer of not only an original master tape, but a safety copy as well. The reason for this was that, in some cases, the original master tapes were either damaged (*Lumpy Gravy* being a notorious example) or incomplete (in the case of *Joe's Garage*, where musical material was removed from the master tape by FZ for reasons unknown).

Unfortunately, not all of the issues with the albums could be addressed initially, and some titles that were issued by Universal were basically clones of the original Ryko CD issues. Priority of issue was given to titles that were deemed to have the greatest number of sonic issues and/or content problems by fans, such as *Fillmore East – June 1971* and *You Are What You Is*. Those original analog masters not issued as part of the 2012 Universal campaign are still held by the ZFT, and will (at least in some cases) see release in some form at a later date.

The following is a rundown of the individual catalog titles included in the Universal reissue campaign (which saw release in the latter half of 2012):

**Freak Out!** – Taken from the Sony 1630 digital tape master prepared by FZ in 1987, making it the same as the original Ryko CD issue. The reason for this is that an excellent transfer of the original 1966 analog edit master reels was issued by the ZFT on the 2006 *MoFO Project/Object* CD set, and the ZFT obviously did not feel the need to force fans to buy that transfer a second time.

**Absolutely Free** – A transfer from the original analog edit master tape, which played well apart from some slight-but-audible tape damage in the opening song "Plastic People." The CD adds the same bonus tracks that were added for the 1989 CD issue, "Big Leg Emma" and "Why Don't You Do Me Right?", this time taken from the master tape for the 1967 mono single release with no additional processing.

***We're Only In It For The Money*** – a reissue of the 1993 digital transfer from a safety copy of the original analog tape. This was done because it was determined that a fresh transfer would not improve on that FZ-approved transfer.

***Lumpy Gravy*** – a complicated title to restore, mainly because the original 1968 master tape is now basically unusable due to poor storage conditions at the MGM vault, where it was stored in the late 1960s. In 1993, FZ and engineer Spencer Chrislu worked to restore the album as much as possible, using several sub-master tapes at their disposal. The major issue in the original master came with the dialogue sections, which had been recorded on a brand of recording tape that did not hold up well over time. By the time Warner Brothers made a safety copy of the tape in 1972 (for reasons unknown, as they did not own this title), the tape had already been damaged. Fortunately, Zappa engineer Dick Kunc had already made a safety copy of the original master tape going back in 1968, so the ZFT had this at their disposal when preparing the album for transfer in 2012. However, it was decided to stick with the 1993 FZ-prepared CD master for the Universal reissue as that tape was correctly deemed to sound fabulous apart from an odd lapse from stereo into mono at one point during the track "Oh No."

***Cruising With Ruben And The Jets*** – Similar to *Freak Out!*, this title was taken from the Sony 1630 digital tape master prepared by FZ in 1987, making it the same as the original Ryko CD issue featuring new bass and drum tracks. The original unaltered 1968 master tape was issued by the ZFT in 2010 on the *Greasy Love Songs* album, although that title suffers from brickwalled mastering wherein the volume the tracks are mastered at is pushed to the limit, squashing some of the dynamics of the original.

***Mothermania*** – A straight copy of the 1969 edit master tape. This title was initially released as a digital download in 2009, but the same master was finally released as a CD by Universal in 2013, the first time this legendary "lost" compilation had been released in that format.

***Uncle Meat*** – This title was a reissue of the 1987 digital master, previously issued by Ryko and including bonus selections in the form of long stretches of dialogue and music from FZ's "Mothers Of Invention movie" *Uncle Meat*. The process of compiling a complete digital version of the original 1968 master tape was not a simple one, as the original analog reels contained a notable amount of tape damage. After the master was transferred, warts and all, into the digital realm, a digital transfer of a safety copy was used to patch up the damaged parts of the original master. From this new digital edit master, a vinyl reissue was prepared and released in 2013. It is likely that this master will be issued on CD at some point in the near future.

***Hot Rats*** – A fresh digital transfer of the original 1969 edit master, which held up beautifully against the ravages of time despite being recorded using tape stock which was susceptible to oxide shedding. By the end of the 1960s, tape stock had switched from acetate tape to back-coat tape, which was at least a bit more durable than acetate. Whereas damaged acetate tape cannot be saved by baking, back-coat tape can. Early back-coat tapes, however, were still fairly fragile as a result of oxide-shedding. Examples of Zappa master tapes from this period subject to oxide-shedding include *Permanent Damage* by the GTOs, *An Evening With Wild Man Fischer*, *Burnt Weeny Sandwich* and *Weasels Ripped My Flesh*. This problem also befell Captain Beefheart & His Magic Band's classic album *Trout Mask Replica*, which was reissued by the ZFT in 2013. On this reissue the opening track, "Frownland," suffers audibly from tape damage, and it could not be repaired or replaced as this was one of two songs from that album for which a safety copy does not exist (the other being "Moonlight On Vermont").

**Burnt Weeny Sandwich** – This title was problematic for the ZFT to restore, as the original 1969 edit master tape is not in the Zappa Vault. Two copies of the album do exist in the Vault, including an EQ copy made by Warner Brothers which is the copy that FZ used for all of the CDs that have been in print prior to 2012. At the beginning of the track "The Little House I Used To Live In," the Warner Brothers EQ copy features an edit where the tape was cut and pieced back together with sticky tape, causing an audible glitch at the start of the track. Unfortunately, when preparing the album for its intial CD issue, FZ apparently missed this glitch. Fortunately, there were other copies made, second-generation copies made from the main master by the Los Angeles mastering facility Artisan Recorders, the company that was making the discs at the time. This Artisan copy, which was free of the glitch, was used to produce the 2012 remaster.

**Weasels Ripped My Flesh** – The original edit master tapes were used, as they were still in usable shape, although a few minor dropouts crept into the remastering process. This was due to the back-coat tape stock being somewhat fragile.

**Chunga's Revenge** – A fresh transfer from the original edit master, replacing a highly deficient (in terms of sound quality) FZ CD master from 1989.

**Fillmore East – June 1971** – Taken from the original edit master, and complete on CD for the first time as previous CD issues dropped "Willie The Pimp, Part Two" from the album so that FZ could eliminate the side 1/side 2 break of the original album.

**Just Another Band From LA** – This was one of the few titles in the reissue project where technical issues with the tapes had to be addressed before the title could be remastered. The primary issue was that the original edit masters were not balanced properly, a process where the channels match in each other in terms of loudness. The balancing of the channels, therefore, had to be manually performed for the 2012 remaster. As a result, there is a slight variation in the sound of the 2012 issue as compared to the original vinyl LP, which some eagle-eared fans immediately picked up on. This is, however, a minor difference at best.

**Waka/Jawaka** – Taken from the original edit masters, and one of the best-sounding CDs in the entire reissue program.

**The Grand Wazoo** – Original edit masters were used again. Another stunning job from the ZFT.

**Over-Nite Sensation** – Original edit masters were used again, reflecting the the original vinyl content precisely.

**Apostrophe (')** – Taken again from the 1974 edit masters, and sounding as good as it gets. The edit masters had previously been used for Ryko's Au20 gold disc CD edition of this title, but this was the first time the ZFT had officially sanctioned their authorizationrelease in a standard, silver CD format.

***Roxy & Elsewhere*** – For this release, the ZFT chose to work with the 1992 FZ-approved CD master previously issued by Ryko, which utilized an EQ-treated copy of the original edit master tapes apart from a remixed "Cheepnis." The full-blown, original, non-EQ'd master was issued on vinyl by the ZFT in 2013.

***One Size Fits All*** – The original, non EQ'd edit master was used, appearing for the first time on CD. The edit master had previously been issued as a Ryko Au20 gold CD, with additional EQ courtesy of Spencer Chrislu.

***Bongo Fury*** – Another stunning upgrade in clarity came from using the original edit master from this title, replacing a noticeably murkier earlier CD master.

***Zoot Allures*** – One of the major victories for the ZFT in this campaign, this was taken from the complete edit master for the first decent mastering of this album on CD. The original FZ-authorized CD mastering was absolutely riddled with problems, and difficult to listen to for anyone who knew how good this album could and should sound.

***Zappa In New York*** – Taken from FZ's 1991 2-CD reconstruction of the album, mainly because that version's many bonus tracks made a convincing argument to keep it in print. The original edit masters for this album were transferred, and are being held back for possible future use.

***Studio Tan*** – A fresh transfer off the edit masters, matching the original vinyl content apart from "The Adventures Of Greggery Peccary," which runs to the end of the track rather than fading as on the original LP.

***Sleep Dirt*** – Reverts to the analog edit master for the first time on CD. Earlier CD pressings were taken from a new digital master tape FZ had created, including vocal overdubs on several tracks that had been left as instrumentals on vinyl versions of the album.

***Sheik Yerbouti*** – The original, first-generation edit master tapes were used for the Universal release, giving fans the first complete version of the album on CD since the European EMI pressings of the late 1980s (which were made from a higher-generation analog tape). This replaces FZ/Ryko's previous master, which suffered from major sound quality issues and featured a rather grim edit of the track "I'm So Cute." The original edit master tape was recorded on a formulation of Ampex tape which had a tendency to shed oxide, and had to be baked before it could be transferred.

***Orchestral Favorites*** – FZ's 1991 master was made use of once again. The content basically matches the original vinyl, apart from the stereo channels being mysteriously reversed and the material being treated to additional EQ work.

***Joe's Garage Acts I, II & III*** – Most of this title is a fresh transfer from the original edit masters. Unfortunately, for some reason FZ cut the track "On The Bus" out of the edit master tape, and that first-generation tape could not be found. A safety backup was employed to restore the missing track, which was fitted seamlessly into the program material. As noted earlier, the edit masters were on an Ampex tape stock that had to be baked in order to transfer the tapes to digital.

***Tinsel Town Rebellion*** – Taken from the analog edit master tapes, making this the first issue of the album to be a 100% accurate reproduction of the original vinyl album content on CD (this includes the 1986 EMI European CD issue, which suffered from an edit in the track "Easy Meat").

***Shut Up 'N Play Yer Guitar*** – Original edit master tapes used again. Finally this album (actually originally issued as three single LPs) is available in a CD version that is 100% faithful to the vinyl. Sound quality is a marked improvement over previoius digital issues as well.

***You Are What You Is*** – This was one of the most infamous titles in the original Ryko-era Zappa CD catalog, with sound quality issues a-go-go and the guitar solo in the song "Dumb All Over" edited out. This release used the original edit master tapes, complete and unexpurgated. Sound quality is great, and the content is 100% faithful to the original vinyl issue (EMI had released a similarly musically complete CD in 1986, but the sound quality of this version is superior as the EMI release was taken from an analog sub-master tape used for LP production).

***Ship Arriving Too Late To Save A Drowning Witch*** – Taken from the analog edit master. Previous digital versions of this title were also taken from this source, so the content of the two versions is basically the same.

***The Man From Utopia*** – Taken from the Sony 1630 digital master tape for the CD remix of this album prepared by FZ in 1991, complete with bonus track. The original analog edit master of this album was transferred, and may be issued at some point.

***Baby Snakes*** – This "CD mix" of this title was used for this project, although it had actually been released without fanfare as the second vinyl pressing of this title in 1985. The original analog edit master tape was also transferred, and could be reissued someday, perhaps on vinyl.

***London Symphony Orchestra*** – A reissue of the 1993/1995 "house master" 2-CD remix/reassembly of this title. The original digital edit masters of the two LP releases of this material were transferred, and could be reissued at some point.

***Boulez Conducts Zappa: The Perfect Stranger*** – The 1991 FZ remix of this album was again used for this reissue. The vinyl mix has only been issued digitally on the 1985 EMI CD of this title, which was the very first Frank Zappa compact disc. The original edit master has been transferred as part of this project, and may surface someday.

***Them Or Us*** – Reverts to the original vinyl mix, replacing a sonically problematic 1990 digital remaster that had become the standard Ryko version. The 1990 disc contained an extended version of the title track however, so that is one instance where the Ryko CD is still of value.

***Thing-Fish*** – The same FZ-approved remixed/reedited master that had been issued by Ryko in 1995 was reissued here. The original digital edit master was also transferred and could be reissued on vinyl, although this would likely not be a priority release for the ZFT.

***Francesco Zappa*** – The same master used for every digital version of this title was used again here, though as it matches the 1984 vinyl release exactly, there never was any real variation here.

***Frank Zappa Meets The Mothers Of Prevention*** – The 1995 digital CD master was employed again here. The mix/material content matches the original US and European vinyl LPs, which prior to 1995 had been spread out over two different CD pressings (and was still not as complete as the 1995 CD).

***Does Humor Belong In Music?*** – The 1993 digital remix (first issued in 1995) was reissued for this series. The original digital CD mix, previously available only on the initial 1986 release of this title, was transferred as part of this archiving project, though it probably isn't high on the list of reissue contenders.

***Jazz From Hell*** – The 1995 CD master was employed again here. It is supposed to be a copy of the 1990 European Zappa Records CD, which was labeled as a "U.M.R.K. Digital Remix." There appears to be no difference between the "remix" and the original mix at all. The "remix" tag was probably a bit of hype to help sell the 1990 reissue.

***Guitar, You Can't Do That On Stage Anymore Vol. 1, You Can't Do That On Stage Anymore Vol. 2, Broadway The Hard Way, You Can't Do That On Stage Anymore Vol. 3, The Best Band You Never Heard In Your Life, Make A Jazz Noise Here, You Can't Do That On Stage Anymore Vol. 4, You Can't Do That On Stage Anymore Vol. 5, You Can't Do That On Stage Anymore Vol. 6, Playground Psychotics, Ahead Of Their Time, The Yellow Shark, The Lost Episodes*** – These titles all used the 1995 "house masters" that had previously been issued by Ryko.

***Läther*** – This title (which featured completely new cover art) used the same master that had been issued in 1996 by Ryko, minus the bonus tracks which had never been authorized for release by the ZFT in the first place. In 1995, engineer Spencer Chrislu was charged with the task of re-creating a releasable digital master of the *Läther* album, but immediately ran into problems with the tapes. Much of the edit masters had been recorded on a tape formulation that had deteriorated greatly, and Spencer was forced to cobble together a digital master wth the help of safety copies. The result was a spiffy-sounding CD master for the album, to which Chrislu added a few bonus tracks. Unfortunately, the ZFT were reportedly not happy with the bonus tracks, and as a result these were removed from the 2012 reissue of *Läther*. The new issue is otherwise the same as the 1996 CD, because it was determined that little could be done to improve on the Chrislu master.

***Have I Offended Someone?, Mystery Disc*** – These titles used the same digital masters that had previously been issued by Rykodisc.

(NOTE: Many thanks to Joe Travers, who assisted greatly in the preparation of this article.)

# FRANK ZAPPA ON COMPACT DISC: A TIMELINE

Titles in bold feature the original vinyl LP mix or are definitive representations of FZ's original intention for a given title; all other discs are altered in some way. The catalog numbers are those of the initial US releases only, apart from two early titles which were not released on CD in the US.

April 1985 (approximate date):
**The Perfect Stranger (EMI CDC 7 47125 2)**

August 1986:
Thing-Fish (Ryko RCD 10020/21)
London Symphony Orchestra (Ryko RCD 10022)
**Frank Zappa Meets The Mothers Of Prevention (Ryko RCD 10023)**
We're Only In It For The Money/**Lumpy Gravy\*** (Ryko RCD 40024)
Apostrophe(')/**Over-Nite Sensation** (Ryko RCD 40025)
The Grand Wazoo (Ryko RCD 10026)
**Them Or Us (Ryko RCD 40027)**
**Shut Up 'N Play Yer Guitar (Ryko RCD 10028/29)**

February 1987:
**Jazz From Hell (Ryko RCD 10030)**

September 1987:
**Joe's Garage Acts I, II & III (Ryko RCD 10060/61)**

October 1987:
Freak Out! (Ryko RCD 40062)
Cruising With Ruben & The Jets (Ryko RCD 10063)
Uncle Meat (Ryko RCD 10064/65)
Hot Rats (Ryko RCD 10066)

April 26, 1988:
**Guitar (Ryko 10079/80)**
**You Can't Do That On Stage Anymore Vol. 1 (Ryko 10081/82)**

October 25, 1988:
**You Can't Do That On Stage Anymore Vol. 2 – The Helsinki Concert (Ryko 10083/84)**

November 22, 1988:
Baby Snakes (Barking Pumpkin D2 74219)

January 1989:
Absolutely Free (Ryko RCD 10093)
Waka/Jawaka (Ryko RCD 10094)
One Size Fits All (Ryko RCD 10095)

May 1989:
Broadway The Hard Way (Ryko RCD 40096)
Bongo Fury (Ryko RCD 10097)

November 13, 1989:
**You Can't Do That On Stage Anymore Vol. 3 (Ryko RCD 10085/86)**

April 16, 1991:
**The Best Band You Never Heard In Your Life (Barking Pumpkin D2 74233)**

May 1990:
Zoot Allures (Ryko RCD 10160)
Just Another Band From LA (Ryko RCD 10161)
Sheik Yerbouti (Ryko RCD 40162)
Weasels Ripped My Flesh (Ryko RCD 10163)
Chunga's Revenge (Ryko RCD 10164)
You Are What You Is (Ryko RCD 40165)
Tinsel Town Rebellion (Ryko RCD 40166)
Fillmore East – June 1971 (Ryko RCD 10167)

June 4, 1991:
**Make A Jazz Noise Here (Barking Pumpkin D2 74234)**

June 14, 1991:
**You Can't Do That On Stage Anymore Vol. 4 (Ryko RCD 10087/88)**

June 1991:
**Ship Arriving Too Late To Save A Drowning Witch (Barking Pumpkin D2 74235)**

September 24, 1991:
Orchestral Favorites (Barking Pumpkin D2 74236)
Studio Tan (Barking Pumpkin D2 74237)
Sleep Dirt (Barking Pumpkin D2 74238)

October 1991:
Zappa In New York (Barking Pumpkin D2 74240)
Burnt Weeny Sandwich (Barking Pumpkin D2 74329)

February 1992:
Roxy & Elsewhere (Barking Pumpkin D2 74241)

April 1992:
Francesco Zappa (Barking Pumpkin D2 74202)
Boulez Conducts Zappa: The Perfect Stranger (Barking Pumpkin D2 74242)

July 10, 1992:
**You Can't Do That On Stage Anymore Vol. 5 (Ryko RCD 10089/90)**
**You Can't Do That On Stage Anymore Vol. 6 (Ryko RCD 10091/92)**

October 27, 1992:
**Playground Psychotics (Barking Pumpkin D2 74244)**

January 1993:
The Man From Utopia (Barking Pumpkin D2 74245)

April 20, 1993:
**Ahead Of Their Time (Barking Pumpkin D2 74246)**

November 2, 1993:
**The Yellow Shark (Barking Pumpkin R2 71600)**

December 2, 1994:
**Civilization Phaze III (Barking Pumpkin UMRK 01)**

April 18
**We're Only In It For The Money (Ryko RCD 10503)**
**Lumpy Gravy (Ryko RCD 10504)\***
Over-Nite Sensation (Ryko RCD 10518)
Apostrophe (') (Ryko RCD 10510)
The London Symphony Orchestra Volumes I & II (Ryko RCD 10540/41)

May 2, 1995:
Freak Out! (Ryko RCD 10501)
Absolutely Free (Ryko RCD 10502)
Uncle Meat (Ryko RCD 10506/07)
Hot Rats (Ryko RCD 10508)
Burnt Weeny Sandwich (Ryko RCD 10509)
Weasels Ripped My Flesh (Ryko RCD 10510)
Chunga's Revenge (Ryko RCD 10511)
Just Another Band From LA (Ryko RCD 10515)
Waka/Jawaka (Ryko RCD 10516)
Roxy & Elsewhere (Ryko RCD 10520)
One Size Fits All (Ryko RCD 10521)
Bongo Fury (Ryko RCD 10522)
Zoot Allures (Ryko RCD 10523)
Zappa In New York (Ryko RCD 10524/25)
Studio Tan (Ryko RCD 10526)

Sleep Dirt (Ryko RCD 10527)
Sheik Yerbouti (Ryko RCD 10528)
Orchestral Favorites (Ryko RCD 10529)
**Joe's Garage Acts I, II & III (Ryko RCD 10530/31)**
Tinsel Town Rebellion (Ryko RCD 10532)
You Are What You Is (Ryko RCD 10536)
**Ship Arriving Too Late To Save A Drowning Witch (Ryko RCD 10537)**
The Man From Utopia (Ryko RCD 10538)
Baby Snakes (Ryko RCD 10539)
Them Or Us (Ryko RCD 10543)
Thing-Fish (Ryko RCD 10544/45)
**Francesco Zappa (Ryko RCD 10546)**
**Guitar (Ryko RCD 10550/51)**
Broadway The Hard Way (Ryko RCD 10552)
**Make A Jazz Noise Here (Ryko RCD 10555/56)**

May 16, 1995:
Cruising With Ruben & The Jets (Ryko RCD 10505)
The Grand Wazoo (Ryko RCD 10517)
Boulez Conducts Zappa: The Perfect Stranger (Ryko RCD 10542)
**Frank Zappa Meets The Mothers Of Prevention (Ryko RCD 10547)**
Does Humor Belong In Music? (Ryko RCD 10548)
**Jazz From Hell (Ryko RCD 10549)**
**You Can't Do That On Stage Anymore Vol. 1 (Ryko RCD 10561/62)**
**You Can't Do That On Stage Anymore Vol. 2 (Ryko RCD 10563/64)**

May 30, 1995:
Fillmore East – June 1971 (Ryko RCD 10512)
Shut Up 'N Play Yer Guitar (Ryko RCD 10533/34/35)
**The Best Band You Never Heard In Your Life (Ryko RCD 10553/54)**
**Playground Psychotics (Ryko RCD 10557/58)**
**Ahead Of Their Time (Ryko RCD 10559)**
**The Yellow Shark (Ryko RCD 40560)**
**You Can't Do That On Stage Anymore Vol. 3 (Ryko RCD 10565/66)**
**You Can't Do That On Stage Anymore Vol. 4 (Ryko RCD 10567/68)**
**You Can't Do That On Stage Anymore Vol. 5 (Ryko RCD 10569/70)**
**You Can't Do That On Stage Anymore Vol. 1 (Ryko RCD 10571/72)**

February 27, 1996:
**The Lost Episodes (Ryko RCD 40573)**

July 2, 1996:
**Apostrophe (') (Ryko RCD 80519 – Au20 Gold Disc)**
**One Size Fits All (Ryko RCD 80520 – Au20 Gold Disc)**

September 24, 1996:
**Läther (Ryko RCD 10574/75/76)**

October 31, 1996:
**Frank Zappa Plays The Music Of Frank Zappa, a memorial tribute (Barking Pumpkin UMRK 02)**

April 8, 1997:
**Have I Offended Someone? (Ryko RCD 10577)**

October 14, 1997:
**200 Motels (Ryko RCD 10513/14)**

September 15, 1998:
**Mystery Disc (Ryko RCD 10580)**

December 21, 1999:
**Everything Is Healing Nicely (Barking Pumpkin UMRK 03)**
August 16, 2002:
**FZ:OZ (Vaulternative VR 2002-1)**

February 4, 2003:
**Halloween (Vaulternative/DTS 1101—DVD-Audio only, no CD issue)**

May 30, 2004
**Joe's Corsage (Vaulternative VR 20041)**

September 14, 2004:
**QuAUDIOPHILIAc (Barking Pumpkin/DTS 1125—DVD-Audio only, no CD issue)**

October 1, 2004:
**Joe's Domage (Vaulternative VR 20042)**

December 21, 2005:
**Joe's XMASage (Vaulternative VR 20051)**

January 13, 2006:
**Imaginary Diseases (Zappa Records ZR 20001)**

November 7, 2006:
**Trance-Fusion (Zappa Records ZR 20002)**

December 5, 2006:
**The MOFO Project/Object (fazedooh) (Zappa Records ZR 20005)**

December 12, 2006:
**The MOFO Project/Object (Zappa Records ZR 20004)**

April 1, 2007:
**Buffalo (Vaulternative VR 2007-1)**

August 24, 2007:
**The Dub Room Special! (Zappa Records ZR 20006)**

October 31, 2007:
**Wazoo (Vaulternative VR 2007-2)**

June 13, 2008:
**One Shot Deal (Zappa Records ZR 20007)**

September 26, 2008:
**Joe's Menage (Vaulternative Records VR 20081)**

January 21, 2009:
**The Lumpy Money Project/Object (Zappa Records ZR 20008)**

December 15, 2009:
**Philly '76 (Vaulternative Records VR 20091)**

April 19, 2010:
**Greasy Love Songs (Zappa Records ZR 20010)**

September 19, 2010:
**"Congress Shall Make No Law . . . " (Zappa Records ZR 20011)**

November 6, 2010:
**Hammersmith Odeon (Vaulternative Records VR 20101)**

September 22, 2011:
**Feeding The Monkies At Ma Maison (Zappa Records ZR 20012)**

November 17, 2011:
**Carnegie Hall (4CD, Vaulternative Records VR 2011-1)**

July 31, 2012:
Freak Out! (Zappa Records ZR 3834)
**Absolutely Free (Zappa Records ZR 3835)**
**Lumpy Gravy (Zappa Records ZR 3836)***
**We're Only In It For The Money (Zappa Records ZR 3837)**
Cruising With Ruben & The Jets (Zappa Records ZR 3838)
Uncle Meat (Zappa Records ZR 3839)
**Hot Rats (Zappa Records ZR 3841)**
**Burnt Weeny Sandwich (Zappa Records ZR 3842)**
**Weasels Ripped My Flesh (Zappa Records ZR 3843)**
**Chunga's Revenge (Zappa Records ZR 3844)**
**Fillmore East – June 1971 (Zappa Records ZR 3845)**
**Just Another Band From LA (Zappa Records ZR 3847)**

August 28, 2012:
**Waka/Jawaka (Zappa Records ZR 3848)**
**The Grand Wazoo (Zappa Records ZR 3849)**
**Over-Nite Sensation (Zappa Records ZR 3850)**
**Apostrophe (') (Zappa Records ZR 3851)**
Roxy & Elsewhere (Zappa Records ZR 3852)
**One Size Fits All (Zappa Records ZR 3853)**
**Bongo Fury (Zappa Records ZR 3854)**
**Zoot Allures (Zappa Records ZR 3855)**
Zappa In New York (Zappa Records ZR 3856)
**Studio Tan (Zappa Records ZR 3857)**
**Sleep Dirt (Zappa Records ZR 3858)**
**Sheik Yerbouti (Zappa Records ZR 3859)**

September 25, 2012:
Orchestral Favorites (Zappa Records ZR 3860)
**Joe's Garage Acts I, II & III (Zappa Records ZR 3861)**
**Tinsel Town Rebellion (Zappa Records ZR 3862)**
**Shut Up 'N Play Yer Guitar (Zappa Records ZR 3863)**
**You Are What You Is (Zappa Records ZR 3864)**
**Ship Arriving Too Late To Save A Drowning Witch (Zappa Records ZR 3865)**
The Man From Utopia (Zappa Records ZR 3866)
Baby Snakes (Zappa Records ZR 3867)
The London Symphony Orchestra Volumes I & II (Zappa Records ZR 3868)
Boulez Conducts Zappa: The Perfect Stranger (Zappa Records ZR 3869)
**Them Or Us (Zappa Records ZR 3870)**
Thing-Fish (Zappa Records ZR 3871)

October 26, 2012:
**Mothermania (Zappa Records ZR 3840)**

October 30, 2012:
**Francesco Zappa (Zappa Records ZR 3872)**
**Frank Zappa Meets The Mothers Of Prevention (Zappa Records ZR 3873)**
Does Humor Belong In Music? (Zappa Records ZR 3874)
**Jazz From Hell (Zappa Records ZR 3875)**
**Guitar (Zappa Records ZR 3876)**
**You Can't Do That On Stage Anymore Vol. 1 (Zappa Records ZR 3877)**
**You Can't Do That On Stage Anymore Vol. 2 (Zappa Records ZR 3878)**
Broadway The Hard Way (Zappa Records ZR 3879)
**You Can't Do That On Stage Anymore Vol. 3 (Zappa Records ZR 3880)**
**The Best Band You Never Heard In Your Life (Zappa Records ZR 3881)**
**You Can't Do That On Stage Anymore Vol. 4 (Zappa Records ZR 3882)**
**Make A Jazz Noise Here (Zappa Records ZR 3883)**
**Understanding America (Zappa Records ZR 3892)**

November 7, 2012:
**Road Tapes, Venue #1 (Vaulternative Records VR 20122)**

November 19, 2012:
**You Can't Do That On Stage Anymore Vol. 5 (Zappa Records ZR 3884)**
**You Can't Do That On Stage Anymore Vol. 6 (Zappa Records ZR 3885)**
**Playground Psychotics (Zappa Records ZR 3886)**
**The Yellow Shark (Zappa Records ZR 3888)**
**Have I Offended Someone? (Zappa Records ZR 3890)**
**Mystery Disc (Zappa Records ZR 3891)**

December 12, 2012:
**Finer Moments (Zappa Records/UMe ZR 3894)**

December 14, 2012:
**Läther (Zappa Records ZR 3893)**

December 18, 2012:
**Ahead Of Their Time (Zappa Records ZR 3887)**
**The Lost Episodes (Zappa Records ZR 3889)**

December 21, 2012:
**AAAFNRAA—Baby Snakes—The Compleat Soundtrack (Zappa Records—Direct Download only, no CD release or catalog number)**

October 31, 2013:
**Road Tapes, Venue #2 (Vaulternative Records VR 2013-1)**

November 25, 2013:
**A Token Of His Extreme Soundtrack (Zappa Records ZR 20015)**

January 30, 2014:
**Joe's Camouflage (Vaulternative Records VR 2013-02)**

March 13, 2014:
**Roxy By Proxy (Zappa Records ZR 20017)**

June 1, 2015:
**Dance Me This (Zappa Records)**


*The 1995 and 2012 CD reissues of Lumpy Gravy basically reflect the content of the original vinyl, apart from a section in "Part One" which is in mono on these issues. The 1986 "2-fer" CD presents the full album in stereo, but the sound quality is not quite as good as the 1995 and 2012 issues.

Zappa CD number : 1

**Freak Out!** (June 1966)

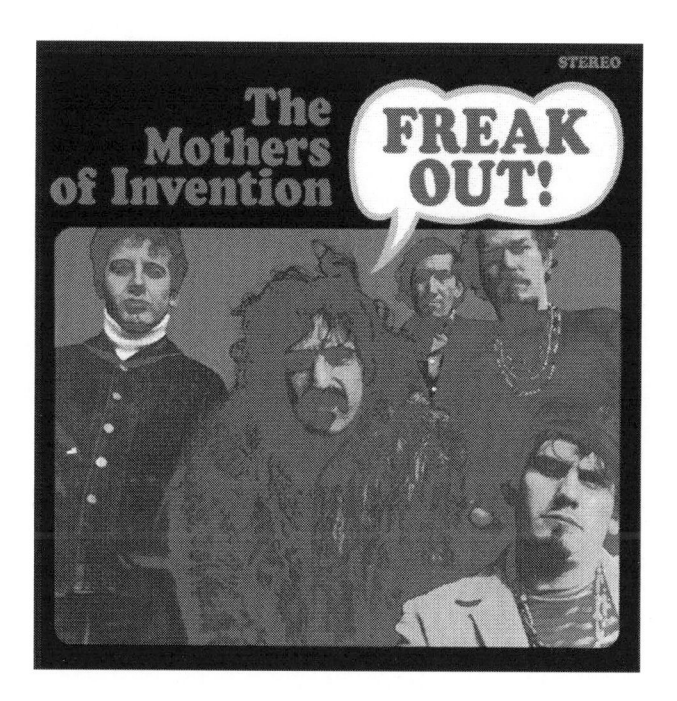

Performers:

The Mothers of Invention:
Frank Zappa (guitar, vocals)
Ray Collins (lead vocalist, harmonica, percussion)
Jim Black (drums, vocals)
Roy Estrada (bass, vocals)
Elliot Ingber (guitar)

"The Mothers' Auxiliary":
Gene Estes (percussion)
Eugene Di Novi (piano)
Neil Le Vang (guitar)
John Rotella (clarinet, saxophone)
Kurt Reher (cello)
Raymond Kelley (cello)
Paul Bergstrom (cello)
Emmet Sargeant (cello)
Joseph Saxon (cello)
Edwin Beach (cello)
Arthur Maebe (French horn, tuba)
George Price (French horn)

John Johnson (tuba?)
Carol Kaye (12-string guitar)
Virgil Evans (trumpet)
David Wells (trombone)
Kenneth Watson (percussion)
Plas Johnson (sax, flute)
Roy Caton (copyist)
Carl Franzoni (voice)
Vito (voice)
Kim Fowley (hyophone)
Benjamin Barrett (contractor)
David Anderle
Motorhead Sherwood (noises)
Mac Rebenack "Dr. John" (piano)
Paul Butterfield
Les McCann (piano)
Jeannie Vassoir (voice of Suzy Creamcheese)

Tom Wilson (producer)

All tracks recorded March 9-12, 1966, Sunset-Highland Studios of T.T.G, Los Angeles CA

1. Hungry Freaks, Daddy 3:27 ("Mr. America, walk on by your schools that do not teach")
2. I Ain't Got No Heart  2:30  ("Ain't got no heart, I ain't got no heart to give away")
3. Who Are The Brain Police?  3:22  ("What will you do if we let you go home?")
4. Go Cry On Somebody Else's Shoulder 3:31 (Zappa/Collins)  (spoken: "A year ago today, was when you went away") (sung: "Go cry, on somebody else's shoulder")
5. Motherly Love 2:45 ("Motherly love, motherly love")
6. How Could I Be Such A Fool 2:12 ("When I won your love, I was very glad")
7. Wowie Zowie 2:45  ("Wowie zowie, your love's a treat")
8. You Didn't Try To Call Me  3:17 ("You didn't try to call to me")
9. Any Way The Wind Blows  2:52  ("Any way the wind blows...")
10. I'm Not Satisfied  2:37  ("Got no place to go")
11. You're Probably Wondering Why I'm Here  3:37  ("You're probably wondering why I'm here")
12. Trouble Every Day 6:16 ("Well I'm about to get upset, from watching my T.V.")
13. Help, I'm A Rock  (I. Okay to Tap Dance  II. In memoriam Edgar Varese  III. It Can't Happen Here) 8:37 (I. "Help I'm a rock, help I'm a rock" III. "It can't happen here, it can't happen here")
14. The Return of the Son of Monster Magnet (Unfinished ballet in two tableaux: I. Ritual Dance of the Child Killer II. Nullis Pretti [No Commercial Potential]) (spoken: "Suzy?" "Yes?" "Suzy Creamcheese?" "Yes?")

Issues:     ZFT reissue   Zappa Records ZR3834
            Original issue : Stereo: Verve V-65005-2 and/or V-65005-2X; Mono: Verve V-5005
            Rykodisc reissue: Rykodisc RCD 10501

Transcriptions:

Piano/vocal arrangements of "How Could I Be Such A Fool" and "I'm Not Satisfied" may be in *The Frank Zappa Songbook* volume 1 (Los Angeles: Frank Zappa Music; Astoria NY: Big 3, 1973; reprinted in Cologne and Frankfurt, West Germany: Amsco/Melodie der Welt, 1982).

Inquiries about the lead-sheet collection for *Freak Out!* may be made in writing to Zappa's music publishing firm Munchkin Music at <munchkinmusic@zappa.com> .

HERE'S THE DEAL: The debut album by Frank Zappa and The Mothers Of Invention remains one of the classic albums of its era, and functions as a true Statement Of Intent for the young composer. It is certainly, in both musical and lyrical content, a preview of things to come while at the same time working as a truly cohesive statement on its own terms. If Zappa had stopped here, this would still be a highly regarded work. Lyrically, Zappa rails against both the conservative establishment and typical American teenage life. He promotes the emergent underground "Freak" scene as offering an alternative to these values, but also cannot resist puncturing some of the Freaks' proclivities. An essential album for any Zappa fan.

RATING: *****

DOWNLOAD THESE: Hungry Freaks Daddy, Who Are The Brain Police?, Wowie Zowie, Trouble Every Day, Help I'm A Rock, It Can't Happen Here

DIFFERENCES BETWEEN THE ZFT CD REISSUE AND PREVIOUS CD REISSUES: None. All CD issues of this album use the same 1987 digital master tape created by FZ for CD release. This features additional editing and reverb added to the tracks, as well as remixes of "Hungry Freaks, Daddy," "Who Are The Brain Police?" and "The Return Of The Son Of Monster Magnet." The original 1966 stereo LP master of *Freak Out!* was included as one did of the *MoFO Project/Object* albums (CD nos. 77 and 78), released by the ZFT in 2006. A mono mix of this album was also issued on vinyl, but has not seen reissue in digital form.

Zappa CD number: 2

Absolutely Free (April 1967)

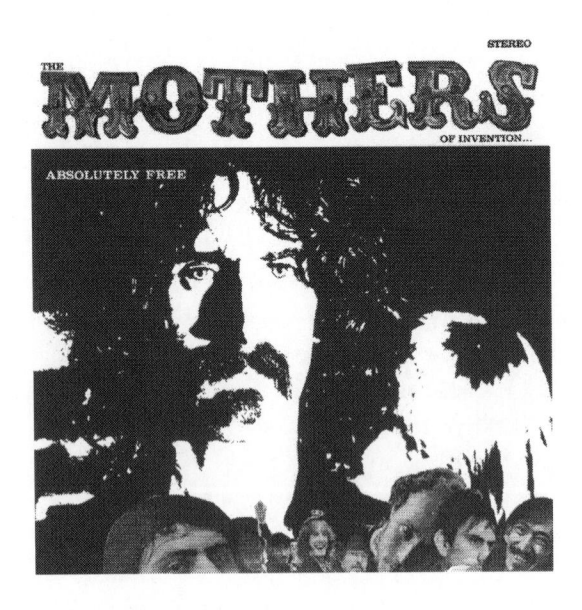

Performers:

Frank Zappa (guitar, vocals)
Ray Collins (lead vocals, tambourine, Duke of Prunes)
Jim Fielder: (guitar, piano)
Don Preston (keyboards)
Bunk Gardner (woodwinds)
Roy Estrada (bass, vocals)
Jim Black (drums, vocals)
Billy Mundi (drums, percussion)

Tom Wilson (producer)

All tracks recorded November 15-18, 1966, Sunset-Highland Studios of T.T.G, Los Angeles CA

Tracks 1-7: "Absolutely Free (1st in a series of underground oratorios)"
Tracks 10-15: "The M.O.I. American Pageant (2nd in a series of underground oratorios)"

1. Plastic People 3:42 (spoken: "Ladies and gentlemen, the President of the United States!" sung: "Plastic people, oh baby now, you're such a drag")
2. The Duke Of Prunes 2:13 ("A moon beam through the prune, in June")
3. Amnesia Vivace 1:01 ("La la lala la la lala lah lah...")
4. The Duke Regains His Chops 1:50 ("And you'll be my duchess, my Duchess of Prunes")
5. Call Any Vegetable 2:20 (spoken: "This is a song about vegetables. They keep you regular, they're real good for ya." sung: "Call any vegetable!")

6. Invocation And Ritual Dance Of The Young Pumpkin 7:00  (instrumental)
7. Soft-Sell Conclusion 1:40  (spoken: "A lot of people don't bother about their friends in the vegetable kingdom")
8. Big Leg Emma 2:32  ("I got a big dilemma, about my Big Leg Emma, uh huh.")
9. Why Don'tcha Do Me Right? 2:37  ("Why don'tcha do me right?")
10. America Drinks 1:53   ("I tried to find how my heart could be so blind, dear")
11. Status Back Baby 2:54 ("I'm losin' status at the high school")
12. Uncle Bernie's Farm 2:11  (lead-in: "I'm dreaming, of a" [Oh no-o-o!]" sung: "There's a bomb to blow your mommy up, a bomb for your daddy too")
13. Son Of Suzy Creamcheese 1:34  ("Suzy Creamcheese, oh mama now, what's got into you?")
14. Brown Shoes Don't Make It 7:30 ("Brown shoes, don't make it")
15. America Drinks and Goes Home 2:46  (spoken: "This is a special request, hope you enjoy it" sung: "I tried to find how my heart could be so blind, dear")

Issues:   ZFT reissue   Zappa Records ZR3835
          Original issue  Stereo: Verve V65013; Mono: Verve V 5013
          Rykodisc reissued: Rykodisc RCD 10502

Transcriptions:  Piano/vocal arrangements of "Son of Suzy Creamcheese," "Brown Shoes Don't Make It," and "America Drinks and Goes Home" are in *The Frank Zappa Songbook* volume 1 (Los Angeles: Frank Zappa Music; Astoria NY: Big 3, 1973; reprinted in Cologne and Frankfurt, West Germany: Amsco/Melodie der Welt, 1982).

Note: Tracks 8 and 9 were issued originally in April 1967 as a 45-rpm single (Verve VK 10513); they were not included in the LP issues of *Absolutely Free*. They were inserted at the LP's side break for the 1988 Rykodisc CD issue.

HERE'S THE DEAL: The second Mothers Of Invention album was recorded with (and despite) a slashed budget courtesy of their record label MGM/Verve, who did not consider their investment in the *Freak Out!* album to have produced significant returns. Despite the obviously rushed nature of the production, this album is an extension of the first album in many ways, with FZ railing against the plastic nature of American society, drinkers, advertisers and even the hip, young crowd who made up The Mothers' audience. The towering moment comes with "Brown Shoes Don't Make It," a scathing attack on perversion and corruption of all sorts in American politics that still rings sadly true today.

RATING: ****

DOWNLOAD THESE: Plastic People, Call Any Vegetable, Brown Shoes Don't Make It

DIFFERENCES BETWEEN THE ZFT CD REISSUE AND PREVIOUS CD REISSUES: The ZFT CD reissue utilizes the original 1967 analog stereo LP master for the first time on CD. Previous CD issues used a reverb-laden digital master, prepared by FZ in 1987. This album was also issued in a mono mix format on vinyl, but this mix has not been reissued in the digital domain as the mono mixdown master tapes are missing from the Zappa Vault.

Zappa CD number: 3

Lumpy Gravy (May 1968)

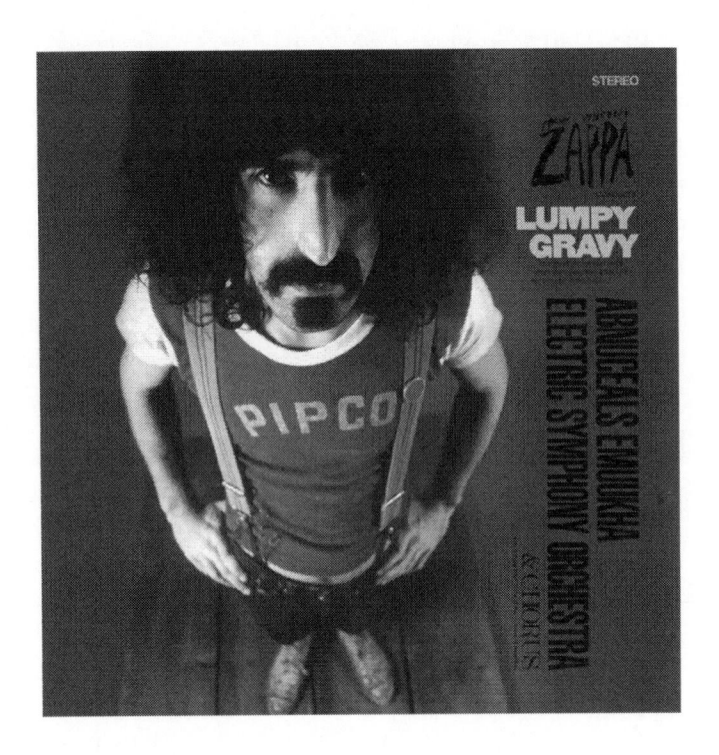

Performers:

Frank Zappa (composer, conductor)
Abnuceals Emuukha Electric Symphony Orchestra and Chorus
selected members:
Shelly Manne (drums)
Victor Feldman (percussion)
Bunk Gardner (woodwinds)
Louie The Turkey (chorus speaker)
Ronnie Williams (chorus speaker)
Dick Barber
Roy Estrada
Motorhead Sherwood
Pumpkin (Gail Zappa)
Jimmy Carl Black

Orchestral music at Capitol Studios, Hollywood, February 13 and March 14-16, 1967.
People inside the piano recorded at Apostolic Studios, NYC, October, 1967.

Lumpy Gravy Part One (15:46 total)

1. The Way I See It, Barry (0:06) ("The way I see it, Barry, this should be a very dynamite show")
2. Duodenum (1:32)
3. Oh No (2:03)
4. Bit Of Nostalgia (1:35) ("Bit of nostalgia for the old folks! ")
5. It's From Kansas (0:29)
6. Bored Out 90 Over (0:32)
7. Almost Chinese (0:25) ("Almost Chinese, huh?")
8. Switching Girls (0:29) ("I keep switching girls all the time")
9. Oh No Again (1:12)
10. At The Gas Station (2:41) ("I worked in a cheesy newspaper company for a while but that was terrible")
11. Another Pickup (0:53)
12. I Don't Know If I Can Go Through This Again (3:52)

Lumpy Gravy Part Two (15:51 total)

13. Very Distraughtening (1:34) ("Buh-bah-bahdn" "Oh!" "There it went again.")
14. White Ugliness (2:21) ("Grrr . . . Arf arf arf ar-ar-ar-ar-ar! Teeth out there, and ready to attack 'em.")
15. Amen (1:33) ("Oh yeah! That's just fine! Come on boys! Just one more time!")
16. Just One More Time (0:58)
17. A Vicious Circle (1:12)
18. King Kong (0:42)
19. Drums Are Too Noisy (0:58) ("Drums are too noisy, 'n you've got no corners to hide in!")
20. Kangaroos (0:57)
21. Envelops The Bath Tub (3:42) ("'Cause round things are . . . are boring")
22. Take Your Clothes Off (1:52)


Issues:    ZFT reissue Zappa Records ZR3836
           Original issue: Stereo: Verve V6-8741; Mono: Verve V8741
           Rykodisc reissue: Ryko RCD40024 (1986 twofer with We're Only In It For The Money [no. 4]), Ryko RCD 10504 (1995; first issue with 22 titled tracks)

Transcriptions: None

HERE'S THE DEAL: Frank Zappa's first solo album is a largely instrumental affair, punctuated by bizarre spoken passages from people conversing with each other inside a grand piano. An important and vital album as it presents Zappa's compositional insignia in pure form for the first time. *Lumpy Gravy* was also an important work for Zappa himself, one whose concepts he would return to on several occasions throughout his career.

RATING: *****

DOWNLOAD THESE: Duodenum, I Don't Know If I Can Go Through This Again, Take Your Clothes Off When You Dance

DIFFERENCES BETWEEN THE ZFT CD REISSUE AND PREVIOUS CD REISSUES: The ZFT reissue of the album uses the same 1967 safety master tape as the 1995 CD reissue, which oddly lapses into mono at one point during the first half of the album. The original 1986 Ryko CD (packaged as a "two-fer" with *We're Only In It For The Money* [no. 4]) is stereo throughout (although it is missing two bass notes during "King Kong" which can be heard on the 1995 CD, a minor detail but important to obsessive completists). The 1986 CD presents the album as "Part I" and "Part II" as per the original vinyl, while the 1995 CD breaks up the album into small individually titled segments.

Zappa CD number: 4

We're Only In It For The Money (March 1968)

Performers:

Frank Zappa (guitar, piano, lead vocals, weirdness and editing)
Billy Mundi (drums, vocal)
Roy Estrada (bass, vocals)
Jimmy Carl Black (vocals)
Ian Underwood (piano, woodwinds)
Suzy Creamcheese (telephone)
Dick Barber (snorks)
Gary Kellgren (engineer, whispering)
Eric Clapton (spoken exclamation)
Sid Sharp (orchestra conductor)
(Note: performing personnel from the Mothers verified from www.zappa.com)

Arthur Barrow (bass on 1984 overdubs)
Chad Wackerman (drums on 1984 overdubs)


Recorded August-September 1967, Mayfair Studios, New York City, and October 1967, Apostolic Studios, New York City.

1. Are You Hung Up? 1:24 ("Are you, Are you hung up? Are you hung up?")
2. Who Needs The Peace Corps? 2:34 ("What's there to live for? Who needs the peace corps?")
3. Concentration Moon 2:22 ("Concentration Moon, over the camp in the valley")
4. Mom and Dad 2:16 ("Mama! Mama! Someone said they made some noise")
5. Telephone Conversation 0:48 ("Well, operator? Hold for a minute, please")
6. Bow Tie Daddy 0:33 ("Bow tie daddy, don't you blow your top")
7. Harry, You're A Beast 1:21 ("I'm gonna tell you the way it is")
8. What's The Ugliest Part Of Your Body? 1:03 ("What's the ugliest part of your body?")
9. Absolutely Free 3:24 (spoken: "I don't do publicity balling for you anymore" "The first word in this song is 'discorporate.' It means 'to leave your body.'" sung: "Discorporate and come with me")
10. Flower Punk 3:03 ("Hey punk, where you goin' with that flower in your hand?")
11. Hot Poop 0:26
12. Nasal Retentive Calliope Music 2:02 (spoken: "Oh my God" "Beautiful! God! It's God! I see God!")
13. Let's Make The Water Turn Black 2:01 ("Now believe me when I tell you that my song is really true")
14. The Idiot Bastard Son 3:18 ("The idiot bastard son")
15. Lonely Little Girl 1:09 ("You're a lonely little girl")
16. Take Your Clothes Off When You Dance 1:32 ("There will come a time when everybody Who is lonely will be free to sing and dance and love")
17. What's The Ugliest Part Of Your Body? (Reprise) 1:02 ("What's the ugliest part of your body?")
18. Mother People 2:26 ("We are the other people")
19. The Chrome Plated Megaphone Of Destiny 6:25

Issues:  ZFT reissue   Zappa Records ZR3837
         Original issue: Stereo: Verve V65045(X); Mono: Verve V5045
         Rykodisc reissue: Ryko RCD 10503 (1995)

Transcriptions:  Piano/vocal arrangements of "Mom and Dad," "Absolutely Free," "Let's Make The Water Turn Black," "The Idiot Bastard Son," and "Mother People" were published in *The Frank Zappa Songbook* volume 1 (Los Angeles: Frank Zappa Music; Astoria NY: Big 3, 1973; reprinted in Cologne and Frankfurt, West Germany: Amsco/Melodie der Welt, 1982).

HERE'S THE DEAL: Building on the lyrical themes contained in the first two Mothers albums (nos. 1-2), Zappa unleashed a mighty assault on nearly everyone on this classic album. Nothing escapes his withering commentary, from the hippie subculture to bored housewives and conservative bow tie-wearing men. The final track, "The Chrome-Plated Megaphone Of Destiny," is a warning to the hippies that the government may not take too kindly to their aspirations for a truly free society (albeit in instrumental form). Set these lyrics to some of the most complex music and production being dealt out by anyone at the time, and you have what is arguably Frank Zappa's first truly genius work.

RATING: *****

DOWNLOAD THESE: The whole thing! But if you must dip your toe in the water before diving in try these: Who Needs The Peace Corps?, Concentration Moon, Mom And Dad, What's The Ugliest Part Of Your Body?, Let's Make The Water Turn Black, The Idiot bastard Son, Mother People

DIFFERENCES BETWEEN THE ZFT CD REISSUE AND PREVIOUS CD REISSUES: The ZFT CD issue utilizes the original 1967 stereo LP master, as had the second Ryko CD release of the album in 1995. The first Ryko CD issue of the album, released in 1986 as a "two-fer" with *Lumpy Gravy* (no. 3), used a thoroughly reconstructed version of the album, assembled in 1984 by FZ. This replaced the original Roy Estrada/Billy Mundi bass and drum parts with new recordings by bassist Arthur Barrow and drummer Chad Wackerman. This overdubbed/reconstructed version, out of print since 1995, was reissued by the ZFT as part of the *Lumpy Money Project/Object* album (no.85) in 2009.

Zappa CD number: 5

Cruising With Ruben & the Jets (February/March 1968, rev. 1984)

Performers:

Frank Zappa (lead guitar, vocals)
Jimmy Carl Black (drums)
Ray Collins (lead vocals)
Roy Estrada (electric bass, vocals)
Bunk Gardner (tenor and alto saxophones)
Don Preston (keyboards)
Motorhead Sherwood (baritone saxophone, tambourine)
Arthur Dyer Tripp III (drums)
Ian Underwood (keyboards, tenor and alto saxophones)

Jay Anderson (string bass on 1984 overdubs)
Arthur Barrow (electric bass on 1984 overdubs)
Chad Wackerman (drums on 1984 overdubs)

Recorded December 1967-February 1968, Apostolic Studios, New York City; overdubs 1984, Utility Muffin Research Kitchen studio, California)

Durations follow 1984 revision.

1. Cheap Thrills 2:39 ("Darling, darling, please hear my plea")
2. Love Of My Life 3:08 ("Love of my life, I love you so")
3. How Could I Be Such A Fool 3:34 ("When I won your love, I was very glad")
4. Deseri 2:09 ("When I'm dancing with Deseri")
5. I'm Not Satisfied 4:08 ("Got no place to go, No love left for me to give")
6. Jelly Roll Gum Drop 2:24 ("Jelly Roll Gum Drop, got my eyes on you")
7. Anything 3:06 ("For you, I could do anything")
8. Later That Night 3:00 ("You surely must be trying to break this heart of mine")
9. You Didn't Try To Call Me 3:58 ("You didn't try to call me, why didn't you try?")
10. Fountain Of Love 3:22 ("It was September, the leaves were gold")
11. No. No. No. 2:16 ("Boppa dooayyydoo, boppa dooayyydoo")
12. Anyway The Wind Blows 3:02 ("Any way the wind blows, is fine with me")
13. Stuff Up The Cracks 4:38 ("If you decide to leave me, it's all over")

Issues:   ZFT reissue  Zappa Records ZR3838
          Original issue  Verve V6-5055-X
          Rykodisc reissue  RCD 10505

For ZFT release of 1968 Verve arrangement and mix, see *Greasy Love Songs* (no.87).

Transcriptions: Piano/vocal arrangements of "How Could I Be Such A Fool" and "I'm Not Satisfied" may be in *The Frank Zappa Songbook* volume 1 (Los Angeles: Frank Zappa Music; Astoria NY: Big 3, 1973; reprinted in Cologne and Frankfurt, West Germany: Amsco/Melodie der Welt, 1982).

HERE'S THE DEAL: While recording the sprawling and complex *Uncle Meat* album (no. 6), Zappa recorded an album of 1950s-styled R&B tracks, initially intending to pass the resulting Mothers album off as an album by an obscure R&B combo. It didn't work, but the album itself is a joyous celebration of R&B and 1950s American culture, concluding with a sudden shift to the present day with a mean FZ guitar solo. The star here is Ray Collins, who furthered his credentials as perhaps the finest lead vocalist Zappa ever worked with.

RATING: ****

DOWNLOAD THESE: Love Of My Life, Deseri, Stuff Up The Cracks

DIFFERENCES BETWEEN THE ZFT CD REISSUE AND PREVIOUS CD REISSUES: None. The ZFT CD reissue utilizes the same 1987 digital master tape as all previous CD reissues, wherein the original Roy Estrada/Jimmy Carl Black bass and drum parts were replaced with new recordings by bassist Arthur Barrow and drummer Chad Wackerman. The original 1968 stereo album master was issued on CD as part of the 2010 ZFT release *Greasy Love Songs* (no. 87).

Zappa CD number: 6

Uncle Meat (April 1969)

Performers:

Frank Zappa (guitar, vocals, percussion)
Ray Collins (vocals)
Jimmy Carl Black (drums)
Roy Estrada (electric bass, "Pachuco" vocals)
Don Preston (electric piano)
Billy Mundi (drums)
Bunk Gardner (piccolo, flute, clarinet, bass clarinet, soprano saxophone, alto saxophone, tenor saxophone, bassoon)
Ian Underwood (electric organ, piano, harpsichord, celeste, flute, clarinet, alto saxophone, baritone saxophone)
Art Tripp (drums, timpani, vibes, marimba, xylophone, wood blocks, bells, small chimes)
Euclid James (Motorhead) Sherwood (tenor saxophone, tambourine)

Pamela Zarubica as Suzy Creamcheese, uncredited (vocals)
Ruth Komanoff (marimba and vibes with Artie 'on many of the tracks')
Nelcy Walker (soprano voice on "Dog Breath" and "The Uncle Meat Variations")

Massimo Bassoli (vocal on "Tengo Na Minchia Tanta"; undated but likely 1980s)

Recorded October 1967 - February 1968 at Apostolic Studios, New York City. Percussion overdubs recorded March-April 1968 at Sunset Sound, Los Angeles. Live recording dates where noted.

1. Uncle Meat: Main Title Theme 1:55
2. The Voice Of Cheese 0:26 (spoken: "Hello, teenage America, my name is Suzy Creemcheese")
3. Nine Types Of Industrial Pollution 6:00
4. Zolar Czakl 0:54
5. Dog Breath, In The Year Of The Plague 3:59 ("Cucuroo carucha Chevy '39, going to El Monte Legion Stadium")
6. The Legend Of The Golden Arches 3:27
7. Louie Louie (At the Royal Albert Hall in London) (Berry) 2:18 ("Ah! I know the perfect thing to accompany this man's trumpet") rec. 23 September 1967
8. The Dog Breath Variations 1:48
9. Sleeping In A Jar 0:50 ("It's the middle of the night")
10. Our Bizarre Relationship 1:05 (spoken: "Bizarre!" "Bizarre!")
11. The Uncle Meat Variations 4:46 ("Fuzzy dice and bongos, fuzzy dice")
12. Electric Aunt Jemima 1:46 ("Ow ow ow ow, rundee rundee rundee dinny wop wop" "Electric Aunt Jemina, goddess of love")
13. Prelude To King Kong 3:38
14. God Bless America (Live at the Whisky A Go Go) (Berlin) 1:10 ("God bless America, land that I love")
15. A Pound For A Brown On The Bus 1:29
16. Ian Underwood Whips It Out (Live on stage in Copenhagen) 5:05 (spoken: "My name is Ian Underwood and I am the straight member of the group") rec. 1 October 1967
17. Mr. Green Genes 3:14 ("Eat your greens")
18. We Can Shoot You 2:03 (spoken: "Dee . . . dee bah dam . . .")
19. "If We'd All Been Living In California..." 1:14 (spoken: "Okay? Now if you still want to get your name in magazines")
20. The Air 2:57 ("The air escaping from your mouth")
21. Project X 4:48
22. Cruising For Burgers 2:18 ("I must be free")
23. Uncle Meat Film Excerpt Part I 37:34 ("We're shooting the uh, title sequence for Uncle Meat right now")
24. Tengo Na Minchia Tanta 3:46 ("Ah, tengo na minchia tanta")
25. Uncle Meat Film Excerpt Part II 3:51 ("I used to watch him eat")
26. King Kong Itself (as played by the Mothers in a studio) 0:51
27. King Kong (its magnificence as interpreted by Dom DeWild) 1:19
28. King Kong (as Motorhead explains it) 1:45
29. King Kong (the Gardner Varieties) 6:17
30. King Kong (as played by 3 deranged Good Humor Trucks) 0:33
31. King Kong (live on a flat bed diesel in the middle of a race track at a Miami Pop Festival... the Underwood ramifications) 7:25 rec. May 18, 1968

Issues:   ZFT reissue  Zappa Records ZR3839
         Original issue  Warner Bizarre/Reprise 2MS 2024 (contains 1-22, 26-31)
         Rykodisc reissue  RCD 10506-07

Transcriptions: Piano arrangement of "Uncle Meat" was published in *The Frank Zappa Songbook* volume 1 (Los Angeles: Frank Zappa Music; Astoria NY: Big 3, 1973; reprinted in Cologne and Frankfurt, West Germany: Amsco/Melodie der Welt, 1982).

HERE'S THE DEAL: The first album to be originally issued under Zappa's new contract with Warner Brothers/Reprise, *Uncle Meat* is a sprawling, largely instrumental work that furthered the musical and assembling/editing concepts heard on *Lumpy Gravy* (no. 3). Add to this a few truly bizarre lyrical numbers and you have an amazingly satisfying whole, the final great statement from the original Mothers as an active unit (they would disband four months after the release of this album. Brilliant.

RATING: *****

DOWNLOAD THESE: Uncle Meat: Main Title Theme, Dog Breath In The Year Of The Plague, The Dog Breath Variations, A Pound For A Brown On The Bus, Mr. Green Genes, Cruising For Burgers, King Kong (live)

DIFFERENCES BETWEEN THE ZFT CD REISSUE AND PREVIOUS CD REISSUES: None. All CD releases use a 1987 digital master of the album, which added bonus material in the form of lengthy audio tracks taken from FZ's movie *Uncle Meat* as well as being loaded with digital reverb. The original 1969 album master has yet to be reissued on CD as of this writing, although it was reissued on vinyl LP by the ZFT in 2013.

Zappa CD number: 7

Mothermania   (March 1969)

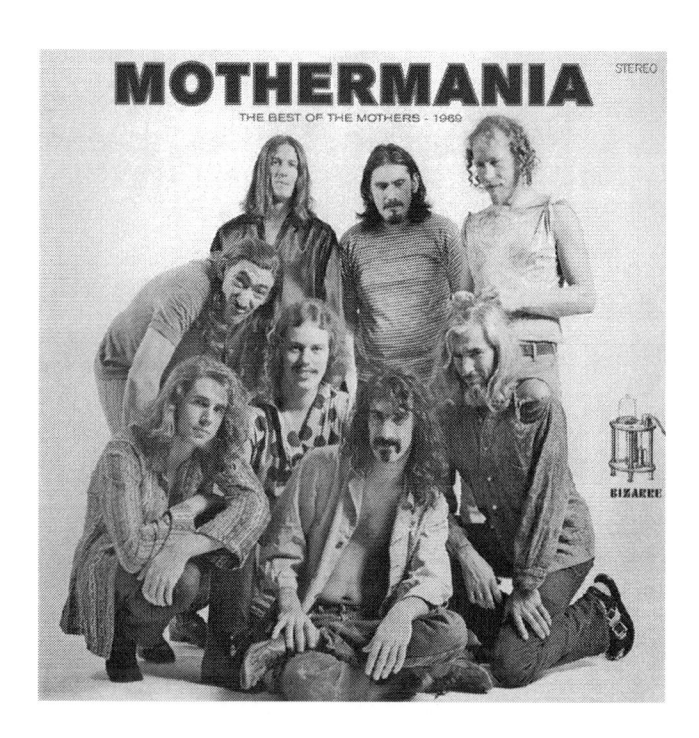

Performers:

Frank Zappa (guitar, vocals)
Ray Collins (lead vocalist, harmonica, percussion)
Jim Black (drums, vocals)
Roy Estrada (bass, vocals)
Elliot Ingber (guitar)
Jim Fielder: (guitar, piano)
Don Preston (keyboards)
Bunk Gardner (woodwinds)
Billy Mundi (drums, percussion)
Ian Underwood (piano, woodwinds)

All tracks previously issued and drawn from *Freak Out!* (no. 1), *Absolutely Free* (no. 2), and *We're Only In It For The Money* (no. 4).

1. Brown Shoes Don't Make It 7:26 ("Brown shoes, don't make it")
2. Mother People 1:41  ("We are the other people")
3. Duke Of Prunes 5:09  ("A moon beam through the prune, in June")

4. Call Any Vegetable 4:31  (spoken: "This is a song about vegetables. They keep you regular, they're real good for ya." sung: "Call any vegetable!")
5. The Idiot Bastard Son 2:26  ("The idiot bastard son")
6. It Can't Happen Here 3:13  ("It can't happen here, it can't happen here")
7. You Are Probably Wondering Why I'm Here 3:37  ("You're probably wondering why I'm here")
8. Who Are The Brain Police? 3:22  ("What will you do if we let you go home?")
9. Plastic People 3:40  (spoken: "Ladies and gentlemen, the President of the United States!" sung: "Plastic people, oh baby now, you're such a drag")
10. Hungry Freaks, Daddy 3:27  ("Mr. America, walk on by your schools that do not teach")
11. America Drinks And Goes Home 2:43  (spoken: "This is a special request, hope you enjoy it" sung: "I tried to find how my heart could be so blind, dear")

Issues:    ZFT reissue  Zappa Records ZR 3840
           Original issue: Verve V6-5068X
           Rykodisc reissue: None

Transcriptions: Piano/vocal arrangements of "Brown Shoes Don't Make It," "The Idiot Bastard Son," "Mother People" and "America Drinks and Goes Home" were published in *The Frank Zappa Songbook* volume 1 (Los Angeles: Frank Zappa Music; Astoria NY: Big 3, 1973; reprinted in Cologne and Frankfurt, West Germany: Amsco/Melodie der Welt, 1982).

HERE'S THE DEAL: *Mothermania* was a compilation album assembled by FZ to fulfill a contractual obligation with MGM/Verve before his departure for the supposedly greener pastures of Warner Brothers/Reprise. Essential as the only place to hear the uncensored version of "Mother People," which had been altered for *We're Only In It For The Money*. Also contains a remixed and re-edited version of "The Idiot Bastard Son." The other tracks appear in these same mixes on the first two Mothers albums.

RATING: ***

DOWNLOAD THESE: Mother People

DIFFERENCES BETWEEN THE ZFT CD REISSUE AND PREVIOUS CD REISSUES: This album, assembled by FZ and utilizing a number of mix and edit variations of previously released tracks, was reissued by the ZFT as a digital download in 2009 and finally on CD in 2012, though not as part of the ZFT/Universal deal. Amazingly enough, this marked the highly enjoyable *Mothermania*'s first appearance on CD.

Zappa CD number: 8

Hot Rats (October 1969)

Performers:

Frank Zappa (guitar, octave base, percussion)
Captain Beefheart (vocals)
Sugarcane Harris (electric violin)
Jean-Luc Ponty (electric violin)
John Guerin (drums)
Paul Humphrey (drums)
Ron Selico (drums)
Max Bennett (bass)
Shuggy Otis (bass)
Ian Underwood (piano, organ, flute, clarinets, saxes)
Lowell George, uncredited (guitar)

Recorded: T.T.G., LA; Sunset Sound, LA; Whitney Studios, Glendale, July-August, 1969.

Song titles  Duration  (first line)  year of source recording(s)
1. Peaches En Regalia 3:37
2. Willie The Pimp 9:16 ("I'm a little pimp with my hair gassed back")

3. Son Of Mr. Green Genes 8:58
4. Little Umbrellas 3:03
5. The Gumbo Variations 16:57
6. It Must Be A Camel 5:16

Issues:   ZFT reissue  Zappa Records ZR3841
          Original issue  Warner/Bizarre/Reprise RS 6356
          Rykodisc reissue Rykodisc RCD 10066, 10508

Transcriptions: guitar parts for the complete album transcribed in staff notation and in tablature on Zappa, *Hot Rats* (Milwaukee, WI: Hal Leonard, 2001).

HERE'S THE DEAL: As the original Mothers Of Invention era was coming to a close, Zappa came up trumps with his second solo effort. *Hot Rats* had FZ steering away from the complex collages of the last several albums and into the area of jazz-tinged rock. The result was another brilliant work from start to finish, and one that showcased FZ's lead guitar in its full-blown glory for the first time. This remains one of Zappa's most beloved albums, one which must be heard in its entirety to be fully appreciated. FZ's buddy Don Van Vliet (a.k.a. Captain Beefheart) provides a stunning lead vocal for the album's only vocal track, "Willie The Pimp."

RATINGS: *****

DOWNLOAD THESE: Peaches En Regalia, Willie The Pimp, Son Of Mr. Green Genes (though really you should get the whole thing)

DIFFERENCES BETWEEN THE ZFT CD REISSUE AND PREVIOUS CD REISSUES: The ZFT CD reissue uses, for the first time on the CD format, the original 1969 analog master tape mix and edit of the album. All previous CD reissues used a substantially remixed and expanded digital master, including an extended version of "The Gumbo Variations."

Zappa CD number: 9

Burnt Weeny Sandwich (February 1970)

Performers:

Frank Zappa (guitar, vocals)
Lowell George (guitar, vocals)
Roy Estrada (bass, vocals)
Don Preston (keyboards, Minimoog)
Ian Underwood (keyboards, clarinet, piano)
Buzz Gardner (trumpet)
Bunk Gardner (woodwinds)
Motorhead Sherwood (saxophone, vocals)
Jimmy Carl Black (drums, trumpet, vocals)
Art Tripp (drums, percussion)
Sugar Cane Harris (violin solo on "Little House I Used To Live In")
Janet Ferguson( backing vocals on "Dit-Dit-Doo-Way-Doo")

Material recorded unspecified dates in 1968-1969, but tracks 3 and 6 are believed to have been recorded in July-August 1969.

1. WPLJ (R. Dobard/L. McDaniels) 2:52 ("I say WPLJ, really taste good to me")
2. Igor's Boogie, Phase One 0:37

3. Overture To A Holiday In Berlin 1:27
4. Theme From Burnt Weeny Sandwich 4:32
5. Igor's Boogie, Phase Two 0:37
6. Holiday In Berlin, Full-Blown 6:23
7. Aybe Sea 2:46
8. The Little House I Used To Live In 18:42
9. Valarie 3:14  (Clarence Lewis-Bobby Robinson) (spoken: "Thank you, good night . . . Thank you, if you'll . . . if you sit down and be quiet, we'll make an attempt to, ah, perform Brown Shoes Don't Make It"  sung: "La la la la la la la" "Although you don't want me no more")

Issues:    ZFT reissue  Zappa Records ZR3842
           Original issue  Warner/Bizarre/Reprise RS 6370
           Rykodisc reissue  Rykodisc RCD 10509


Transcriptions:

Manuscript source material for "Little House I Used To Live In" reproduced in facsimile as "DB [Down Beat] Music Workshop: Frank Zappa's 'Little House,'" *Down Beat* 36 no. 22 (30 October 1969): 30, 32-33.

Piano arrangements of "Igor's Boogie" and "Little House I Used To Live In" were published in *The Frank Zappa Songbook* volume 1 (Los Angeles: Frank Zappa Music; Astoria NY: Big 3, 1973; reprinted in Cologne and Frankfurt, West Germany: Amsco/Melodie der Welt, 1982).

HERE'S THE DEAL: This was the first of two albums to be released by FZ following the breakup of the original Mothers Of Invention. Here he reverts to his standard collage style of editing, and the effect is harmonious and cohesive, bookened by two 1950s R&B covers (the bread in the sandwich, as it were). Packed top to bottom with musical delights.

RATING: ****

DOWNLOAD THESE: Holiday In Berlin Full Blown, The Little House I Used To Live In, Valarie

DIFFERENCES BETWEEN THE ZFT CD REISSUE AND PREVIOUS CD REISSUES: The ZFT CD reissue uses, for the first time on the CD format, the original 1969 analog master tape for the album. All previous CD reissues used a master which had been "enhanced" with digital reverb and featured a brief but audible moment of tape damage at the beginning of "The Little House I Used To Live In."

Zappa CD number: 10

Weasels Ripped My Flesh (August 1970)

Performers:

Frank Zappa (lead guitar, vocals)
Ray Collins (vocals on "Oh No")
Lowell George (rhythm guitar, vocals)
Don "Sugarcane" Harris (electric violin and vocals on "Directly From My Heart To You")
Ian Underwood (alto saxophone)
Bunk Gardner (tenor saxophone)
Motorhead Sherwood (baritone saxophone)
Buzz Gardner (trumpet, flugelhorn)
Roy Estrada (bass guitar, vocals)
Don Preston (keyboards, electronics)
Jimmy Carl Black (drums)

1. Didja Get Any Onya? 6:51 ("MOO-AHHH, MOO-AHHH, MOO-AHHH! Years ago in Germany...") rec. March 2, 1969, Philadelphia Arena, Philadelphia PA
2. Directly From My Heart To You (Penniman) 5:16 ("Direct, directly from my heart to you") rec. July 1969, T.T.G Studios, Los Angeles CA

3. Prelude to the Afternoon of a Sexually Aroused Gas Mask 3:48  rec. October 25, 1968, Royal Festival Hall, London, England

4. Toads of the Short Forest 4:48 ("At this very moment on stage we have drummer A playing in ⅞...") rec. August 1969, Whitney Studios, Glendale, CA, and February 7-8, 1969, Thee Image, Miami, FL)

5. Get a Little 2:31  ("Yes . . . be hot . . . and everybody workin' on it . . .") rec. February 13, 1969, The Factory, The Bronx, New York City

6. The Eric Dolphy Memorial Barbecue 6:52  rec. June 1969 A&R Studios, New York City

7. Dwarf Nebula Processional March and Dwarf Nebula 2:12  rec. December 1967 - February 1968, Apostolic Studios, New York City

8. My Guitar Wants To Kill Your Mama 3:32 ("You know, your mama and your daddy") rec. February 1969, Criteria Studios, Miami FL, and August-September 1969, T.T.G. Studios, Los Angeles, CA

9. Oh No 1:45  ("Oh no I don't believe it") rec. December 1967 - February 1968, Apostolic Studios, New York City

10. The Orange County Lumber Truck 3:21  rec. October 25, 1968, Royal Festival Hall, London, England

11. Weasels Ripped My Flesh 2:08 rec. May 30, 1969, Town Hall, Birmingham, England

Issues:   ZFT reissue  Zappa Records ZR3843
          Original issue  Warner/Bizarre/Reprise MS 2028
          Rykodisc reissue  Rykodisc RCD 10510

Transcriptions: Piano/vocal arrangement of "Oh No" was published in *The Frank Zappa Songbook* volume 1 (Los Angeles: Frank Zappa Music; Astoria NY: Big 3, 1973; reprinted in Cologne and Frankfurt, West Germany: Amsco/Melodie der Welt, 1982).

HERE'S THE DEAL: The second and last "in memoriam" album for the original Mothers Of Invention, this one focuses on the group's more difficult, demanding side. There are also moments of beauty among the dissonance, such as "Toads Of The Short Forest" and the gorgeous "Oh No" featuring a breathtaking vocal from Ray Collins.

RATING: ***1/2

DOWNLOAD THESE: Toads Of The Short Forest, The Eric Dolphy Memorial Barbecue, Oh No

DIFFERENCES BETWEEN THE ZFT CD REISSUE AND PREVIOUS CD REISSUES: The ZFT CD reissue uses, for the first time on the CD format, the original 1970 analog master tape mix and edit of the album. All previous CD reissues used an expanded digital master, including an extended version of "Didja Get Any Onya?" as well as additional digital reverb.

Zappa CD number: 11

Chunga's Revenge (October 1970)

Performers:

Frank Zappa (guitar, vocals, Condor, harpsichord, drum set, wood blocks, temple blocks, boobams, tom-toms, etc.)
Max Bennett (bass)
George Duke (electric piano, vocal drum imitations, organ, trombone)
Aynsley Dunbar (drums, tambourine)
John Guerin (drums)
Don "Sugarcane" Harris (organ)
Mark Volman as The Phlorescent Leech (vocals)
Jeff Simmons (bass, vocals)
Ian Underwood (rhythm guitar, alto sax, electric piano, electric alto sax with wah-wah pedal, grand piano, tenor sax, organ, piano, pipe organ)
Howard Kaylan as Eddie (vocals, rhythm guitar)

Known locations and dates: T.T.G., Los Angeles, c. July 1969; The Record Plant, Los Angeles, March 1970; Minneapolis MN July 5, 1970; Whitney Studios, Glendale The Record Plant, LA, August 28-29, 1970;

1. Transylvania Boogie 5:01 March, 1970
2. Road Ladies 4:10 ("Don't it ever get lonesome?") August 28-29, 1970

3. Twenty Small Cigars 2:17  July, 1969
4. The Nancy and Mary Music 9:27  (spoken: "Everybody sing!") Recorded live at the Tyrone Guthrie Theater, Minneapolis, MN on July 5, 1970
5. Tell Me You Love Me 2:33  ("Tell me you love me") August 28-29, 1970
6. Would You Go All The Way? 2:29  ("Remember Freddie and Jo?") August 28-29, 1970
7. Chunga's Revenge 6:15 March, 1970
8. The Clap 1:23 March, 1970
9. Rudy Wants To Buy Yez A Drink 2:44  ("Hi and howdy doody, I'm the union man") August 28-29, 1970
10. Sharleena 4:03  ("I'm cryin', I'm cryin', cryin' for Sharleena") June, 1970

Issues:   ZFT reissue  Zappa Records ZR 3844
          Original issue  Warner/Bizarre/Reprise MS 2030
          Rykodisc reissue  Rykodisc RCD 10511

Transcriptions: None

HERE'S THE DEAL: Frank Zappa began 1970 doing a few shows with a five-man group known as Hot Rats. This band went into the studio and cut some tracks in March of 1970, with a view toward putting together an album. Fate intervened however, and in May FZ found himself playing with a partially-reunited Mothers Of Invention for a series of shows leading up to a major concert with the Los Angeles Philharmonic orchestra. Backstage at that show, Frank was introduced to Mark Volman and Howard Kaylan, the former lead singers for 1960s hitmakers The Turtles. Shortly thereafter, FZ put together a new version of The Mothers with Volman and Kaylan (rechristened The Phlorescent Leech and Eddie for contractual reasons, a name which was typically shortened to Flo and Eddie), and set out on tour with the new group (which is known as the "Vaudeville" era of The Mothers). They also went into the studio and cut some tracks over the next few months, and out of these sessions (and one live cut from the new Mothers) Frank was able to construct his next solo album, adding some of the Hot Rats material from March 1970. The result was *Chunga's Revenge*, an album which was more of a hodgepodge than any previous Zappa/Mothers album. While the album contains a number of major musical moments with many great songs, as a totality it doesn't quite jell being neither "this" nor "that" in terms of concept. It was an important album however, in that it pointed the way toward the major film project that FZ was engrossed in at the time, a project known as *200 Motels* (no. 13).

RATING: ***

DOWNLOAD THESE: Transylvania Boogie, Road Ladies, Twenty Small Cigars, Tell Me You Love Me, Chunga's Revenge, Sharleena

DIFFERENCES BETWEEN THE ZFT CD REISSUE AND PREVIOUS CD REISSUES: The ZFT CD reissue uses, for the first time on the CD format, the original 1970 analog master tape of the album. All previous CD reissues used a substandard digital master "re-tweezed" by FZ and incorporating, you guessed it, a generous amount of the dreaded digital reverb. An absolutely stunning remaster from the ZFT.

Zappa CD number: 12

Fillmore East - June 1971   (August 1971)

*THE* MOTHERS
*Fillmore East - June 1971*

Performers:
Frank Zappa (guitar, dialogue)
Aynsley Dunbar (drums)
Bob Harris (second keyboard, vocals)
Howard Kaylan (lead vocals, dialogue)
Jim Pons (bass, vocals, dialogue)
Don Preston (minimoog)
Ian Underwood (winds, keyboards, vocals)
Mark Volman (lead vocals, dialogue)

All titles performed at the Fillmore East, New York City, June 5-6, 1971

1. Little House I Used To Live In 4:41
2. The Mud Shark 5:22  ("Mud shark")
3. What Kind of Girl Do You Think We Are? 4:17 ("What's a girl like you, doin' in a place like this?")
4. Bwana Dik 2:21 ("And if his dick is a monster")
5. Latex Solar Beef 2:38  ("Mud shark, mud shark, you could hear the steam baby")
6a. Willie The Pimp Part One 4:03
6b. Willie The Pimp Part Two 1:54
7. Do You Like My New Car? 7:08  ("You are, you gotta tell me something")
8. Happy Together (Bonner/Gordon) 2:57 ("Imagine me and you, I do")
9. Lonesome Electric Turkey 2:32

10. Peaches En Regalia 3:22
11. Tears Began To Fall 2:46 ("Tears began to fall")

Issues:   ZFT reissue  Zappa Records ZR3845
          Original issue  Warner/Bizarre/Reprise  MS 2042
          Rykodisc reissue  Rykodisc RCD 10512

Transcriptions: None

HERE'S THE DEAL: Recorded live at promoter Bill Graham's legendary New York concert venue, *Fillmore East – June 1971* features FZ and the Vaudeville-era Mothers performing a lengthy oratorio about the life of rock and roll musicians on the road (focusing on the sexual escapades made available to young rock star types). The album, while being considered by older fans to be more "lowbrow" than any previous Zappa album, managed to gain Zappa a new following of young males, who found the "dirty" texts to be found within quite appealing. As a piece of folklore, it is certainly one of the high points in the Zappa catalog.

RATING: ****

DOWNLOAD THESE: The Mud Shark, Willie the Pimp Parts One and Two, Do You Like My New Car?

DIFFERENCES BETWEEN THE ZFT CD REISSUE AND PREVIOUS CD REISSUES: One of the major wins for the ZFT in their 2012 reissue series was this album, which for the first time in the digital format utilized the 1971 analog master tape in its complete form. All previous CD issues used a substandard digital master featuring a touch of digital reverb this album never needed as well as omitting "Willie The Pimp Part Two," largely because FZ did not want a break in the programming (and allegedly because he didn't like the guitar solo, although I can't imagine why!). The 2012 is far and away the definitive digital release of this album.

Zappa CD number: 13

200 Motels   (October 1971)

Performers:

Frank Zappa (bass, guitar, producer, orchestration)
Mark Volman (vocals)
Howard Kaylan (vocals)
Jimmy Carl Black (vocals)
Jim Pons (vocals)
George Duke (trombone, keyboards)
Ian Underwood (keyboards, woodwind)
Ruth Underwood (percussion)
Aynsley Dunbar (drums)
Royal Philharmonic Orchestra, Elgar Howarth (conductor)
The Top Score Singers, David Van Asch (conductor)
Phyllis Bryn-Julson (soprano)
John Williams (supervisor of guitar ensemble)
Theodore Bikel (narrator)

All titles recorded February and March 1971

1. Semi-Fraudulent/Direct-From-Hollywood Overture 1:59 (spoken: "Ladies and gentlemen!" sung: "200 motels!")
2. Mystery Roach 2:32 ("How long? How long? Till that mystery roach be arrivin' soon")
3. Dance Of The Rock and Roll Interviewers 0:48
4. This Town Is A Sealed Tuna Sandwich (Prologue) 0:55 ("This town we're in is just a Sealed Tuna Sandwich with the wrapper glued")
5. Tuna Fish Promenade 2:29 ("This town we're in is just a Sealed Tuna Sandwich with the wrapper glued")
6. Dance Of The Just Plain Folks 4:40
7. This Town Is A Sealed Tuna Sandwich (Reprise) 0:58 ("This town we're in is just a Sealed Tuna Sandwich with the wrapper glued")
8. The Sealed Tuna Bolero 1:40 ("This town we're in is just a Sealed Tuna Sandwich with the wrapper glued")
9. Lonesome Cowboy Burt 3:59 ("My name is Burtram, I am a redneck")
10. Touring Can Make You Crazy 2:52
11. Would You Like A Snack? 1:23 ("Went on the road for a month touring")
12. Redneck Eats 3:02 (spoken: "Hey, who are these dudes? Are you a boy, or a girl?")
13. Centerville 2:31 ("Centerville: A real nice place to raise your kids up")
14. She Painted Up Her Face 1:41 ("She painted up her face")
15. Janet's Big Dance Number 1:18 ("The clock upon the wall, has struck the midnight hour")
16. Half A Dozen Provocative Squats 1:57 ("She painted up her face, she sat before the mirror")
17. Mysterioso 0:48
18. Shove It Right In 2:32 ("She chooses all the clothes ")
19. Lucy's Seduction of A Bored Violinist and Postlude 4:01
20. I'm Stealing The Towels 2:14 ("I'm stealing the towels!")
21. Dental Hygiene Dilemma 5:11 (spoken: "No, Jeff" "Man! This stuff is great!")
22. Does This Kind of Life Look Interesting To You? 2:59 ("Does this kind of life look interesting to you?)
23. Daddy, Daddy, Daddy 3:11 ("Ooo-ooo, do you like my new car?")
24. Penis Dimension 4:37 ("Penis dimension")
25. What Will This Evening Bring Me This Morning 3:32 ("What will this evening Bring me this morning?")
26. A Nun Suit Painted On Some Old Boxes 1:08 ("Why don't you strap on this here bunch Of cardboard boxes, daddy-o?")
27. Magic Fingers 3:53 ("Ooh, the way you love me, lady, I get so hard now I could die")
28. Motorhead's Midnight Ranch 1:28
29. Dew On The Newts We Got 1:09 ("Dew, on the newts we got")
30. The Lad Searches The Night For His Newts 0:41 ("The lad searches the night for his newts")
31. The Girl Wants To Fix Him Some Broth 1:10 ("The girl wants to fix him some broth.")
32. The Girl's Dream 0:54 (spoken: "The girl" sung: "The girl wants to fix him some broth")
33. Little Green Scratchy Sweaters and Courduroy Ponce 1:00 ("Broth reminds me of nuns")
34. Strictly Genteel (The Finale) 11:10 (spoken: "This, as you might have guessed, is the end of the movie." sung: "Lord, have mercy on the people of England" the finale: "They're gonna clear out the studio")

Additional tracks added for CD

35. "Coming Soon!..." (0:55)
36. "The Wide Screen Erupts..." (0:58)
37. "Coming Soon!..." (0:31)
38. "Frank Zappa's 200 Motels..." (0:13)
39. Magic Fingers (Single Edit) (2:56) ("Ooh, the way you love me, lady, I get so hard now I could die")

Issues:   ZFT reissue - none
          Original issue United Artists UAS 9956
          Rykodisc reissue: Rykodisc RCD 10513/14

Transcriptions: Piano arrangement of "Penis Dimension" was published in *The Frank Zappa Songbook* volume 1 (Los Angeles: Frank Zappa Music; Astoria NY: Big 3, 1973; reprinted in Cologne and Frankfurt, West Germany: Amsco/Melodie der Welt, 1982).

HERE'S THE DEAL: Frank Zappa spent most of 1970 working on this, his first major film project, for United Artists. The music consisted mainly of pieces dating back to at least 1968. Most of the soundtrack album, which alternates ballsy rock and roll songs from the Vaudeville-era Mothers with stunning classical music brought to life by London's Royal Philharmonic Orchestra, was recorded live during the film shoot in early 1971. The entire album is strongly recommended as a good overview of Frank Zappa as composer/creative genius.

RATING: ****

DOWNLOAD THESE: Semi-Fraudulent/Direct-From-Hollywood Overture, Lonesome Cowboy Burt, Centerville, Shove It Right In, Dental Hygiene Dilemma, Daddy Daddy Daddy, Penis Dimension, What Will This Evening Bring Me This Morning, Magic Fingers, Strictly Genteel (The Finale)

NOTE: This album was not reissued as part of the ZFT reissue campaign, as the ZFT do not own the rights to the soundtrack (which have been held by United Artists since day one). This album was given its first and only CD release in 1997, issued by Rykodisc and licensed from United Artists. Unfortunately, while the tape utilized for this release was indeed the original 1971 2-track analog master tape, it is the master itself which was substandard. This resulted in a muddy, boxy sound for the CD which was made worse by adding additional compression in the mastering stage. A true disappointment and an obvious example of a situation where the original vinyl album sounds better than the digital reproduction – though this applies only to the first pressings of the album, as subsequent vinyl reissues are actually of poorer quality than the CD! Sadly, the only way that this album will ever sound good in the digital domain is if it were remixed from the original multitrack tapes, and this is unlikely to *ever* happen, given the ZFT's lack of ownership of the album.

Zappa CD number: 14

Just Another Band From L.A. (March 1972)

Performers:

Frank Zappa (guitar, vocals)
Aynsley Dunbar (drums)
Howard Kaylan (lead vocals)
Jim Pons (bass, vocals)
Don Preston (keyboards, minimoog)
Ian Underwood (winds, keyboards, vocals)
Mark Volman (lead vocals)

All titles recorded at Pauley Pavilion, UCLA, Los Angeles, California, August 7, 1971.

1. Billy The Mountain 24:47 ("Billy The Mountain! Billy The Mountain!")
2. Call Any Vegetable 7:22 ("Call any vegetable! Call it by name!")
3. Eddie, Are You Kidding? 3:09 ("Eddie, are you kidding? I've seen you on my TV")
4. Magdalena 6:24 ("Hey! Ha! Ooh! There was a man, a little ole man")
5. Dog Breath 3:38 ("Primer mi carucha, Chevy 39")

Issues:   ZFT reissue  Zappa Records ZR3847
          Original issue Warner/Bizarre/Reprise MS 2075
          Rykodisc reissue  Rykodisc RCD 10161, RCD 10515

Transcriptions: None

HERE'S THE DEAL: This was the final album to be issued from the Vaudeville era of The Mothers, which broke up after FZ was seriously injured following an assault from an audience member at a show in London in December of 1971. *Just Another Band From LA* was another live album, recorded in August 1971 before a packed house at UCLA's Pauley Pavilion. The main track here is the lengthy concept piece "Billy The Mountain," about a mountain who travels (with his wife, who happens to be a tree growing off of his shoulder) across the country on vacation, destroying everything in his path. The rest of the album features two revisits of older Mothers material, as well as two new songs co-written with Howard Kaylan.

RATING: ***1/2

DOWNLOAD THESE: Billy The Mountain, Call Any Vegetable

DIFFERENCES BETWEEN THE ZFT CD REISSUE AND PREVIOUS CD REISSUES: The ZFT CD reissue uses, for the first time on the CD format, the original 1972 analog master tape of the album. All previous CD reissues used an "re-tweezed" digital master which featured evidence of tape damage and EQ work. Unfortunately, while there are improvements made in the 2012 remaster (the fade at the end of "Dog Breath" is slightly longer for one), this has also been subjected to the application of EQ, resulting in a "boomier" sound for the new CD that is not to every fan's taste.

Zappa CD number: 15

Waka/Jawaka (July 1972)

Performers:
Frank Zappa (acoustic guitar, electric bed springs, vocals, guitar, percussion)
Mike Altschul (baritone sax, piccolo, bass flute, bass clarinet, tenor sax, baritone sax)
Bill Byers (trombone, baritone horn)
George Duke (ring-modulated and echoplexed electric piano, tack piano)
Aynsley Dunbar (drums, washboard, tambourine)
Tony Duran (slide guitar, vocals)
Erroneous (electric bass, vocals, fuzz bass)
Janet Ferguson (vocals)
"Sneaky Pete" Kleinow (pedal steel solo)
Sal Marquez (trumpets, vocals, flugelhorn, chimes)
Joel Peskin (tenor sax)
Kris Peterson (vocals)
Don Preston (piano, Minimoog)
Ken Shroyer (trombone, baritone horn)
Jeff Simmons (Hawaiian guitar, vocals)

All tracks recorded April-May 1972, Paramount Studios, Los Angeles.

1. Big Swifty 17:22
2. Your Mouth 3:12 ("Your mouth is your religion")
3. It Just Might Be A One-Shot Deal 4:16 ("If the froggy come up a--with his satchel in his hand")
4. Waka/Jawaka 11:19


Issues:   ZFT reissue  Zappa Records ZR3848
             Original issue Warner/Bizarre/Reprise 2094
             Rykodisc reissue  Rykodisc RCD 10516

Transcriptions: None

HERE'S THE DEAL: Written and recorded while FZ was in a wheelchair recuperating from the assault in London, *Waka/Jawaka* was a return to the jazzy feel of *Hot Rats* (no.8). It is another stunner from start to finish, spearheaded by the towering "Big Swifty." The rest of the album is no slouch either.

RATING: *****

DOWNLOAD THESE: The whole thing, although "Big Swifty" is a must.

DIFFERENCES BETWEEN THE ZFT CD REISSUE AND PREVIOUS CD REISSUES: The ZFT CD reissue uses, for the first time on the CD format, the original 1972 analog master tape of the album. All previous CD reissues used a "re-tweezed" digital master that was given a coating of digital reverb. The CD is the ultimate digital presentation of this towering work.

Zappa CD number: 16

The Grand Wazoo (November 1972)

Performers:

Frank Zappa (guitars, percussion, vocals)
Mike Altschul (woodwinds)
JoAnn Caldwell-McNab (woodwinds)
Earle Dumler (woodwinds)
Fred Jackson (woodwinds)
Tony Ortega (woodwinds)
Joel Peskin (woodwinds)
Johnny Rotella (woodwinds)
Ernie Watts (woodwinds)
Bill Byers (brass)
Malcolm McNabb (brass)
Ernie Tack (brass)
Chunky (vocals)
Lee Clement (percussion, gong)
George Duke (keyboards, vocals)
Aynsley Dunbar (drums)
Tony Duran (guitars)
Erroneous (bass)
Alan Estes (percussion)

Bob Zimmitti (percussion)
Sal Marquez (woodwinds, vocals, brass, 'multiple toots')
Janet Neville-Ferguson (woodwinds, vocals)
Don Preston (mini-moog)
Ken Shroyer (brass, multiple trombones)

All tracks recorded April-May 1972, Paramount Studios, Los Angeles.

1. For Calvin (And His Next Two Hitch-Hikers) 6:06 ("Where did they go? When did they come from?")
2. The Grand Wazoo 13:20
3. Cletus Awreetus-Awrightus 2:57
4. Eat That Question 6:42
5. Blessed Relief 8:00

Issues:   ZFT reissue  Zappa Records ZR3849
          Original issue  Warner/Bizarre/Reprise MS 2093
          Rykodisc reissue  Rykodisc RCD 10517

Completist remarks: Track listing follows the 1972 LP. On the Zappa.com site, the track listing for all CD versions reverses the order of "For Calvin and His Next Two Hitch-hikers" and "The Grand Wazoo."

Transcriptions: None

HERE'S THE DEAL: Another "wheelchair era" album. *The Grand Wazoo* continues in the primarily instrumental vein of *Waka/Jawaka* (no.15), this time assembling a large ensemble of L.A.'s best studio musicians for a more big band/orchestral feel. The resulting album is no less brilliant than its predecessor, being some of the most breathtakingly beautiful music Frank Zappa ever produced. The album did not fare well commercially at the time of release, but that did not prevent it from becoming one of Zappa's most classic works.

RATING: *****

DOWNLOAD THESE: Everything, but if you must select, then For Calvin, The Grand Wazoo, Blessed Relief

DIFFERENCES BETWEEN THE ZFT CD REISSUE AND PREVIOUS CD REISSUES: The ZFT CD reissue uses, for the first time on the CD format, the original 1972 analog master tape of the album. All previous CD reissues used a digital master featuring the dreaded digital reverb again – though in this case, FZ's original digital master was not substandard to begin with. Still, the 2012 CD is the ultimate digital presentation of this classic album.

Zappa CD number: 17

Over-Nite Sensation (September 1973)

Performers:

Frank Zappa (guitar, vocals)
George Duke (keyboards, synthesizer)
Bruce Fowler (trombone)
Tom Fowler (bass)
Ralph Humphrey (drums)
Sal Marquez (trumpet, vocals)
Jean-Luc Ponty (violin, baritone violin)
Tina Turner, Lynn (Linda Sims) ahd Debbie (Wilson), uncredited (backing vocals)
Ian Underwood (flute, clarinet, alto and tenor sax)
Ruth Underwood (percussion)
Kin Vassy, uncredited (backing vocals)
Ricky Lancelotti (backing vocals)

Recorded at Bolic Sound, Inglewood, CA; Whitney, Glendale, CA; and Paramount Studios, LA, CA, March-June, 1973.

Song titles  Duration  (first line)  year of source recording(s)
1. Camarillo Brillo 3:59 ("She had that Camarillo brillo")
2. I'm The Slime 3:34 ("I am gross and perverted")
3. Dirty Love 2:58 ("Give me your dirty love")
4. Fifty-Fifty 6:10 ("Well, my dandruff is loose")

5. Zomby Woof 5:10 ("Three hundred years ago I thought I might get some sleep")
6. Dinah-Moe Humm 6:02 ("I couldn't say where she's comin' from")
7. Montana 6:33 ("I might be movin' to Montana soon")

Issues:  ZFT reissue Zappa Records ZR3850
Original issue Warner/Bizarre/Reprise MS 2149
Rykodisc reissue RCD 40025, RCD 10518

Transcriptions: vocal melodies and guitar parts for the complete album transcribed in staff notation and in tablature on Zappa, *Over-nite Sensation* (Milwaukee, WI: Hal Leonard, 2010).

HERE'S THE DEAL: After the commercial failures of his last two albums, FZ went back to vocal tunes on his next album, recorded by a new Mothers lineup that featured some of the best musicians in any musical field (keyboardist George Duke, violinist Jean-Luc Ponty and percussionist Ruth Underwood to name but three). Lyrically, the album returns to the sexual themes of the Vaudeville era group, and also takes pot shots at television ("I'm The Slime") and wraps up with one of FZ's best-known songs about a wannabe dental floss rancher ("Montana"). A true Classic Album (they've even made a documentary about the making of it), featuring one of FZ's most beloved bands.

RATING: *****

DOWNLOAD THESE: Camarillo Brillo, I'm The Slime, Zomby Woof, Dinah-Moe-Humm, Montana

DIFFERENCES BETWEEN THE ZFT CD REISSUE AND PREVIOUS CD REISSUES: The ZFT CD reissue uses, for the first time on the CD format, the original 1973 analog master tape mix and edit of the album. All previous CD reissues used a digital master that featured additional digital reverb (standard operating procedure for FZ's intial CD catalog releases as I'm sure you understand by now!). For some reason, the 2012 CD switches the stereo channels around (right for left, left for right). But this is still far and away the ultimate digital presentation of this indisputable classic album.

Zappa CD number: 18

Apostrophe (') (March 1974)

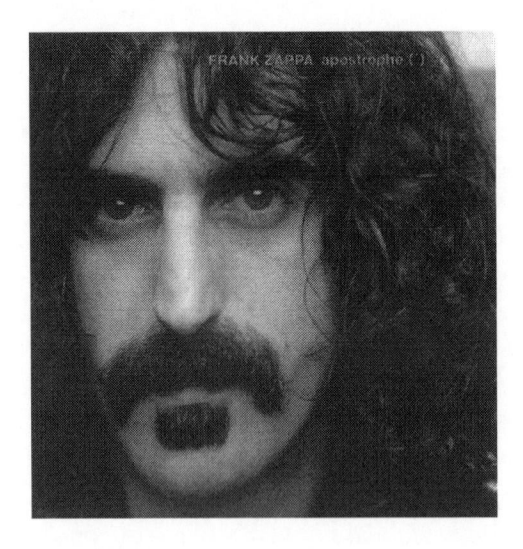

Performers:

Frank Zappa (guitars, bass, lead vocals)
Napoleon Murphy Brock (saxophone, back-up vocals)
Jack Bruce (bass)
Robert "Frog" Camarena (back-up vocals)
Ray Collins (back-up vocals)
Debbie (back-up vocals)
Ruben Ladron de Guevara (back-up vocals)
Alex Dmochowski (Erroneous) (bass)
George Duke (keyboards, back-up vocals)
Aynsley Dunbar (drums)
Tony Duran (rhythm guitar)
Bruce Fowler (trombone)
Tom Fowler (bass)
Susie Glover (back-up vocals)
Jim Gordon (drums)
Johnny Guerin (drums)
Sugar Cane Harris (violin)
Ralph Humphrey (drums)
Lynn (back-up vocals)
Sal Marquez (trumpet)
Kerry McNabb (back-up vocals)
Jean-Luc Ponty (violin)
Ian Underwood (saxophone)
Ruth Underwood (percussion)

1. Don't Eat The Yellow Snow 2:07  ("Dreamed I was an Eskimo") summer 1973
2. Nanook Rubs It 4:37 ("Well right about that time, people, a fur trapper") summer 1973
3. St. Alfonzo's Pancake Breakfast 1:51 ("Yes indeed, here we are! At Saint Alfonzo's Pancake Breakfast")    summer 1973
4. Father O'Blivion 2:18  ("Get on your feet an' do the funky Alfonzo! Father Vivian O'Blivion resplendent in his frock")   summer 1973
5. Cosmik Debris 4:13     ("The Mystery Man came over")  Bolic Sound, Inglewood  May 26, 29 and June 1, 1973
6. Excentrifugal Forz 1:33 ("The clouds are really cheap")  Basic track probably recorded c. August-September, 1969
7. Apostrophe' 5:50  Recorded at Electric Ladyland Studios, NYC  November 7, 1972
8. Uncle Remus 2:44  ("Wo, are we movin' too slow?")  Paramount Studios, LA   April-May, 1972
9. Stink-Foot 6:34  ("In the dark, where all the fevers grow") The Record Plant, LA   March 1970

Issues:    ZFT reissue  Zappa Records ZR3851
           Original issue  Warner/Bizarre/Reprise DS 2175
           Rykodisc reissue  Rykodisc RMD 40025, RCD 80519

Transcriptions: Vocal melodies and guitar parts for the complete album transcribed in staff notation and in tablature on Zappa, *Apostrophe (')* (Milwaukee, WI: Hal Leonard, 2003).

HERE'S THE DEAL: Another classic-album-that-they-made-a-documentary-about-the-making-of, *Apostrophe (')* is loaded from top to bottom with tracks that are among any even casual Zappa fan's favorites. Also contained FZ's only top ten hit single "Don't Eat The Yellow Snow." Another must have album, without a doubt.

RATING: *****

DOWNLOAD THESE: Don't Eat The Yellow Snow, Cosmik Debris, Uncle Remus, Stink-Foot

DIFFERENCES BETWEEN THE ZFT CD REISSUE AND PREVIOUS CD REISSUES: This one has a long and confusing digital release history. The original CD, released in 1986, was coupled with *Over-Nite Sensation* (no.17) as a "two-fer" disc. This suffered from the addition of Ye Olde Digital Reverb, and it was poorly mastered. A 1990 European reissue of the "two-fer" CD offered a "UMRK digital remix," which essentially featured less reverb and improved sonics in the mastering. Unfortunately there were a number of additional problems, such as dropouts, present on the 1990 disc. The 1995 Ryko CD reissue – which was issued as a stand-alone disc – used the 1990 remix, this time with improved mastering but, oddly, with additional digital reverb. In 1998, the original 1974 analog master tape was issued by Ryko as part of its "Au20" gold disc series, albeit with one noticeable tape glitch. This master eventually was used for the standard silver CD pressing of the CD, issued without fanfare in 1999. Finally, the 2012 ZFT reissue again uses the analog master tape, without the tape glitch. That makes this the ultimate digital presentation of the album, and a win for the ZFT.

Zappa CD number: 19

Roxy and Elsewhere  (July 1974)

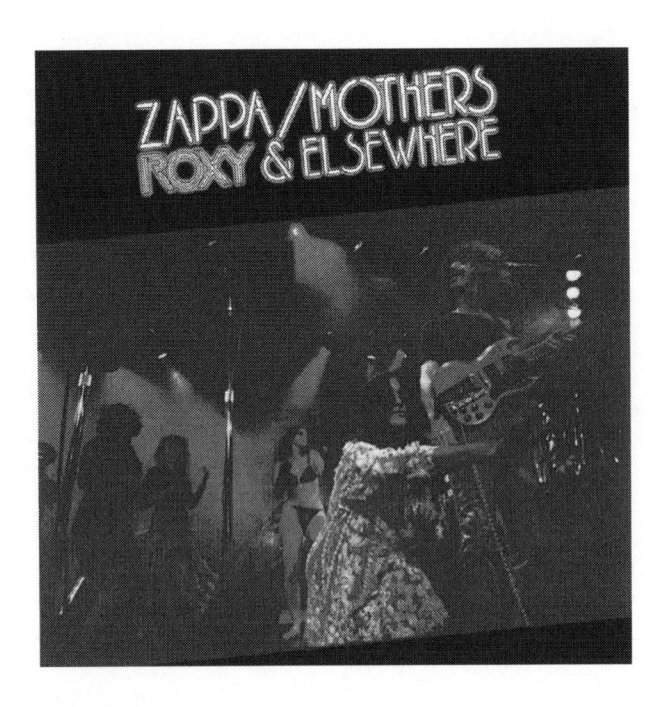

Performers:

Frank Zappa (guitar, vocals)
Napoleon Murphy Brock (tenor sax, flute, vocals)
George Duke (keyboards, vocals)
Bruce Fowler (trombone)
Tom Fowler (bass)
Walt Fowler (trumpet)
Don Preston (synthesizer)
Jeff Simmons (rhythm guitar, vocals)
Chester Thompson (drums)
Ralph Humphrey (drums)
Ruth Underwood (percussion)
Debbi Wilson (overdub backing vocals)
Lynn (Linda Sims)  (overdub backing vocals)
Ruben Guevara  (overdub backing vocals)
Robert Camarena  (overdub backing vocals)

All material recorded December 7-12, 1973 at the Roxy, Los Angeles, except where noted. Some overdubs (mostly of vocals) done at Bolic Studios and Paramount Studios, Hollywood, summer 1974.

1. Penguin In Bondage 6:48 ("Thank you. Brian, I could use a little bit more monitor.")
 portion from Auditorium Theater in Chicago, Illinois, May 11, 1974

2. Pygmy Twylyte 2:12 ("Green hocker croakin' in the Pygmy Twylyte")
3. Dummy Up 6:03 ("Sunrise, get up in the mornin'")
4. Village Of The Sun 4:17 ("Thank you ...thank you very much ...awright, does anybody here know where Palmdale is?")
5. Echidna's Arf (Of You) 3:53
6. Don't You Ever Wash That Thing? 9:40 ("Ladies and gentlemen, watch Ruth!")
7. Cheepnis 6:31 (""Cheepnis." Let me tell you something, do you like monster movies?" sung: "I ate a hot dog")
8. Son Of Orange County 5:53 ("And in your dreams, you can see yourself") Edinboro State College in Pennsylvania on May 8, 1974
9. More Trouble Every Day 6:00 ("Well I'm about to get sick, from watchin' my TV") Edinboro State College in Pennsylvania on May 8, 1974
10. Be-Bop Tango (Of The Old Jazzmen's Church) 16:41 (spoken: "Some of you may know that the tango")

Issues:   ZFT reissue  Zappa Records ZR3852
          Original issue  Warner Discreet 2DS 2202
          Rykodisc reissue Rykodisc RCD 10520

Transcriptions: None

HERE'S THE DEAL: *Roxy & Elsewhere* is a legendary album among Zappa fans, featuring a band that is among FZ's most beloved and several equally loved songs. Recorded live (mostly) at the legendary Los Angeles club The Roxy, the shows were also filmed for a television special which remains at the top of every Zappa fan's want list 40 years later. Stunning in its musical complexity, this is another major Zappa classic. For more music from these dates, see Roxy By Proxy (no.99).

RATING: *****

DOWNLOAD THESE: Penguin In Bondage, Pygmy Twylyte, Village Of The Sun, Don't You Ever Wash That Thing?, Cheepnis, Be-Bop Tango (Of The Old Jazzmen's Church)

DIFFERENCES BETWEEN THE ZFT CD REISSUE AND PREVIOUS CD REISSUES: The original 1992 CD reissue was actually available in two varieties: the European issue, which used the original 1974 analog master tape unaltered, and the American issue. The first pressing of the American issue was identical to the European release (and the original vinyl LP), but this was quickly replaced with a second pressing which featured a new (and very slightly longer) remix of "Cheepnis". The version with the "Cheepnis" remix was made the standard CD version of the album with the 1995 Ryko CD reissue, and was issued again by the ZFT in 2012. This means that the original Zappa Records European-only issue version of the CD, from 1992, is the current ultimate digital presentation of this album (unless you like the "Cheepnis" remix [most fans do not]).

Zappa CD number: 20

One Size Fits All (June 1975)

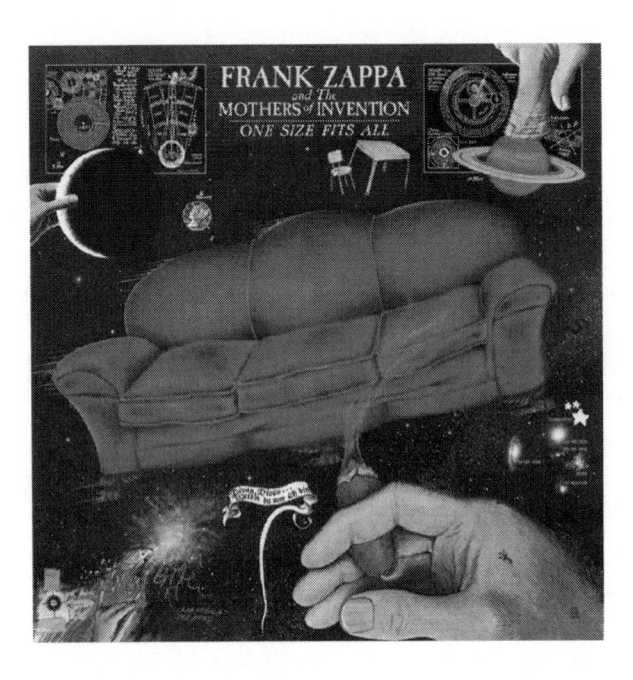

Performers:

Frank Zappa (guitars, vocals)
George Duke (keyboards, synthesizers, vocals)
Napoleon Murphy Brock (flute, tenor sax, vocals)
Chester Thompson (drums)
Tom Fowler (bass)
Ruth Underwood (percussion)
James Youman (bass)
Johnny "Guitar" Watson (flambe vocals)
Bloodshot Rollin' Red (Captain Beefheart) (harmonica)

Recorded: The Record Plant, Los Angeles; Caribou, Nederland, Colorado; Paramount Studios, Los Angeles, December, 1974-April, 1975.


1. Inca Roads 8:45 ("Did a vehicle come from somewhere out there?")
2. Can't Afford No Shoes 2:38 ("Have you heard the news?")
3. Sofa No. 1 2:39
4. Po-Jama People 7:39 ("Some people's hot, some people's cold")
5. Florentine Pogen 5:27 ("She was the daughter of a wealthy Florentine Pogen")

6. Evelyn, A Modified Dog 1:04 ("Evelyn, a modified dog")
7. San Ber'dino 5:57 ("She lives in Mojave in a Winnebago")
8. Andy 6:04 ("Is there anything good inside of you")
9. Sofa No. 2 2:42 ("I am the heaven")

Issues:   ZFT reissue  Zappa Records ZR 3853
          Original issue  Warner DiscReet DS 2216
          Rykodisc reissue  Rykodisc RCD 80521

Transcriptions: Vocal melodies and guitar parts for the complete album transcribed in staff notation and in tablature on Zappa, *One Size Fits All* (Milwaukee, WI: Hal Leonard, 2011).

HERE'S THE DEAL: 1974 wrapped up with FZ touring a slimmed-down version of the *Roxy*-era Mothers, performing incredible shows night after night with a group that would become a great many Zappa fan's all-time favorite lineup. *One Size Fits All* was recorded primarily with that group, with parts of the album tracked live during the taping of another failed TV special (see also CDs nos. 81 and 97). Some of the best musicianship a Zappa band ever had is in full evidence here, and the pieces they are playing are as musically complex and diverse as any you will find in the Zappa catalog. Mind-blowing, and another obvious must have.

RATING: *****

DOWNLOAD THESE: Inca Roads, Sofa No. 1, Florentine Pogen, San Ber'Dino, Andy

DIFFERENCES BETWEEN THE ZFT CD REISSUE AND PREVIOUS CD REISSUES: The original 1989 CD reissue of the album uses a digital master tape which adds a coating of digital reverb but is otherwise the same as the original vinyl mix. This "re-tweezed" version was issued a second time as part of Ryko's 1995 reissue campaign. In 1998, Ryko reissued this album as part of their "Au20" gold disc series, this time using the original 1975 analog tape master without the digital reverb. The 2012 ZFT CD master again ultilized the original analog tape master.

Zappa CD number: 21

Bongo Fury (October 1975)

Performers:

Frank Zappa (lead guitar, vocals)
Terry Bozzio (drums)
Robert "Frog" Camarena, uncredited (vocals on Debra Kadabra)
Napoleon Murphy Brock (sax, vocals)
George Duke (keyboards, vocals)
Bruce Fowler (trombone)
Tom Fowler (bass)
Chester Thompson (drums on "200 Years Old" and "Cucamonga")
Captain Beefheart (harp, vocals)
Denny Walley (slide guitar, vocals)

Recorded live at Armadillo World Headquarters, Austin Texas 20th and 21st of May 1975.

1. Debra Kadabra 3:54 ("Debra Kadabra, say she's a witch")
2. Carolina Hard-core Ecstasy 5:59 ("I coulda swore her hair was made of rayon")
3. Sam With The Showing Scalp Flat Top 2:51 ("Sam with the showing scalp flat top")
4. Poofter's Froth Wyoming Plans Ahead 3:03 (spoken: "While we're at it, we have a sort of a cowboy song we'd like to do for ya" sung: "Poofter's Froth, Wyoming")
5. 200 Years Old 4:32 ("I was sitting in a breakfast room in Allentown, Pennsylvania")

6. Cucamonga 2:24  ("Out in Cucamonga")
7. Advance Romance 11:17  ("No more credit from the liquor store")
8. Man With The Woman Head 1:28  (spoken: "Are you with me on this, people?"  sung: "The man with the woman head")
9. Muffin Man 5:32  (spoken: "The Muffin Man is seated at the table"  sung: "Girl, you thought he was a man, but he was a muffin")


Issues:    ZFT reissue  Zappa Records ZR 3854
           Original issue  Warner DiscReet DS 2234
           Rykodisc reissue  Rykodisc RCD 10097, Rykodisc RCD 10522

Transcriptions: None

HERE'S THE DEAL: The relationship between Frank Zappa and Don Van Vliet (a.k.a. Captain Beefheart) is legendary for several reasons, the first and foremost of which is the fact that both were mavericks in their field, and both were geniuses. Their relationship was also legendarily rocky, with periods of savage trashing in the press (mostly by Vliet) followed by periods of reconciliation. In early 1975, Vliet was down on his luck – his beloved Magic Band had folded, to be replaced by a so-called "Tragic Band" of skilled session musicians who lacked the imagination and intensity of previous lineups. Two albums recorded with these musicians, in an move toward greater commercial acceptance, had failed to achieve their goals. Without a record deal and near destitute, Vliet looked to his old buddy Frank for help. FZ assembled a band, wrote some new songs and took Vliet on the road with him, a tour that would result in the primarily live *Bongo Fury* album. While the tour was typically rocky with most shows not using the Captain to his full potential, a better balance is achieved here with several Beefheart lead vocals. The rest of the album contains some of the better Zappa songs from the period, including one indisputable guitar classic, "Muffin Man."

RATING: ****

DOWNLOAD THESE: Debra Kadabra, Carolina Hard-Core Ecstasy, Advance Romance, Muffin Man

DIFFERENCES BETWEEN THE ZFT CD REISSUE AND PREVIOUS CD REISSUES: All digital issues of this album are sourced from the original 1975 analog tape master. The original 1989 Ryko CD had a number of mastering errors, which have been corrected for the 2012 ZFT issue. However, the ZFT remaster has apparently been subjected to additional EQ work, changing the sound of the album somewhat (for those fetishists who notice such things).

Zappa CD number: 22

Zoot Allures  (October 1976)

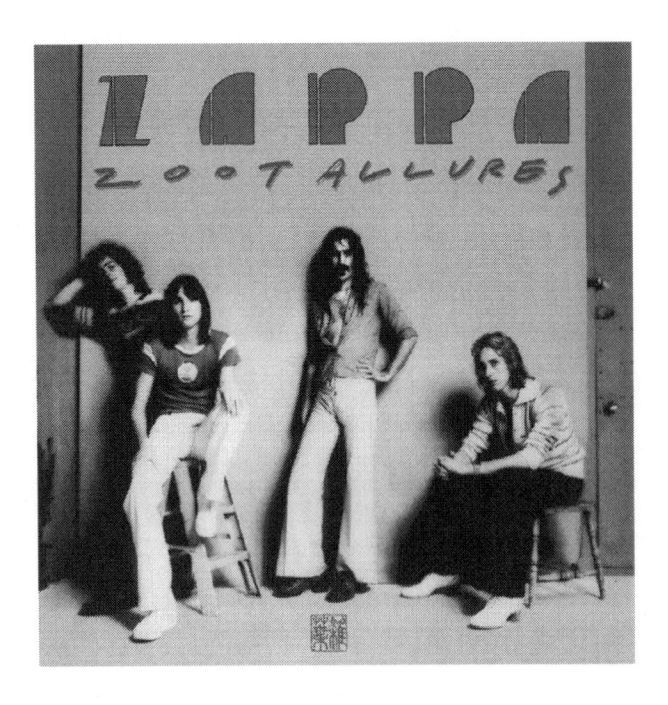

Performers:

Frank Zappa (guitar, bass, synth, vocals, keyboards)
Terry Bozzio (drums, vocals)
Napoleon Murphy Brock (sax, vocals)
Ruben Ladron de Guevara (vocals)
Roy Estrada (bass, vocals)
Andre Lewis (organ, vocals)
Davey Moire (vocals)
Lu Ann Neill (harp)
Sparkie Parker as Sharkie Barker (vocals)
Dave Parlato (bass)
Ruth Underwood (synth, marimba)
Captain Beefheart as Donnie Vliet (harmonica)

Recorded May-June 1976 at the Record Plant, Los Angeles unless noted otherwise.


1. Wind Up Workin' In A Gas Station 2:30  ("This here song might offend you some")
2. Black Napkins 4:15   Kosei Nenkin Kaikan, Osaka, Japan February 3, 1976
3. The Torture Never Stops 9:45  ("Flies all green 'n buzzin' in his dungeon of despair")
4. Ms Pinky 3:40 ("I got a girl with a little rubber head")
5. Find Her Finer 4:07  ("Find her finer, sneak up behind her")

6. Friendly Little Finger 4:17   Basic track: Hofstra University, Hempstead, October 26, 1975  (brass recorded May 30-June 1, 1973)
7. Wonderful Wino (FZ/Simmons) 3:38  ("L.A. in the summer of '69") 1973 (brass recorded May 30-June 1, 1973)
8. Zoot Allures 4:12  basic track recorded  Kosei Nenkin Kaikan, Osaka, Japan February 3, 1976
9. Disco Boy 5:10  ("Disco boy")

Issues:    ZFT reissue  Zappa Records ZR3855
           Original issue  Warner Bros. BS 2970
           Rykodisc reissue  Rykodisc RCD 10160, RCD 10523

Transcriptions: The guitar part for "Black Napkins" transcribed in staff notation by Steve Vai and published in Zappa, *The Frank Zappa Guitar Book* (Los Angeles: Munchkin Music, distributed by Milwaukee, WI: Hal Leonard, 1982).

HERE'S THE DEAL: In the fall of 1975, Zappa toured with a scaled-down Mothers lineup, which would turn out to be the last incarnation of The Mothers Of Invention. Frank got this lineup into the studio early in 1976 to cut a few tracks, and along with some outtakes dating back to 1973 and a couple of live tracks from the last Mothers lineup, he produced *Zoot Allures*. This would turn out to be his final non-contractual obligation album he would produce for Warner Brothers, with whom things were about to get very bad indeed. While many of the individual songs are fine, the album suffers from *Chunga's Revenge* (no. 11) syndrome in that it doesn't quite add up to a convincing whole. It's almost too much of a hodgepodge, but it did produce two of FZ's finest guitar vehicles in the title track and "Black Napkins," and one of his best songs, "The Torture Never Stops."

RATING: ***1/2

DOWNLOAD THESE: Black Napkins, The Torture Never Stops, Zoot Allures, Disco Boy

DIFFERENCES BETWEEN THE ZFT CD REISSUE AND PREVIOUS CD REISSUES: The original 1989 Ryko CD reissue of the album was treated to gobs of digital reverb by FZ. This resulted in a soupier, less clear sound overall and was compounded by poor digital mastering. It also chopped off the first few seconds of "Disco Boy." The 2012 ZFT reissue uses the original 1976 analog master tape for the first time on CD, which corrects all these issues. A must have for sure!

Zappa CD number: 23

Zappa in New York   (March 1978)

Performers:

Frank Zappa (conductor, lead guitar, vocals)
John Bergamo (percussion overdubs)
Terry Bozzio (drums, vocals)
Mike Brecker (tenor sax, flute)
Randy Brecker (trumpet)
Ronnie Cuber (baritone sax, clarinet)
Eddie Jobson (keyboards, violin, vocals)
Tom Malone (trombone, trumpet, piccolo)
Ed Mann (percussion overdubs)
Lou Marini (alto sax, flute)
Lou Anne Neill (osmotic harp overdubs)
Patrick O'Hearn (bass, vocals)
Don Pardo (sophisticaded narration)
David Samuels (timpani, vibes)
Ruth Underwood (percussion, synthesizer)
Ray White (rhythm guitar, vocals)

Recorded at The Palladium, New York, 26th - 29th December 1976.


1. Titties and Beer 7:36   ("It was the blackest night")
2. Cruisin' For Burgers 9:12   ("I must be free")

3. I Promise Not To Come In Your Mouth 3:31
4. Punky's Whips 10:50   (spoken: "In today's rapidly changing world, musical groups appear almost every day with some new promotional device " sung:  "I can't stand the way he pouts")
5. Honey, Don't You Want A Man Like Me? 4:11   ("Honey honey, hey, baby don't you want a man like me")
6. The Illinois Enema Bandit 12:41   (spoken: "And now folks, it's time for Don Pardo to deliver our special Illinois Enema Bandit-type announcement. Take it away, Don!" "This is a true story about a famous criminal from right around Chicago. " sung: "The Illinois Enema Bandit")
7. I'm The Slime 4:24   ("I am gross and perverted")
8. Pound For A Brown 3:41
9. Manx Needs Women 1:50
10. The Black Page Drum Solo/Black Page #1 3:50
11. Big Leg Emma 2:17   ("There's a big dilemma about my Big Leg Emma")
12. Sofa 2:56
13. Black Page #2 5:36
14. The Torture Never Stops 12:34   ("Flies all green 'n buzzin' in his dungeon of despair")
15. The Purple Lagoon/Approximate 16:40

Issues:   ZFT reissue  Zappa Records ZR 3856
          Original issue  Warner DiscReet D2 2290
          Rykodisc reissue Rykodisc RCD 10524/25

Transcriptions: none

HERE'S THE DEAL: The first of four contractural-obligation albums that FZ delivered to Warner Brothers upon leaving the label in 1977, *Zappa In New York* is probably also the most fully realized. A live album recorded with a top-shelf live band (FZ's first "solo" group) during a four-show holiday run in New York in December 1976, *Zappa In New York* oozes with virtuostic musicianship and several well-loved Zappa songs. Unfortunately, Warner Brothers censored the original album, removing the track "Punky's Whips" (a song about Angel guitarist Punky Meadows) out of fear of a lawsuit, censoring "Titties And Beer" and shuffling the track order around. This tampering with his art incensed FZ greatly, and the remaining three obligation albums were dumped onto Warners' lap without artwork or liner notes. The 1991 CD reissue of the album not only restores the censored bits but contains much in the way of previously-unreleased material from these shows. This would be a rare case where the CD issue of the album is probably the one to get.

RATING: ****1/2

DOWNLOAD THESE: Titties And Beer, Honey, Don't You Want A Man Like Me?, The Illinois Enema Bandit, Sofa, Black Page #2, The Purple Lagoon/Approximate

DIFFERENCES BETWEEN THE ZFT CD REISSUE AND PREVIOUS CD REISSUES: None. All digital versions of this album are sourced from an expanded and remixed Sony 1630 digital master tape, prepared by FZ in 1991. The original vinyl mix and edit has yet to appear in a digital format.

Zappa CD number: 24

Studio Tan (September 1978)

Performers:

Frank Zappa (guitar, keyboards)
Davey Moire (vocals)
Eddie Jobson (keyboards, yodeling)
George Duke (keyboards)
Max Bennett (bass)
Paul Humphrey (drums)
Chester Thompson (drums)
Don Brewer (bongos)
James Youman (bass)
Ruth Underwood (percussion, synthesizer)

1. The Adventures Of Greggery Peccary 20:34 ("The adventures of Greggery Peccary!")  The Record Plant on 3-14 January 1975 and at at the Royce Hall, UCLA on 18-19 September 1975
2. Revised Music For Guitar And Low-Budget Orchestra 7:36  January-February 1975
3. Lemme Take You To The Beach 2:44  ("Lemme take you to the beach")  Basic tracks August-September 1969, overdubs c.1976
4. RDNZL 8:13  Caribou Studios, December 1974

Issues:   ZFT reissue  Zappa Records ZR 3857
          Original issue  DiscReet DSK 2291
          Rykodisc reissue   Rykodisc RCD 10526

Transcriptions: none

HERE'S THE DEAL: Album #2 in FZ's contractual obligation series to fulfill his Warner Brothers contract. This one was doozy from start to finish, taken from sessions stretching back to 1969 and containing FZ's last extended concept piece "The Adventures Of Greggery Peccary" and two of his more beautiful instrumental compositions, "Revised Music For Guitar And Low-Budget Orchestra" and "RDNZL."

RATING: ****

DOWNLOAD THESE: The Adventures Of Greggery Peccary, Revised Music For Guitar And Low-Budget Orchestra, RDNZL

DIFFERENCES BETWEEN THE ZFT CD REISSUE AND PREVIOUS CD REISSUES: The original 1991 CD reissue of the album uses a digital master tape featuring a remix of "The Adventures Of Greggery Peccary." The 2012 ZFT CD reissue is sourced from the original 1976 analog master tape, including the original mix of "Greggery Peccary." One minor variation from the vinyl is that this CD track does not fade out as it does on the LP. Another win for the ZFT.

Zappa CD number: 25

Sleep Dirt  (January 1979)

Performers:

Frank Zappa (guitar, keyboards)
Dave Parlato (bass)
Terry Bozzio (drums)
George Duke (keyboards)
Patrick O'Hearn (bass)
Ruth Underwood (percussion)
Chad Wackerman (drum overdubs on CD)
Thana Harris (vocals overdubs on CD)
Bruce Fowler (all brass)
James Youman (bass)
Chester Thompson (drums)

Tracks 1 and 7 recorded at the Record Plant, Los Angeles, May-June, 1976
Tracks 2-6 recorded at the Caribou Studios, Nederland, Colorado, December, 1974

Song titles  Duration  (first line)  year of source recording(s)
1. Filthy Habits 7:33
2. Flambay 4:54  ("He used to be very kind in his own crude way")
3. Spider Of Destiny 2:33  ("Listen carefully, spider of destiny")
4. Regyptian Strut 4:13

5. Time Is Money 2:49  ("Time is money ... but space is a long, long time")
6. Sleep Dirt 3:21
7. The Ocean Is The Ultimate Solution 13:17

Issues:   ZFT reissue  Zappa Records ZR3858
          Original issue  Warner DiscReet DSK 2292
          Rykodisc reissue  Rykodisc RCD 10527

Transcriptions: none

HERE'S THE DEAL: The third installment in the "Ugly Albums" contractral-obligation series for Warner Brothers, *Sleep Dirt* contains a number of wonderful instrumental compositions, several of which were written for a never-realized Zappa play titled *Hunchentoot*. The *Hunchentoot* tracks were later overdubbed with vocals for their 1991 CD release.

RATING: ***

DOWNLOAD THESE: Filthy Habits, Regyptian Strut, Sleep Dirt

DIFFERENCES BETWEEN THE ZFT CD REISSUE AND PREVIOUS CD REISSUES: Another complicated one. All Rykodisc CD issues were sourced from a digital master tape prepared by FZ, which featured vocal overdubs on "Flambay," "Spider Of Destiny" and "Time Is Money," all of which were entirely instrumental on the original vinyl LP. The first pressing of the Ryko CD, issued in 1991, featured Chester Thompson's original drum track on "Regyptian Strut." This was replaced on later pressings by a Chad Wackerman overdub. The 2012 ZFT reissue uses the original 1976 analog master tape for the first time on CD. This is, of course, wonderful—but you still need both versions to have everything.

Zappa CD number: 26

Sheik Yerbouti   (March 1979)

Performers:
Frank Zappa (lead guitar, vocals)
Adrian Belew (rhythm guitar, vocals)
Tommy Mars (keyboards, vocals)
Peter Wolf (keyboards)
Patrick O'Hearn (bass, vocals)
Terry Bozzio (drums, vocals)
Ed Mann (clarinet)
David Ocker (clarinet)
Napoleon Murphy Brock (background vocals)
Andre Lewis (background vocals)
Randy Thornton (background vocals)
Davey Moire (background vocals)

1. I Have Been In You 3:34 ("Well, I have been in you, baby")  January 25, 1978, London
2. Flakes 6:41 ("Flakes! Flakes! Flakes! Flakes!") January 25, 1978, London
3. Broken Hearts Are For Assholes 3:42  (spoken: "Hey, now, hey! Hey! Do you know what you are?"  sung: "Some of you might not agree")  January 27, 1978, London
4. I'm So Cute 3:09 ("Feelin' sorry, feelin' sad")  January or February 1978
5. Jones Crusher 2:49 ("My baby's got Jones crushin' love")  October 31, 1977 NYC
6. What Ever Happened To All The Fun In The World 0:33 (spoken: "What ever happened to all the fun in the world?")
7. Rat Tomago 5:17  February 15, 1978 Berlin
8. Wait A Minute 0:31 (LP title: We've Got To Get Into Something Real) ("Wait a minute; we gotta get somethin' happenin' here")

9. Bobby Brown Goes Down 2:49 ("Hey there, people, I'm Bobby Brown") January or February 1978
10. Rubber Shirt 2:43 September 25, 1974, Goteborg, Sweden
11. The Sheik Yerbouti Tango 3:58 (spoken: "Why don't you take it down to C-sharp, Ernie?") February 15, 1978 Berlin
12. Baby Snakes 1:50 ("Baby snakes") February 28, 1978 London
13. Tryin' To Grow A Chin 3:32 ("Hey! I'm only fourteen, sickly 'n thin") January or February 1978
14. City Of Tiny Lites 5:31 ("City of tiny lites") January or February 1978
15. Dancin' Fool 3:43 ("I don't know much about dancin'") February 28, 1978 London
16. Jewish Princess 3:16 ("I want a nasty little Jewish Princess") October 30, 1977 NYC
17. Wild Love 4:09 ("Many well-dressed people in several locations") February 28, 1978 London
18. Yo' Mama 12:35 ("Maybe you should stay with yo' mama") vocal sections from February 28, 1978 London

Issues:   ZFT reissue Zappa Records ZR3859
          Original issue Zappa SRZ-2-1501
          Rykodisc reissue Rykodisc RCD 10528

Transcriptions: Guitar parts for "Sheik Yerbouti Tango," "Rat Tomago," and "Mo' Mama" transcribed in staff notation by Steve Vai and published in Zappa, *The Frank Zappa Guitar Book* (Los Angeles: Munchkin Music, distributed by Milwaukee, WI: Hal Leonard, 1982).

HERE'S THE DEAL: After two years in the wilderness wherein FZ could not sign to another label due to the ongoing legal dispute with the Brothers Warner, *Sheik Yerbouti* finally made its way to the public in early 1979, released on FZ's own Zappa Records label. Fittingly, this album was one of Zappa's very finest, featuring a slew of songs that even the casual Zappa fan will know and love. A fine comeback indeed, and a classic album to boot. FZ even got a hit single out of it with his put-down of disco culture "Dancin' Fool."

RATING: *****

DOWNLOAD THESE: Flakes, Broken Hearts Are For Assholes, Tryin' To Grow A Chin, City Of Tiny Lites, Dancin' Fool, Wild Love, Yo' Mama

DIFFERENCES BETWEEN THE ZFT CD REISSUE AND PREVIOUS CD REISSUES: The initial CD issue of this album, released in Europe in 1986, utilized an analog sub-master tape that had been sent to EMI and was issued without FZ's consent. This issue matched the content of the original vinyl release exactly. This issue was subsequently withdrawn, and replaced in 1990 with a Rykodisc pressing sourced from a 1630 digital master tape prepared by FZ. This pressing severely edits "I'm So Cute," shortens most everything else by a second or two and is poorly mastered to boot. The 2012 ZFT reissue is sourced from the original 1978 analog master tape, and corrects all of the problems with the Rykodisc version. This is the definitive version of the album, and a major win for the ZFT.

Zappa CD number: 27

Orchestral Favorites (May 1979)

Performers:

Frank Zappa (guitar)
Terry Bozzio (drums)
Dave Parlato (bass)
Mike Lang (keyboards)
Emil Richards (percussion)
Pamela Goldsmith (viola)
John Wittenberg (violin)
Bobby Dubow (violin)
Jerry Kessler (cello)
Bruce Fowler (trombone)
Earle Dumler (oboe)
Mike Altschul (flute, trumpet)
Malcolm McNabb (trumpet)
David Duke (french horn)
Dana Hughes (bass trombone)
Ray Reed (flute)
David Shostak (flute)
Tommy Morgan (harmonica)
Marty Perellis
Captain Beefheart (dancing)

Recorded at the Royce Hall, UCLA, September 18-19, 1975.

Song titles  Duration  (first line)  year of source recording(s)

1. Strictly Genteel 7:04
2. Pedro's Dowry 7:41
3. Naval Aviation In Art? 1:22
4. Duke Of Prunes 4:20
5. Bogus Pomp 13:27

Issues:   ZFT reissue  Zappa Records ZR 3860
          Original issue Warner DiscReet DSK 2294
          Rykodisc reissue  Rykodisc RCD 10529


Scores: The chamber version of "Pedro's Dowry" is available for rental only from Schott Music.

HERE'S THE DEAL: *Orchestral Favorites* was the final "contractual obligation" album that FZ delivered to Warner Brothers. It consists of compositions performed by a cobbled-together orchestra which performed these pieces live over two shows in 1975. Includes gorgeous reworkings of older pieces alongside a couple of newer compositions. Recommended for fans of FZ's classical side.

RATING: ***

DOWNLOAD THESE: Naval Aviation In Art?

DIFFERENCES BETWEEN THE ZFT CD REISSUE AND PREVIOUS CD REISSUES: None. All digital issues of this album are sourced from a 1630 digital master tape prepared by FZ, with additional EQ work and a reversed stereo image as compared to the vinyl LP. The original 1976 analog master tape has yet to appear in a digital format.

Zappa CD number: 28

Joe's Garage Act I (September 1979)

Performers:

Frank Zappa (lead guitar, vocals)
Warren Cuccurullo (rhythm guitar, vocals)
Denny Walley (slide guitar, vocals)
Ike Willis (lead vocals)
Peter Wolf (keyboards)
Tommy Mars (keyboards)
Arthur Barrow (bass, guitar (on "Joe's Garage"), vocals)
Ed Mann (percussion, vocals)
Vinnie Colaiuta (drums, combustible vapors, optometric abandon)
Jeff (tenor sax)
Marginal Chagrin (baritone sax)
Stumuk (bass sax)
Dale Bozzio (vocals)
Al Malkin (vocals)
Craig Steward (harmonica)

Recorded at Village Recorders "B," Los Angeles, April-June 1979

1. The Central Scrutinizer 3:28 ("This is the CENTRAL SCRUTINIZER")
2. Joe's Garage 6:10 ("It wasn't very large")
3. Catholic Girls 4:19 ("Catholic Girls! With a tiny little mustache")
4. Crew Slut 6:38 ("Hey Hey Hey all you girls in these industrial towns")
5. Fembot In A Wet T-Shirt 4:44 ("Looks to me like something funny is goin on around here")
6. On The Bus 4:31
7. Why Does It Hurt When I Pee? 2:23 ("Why does it hurt when I pee?")
8. Lucille Has Messed My Mind Up 5:42 ("Lucille has messed my mind up")
9. Scrutinizer Postlude 1:35 ("This is the CENTRAL SCRUTINIZER... again. Hi!...It's me again, the CENTRAL SCRUTINIZER.")

Issues:   ZFT reissue  Zappa Records ZR 3861
          Original issue Zappa SRZ-1-1603
          Rykodisc reissue Rykodisc RCD 10060

Transcriptions: none

HERE'S THE DEAL: *Joe's Garage Act I* was the first volume of a three-act "play" of sorts, which essentially details in allegorical form the years of depression FZ experienced after being blocked from getting himself a record deal by various legal machinations. Another MAJOR favorite album of Zappa fans everywhere, featuring several beloved Zappa songs. Certainly a must-have along with its follow-up *Acts II & III* (no.29).

RATING: *****

DOWNLOAD THESE: Joe's Garage, Catholic Girls, Crew Slut, Why Does It Hurt When I Pee?, Lucille Has Messed My Mind Up

DIFFERENCES BETWEEN THE ZFT CD REISSUE AND PREVIOUS CD REISSUES: All digital versions of this album (issued with *Joe's Garage Acts II & III* on two CDs) are essentially the same, and are faithful reproductions of the original vinyl LP. The one minor difference is that the original 1987 Rykodisc CD fixes an out-of-sync Central Scutinizer intro to the song "Joe's Garage" which had appeared on the vinyl LP. The 2012 ZFT CD uses the original 1979 analog tape master, and restores this Scrutinizer prelude to its original out-of-sync glory.

Zappa CD number: 29

Joe's Garage Acts II and III (November 1979)

Performers:

Frank Zappa (lead guitar, vocals)
Warren Cuccurullo (rhythm guitar, vocals)
Denny Walley (slide guitar, vocals)
Ike Willis (lead vocals)
Peter Wolf (keyboards)
Tommy Mars (keyboards)
Arthur Barrow (bass, guitar (on Joe's Garage), vocals)
Patrick O'Hearn (bass on Outside Now and He Used To Cut The Grass)
Ed Mann (percussion, vocals)
Vinnie Colaiuta (drums, combustible vapors, optometric abandon)
Jeff (tenor sax)
Marginal Chagrin (baritone sax)
Stumuk (bass sax)
Dale Bozzio (vocals)
Al Malkin (vocals)
Craig Steward (harmonica)
Geordie Hormel (chorus vocals)
Barbara Isaak (chorus vocals)

Recorded at Village Recorders "B," Los Angeles, April-June 1979

1. A Token Of My Extreme (5:29) ("Welcome to the First Church of Appliantology!")
2. Stick It Out (4:34) ("Fick mich, du miserabler Hurensohn")
3. Sy Borg (8:55) ("Sy Borg, gimme dat, gimme dat")
4. Dong Work For Yuda (5:03) ("This is the story 'bout Bald-Headed John")
5. Keep It Greasey (8:21) ("Keep it greasey so it'll go down easy")
6. Outside Now (5:49) ("These executives have plooked the fuck out of me")
7. He Used To Cut The Grass (8:35) ("I'm out at last")
8. Packard Goose (11:31) ("Maybe you thought I was the Packard Goose")
9. Watermelon In Easter Hay (9:05)
10. A Little Green Rosetta (8:14) ("A little green rosetta")

Issues:   ZFT reissue  Zappa Records ZR 3861
          Original issue Zappa SRZ-2-1502
          Rykodisc reissue Rykodisc RCD 10060

Transcriptions: Guitar parts for "Outside Now," "He Used To Cut The Grass," "Packard Goose," and "Watermelon in Easter Hay" transcribed in staff notation by Steve Vai and published in Zappa, *The Frank Zappa Guitar Book* (Los Angeles: Munchkin Music, distributed by Milwaukee, WI: Hal Leonard, 1982).

HERE'S THE DEAL: The conclusion of the *Joe's Garage* saga, again containing many familiar and well-loved songs, including what is arguably FZ's finest moment as a guitarist in "Watermelon In Easter Hay."

RATING: ****

DOWNLOAD THESE: Outside Now, Packard Goose, Watermelon In Easter Hay

DIFFERENCES BETWEEN THE ZFT CD REISSUE AND PREVIOUS CD REISSUES: All digital versions of this album (issued with *Joe's Garage Act I* on two CDs) are essentially the same, and are faithful reproductions of the original vinyl LP.

Zappa CD number: 30

Tinsel Town Rebellion  (May 1981)

Performers:

Frank Zappa (lead guitar, vocals)
Ike Willis (rhythm guitar, vocals)
Ray White (rhythm guitar, vocals)
Steve Vai (rhythm guitar, vocals)
Warren Cuccurullo (rhythm guitar, vocals)
Denny Walley (slide guitar, vocals)
Tommy Mars (keyboards, vocals)
Peter Wolf (keyboards)
Bob Harris (keyboards, trumpet, vocals)
Ed Mann (percussion)
Arthur Barrow (bass, vocals)
Patrick O'Hearn (bass)
Vinnie Colaiuta (drums)
David Logeman (drums)
Creg Cowan (voice)

1. Fine Girl 3:31 ("Well, yeah, well, oh yeah, she was a fine girl")  July-September, 1980
2. Easy Meat 9:19 ("This girl is easy meat") Tower Theater, Upper Darby, PA, April 29, 1980; orchestral section: Royce Hall, UCLA, Los Angeles CA, September 18, 1975; guitar solo: Santa Monica Civic Auditorium, Santa Monica, CA, December 11, 1980 (early show)
3. For The Young Sophisticate 2:48 ("Baby baby why you cryin'") Hammersmith Odeon, London, England, February 18, 1979 (late show)
4. Love Of My Life 2:15 ("Love of my life, I love you so")  Berkeley Community Theater, Berkeley, CA, December 5, 1980 (early show)
5. I Ain't Got No Heart 1:59 ("Ain't got no heart")  Berkeley Community Theater, Berkeley, CA, December 5, 1980 (late show)
6. Panty Rap 4:35 ("Hello there, welcome to the show. No, we're not going to play 'Cheepnis'") Berkeley Community Theater, Berkeley, CA, December 5, 1980 (late show)
7. Tell Me You Love Me 2:07  ("Tell me you love me")  Berkeley Community Theater, Berkeley, CA, December 5, 1980 (late show)
8. Now You See It--Now You Don't 4:54  Southern Illinois University, Carbondale, IL, November 15, 1980
9. Dance Contest 2:58 ("One of the . . . One of the things that I like best about playing in New York is this particular place, because it has") The Palladium, New York City, NYC October 27, 1978 (early show)
10. The Blue Light 5:27 ("Your ethos, your pathos")  Berkeley Community Theater, Berkeley, CA, December 5, 1980 (early and late shows) and, Santa Monica Civic Auditorium, Santa Monica, CA, December 11, 1980 (late show)
11. Tinsel Town Rebellion 4:35 ("From Madam Wong's to Starwood") Berkeley Community Theater, Berkeley, CA, December 5, 1980 (early and late shows)
12. Pick Me, I'm Clean 5:07 ("Why not come over?")  Berkeley Community Theater, Berkeley, CA, December 5, 1980 (early and late shows), and Dallas Convention Center, Dallas, TX, October 17, 1980
13. Bamboozled By Love 5:46 ("Bamboozled by love") Hammersmith Odeon, London, England, February 19, 1979
14. Brown Shoes Don't Make It 7:14  ("Brown shoes, don't make it") Hammersmith Odeon, London, England, February 18, 1979 (late show)
15. Peaches III 5:03  Hammersmith Odeon, London, England, February 18, 1979 (early and late shows)

Issues:   ZFT reissue Zappa Records ZR 3862
Original issue Barking Pumpkin PW2 37336
Rykodisc reissue Rykodisc RCD 40166, RCD 10532

Transcriptions: none

HERE'S THE DEAL: *Tinsel Town Rebellion* was the first album FZ would release on his new label Barking Pumpkin Records, and consisted primarily of live tracks recorded on his early 1979 European tour. While fairly cohesive as an album, there is a fair amount filler/padding present here (in order to make this a 2-LP set) which detracts from the end product. Still, there are a number of fine pieces to be heard here, and much in the way of fine musicianship.

RATING: ***

DOWNLOAD THESE: Fine Girl, Easy Meat, Pick Me I'm Clean, Bamboozled By Love

DIFFERENCES BETWEEN THE ZFT CD REISSUE AND PREVIOUS CD REISSUES: Yet another title with a confusing digital release history. The initial CD issue of this album, released in Europe in 1987, was sourced from an analog sub-master tape that had been sent to EMI and was issued without FZ's consent. This issue matched the content of the original vinyl release apart from a terrible cut at the end of "Easy Meat" which brought the proceedings to a dead stop (this track segued into "For The Young Sophisticate" on the original vinyl LP). This issue was subsequently withdrawn, and replaced in 1990 with a Rykodisc pressing sourced from a 1630 digital master tape prepared by FZ. This CD is VERY poorly mastered, and one of the worst of the original batch of FZ CD remasters. The 1995 Rykodisc CD issue was taken from this same source. This title, along with the equally poorly mastered *You Are What You Is*, were replaced without fanfare in 1998 with a version prepared from the original 1979 analog master tape by Zappa engineer Spencer Chrislu. Unfortunately this release featured crossfades between the tracks that began and ended the four sides of the original LP. The 2012 ZFT reissue is again sourced from the original 1979 analog master tape without the crossfading, and stands as the definitive digital release of the album.

Zappa CD number: 31

Shut Up 'N Play Yer Guitar  (May 1981)

Performers and Dates:

Unspecified studio(s), 1979

Frank Zappa (lead guitar)
Warren Cuccurullo (rhythm guitar)
Vinnie Colaiuta (drums)

Hammersmith Odeon, London, UK, February 17, 1979
Hammersmith Odeon, London, UK, February 19, 1979

Frank Zappa (lead guitar)
Warren Cuccurullo (rhythm guitar)
Denny Walley (rhythm guitar)
Ike Willis (rhythm guitar)
Tommy Mars (keyboards)
Peter Wolf (keyboards)
Ed Mann (percussion)
Arthur Barrow (bass)
Vinnie Colaiuta (drums)

Brady Theater, Tulsa, October 18, 1980
Berkeley Community Theater, December 5, 1980 (late show)
Santa Monica Civic Auditorium, December 11, 1980 (late show)

Frank Zappa (lead guitar)
Steve Vai (rhythm guitar)
Ray White (rhythm guitar)
Ike Willis (rhythm guitar)
Tommy Mars (keyboards)
Bob Harris (keyboards)
Arthur Barrow (bass)
Vinnie Colaiuta (drums)


Song titles Duration (Solo sources) Recording dates

1. five-five-FIVE 2:35 (Conehead) February 19, 1979
2. Hog Heaven 2:49 (Easy Meat) October 18, 1980
3. Shut Up 'N Play Yer Guitar 5:38 (Inca Roads) February 17, 1979
4. While You Were Out 6:00  1979
5. Treacherous Cretins 5:34  February 17, 1979
6. Heavy Duty Judy 4:42 December 5, 1980 (late show)
7. Soup 'N Old Clothes 7:53 (Illinois Enema Bandit) December 11, 1980 (late show)


Issues:    ZFT reissue Zappa Records ZR 3863
           Original issue Barking Pumpkin BPR 1111
           Rykodisc reissue Rykodisc RCD 10028/29, RCD 10533/34/35

Transcriptions: Guitar parts for the complete album transcribed in staff notation by Steve Vai and published as Zappa, *The Frank Zappa Guitar Book* (Los Angeles: Munchkin Music, distributed by Milwaukee, WI: Hal Leonard, 1982).

HERE'S THE DEAL: Frank Zappa's solos on guitar were highlights of his concerts. Since his motivic melodies were often based on the chords and/or bass guitar part of a song – but not on the song's melody—the solos had the potential to take on lives of their own. Which is exactly what Zappa achieved by extracting the solos from the live performances of various songs, giving each a new title, and presenting them on record. The original issue of this and the two companion LPs (nos. 32 and 33) were among the first to be offered by Zappa through the Barking Pumpkin mail order service. Also, most of the solos in the series (including all of them on this album) were transcribed into music notation by Steve Vai for publication by Hal Leonard as *The Frank Zappa Guitar Book*, which has become a valuable collector's item.

RATING:  ****

DOWNLOAD THESE: five-five-FIVE, Shut Up 'N Play Yer Guitar

DIFFERENCES BETWEEN THE ZFT CD REISSUE AND PREVIOUS CD REISSUES: The original Rykodisc CD issue of this album was packaged as a 2-CD set along with *Shut Up 'N Play Yer Guitar Some More* and *The Return Of The Son Of Shut Up 'N Play Yer Guitar*. The source for this initial CD release was a Sony 1630 digital master which corrected an issue present on the original vinyl LPs wherein all of the material apart from "Stucco Homes" and "Carnard Du Jour" ran slightly fast. The 1995 Rykodisc reissue separated the albums back into a 3 disc configuration, and packaged it as a box set. This issue made use of the original 1980 analog master tapes, all at the correct speed but including a crossfade from the end of "Why Johnny Can't Read" into "Stucco Homes." The 2012 ZFT CD remaster uses the original analog masters again, packages the set as 2 CDs and eliminates the 1995 CD crossfade. That makes this the definitive digital version of these albums.

Zappa CD number: 32

Shut Up 'N Play Yer Guitar Some More (May 1981)

Performers and Dates:

Kosei Nenkin Kaikan, Osaka, Japan, February 3, 1976

Frank Zappa (lead guitar)
André Lewis (keyboards)
Roy Estrada (bass)
Terry Bozzio (drums)


Hammersmith Odeon, London, UK, February 17, 1977

Frank Zappa (lead guitar)
Ray White (rhythm guitar)
Eddie Jobson (keyboards)
Patrick O'Hearn (bass)
Terry Bozzio (drums)

Hammersmith Odeon, London, UK, February 18, 1979
Hammersmith Odeon, London, UK, February 19, 1979

Frank Zappa (lead guitar)
Warren Cuccurullo (rhythm guitar)
Denny Walley (rhythm guitar)
Ike Willis (rhythm guitar)
Tommy Mars (keyboards)
Peter Wolf (keyboards)
Ed Mann (percussion)
Arthur Barrow (bass)
Vinnie Colaiuta (drums)


Santa Monica Civic Auditorium, December 11, 1980 (late show)

Frank Zappa (lead guitar)
Steve Vai (rhythm guitar)
Ray White (rhythm guitar)
Ike Willis (rhythm guitar)
Tommy Mars (keyboards)
Bob Harris (keyboards)
Arthur Barrow (bass)
Vinnie Colaiuta (drums)


Song titles Duration (Solo sources) Recording dates

1. Variations On The Carlos Santana Secret Chord Progression 3:58 (City of Tiny Lites) December 11, 1980 (late show)
2. Gee, I Like Your Pants 2:35 (Inca Roads) February 18, 1979 (late show)
3. Canarsie 6:05 February 19, 1979
4. Ship Ahoy 5:20 (Zoot Allures) February 3, 1976
5. The Deathless Horsie 6:20 February 19, 1979
6. Shut Up 'N Play Yer Guitar Some More 6:53 (Inca Roads) February 18, 1979 (early show)
7. Pink Napkins 4:38 (Black Napkins) February 17, 1977


Issues:   ZFT reissue Zappa Records ZR 3863
          Original issue Barking Pumpkin BPR 1112
          Rykodisc reissue Rykodisc RCD 10028/29, RCD 10533/34/35

Transcriptions: Guitar parts for "Variations on the Carlos Santana Secret Chord Progression," "Gee, I Like Your Pants," "The Deathless Horsie," "Shut Up 'N Play Yer Guitar Some More," and "Pink Napkins" transcribed in staff notation by Steve Vai and published as Zappa, *The Frank Zappa Guitar Book* (Los Angeles: Munchkin Music, distributed by Milwaukee, WI: Hal Leonard, 1982).

HERE'S THE DEAL: A continuation of *Shut Up 'N Play Yer Guitar* (see no. 32). Most of the album was transcribed to sheet music by Steve Vai except for "Canarsie" and "Ship Ahoy."

RATING: ****

DOWNLOAD THESE: Variations On The Carlos Santana Secret Chord Progression, The Deathless Horsie, Pink Napkins.

DIFFERENCES BETWEEN THE ZFT CD REISSUE AND PREVIOUS CD REISSUES: See comments for *Shut Up 'N Play Yer Guitar* (no. 32).

Zappa CD number: 33

Return of the Son of Shut Up N' Play Yer Guitar  (May 1981)

Performers and Dates:

Paramount Studios, LA, 1972

Frank Zappa (bouzouki)
Jean-Luc Ponty (baritone violin)

Unspecified studio(s), 1979

Frank Zappa (lead guitar)
Warren Cuccurullo (rhythm guitar)
Vinnie Colaiuta (drums)

Hammersmith Odeon, London, UK, February 17, 1979
Hammersmith Odeon, London, UK, February 19, 1979

Frank Zappa (lead guitar)
Warren Cuccurullo (rhythm guitar)
Denny Walley (rhythm guitar)
Ike Willis (rhythm guitar)
Tommy Mars (keyboards)
Peter Wolf (keyboards)
Ed Mann (percussion)
Arthur Barrow (bass)
Vinnie Colaiuta (drums)

The Palladium, NYC, October 30, 1980
Berkeley Community Theater, December 5, 1980 (early show)

Frank Zappa (lead guitar)
Steve Vai (rhythm guitar)
Ray White (rhythm guitar)
Ike Willis (rhythm guitar)
Tommy Mars (keyboards)
Bob Harris (keyboards)
Arthur Barrow (bass)
Vinnie Colaiuta (drums)


Song titles Duration (Solo sources) Recording dates

1. Beat It With Your Fist 1:58 (The Torture Never Stops) October 30, 1980
2. Return Of The Son Of Shut Up 'N Play Yer Guitar 8:30 (Inca Roads) February 19, 1979
3. Pinocchio's Furniture 2:05 (Chunga's Revenge) December 5, 1980 (early show)
4. Why Johnny Can't Read 4:15 (Pound For A Brown) February 17, 1979
5. Stucco Homes 9:08  1979
6. Canard Du Jour 9:57 1972


Issues:   ZFT reissue  Zappa Records ZR 3863
          Original issue Barking Pumpkin BPR 1113
          Rykodisc reissue Rykodisc RCD 10028/29, RCD 10533/34/35

Transcriptions: The guitar part for "Stucco Homes" transcribed in staff notation by Steve Vai and published in Zappa, *The Frank Zappa Guitar Book* (Los Angeles: Munchkin Music, distributed by Milwaukee, WI: Hal Leonard, 1982).


HERE'S THE DEAL: The concluding volume to Zappa's three-part *Shut Up 'N Play Yer Guitar* (see no. 32).

RATING: ***1/2


DOWNLOAD THESE: Stucco Homes, Canard Du Jour


DIFFERENCES BETWEEN THE ZFT CD REISSUE AND PREVIOUS CD REISSUES: See comments for *Shut Up 'N Play Yer Guitar* (no. 32).

Zappa CD number: 34

You Are What You Is   (September 1981)

Performers:

Frank Zappa (lead guitar, vocals)
Ike Willis (rhythm guitar, vocals)
Ray White (rhythm guitar, vocals)
Bob Harris (boy soprano, trumpet)
Steve Vai ("strat abuse")
Tommy Mars (keyboards)
Arthur Barrow (bass)
Ed Mann (percussion)
David Ocker (clarinet, bass clarinet)
Motorhead Sherwood (tenor saxophone, vocals)
Denny Walley (slide guitar, vocals)
David Logeman (drums)
Craig Steward (harmonica)
Jimmy Carl Black (vocals)
Ahmet Zappa (vocals)
Moon Zappa (vocals)

All songs recorded July-September, 1980 unless noted otherwise

1. Teen-age Wind 3:02 ("It's a miserable Friday night")
2. Harder Than Your Husband 2:28 ("We must say good-bye")
3. Doreen 4:44 ("Doreen . . . don't make me wait ")
4. Goblin Girl 4:06 ("Hob-noblin, wit de goblin")
5. Theme From The 3rd Movement Of Sinister Footwear 3:31 (The Palladium, NYC, October 27, 1978)
6. Society Pages 2:26 ("You're the ol' lady from the society pages")
7. I'm A Beautiful Guy 1:56 ("I'm a beautiful guy") (basic track: Tower Theater, Upper Darby, PA
April 29, 1980)
8. Beauty Knows No Pain 3:01 ("Beauty knows no pain")
9. Charlie's Enormous Mouth 3:36 ("Charlie's enormous mouth, well, it's awright")
10. Any Downers? 2:08 ("And all around, at the side of the grave")
11. Conehead 4:18 ("Conehead . . . she ain't really dumb")
12. You Are What You Is 4:23 ("Do you know what you are? You are what you is")
13. Mudd Club 3:11 ("And here we are, at the Mudd Club, y'all")
14. The Meek Shall Inherit Nothing 3:10 ("Work the wall, work the floor")
15. Dumb All Over 4:03 ("Whoever we are, wherever we're from")
16. Heavenly Bank Account 3:44 ("And if these words you do not heed, your pocketbook just kinda might recede")
17. Suicide Chump 2:49 ("You say there ain't no use in livin'")
18. Jumbo Go Away 3:43 ("Jumbo, go away")
19. If Only She Woulda 3:47 ("You took a chance, on Jumbo's love") (basic track: Tower Theater, Upper Darby, PA, April 29, 1980)
20. Drafted Again 3:07 ("Special delivery . . . registered mail . . .OH NO" "I don't wanna get drafted")

Issues:    ZFT reissue  Zappa Records ZR3864
           Original issue  Barking Pumpkin PW2 37537
           Rykodisc reissue  Rykodisc RCD 40165, RCD 10536


Transcriptions: The guitar part for "Theme from the 3rd Movement of Sinister Footwear" transcribed in staff notation by Steve Vai and published as Zappa, *The Frank Zappa Guitar Book* (Los Angeles: Munchkin Music, distributed by Milwaukee, WI: Hal Leonard, 1982).

HERE'S THE DEAL: This was Zappa's first collection of new songs that he released on his Barking Pumpkin label. "You Are What You Is" became something of a signature song for Zappa, as it was used on many news items about him through the mid-1980s. This album also documents the shift of Steve Vai from music transcriber to "stunt guitarist." Apparently long-time Zappa fans have treasured the original vinyl release, as it is not easy to find in used LP stores.

RATING: \*\*\*\*

DOWNLOAD THESE: Society Pages, You Are What You Is, The Meek Shall Inherit Nothing, Drafted Again

DIFFERENCES BETWEEN THE ZFT CD REISSUE AND PREVIOUS CD REISSUES: One more time for the world! The initial CD issue of this album, released in Europe in 1987, was sourced from an analog sub-master tape that had been sent to EMI and was issued without FZ's consent. This issue matched the content of the original vinyl release exactly. This issue was subsequently withdrawn, and replaced in 1990 with a Rykodisc pressing sourced from a 1630 digital master tape prepared by FZ. This CD is, like other titles released that year, VERY poorly mastered, and one of the worst of the original batch of FZ CD remasters. FZ also saw fit to remove the guitar solo in "Dumb All Over" for this issue. The 1995 Rykodisc CD issue was taken from this same source. This title, along with the equally poorly mastered *Tinsel Town Rebellion* (no.30), were replaced without fanfare in 1998 with a version prepared from the original 1979 analog master tape by Zappa engineer Spencer Chrislu. Unfortunately this release featured a "Dumb All Over" which, while longer than the original Ryko CD, was still incomplete. The 2012 ZFT reissue is sourced from the original complete and unexpurgated 1981 analog master tape, and stands as the definitive digital release of the album. Victory for the ZFT once again!

Zappa CD number: 35

Ship Arriving Too Late To Save A Drowning Witch (May 1982)

Performers:

Frank Zappa (lead guitar, vocals)
Steve Vai (impossible guitar parts)
Ray White (rhythm guitar, vocals)
Tommy Mars (keyboards)
Bobby Martin (keyboards, sax and vocals)
Ed Mann (percussion)
Scott Thunes (bass on "Drowning Witch," "Envelopes," "Teen-age Prostitute" and "Valley Girl")
Arthur Barrow (bass on "No Not Now" and the first part of "I Come From Nowhere")
Patrick O'Hearn (bass during the guitar solo in "I Come From Nowhere")
Chad Wackerman (drums)
Roy Estrada (vocals)
Ike Willis (vocal)
Bob Harris (vocals)
Lisa Popeil (vocal on "Teen-age Prostitute')
Moon Zappa (vocal on "Valley Girl")

Recorded summer 1981- early 1982 unless specifically noted

1. No Not Now 5:50 ("No not now")
2. Valley Girl 4:50 (FZ/Moon Zappa) ("Valley Girl, she's a Valley Girl")
3. I Come From Nowhere 6:09 ("I come from nowhere")
4. Drowning Witch 12:03 ("There's a ship arriving too late to save a drowning witch")  basic track: Santa Monica, December 11, 1981
5. Envelopes 2:45
6. Teen-age Prostitute 2:41 ("She's only seventeen")  Santa Monica, December 11, 1981

Issues:   ZFT reissue  Zappa Records ZR3865
          Original issue Barking Pumpkin FW 38066
          Rykodisc reissue Rykodisc RCD 15037


Transcriptions: None




HERE'S THE DEAL: For its song structure, "Valley Girl" is much like "Teenage Wind" (on *You Are What You Is*, no. 34), but Moon Unit's dead-on "Val-speak" and Scott Thunes' fat bass line made "Valley Girl" funny in the very places where "Teenage Wind" fell flat. Because of the success of "Valley Girl" as a single, *Ship Arriving Too Late* was the first Zappa album that many people bought in a long time, or at all. It is also the first album with multi-instrumentalist/singer Bobby Martin and drummer Chad Wackerman, two mainstays of the 1980s Zappa touring band.


RATING: ***1/2


DOWNLOAD THESE: Valley Girl, Envelopes, Teen-age Prostitute

DIFFERENCES BETWEEN THE ZFT CD REISSUE AND PREVIOUS CD REISSUES: None. All CD issues of the album match the original vinyl LP exactly (oddly enough). The Rykodisc versions were sourced from a Sony 1630 digital master tape, and it is possible (though uncomfirmed) that the 2012 ZFT CD reissue is sourced from the original 1982 analog master tapes.

Zappa CD number: 36

The Man From Utopia (March 1983)

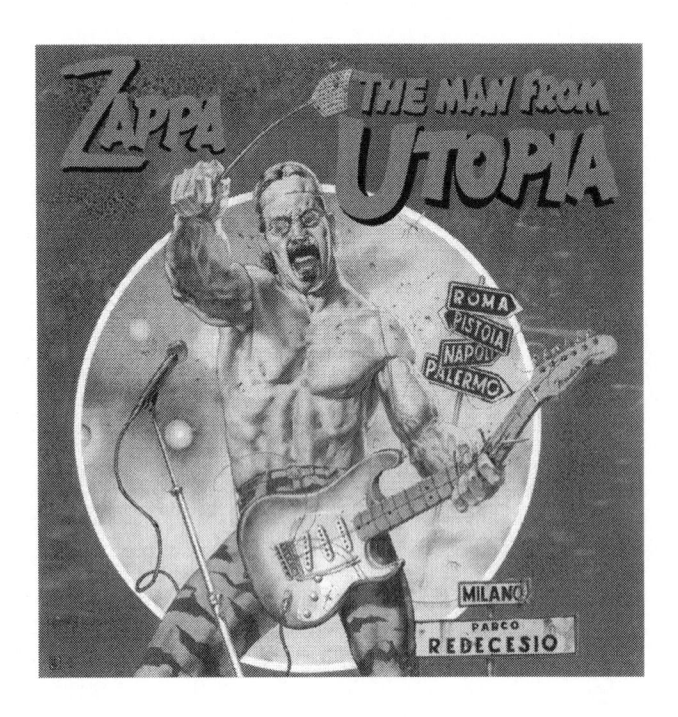

Performers:

Frank Zappa (guitar, vocals, ARP 2600, Linn Drum Machine)
Steve Vai ('impossible' guitar parts on strat and acoustic)
Ray White (guitar, vocals)
Roy Estrada (pachuco falsettos etc)
Bob Harris (boy soprano)
Ike Willis (bionic baritone)
Bobby Martin (keyboards, sax, vocals)
Tommy Mars (keyboards)
Arthur Barrow (keyboards, bass, micro-bass, rhythm guitar)
Ed Mann (percussion)
Scott Thunes (bass)
Chad Wackerman (drums)
Vinnie Colaiuta (drums on "The Dangerous Kitchen")
Dick Fegy (mandolin)
Marty Krystall (sax)

Recordings from 1982 unless otherwise noted

1. Cocaine Decisions 3:54  ("Cocaine decisions")
2. SEX 3:43  ("What's the thing that they's talkin' about everywhere? SEX")
3. Tink Walks Amok 3:38
4. The Radio Is Broken 5:51  ("The cosmos at large")
5. We Are Not Alone 3:18
6. The Dangerous Kitchen 2:51  ("The dangerous kitchen") Armadillo World Headquarters, Austin, Texas, October 16, 1980
7. The Man From Utopia Meets Mary Lou (Donald and Doris Woods/Obie Jessie) 3:22  ("Well, this is the story of a man who lived in Utopia")
8. Stick Together 3:13  ("This is a song about the union, friends")
9. The Jazz Discharge Party Hats 4:28  ("Once upon a time, it was in Albuquerque, New Mexico") Southern Illinois University, Carbondale, November 15, 1980
10. Luigi and The Wise Guys 3:24  ("You-you-you-ooo, look like a dor-r-r-k")
11. Moggio 2:36  Uptown Theatre, Chicago, November 27, 1981

Issues:    ZFT reissue  Zappa Records ZR 3866
           Original issue Barking Pumpkin FW 38403
           Rykodisc reissue Rykodisc RCD 10538

Transcriptions: none

HERE'S THE DEAL: Call silly "The Dangerous Kitchen" and "The Jazz Discharge Party Hats," but they are good examples of the semi-improvisatory exercises that Zappa called "meltdowns" (see *The Real Frank Zappa Book*, pp. 183-185).

RATING: ***1/2

DOWNLOAD THESE: The Dangerous Kitchen, The Jazz Discharge Party Hats, Moggio

DIFFERENCES BETWEEN THE ZFT CD REISSUE AND PREVIOUS CD REISSUES: The initial CD issue of this album, released in Europe in 1986, was sourced from an analog sub-master tape that had been sent to EMI and was packaged as a "two-fer" CD with *Ship Arriving Too Late To Save A Drowning Witch* (no. 35). This issue matched the content of the original vinyl release exactly, apart from containing a remix of "Moggio." This issue was subsequently withdrawn, and replaced in 1990 with a Rykodisc pressing sourced from a 1630 digital master tape prepared by FZ. For this release, FZ saw fit to remix the entire album and add a bonus track with "Luigi and The Wise Guys." This remixed version of the album was reissued by Ryko in 1995, and by the ZFT in 2012. The original vinyl mix of "Moggio" has yet to appear in the digital domain.

Zappa CD number: 37

Baby Snakes   (March 1983)

Performers:

Frank Zappa (guitar, vocals)
Adrian Belew (guitar, vocals)
Terry Bozzio (drums, vocals)
Roy Estrada (gas mask, vocals)
Ed Mann (percussion)
Tommy Mars (keyboards, vocals)
Patrick O'Hearn (bass)
Peter Wolf (keyboards)

All tracks recorded at The Palladium, NYC, October 28-31, 1977 (specific dates noted when known) except for track 1 (same as 26.12)

Song titles  Duration  (first line)  year of source recording(s)
1. Intro Rap/Baby Snakes 2:22 (spoken: "Tonight though I, I tell you one thing . . . 'bout these New York crowds . . . " sung: "Baby snakes") February 28, 1978 London
2. Titties and Beer 6:13  ("It was the blackest night, there was no moon in sight")
3. The Black Page #2 2:50  October 31, 1977
4. Jones Crusher 2:53  ("My baby's got Jones-crushin' love")  October 29, 1977 (early show)
5. Disco Boy 3:51  ("Disco boy") October 30, 1977
6. Dinah-Moe Humm 6:37 ("I couldn't say where she's comin' from, but I just met a lady named Dinah-Moe Humm")

7. Punky's Whips 11:29  (spoken: "In today's rapidly changing world rock groups appear every fifteen minutes..."  sung: "I can't stand the way he pouts")

Issues:    ZFT reissue (pending)
           Original issue  Barking Pumpkin BPR 1115
           Rykodisc reissue Rykodisc RCD 10539

Transcriptions: None


HERE'S THE DEAL: Halloween was Zappa's favorite holiday, on which he often booked concerts in New York City. The 1977 shows were recorded and filmed. By 1983 when the movie was released as *Baby Snakes*, Adrian Belew had emerged as a distinctive singer and guitarist for King Crimson and his own band. When the LP was released in 1983, it was a good memento of the Belew-era Zappa band.


RATING: ***

DOWNLOAD THESE: Titties and Beer. Otherwise, download the whole movie soundtrack (see no. 95).

DIFFERENCES BETWEEN THE ZFT CD REISSUE AND PREVIOUS CD REISSUES: None. Although this would appear to be seldom discussed among collectors, the first vinyl pressing of this album, released in 1983, featured a different mix of the entire album. This was replaced by the more common "CD mix" for the second vinyl pressing of the album around 1984. For the original 1989 Rykodisc CD issue of this album, FZ added the track "Intro Rap" and placed a segue between "Disco Boy" and "Dinah-Moe-Humm" not present on the vinyl. All subsequent CD issues, including the 2012 ZFT reissue, use this same digital master.

Zappa CD number: 38

London Symphony Orchestra Vol. I (June 1983)

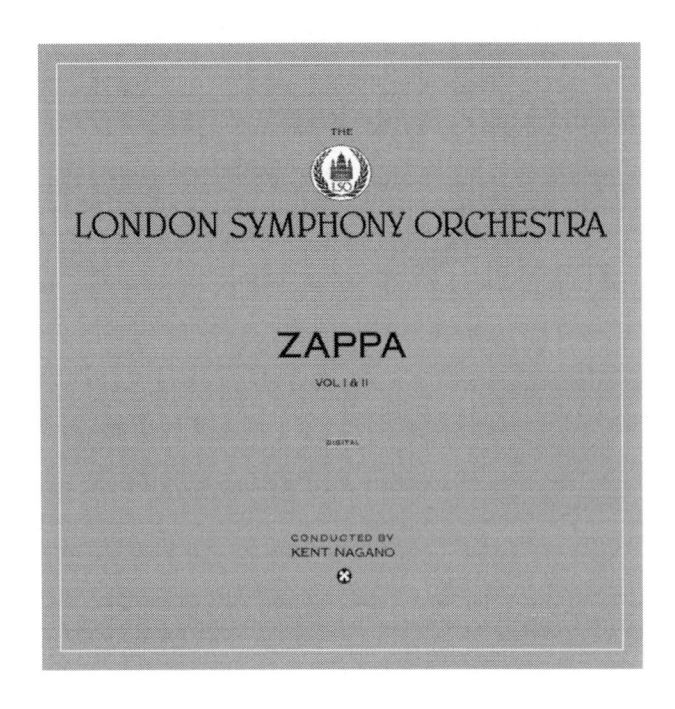

Performers:
The London Symphony Orchestra
Kent Nagano (conductor)
David Ocker (solo clarinet)
Chad Wackerman (drums)
Ed Mann (percussion)


Recorded January 12-14, 1983 at Twickenham Film Studio, London, UK

Song titles  Duration  (track listing from 1983 LP)
1. Sad Jane   9:51
2. Pedro's Dowry  10:26
3. Envelopes  4:11
4. Mo 'N Herb's Vacation I 4:50
5. Mo 'N Herb's Vacation II 10:04
6. Mo 'N Herb's Vacation III 12:52

Issues:    ZFT reissue  Zappa Records ZR 3865
           Original issue Barking Pumpkin FW 38820
           Rykodisc reissue Ryko RCD10022, Ryko RCD 10540/41

Scores: All compositions available for rental only through Schott Music. Note that Nagano conducted the full orchestra version of "Pedro's Dowry," not the chamber version premiered at UCLA in 1975 (for that, see Orchestral Favorites [27.02] or Lather [65.19]).

HERE'S THE DEAL: Zappa thought of himself as a composer who happened to play guitar. Much of his efforts in the mid-1970s to record his latest classical compositions resulted in some uneven or compromised performances (especially those presented on *Studio Tan*, *Sleep Dirt* and *Orchestral Favorites* [nos. 24-25, 27]). The recording sessions with the London Symphony Orchestra among Zappa's greatest financial bids for classical respectability. They were also Kent Nagano's first big break as a conductor.

RATING: \*\*\*\*

DOWNLOAD THESE: Mo 'N Herb's Vacation parts I-III

DIFFERENCES BETWEEN THE ZFT CD REISSUE AND PREVIOUS CD REISSUES: This album was initially released on CD by Rykodisc in 1986, and featured an alternate track listing omitting "Pedro's Dowry" and "Envelopes" while adding "Bogus Pomp" which would appear on the vinyl album *The London Symphony Orchestra, Vol. II* album (no. 48) the following year. In 1993, FZ remixed all of the tracks which had appeared on both vinyl albums and in 1995 these were issued by Ryko as a 2-CD set titled *The London Symphony Orchestra Vols. I & II*. This master was used by the ZFT for their CD reissue in 2012.

Zappa CD number: 39

Boulez conducts Zappa: The Perfect Stranger

Performers:

Ensemble InterContemporain  Tracks 1, 2 and 4
Pierre Boulez (conductor) Tracks 1, 2 and 4

The Barking Pumpkin Digital Gratification Consort

Tracks 1, 2 and 4 recorded IRCAM, Paris, January 10-11, 1984
The remainder at UMRK, Los Angeles, February-April 1984

1. The Perfect Stranger 12:44
2. Naval Aviation In Art? 2:45
3. The Girl In The Magnesium Dress 3:13
4. Dupree's Paradise 7:54
5. Love Story 0:59
6. Outside Now Again 4:06
7. Jonestown 5:27

Issues:     ZFT reissue  Zappa Records ZR3869
            Original issue  Angel DS-38170
            Rykodisc reissue  Ryko RCD 10542

Scores: Tracks 1, 2 and 4 available for hire through Schott Music.

HERE'S THE DEAL: In *The Real Frank Zappa Book* (pp. 194-197), Zappa expressed some mixed feelings for the performances of his classical compositions by Pierre Boulez. On one hand, he recognized Boulez's eminent international standing as a contemporary composer/conductor. On the other hand, he thought the public performances were underrehearsed. That reservation didn't keep Zappa from recording in the studio Boulez and the Ensemble InterContemporain. The album also contained the first releases of Zappa's music for the electronic Synclavier.

RATING: \*\*\*\*

DOWNLOAD THESE: The Perfect Stranger, Dupree's Paradise

DIFFERENCES BETWEEN THE ZFT CD REISSUE AND PREVIOUS CD REISSUES: This album was initially released on CD by EMI in 1985, and matched the contents of the vinyl LP exactly. In 1992, Rykodisc issued a version of this album which had been completely remixed by FZ. This remixed digital master tape was used for both Ryko's 1995 CD reissue and the 2012 CD reissue.

Zappa CD number: 40

Them Or Us   (October 1984)

Performers:

Frank Zappa (guitar and vocals)
Ike Willis, Napoleon Murphy Brock, Roy Estrada (vocals, harmony)
Tommy Mars (keyboards)
Arthur Barrow (bass)
Chad Wackerman (drums)
Scott Thunes (bass)
Ed Mann (percussion)
Steve Vai (stunt guitar, guitar solo on "Ya Hozna" and first guitar solo on "Stevie's Spanking")
Ray White (vocals, rhythm guitar)
Bobby Martin (vocals, keyboards, harmonica)
Dweezil Zappa (guitar solo on "Sharleena" and second guitar solo on "Stevie's Spanking")
Patrick O'Hearn (bass)
Thana Harris (harmony)
George Duke (vocals, piano)
Johnny Guitar Watson (vocals)

Recording dates noted when known; undated tracks are indexed as from 1984.

Song titles  Duration  (first line)  year of source recording(s)
1. The Closer You Are (Lewis/Robinson) 2:58  ("The closer you are")
2. In France 3:30 ("We're playin' in a tent")

3. Ya Hozna 6:26 (backwards: "I am the heaven ")
4. Sharleena 4:33 ("I'm cryin', I'm cryin', cryin' for Sharleena") c. September, 1981-July, 1982
5. Sinister Footwear II 8:40  1st half: Painter's Mill Music Fair, Owings Mills, Maryland, November 15, 1981; Guitar solo: Sporthalle, Boeblingen, Germany, June 23, 1982
6. Truck Driver Divorce 9:03 ("Truck driver divorce!") Basic track recorded live c. May-July, 1982; guitar solo from Zoot Allures: The Ritz, NYC, November 17, 1981
7. Stevie's Spanking 5:24 ("His name is Stevie Vai") Northrop Auditorium, Minneapolis, MN, November 28, 1981; The Ritz, NYC, November 17, 1981; Olympiahalle, Munich, Germany, June 26, 1982
8. Baby, Take Your Teeth Out 1:24 ("Baby take your teeth out") Alte Oper, Frankfurt, Germany, June 11-12, 1982 (soundcheck)
9. Marque-son's Chicken 7:34 Guitar solo:Hammersmith Odeon, London, UK, June 19, 1982, 2nd show
10. Planet Of My Dreams 1:40 ("The planet of my dreams")  Basic track: Caribou Studios, Nederland, Colorado, December, 1974
11. Be In My Video 3:39 ("Be in my video, darling, every night")
12. Them Or Us 5:08 Guitar solo from Black Page, Stadio Communale, Bolzano, Italy, July 3, 1982
13. Frogs With Dirty Little Lips (FZ/Ahmet Zappa) 2:46 ("Frogs with dirty little lips")
14. Whipping Post (Allman) 7:32 ("I been run down")  Santa Monica Civic Auditorium, December 11, 1981; Fox Theater, San Diego, California, December 12, 1981

Issues:   ZFT reissue Zappa Records ZR 3870
          Original issue  Barking Pumpkin SVBO-74200
          Rykodisc reissue  Ryko RCD 40027, Ryko RCD 10543

Transcriptions: none

HERE'S THE DEAL: A fine collection of performances by Zappa's early- to mid-1980s bands. More a potpourri than a cohesive whole, the recordings were well made, whether in the studio or live.

RATING: ****

DOWNLOAD THESE: The Closer You Are, In France, Stevie's Spanking, Be In My Video, Whipping Post

DIFFERENCES BETWEEN THE ZFT CD REISSUE AND PREVIOUS CD REISSUES: The original CD issue of this album, issued by Rykodisc in 1986, was taken from the original Sony 1630 digital master tapes and matched the content of the vinyl LP issue exactly. In 1990, Zappa Records reissued this album on CD in Europe, this time featuring an extended edit of the track "Them Or Us." Unfortunately this version of the album suffers from poor mastering, as did most of FZ's back catalog CDs appearing that year. This poorly-mastered version was then reissued by Rykodisc in 1995. The 2012 ZFT CD reissue utilizes the original 1984 Sony 1630 digital master tape, and like the original EMI CD it matches the content of the vinyl LP exactly.

Zappa CD number: 41

Thing-Fish (November 1984)

Performers:

Frank Zappa (guitar, synclavier)
Steve Vai (guitar)
Ray White (guitar)
Tommy Mars (keyboards)
Chuck Wild (broadway piano)
Arthur Barrow (bass)
Scott Thunes (bass)
Jay Anderson (string bass)
Ed Mann (percussion)
Chad Wackerman (drums)
Steve De Furia (synclavier programmer)
David Ocker (synclavier programmer)

Cast:

Thing-Fish: Ike Willis
Harry: Terry Bozzio
Rhonda: Dale Bozzio
Evil Prince: Napoleon Murphy Brock
Harry-as-a-boy: Bob Harris
Brown Moses: Johnny "Guitar" Watson
Owl-Gonkwin-Jane Cowhoon: Ray White

Specific recording dates noted when known; unspecified 1982-1984 studio tracks are indexed as from 1984.

1. Prologue 2:56 ("Once upon a time, musta been 'round October, few years back")
2. The Mammy Nuns 3:31 ("We got de talkin' shoes! We de MAMMY NUNS!")  guitar outro from: Stadio Ferraris, Genoa, Italy July 5, 1982
3. Harry and Rhonda 3:36 ("HARRY, this is not DREAM GIRLS!")
4. Galoot Up-Date 5:27 ("GALOOT CO-LOG-NUH!") Basic track: Berkeley Community Theater
December 5, 1980; Santa Monica Civic Auditorium, December 11, 1980
5. The 'Torchum' Never Stops 10:33 (spoken: "Now, dis nasty sucker is de respondable party fo de en-whiffment" sung: "Flies all green 'n buzznin' In his dunjing of despair") Basic track: Record Plant, LA c. May-June, 1976
6. That Evil Prince 1:17 ("RHONDA, that EVIL PRINCE . . . he certainly does have a way about him!")
7. You Are What You Is 4:31 ("Straighten up in dat chair and pay ATTENTIUM! People, dis is fo yo' own good! Do YOU know what YOU ARE?") July-September, 1980
8. Mudd Club 3:17 ("And here we are, at the Mudd Club, y'all! ") July-September, 1980
9. The Meek Shall Inherit Nothing 3:14 (spoken: "Boy!" "WORK THE WALL!" sung: "Some take THE BIBLE for what it's worth")  July-September, 1980
10. Clowns On Velvet 1:51 ("Thass right, folks! We talkin' de hypocritical Jeezis-jerknuh parodise dey call LAS VAGRUS NEVADRUH!") The Ritz, NYC November 17, 1981
11. Harry-As-A-Boy 2:34 ("HARRY! HARRY, is that YOU as a BOY?")
12. He's So Gay 2:45 ("He's so gay (He's so gay) He's very very gay")
13. The Massive Improve'lence 5:08 ("Hmmm! Dat quite a massive improve'lence, dah-lin'!")
14. Artificial Rhonda 3:29   (spoken: "Don't look OB'DEWLLA! It's too horrible!" sung: "I got a girl with a little rubber head")  Record Plant, LA, c. May-June, 1976
15. The Crab-Grass Baby 3:47 ("Stroke me pompadour, pompaduooor")
16. The White Boy Troubles 3:34 ("De white boy troubles!")
17. No Not Now 5:49 ("Wooo! Looka-dat! A big ol' truck, 'n a box uh NODOZ") basic track c. late 1981-early 1982
18. Briefcase Boogie 4:10 (spoken: "Anything you say, master! Take me, I'm yours!" sung: "Jingle bells, Jingle bells, Jingle all the way!")
19. Brown Moses 3:00 (spoken: "Oh-oh! Wait a minute! What?" sung: "What wickedness id dis?")
20. Wistful Wit A Fist-Full 4:00 ("What is happenin' to me!")
21. Drop Dead 7:56 ("JESUS, that was terrific!")
22. Won Ton On 4:18 ("Whiff it, Boy! Whiff it good, now!")

Issues:  ZFT reissue  Zappa Records ZR 3871
            Original issue Barking Pumpkin SKCO-74201
            Rykodisc reissue Ryko RCD 10020/21, Ryko RCD 10544/45

Transcriptions: none

HERE'S THE DEAL: Fans regard this full-length musical either as a masterpiece, or as the most self-indulgent derivative muck that Zappa ever made; hence the two ratings given below. In view that Zappa recorded nearly all of the album in the studio instead of at concerts, his effort merits a fair consideration. But even for many Zappa fans, such a consideration may be difficult to give. The lead character Thing-Fish speaks and sings confrontationally to the listener in a thick dialect, the show's plot presents the public humiliation of a self-centered married couple attending the show, and Zappa recycles the melodies of many previously-released songs. But in its favor, Zappa skewers the contemporary issues of racism and AIDS, and he anticipates the absurdities of 2000s trends like multiculturalism and metrosexuality. Also, Ike Willis gives the performance of a lifetime as Thing-Fish; within the Zappa legacy; only Ray Collins' singing in *Cruising With Ruben And The Jets* is as accomplished, if in a different way.

RATING: ***** (or **1/2)

DOWNLOAD THESE: Prologue, Mammy Nuns, He's So Gay

DIFFERENCES BETWEEN THE ZFT CD REISSUE AND PREVIOUS CD REISSUES: The original CD issue of this album, issued in Europe by EMI in 1986, used the same tapes that EMI had used for their vinyl 3-LP box set; this remains the only CD to feature the original vinyl mix of the album. The Rykodisc CD, released the same year, contained a few remixes, notably on "Wistful Wit A Fist-Full." In 1990, the album was reissued on CD by Zappa Records; this featured a complete remix of the album (including the mixes used for the first Ryko pressing). This version has become the standard CD issue of this album, having been reissued by Ryko in 1995 and the ZFT in 2012.

Zappa CD number: 42

Francesco Zappa (November 1984)

Performers:

The Barking Pumpkin Digital Gratification Consort

All music composed by Francesco Zappa (flourished 18th century), arranged for Synclavier by Frank Zappa (1940-1994) with encryption by David Ocker.

All music recorded in February-April 1984.

    01. Op. 1, No. 1: 1st Movement ANDANTE 3:28
    02. Op. 1, No. 1: 2nd Movement ALLEGRO CON BRIO 1:27
    03. Op. 1, No. 2: 1st Movement ANDANTINO 2:14
    04. Op. 1, No. 2: 2nd Movement MINUETTO GRAZIOSO 2:02
    05. Op. 1, No. 3: 1st Movement ANDANTINO 1:52
    06. Op. 1, No. 3: 2nd Movement PRESTO 1:50
    07. Op. 1, No. 4: 1st Movement ANDANTE 2:20
    08. Op. 1, No. 4: 2nd Movement ALLEGRO 3:02
    09. Op. 1, No. 5: 2nd Movement MINUETTO GRAZIOSO 2:26
    10. Op. 1, No. 6: 1st Movement LARGO 2:05
    11. Op. 1, No. 6:2nd Movement MINUET 2:01
    12. Op. 4, No. 1: 1st Movement ANDANTINO 2:42
    13. Op. 4, No. 1: 2nd Movement ALLEGRO ASSAI 1:58
    14. Op. 4, No. 2: 2nd Movement ALLEGRO ASSAI 1:17
    15. Op. 4, No. 3: 1st Movement ANDANTE 2:22
    16. Op. 4, No. 3: 2nd Movement TEMPO DI MINUETTO 1:58
    17. Op. 4, No. 4 1st Movement MINUETTO 2:07

Issues:    ZFT reissue Zappa Records ZR 3872
Original issue Barking Pumpkin ST-74202

Transcriptions: none

HERE'S THE DEAL: Old wine poured in new bottles. Yes, there was a Francesco Zappa who lived and composed in the mid-18th century, as attested by music reference works like *Grove's Dictionary of Music and Musicians* (see especially its third edition in 1928, published 13 years before Frank Zappa's 1941 birth.

RATING: ***

DOWNLOAD THESE: Op. 1 no. 1: ANDANTE.

DIFFERENCES BETWEEN THE ZFT CD REISSUE AND PREVIOUS CD REISSUES: The original CD pressing of this album, issued by Barking Pumpkin in 1992, suffered from poor mastering; this was corrected for the 1995 Rykodisc and the 2012 ZFT CD reissues. The mixes are the same on all titles.

Zappa (release) number: 43

The Old Masters, Box One (April 1985)

LP reissues with some overdubs of:
Freak Out! = no. 1
Absolutely Free = no. 2
We're Only In It For The Money = no. 4
Lumpy Gravy = no. 3
Cruising With Ruben & The Jets = no. 5

First release (partial) of:

Mystery Disc = no. 68

Issues: Original issue: Barking Pumpkin BPR-7777

HERE'S THE DEAL: During the early 1980s, after years of lawsuits, Zappa won back the tape masters for his early albums through 1978. During the meantime, the albums he made for MGM-Verve became collector's items. This first box of "Old Masters" presents a version of every album he delivered to MGM-Verve, and a "Mystery Disc" LP of previously unreleased performances from 1961-1967 (see no. 68).

RATINGS: (*****; keep the set if a copy falls in your lap)

DOWNLOAD THESE: See the suggestions in album nos. 1-5.

DIFFERENCES BETWEEN THE ZFT CD REISSUE AND PREVIOUS CD REISSUES: See the individual CD issues of the albums included in this vinyl-only box set; the set has not been issued on CD in this form. The *Mystery Disc* album, included as a bonus in this set, was reissued on CD in 1998 by Rykodisc, packaged with the *Mystery Disc* from *The Old Masters, Box Two* set and given its own official release number. See that listing (no. 68) for details.

Zappa CD number: 44

Frank Zappa Meets the Mothers of Prevention (November 1985)

**FRANK ZAPPA MEETS THE MOTHERS OF PREVENTION**

Performers:

Frank Zappa (guitar, synclavier)
Steve Vai (guitar)
Johnny "Guitar" Watson (guitar, vocals)
Ike Willis (guitar, vocals)
Ray White (guitar, vocals)
Bobby Martin (keyboards, vocals)
Tommy Mars (keyboards)
Scott Thunes (bass)
Chad Wackerman (drums)
Ed Mann (percussion)

Specific recording dates noted when known; unspecified studio tracks are indexed as from 1985.

1. I Don't Even Care 4:39 ("Would ya b'lieve it") Basic track: soundcheck, circa 1981-82
2. One Man, One Vote 2:35
3. Little Beige Sambo 3:02
4. Aerobics In Bondage 3:16
5. We're Turning Again 4:55 ("Turn turn, turn turn, we're turning again") Santa Monica Civic Auditorium, December 11, 1981
6. Alien Orifice 4:10 circa September 1981-July, 1982
7. Yo Cats 3:33 ("Yo cats, yo yo")

8. What's New In Baltimore? 5:20  Community Theater, Berkeley, California, December 10, 1981; Painter's Mill Music Fair, Owings Mills, Maryland, November 15, 1981; Assembly Hall, University Of Illinois, Champaign, Illinois, November 21, 1981
9. Porn Wars 12:05 ("The reason for this hearing is not to promote any legislation")  Voices from the Committee on Commerce, Science and Transportation, September 19, 1985
10. H.R. 2911 3:35

Issues:   ZFT reissue  Zappa Records ZR 3873
          Original issue Barking Pumpkin ST-74203, EMC 3507
          Rykodisc reissue Ryko RCD 10023, Ryko RCD 10547

Transcriptions: none


HERE'S THE DEAL: The titular "Mothers of Prevention" refers to the Parents Music Resource Center, a group of Washington DC politicians' wives (led by Tipper Gore) who recommended that "Parental Advisory" stickers be affixed to record albums containing adult material. At a U.S. Senate hearing on September 19, 1985, Zappa joined John Denver and Twisted Sister's Dee Snider in giving viewpoints opposing the PMRC agenda. As expected, Zappa spoke eloquently from high and well-researched principles, but Denver surprised and dismayed the PMRC by saying that what the group wished to do would only add to the appeal of the material it wished to "advise" against. "Porn Wars" is Zappa's grand aural collage about the PMRC incident, standing tall among the Synclavier miniatures included on the album.


RATINGS: ****


DOWNLOAD THESE: Porn Wars, We're Turning Again, What's New in Baltimore, Yo Cats.


DIFFERENCES BETWEEN THE ZFT CD REISSUE AND PREVIOUS CD REISSUES: When originally released on vinyl in 1985, this album featured different track listings for each of the American and European markets. The European pressing deleted "Porn Wars" and added the tracks "I Don't Even Care," "One Man – One Vote" and "H.R. 2911." In 1987, this European configuration of the album was issued on CD in that territory by EMI, coupled with the *Jazz From Hell* album. For the 1990 European Zappa Records CD reissue, "Porn Wars" was restored alongside the "Europe only" tracks, albeit in edited form. The first American CD pressing of this album, issued by Rykodisc in 1986, included "Porn Wars," "I Don't Even Care" and "One Man – One Vote" but left off "H.R. 2911." Finally, the 1995 Ryko CD reissue included all of the tracks for the first time. This version of the album was reissued by the ZFT in 2012.

Zappa CD number: 45

Does Humor Belong in Music? (January 1986)

Performers:

Frank Zappa (lead guitar and vocal)
Ray White (rhythm guitar and vocal)
Ike Willis (rhythm guitar and vocal)
Bobby Martin (keyboards, sax, vocal)
Allan Zavod (keyboards)
Scott Thunes (bass)
Chad Wackerman (drums solo on "Let's Move To Cleveland")
Dweezil Zappa (guitar solo on "Whippin' Post")

1. Zoot Allures 5:26 Opening theme: Hammersmith Odeon, London, UK, September 25, 1984; solo from Civic Center, Providence RI October 26, 1984
2. Tinsel-Town Rebellion 4:43 ("From *Madam Wong's* to *Starwood*") Body from Bismarck Theater, Chicago, November 23, 1984, with ending from Queen Elizabeth Theater, Vancouver, December 18, 1984
3. Trouble Every Day 5:31 ("Well I'm about to get sick from watchin' *MTV*") Verses from Bayfront Center Arena, St. Petersburg, Florida, December 1, 1984; solo from Hammersmith Odeon, London, UK, September 25, 1984
4. Penguin In Bondage 6:44 ("She's just like a Penguin in Bondage, boy") Some vocal parts from Bayfront Center Arena, St. Petersburg, Florida, December 1, 1984; solo and the rest from Queen Elizabeth Theater, Vancouver, December 18, 1984

5. Hot-Plate Heaven At The Green Hotel 6:42 ("I used to have a job an' I was doin' fairly well") Queen Elizabeth Theater, Vancouver, December 18, 1984

6. What's New In Baltimore? 4:47 ("Hey! What's new in Baltimore?") Front and solo from Universal Amphitheater, Universal City, CA, December 23, 1984; vocal part from Tower Theater, Upper Darby, PA, November 10, 1984

7. Cock-Suckers' Ball 1:05 (spoken: "Hey, this is for all the Republicans in the audience!" sung: "Cock-sucker Sammy, get your mother fuckin' mammy") Universal Amphitheater, Universal City, CA, December 23, 1984

8. WPLJ 1:30 ("I say WPLJ, won't you take a drink with me") Universal Amphitheater, Universal City, CA, December 23, 1984

9. Let's Move To Cleveland 16:43 ("Let's move to Cleveland") Intro and out-chorus from Universal Amphitheater, Universal City, CA, December 23, 1984; parts of the piano solo from Bayfront Center Arena, St. Petersburg, Florida, December 1, 1984; drum solo from Queen Elizabeth Theatre, Vancouver, December 18, 1984; guitar solo and parts of the piano solo from Fine Arts Center Concert Hall, Amherst, Massachusetts, October 28, 1984.

10. Whippin' Post 8:23 ("I been run down, Lord, 'n I been lied to") Universal Amphitheater, Universal City, CA, December 23, 1984

Issues:   ZFT reissue  Zappa Records ZR 3874
          Original issue EMI CDP 7 46188 2
          Rykodisc reissue Ryko RCD 10548

Transcriptions: none

HERE'S THE DEAL: Zappa's first CD-only release. The contents are drawn from various dates from the 1984 tours. The video release of the same name was of the concert at The Pier in New York City on August 26, 1984.

RATINGS: ***1/2

DOWNLOAD THESE: Hot-Plate Heaven At The Green Hotel

DIFFERENCES BETWEEN THE ZFT CD REISSUE AND PREVIOUS CD REISSUES: The original CD issue of this album, released in Europe in 1986, was the first Zappa album to not be released in the United States. This is the only pressing to feature the original mix of this album. The album was completely remixed by FZ in 1992, and was finally issued in the US as part of Rykodisc's 1995 CD reissue series. This remixed version was reissued by the ZFT in 2012.

Zappa (release) number: 46

Old Masters Box 2 (November 1986)

LP reissues of:

Uncle Meat = no. 6
Hot Rats = no. 8
Burnt Weeny Sandwich = no. 9
Weasels Ripped My Flesh = no. 10
Chunga's Revenge = no. 11
Fillmore East - June 1971 = no. 12
Just Another Band From L.A. = no. 14

First release (partial) of:

Mystery Disc = no. 68

Issues:   Original issue Barking Pumpkin BPR-8888

Transcriptions: none

HERE'S THE DEAL: This sequel to the first *Old Masters* set (no. 43) presents the first 7 albums of Zappa's Bizarre/Warner output (1969-1972). The bonus "Mystery Disc" LP provides live and candid recordings of the Mothers of Invention from 1968 and 1969.

RATINGS: (****; it's good to have if you got it)

DOWNLOAD THESE: See the suggestions for albums nos. 6-14.

DIFFERENCES BETWEEN THE ZFT CD REISSUE AND PREVIOUS CD REISSUES: See the individual CD issues of the albums included in this vinyl-only box set; the set has not been issued on CD in this form. The *Mystery Disc* album, which was included as a bonus in this set, was reissued on CD in 1998 by Rykodisc, packaged along with the *Mystery Disc* from *The Old Masters, Box One* set and given its own official release number. See that listing for details.

Zappa CD number: 47

Jazz From Hell (November 1986)

Performers (for "St. Etienne."):

Frank Zappa (lead guitar)
Steve Vai (rhythm guitar)
Ray White (rhythm guitar)
Tommy Mars (keyboards)
Bobby Martin (keyboards)
Ed Mann (percussion)
Scott Thunes (bass)
Chad Wackerman (drums)

All compositions executed by Frank Zappa on the Synclavier DMS with the exception of "St. Etienne."

Unspecified 1985-1986 studio tracks are indexed as from 1986.

1. Night School 4:50
2. The Beltway Bandits 3:26
3. While You Were Art II 7:18
4. Jazz From Hell 3:00
5. G-Spot Tornado 3:17
6. Damp Ankles 3:45

7. St. Etienne 6:26  Solo from "Drowning Witch," Palais des Sports, St. Etienne, France, May 28, 1982
8. Massaggio Galore 2:31

Issues:   ZFT reissue  Zappa Records ZR 3875
          Original issue  Barking Pumpkin ST-74205

Transcriptions: none

HERE'S THE DEAL: The album won Zappa's lone Grammy, for Best Rock Instrumental Performance, awarded on March 2, 1988. According to an urban legend, the Meyer Music Markets store chain in the northwest U.S. supposedly affixed advisory stickers on this album, even though no lyrics are sung(!).

RATINGS: ****

DOWNLOAD THESE: Night School, Jazz From Hell, G-Spot Tornado, St. Etienne

DIFFERENCES BETWEEN THE ZFT CD REISSUE AND PREVIOUS CD REISSUES: The original CD pressing of this album was issued in Europe in 1986 by EMI, coupled as a "two-fer" with *Frank Zappa vs. The Mothers Of Prevention* (no. 44). The album was issued as a standalone CD in the US in 1987 by Rykodisc. The 1990 European Zappa Records pressing was labeled as a remix, although in fact the mix is identical to the original CD apart from the bass drum downbeat of "Night School," which had been slightly clipped on the previous CD issues, being restored. This minor variation was then reissued by Ryko in 1995 and by the ZFT in 2012.

Zappa (release) number: 48

London Symphony Orchestra Vol. II (June 1987)

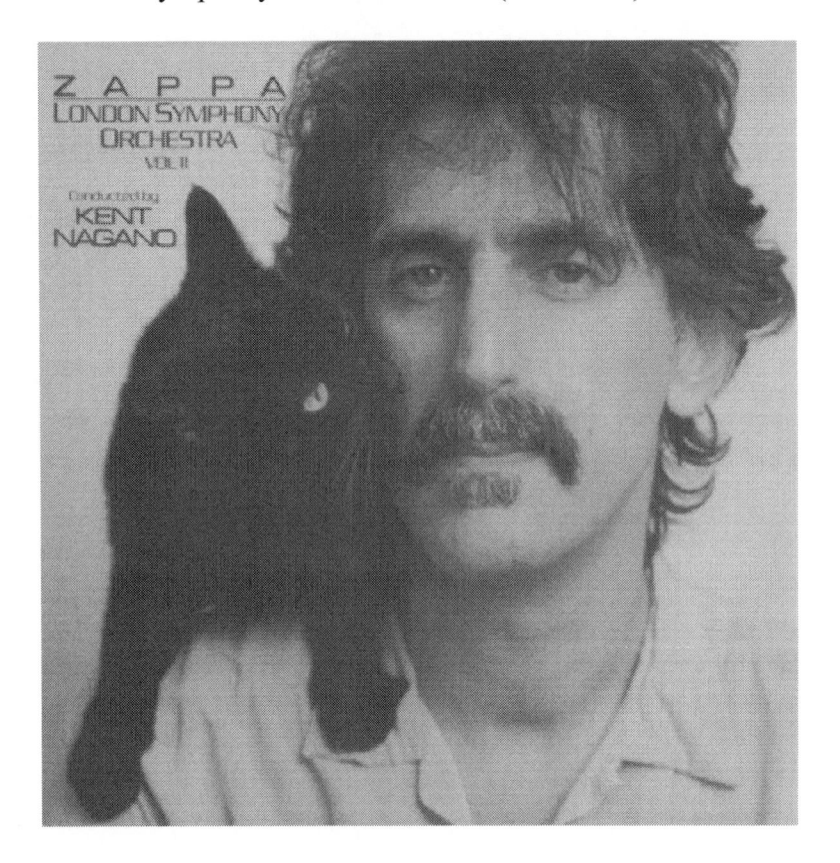

Performers:

The London Symphony Orchestra
Kent Nagano (conductor)

Recorded January 12-14, 1983 at Twickenham Film Studio, London, UK

1. Bogus Pomp 24:35
2. Bob In Dacron 12:11
3. Strictly Genteel 6:56

Issues:  ZFT reissue  Zappa Records 3872
         Original issue Barking Pumpkin SJ-74207
         Rykodisc reissue Ryko RCD 10540/41

Scores: All compositions available for rental only from Schott Music.

HERE'S THE DEAL: Additional performances conducted by Kent Nagano from the 1983 London Symhony Orchestra sessions. "Bogus Pomp" is a fine re-casting of the themes of *200 Motels* (no. 13), enlivened by a wicked solo for viola.

RATINGS: ***

DOWNLOAD THESE: Bogus Pomp.

DIFFERENCES BETWEEN THE ZFT CD REISSUE AND PREVIOUS CD REISSUES: One track from this album, "Bogus Pomp," had previously been issued on *The London Symphony Orchestra* CD, released by Rykodisc in 1986. In 1993, FZ remixed all of the tracks which had appeared on both vinyl albums and in 1995 these were issued by Ryko as a 2-CD set titled *The London Symphony Orchestra Volumes I & II*. This master was used by the ZFT for their CD reissue in 2012.

Zappa (release) number: 49

Old Masters Box 3 (December 1987)

LP reissues of:

Waka/Jawaka = no. 15
The Grand Wazoo = no. 16
Over-Nite Sensation = no. 17
Apostrophe (') = no. 18
Roxy & Elsewhere = no. 19
One Size Fits All = no. 20
Bongo Fury = no. 21
Zoot Allures = no. 22

Issues:   Original issue Barking Pumpkin BPR-9999

Transcriptions: none.

HERE'S THE DEAL: The third and last of Zappa's box sets of his early catalog. This one collects the last Bizarre LP, the DiscReet releases, and his one regular Warners disc.

RATINGS:  (****; keep if a copy is given or willed to you)

DOWNLOAD THESE: See the suggestions for albums nos. 16-22.

DIFFERENCES BETWEEN THE ZFT CD REISSUE AND PREVIOUS CD REISSUES: See the individual CD issues of the albums included in this vinyl-only box set; the set has not been issued on CD in this form.

Zappa CD number: 50

Guitar   (April 1988)

Performers and Dates:

Rhein-Main-Halle, Wiesbaden, Germany, March 27, 1979 (early show)
Rudi-Sedlmeyer Sporthalle, Munich, Germany, March 31, 1979 (late show)

Frank Zappa (guitar solos)
Denny Walley (slide guitar)
Warren Cuccurullo (rhythm guitar)
Ike Willis (rhythm guitar)
Tommy Mars (keyboards)
Peter Wolf (keyboards)
Ed Mann (percussion)
Arthur Barrow (bass)
Vinnie Colaiuta (drums)

Terrace Ballroom, Salt Lake City, Utah, December 7, 1981
Berkeley Community Theater, December 10, 1981 (late show)
Fox Theater, San Diego, California, December 12, 1981 (late show)
Brondbyhallen, Copenhagen, Denmark, May 11, 1982
Sporthalle, Cologne, Germany, May 21, 1982
Philipshalle, Düsseldorf, Germany, May 22, 1982
La Patinoire, Bordeaux, France, June 1, 1982

Alte Oper, Frankfurt, June 11, 1982 (early show)
Hammersmith Odeon, London, UK, June 19, 1982 (late show)
Hallenstadion, Zurich, Switzerland, June 24, 1982
Olympiahalle, Munich, Germany, June 26, 1982
Parco Redecesio, Milan, July 7, 1982
Stadio Communale, Pistoia, Italy, July 8, 1982

Frank Zappa (guitar solos)
Ray White (rhythm guitar)
Steve Vai (stunt guitar)
Tommy Mars (keyboards)
Bobby Martin (keyboards)
Ed Mann (percussion)
Scott Thunes (bass)
Chad Wackerman (drums)

Oscar Mayer Theatre, Madison, Wisconsin, August 11, 1984
Jones Beach Theatre, Wantagh, NY August 16, 1984
Hammersmith Odeon, London, September 25, 1984
Tower Theater, Upper Darby, PA, November 10, 1984 (late show)
Bismarck Theater, Chicago, Illinois November 23, 1984 (late show)
Civic Center, Atlanta, Georgia, November 25, 1984
Sunrise Musical Theatre, Sunrise, Florida, November 30, 1984 (early show)
Orpheum Theater, Memphis, Tennessee, December 4, 1984
Majestic Performing Arts Center, San Antonio, Texas, December 10, 1984
Queen Elizabeth Theatre, Vancouver December 18, 1984 (late show)
Arlene Schnitzer Concert Hall, Portland, Oregon, December 20, 1984

Frank Zappa (guitar solos)
Ike Willis (rhythm guitar)
Ray White (rhythm guitar)
Bobby Martin (keyboards)
Allan Zavod (keyboards)
Scott Thunes (bass)
Chad Wackerman (drums)


1. Sexual Harassment In The Workplace 3:42 December 12, 1981 (late show)
2. Which One Is It? 3:04 (Black Page) June 26, 1982
3. Republicans 5:07 (Let's Move To Cleveland) November 10, 1984 (late show)
4. Do Not Pass Go 3:36 (Drowning Witch) June 19, 1982 (late show)
5. Chalk Pie 4:51 (Zoot Allures) December 7, 1981
6. In-A-Gadda-Stravinsky 2:50 (Let's Move To Cleveland) November 25, 1984
7. That's Not Really Reggae 3:17 (Whipping Post) September 25, 1984
8. When No One Was No One 4:48 (Zoot Allures) May 21, 1982

9. Once Again, Without The Net 3:43  (Let's Move To Cleveland)  December 20, 1984
10. Outside Now (Original Solo) 5:28  (City of Tiny Lites) March 31, 1979 (late show)
11. Jim and Tammy's Upper Room 3:11  (Advance Romance) June 1, 1982
12. Were We Ever Really Safe In San Antonio? 2:49  (Drowning Witch)  December 10, 1984
13. That Ol' G Minor Thing Again 5:02  (City of Tiny Lites) June 24, 1982
14. Hotel Atlanta Incidentals 2:44  (Hot Plate Heaven at the Green Hotel)  November 25, 1984
15. That's Not Really A Shuffle 4:23  (King Kong)  May 11, 1982
16. Move It Or Park It 5:43  (Black Page)  June 11, 1982 (early show)
17. Sunrise Redeemer 3:58     (Let's Move To Cleveland)  November 30, 1984 (early show)
18. Variations On Sinister #3 5:15  (Easy Meat)  August 11, 1984
19. Orrin Hatch On Skis 2:12  (Ride My Face To Chicago) November 30, 1984 (late show)
20. But Who Was Fulcanelli? 2:48  (Drowning Witch)  May 21, 1982
21. For Duane 3:24  (Whipping Post)  November 25, 1984
22. GOA 4:51  (Let's Move To Cleveland)  November 23, 1984 (late show)
23. Winos Do Not March 3:14  (Sharleena) December 4, 1984
24. Swans? What Swans? 4:23  (Pound For A Brown)  December 12, 1981 (late show)
25. Too Ugly For Show Business 4:20 (King Kong)  December 10, 1981 (late show)
26. Systems Of Edges 5:32  (Inca Roads)  March 27, 1979 (early show)
27. Do Not Try This At Home 3:46 (Black Page)  July 7, 1982
28. Things That Look Like Meat 6:57  (City of Tiny Lites)  December 7, 1981
29. Watermelon In Easter Hay 4:02  August 16, 1984
30. Canadian Customs 3:34 (Let's Move To Cleveland)  December 18, 1984 (late show)
31. Is That All There Is? 4:09  (Let's Move To Cleveland) May 22, 1982
32. It Ain't Necessarily The Saint James Infirmary 5:15  (Pound For A Brown) July 8, 1982


Issues:    ZFT reissue  Zappa Records ZR 3876
           Original issue Barking Pumpkin D1 74212
           Rykodisc reissue Ryko RCD 10550/51


Transcriptions: none.


HERE'S THE DEAL: A second collection of Zappa solos to chew on, this time from 1979 through 1984. Included are two mash-ups, "In-A-Gadda-Stravinsky" (the opening solo for bassoon from Stravinsky's "The Rite of Spring" is played to a vamp based on Iron Butterfly's "In-A-Gadda-Vida"), and "It Ain't Necessarily The Saint James Infirmary" ("It Ain't Necessarily So" from George Gershwin's opera *Porgy and Bess* with the traditional blues "St. James Infirmary").

RATINGS: ***

DOWNLOAD THESE:  Sexual Harassment In The Workplace, In-A-Gadda-Stravinsky, It Ain't Necessarily The Saint James Infirmary

DIFFERENCES BETWEEN THE ZFT CD REISSUE AND PREVIOUS CD REISSUES: None. All CD pressings are derived from an expanded-for-CD master tape including 13 extra tracks compared to the original 2-LP vinyl release. Some inter-track edits present on the LP are not heard on the CD, but there is no additional or variant material to be found on the LP that is not present on the CD pressings.

Zappa CD number: 51

You Can't Do That On Stage Anymore Vol. 1

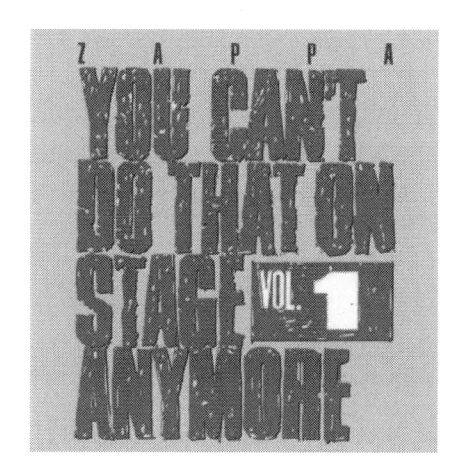

Performers:

February 13, 1969 - The Bronx, New York City
April 1969 - Stratford CT  NOT February 1969
Frank Zappa (lead guitar/vocal)
Lowell George (guitar/vocal)
Roy Estrada (bass/vocal)
Don Preston (keyboard/electronics)
Buzz Gardner (trumpet)
Ian Underwood (alto sax)
Bunk Gardner (tenor sax)
Motorhead Sherwood (baritone sax)
Jimmy Carl Black (drums)
Arthur Dyer Tripp III (drums)

April 1970 - An airport in Florida   NOT June 1970
Frank Zappa (guitar/vocals)
Mark Volman (vocal)
Howard Kaylan (vocal)
Jeff Simmons (bass)
George Duke (keyboards)
Ian Underwood (keyboards/alto sax)
Aynsley Dunbar (drums)

August 7, 1971  NOT July 7 OR July 8, 1971 - UCLA, Los Angeles
December 10, 1971 - London, England
Frank Zappa (guitar/vocals)
Mark Volman (vocal)

Howard Kaylan (vocal)
Jim Pons (bass)
Don Preston (keyboards/electronics)
Ian Underwood (keyboards/alto sax)
Aynsley Dunbar (drums)


December 12, 1973 - Hollywood CA
Frank Zappa (lead guitar/vocal)
Napoleon Murphy Brock (sax/vocal)
George Duke (keyboard/vocal)
Ruth Underwood (percussion)
Tom Fowler (bass)
Chester Thompson (drums)
Ralph Humphrey (drums)

November 8, 1974 - Passaic, NJ NOT November 18, 1974
Frank Zappa (lead guitar/vocal)
Napoleon Murphy Brock (sax/vocal)
George Duke (keyboard/vocal)
Ruth Underwood (percussion)
Tom Fowler (bass)
Chester Thompson (drums)

February 25, 1978 NOT March 1977
Frank Zappa (lead guitar/vocal)
Adrian Belew (guitar/vocal)
Tommy Mars (keyboards)
Peter Wolf (keyboards)
Ed Mann (percussion)
Patrick O'Hearn (bass)
Terry Bozzio (drums)

February 18, 1979 - London, England
Frank Zappa (lead guitar/vocal)
Denny Walley (slide guitar/vocals)
Warren Cucurrullo (guitar)
Tommy Mars (keyboards)
Peter Wolf (keyboards)
Ed Mann (percussion)
Arthur Barrow (keyboards/bass)
Vinnie Colaiuta (drums)

July 3, 1980 - Munich, West Germany
Frank Zappa (lead guitar/vocal)
Ike Willis (guitar/vocal)
Ray White (guitar/vocal)

Tommy Mars (keyboards)
Arthur Barrow (keyboards/bass)
David Logeman (drums)


October 31, 1981 - New York City
July 7, 1982 - Milan, Italy NOT July 6, 1982
July 8, 1982 - Pistoia, Italy NOT July 7, 1982 - Genoa, Italy
July 14, 1982 - Palermo, Sicily NOT July 14, 1982
Frank Zappa (lead guitar/vocal)
Ray White (guitar/vocal)
Steve Vai (stunt guitar)
Tommy Mars (keyboards/vocal)
Bobby Martin (keyboards/sax/vocals)
Ed Mann (percussion)
Scott Thunes (bass)
Chad Wackerman (drums)

August 26, 1984 NOT July 1984 - New York City
Frank Zappa (lead guitar/vocal)
Ike Willis (guitar/vocal)
Ray White (guitar/vocal)
Alan Zavod (keyboards)
Bobby Martin (keyboards/sax/vocals)
Scott Thunes (bass)
Chad Wackerman (drums)

Disc 1:

1. The Florida Airport Tape 1:04 (spoken: "Can I ask some of anybody here, has anyone seen me puke onstage?") April 1970
2. Once Upon A Time 4:38 (spoken: "Once upon a time, way back a long time ago...") December 10, 1971
3. Sofa #1 2:53 ("Ich bin den Himmel...") December 10, 1971
4. The Mammy Anthem 5:41 (instrumental) July 14,1982
5. You Didn't Try To Call Me 3:39 ("You didn't try to call me...") July 3, 1980
6. Diseases of the Band 2:22 (spoken: "Howdy folks. Alright, here's the deal, this is our last show here in London..."), February 18, 1979
7. Tryin' To Grow A Chin 3:44 ("I'm only 14, sickly and thin...") February 18, 1979
8. Let's Make The Water Turn Black / Harry You're A Beast / The Orange County Lumber Truck 3:28 (instrumental performance) April 1969 NOT February 1969
9. The Groupie Routine 5:41 (spoken: "I mean, really. Really! I mean, you guys, what can I say, you guys are my favorite band. You gotta tell me something, are you here in Hollywood long?") August 7, 1971 NOT July 8, 1971
10. Ruthie-Ruthie 2:57 (spoken: "I can't see you, but I know you are out there... " Sung: "Ruthie-Ruthie, where did you go?") November 8, 1974
11. Babbette 3:36 ("Don't you tell me "No," Babbette...") November 8, 1974

12. I'm The Slime  3:13  ("I'm gross and perverted...")  December 12, 1973
13. Big Swifty 8:47  (instrumental)  December 12, 1973
14. Don't Eat The Yellow Snow 20:16  ("Dreamed I was an Eskimo...")  February 18, 1979

Disc 2:

15. Plastic People 4:39  (spoken: "There's a green Chevy..."  sung: "Plastic People, you gotta go...")  February 13, 1969
16. The Torture Never Stops  15:48  ("Flies all green and buzzing...")  February 25, 1978 NOT March 1977
17. Fine Girl  2:55  ("Ooh yeah, she was a fine girl...")  July 7, 1982
18. Zomby Woof 5:39  ("300 years ago, I thought I might get some sleep...")  July 7, 1982
19. Sweet Leilani  2:39  (spoken: "Sweet Leilani, in A. Just pretend it was 30 years ago...")  February 1969 (FZ corrected it to "You Call That Music?" April 1969)
20. Oh No  4:34  (instrumental performance)  April 1969 - Stratford CT  NOT February 1969
21. Be In My Video  3:30  (spoken "I would go to Orlando if you would let me on your plane"  sung: "Be in my video, darling, every night...")  spoken - 1970, sung - August 26, 1984 NOT July 1984
22. The Deathless Horsie  5:29  (instrumental)   sung - August 26, 1984 NOT July 1984
23. The Dangerous Kitchen  1:50  ("The dangerous kitchen, if it ain't one thing, it's another..."  sung - August 26, 1984 NOT July 1984
24. Dumb All Over  4:20  ("Whoever we are, wherever we're from...")  October 31, 1981
25. Heavenly Bank Account 4:06   ("And if with these words, you do not heed...")  October 31, 1981
26. Suicide Chump 4:56 ("You say there ain't no use in living...")  October 31, 1981
27. Tell Me You Love Me 2:09   ("Tell me you love me...")  July 8, 1982
28. Sofa #2 3:01  (instrumental with band names at endl)  July 8, 1982

Issues:    ZFT reissue  Zappa Records ZR 3877
           Original issue: Rykodisc RCD 10081

Transcriptions: none

HERE'S THE DEAL: The first of Zappa's six volumes of live recordings of his touring bands. This one is an overview from 1969 through 1984 and, as such, is a good introduction for new fans to Zappa's music overall.

RATINGS: ****

DOWNLOAD THESE: Once Upon A Time and Sofa no. 1, The Torture Never Stops

DIFFERENCES BETWEEN THE ZFT CD REISSUE AND PREVIOUS CD REISSUES: The original Rykodisc pressing of this CD was sourced from a 1988 Sony 1630 digital master tape. This tape was copied in 1993 under FZ's supervision and issued as part of the 1995 Ryko CD reissue series. The content and mix of the 1988 and 1993 masters are identical. The 1993 1630 digital master was issued again in 2012 by the ZFT.

Zappa CD number 52

You Can't Do That On Stage Anymore Vol. 2

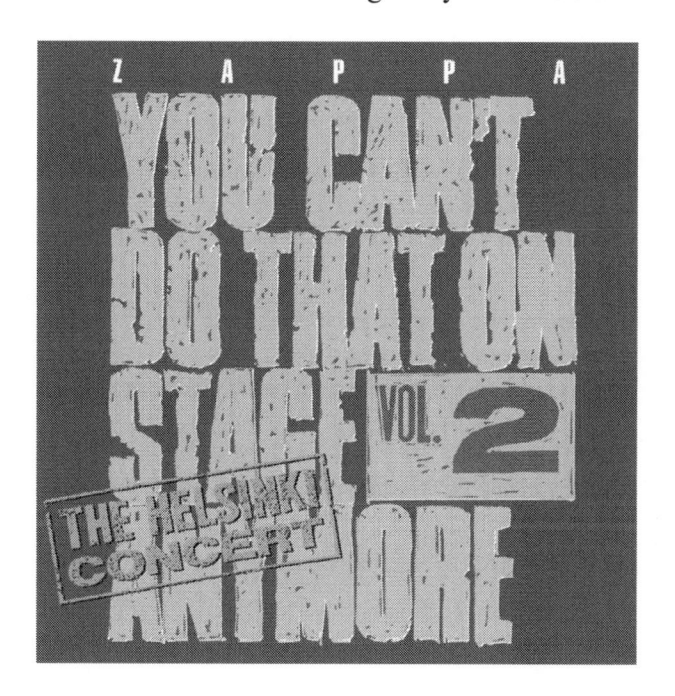

Performers:

Frank Zappa (lead guitar/vocal)
Napoleon Murphy Brock (sax/vocal)
George Duke (keyboard/vocal)
Ruth Underwood (percussion)
Tom Fowler (bass)
Chester Thompson (drums)

All tracks September 22, 1974 Helsinki, Finland


Disc One:
1. Tush Tush Tush (A Token of My Extreme) 2:46 (spoken: "It's about all of the sunshine here in Finland...")
2. Stinkfoot 4:20 ("In the dark, where all the fevers grow..."
3. Inca Roads 10:54 ("Did a vehicle come from somewhere out there?")
4. RDNZL 8:43  ("We could share a love...")
5. Village of the Sun  4:33  ("Goin' back home to the village of the sun...")
6. Echidna's Arf (Of You)  3:30  (instrumental)
7. Don't You Ever Wash That Thing?  4:56  (instrumental)
8. Pygmy Twylyte  8:22   ("Green hocker croakin' In the pygmy twylyte...")
9. Room Service  6:22 ("Honey, honey...")

10. The Idiot Bastard Son  2:39  ("The idiot bastard son, the father's a Nazi in Congress today...")
11. Cheepnis  4:28  ("I ate a hot dog, it tasted real good...")

Disc Two:
12. Approximate  8:11   (spoken: "Come on Ruth, come on, aw come on Ruth, sing along, aw come on Ruth sing along with me.:
13. Dupree's Paradise  23:59 (spoken introduction: "Ladies and gentlemen, the name of this song, seeing as we are confronted with a partial, how shall we say, language barrier here, we don't want to press the issue too much...")
14. Satumaa (Finnish Tango)  3:51   (spoken introduction: "We have now a special request, now you better leave the lights on onstage because we have to read this music, we've never played it before..." sung: "Aavan meren tuolla puolen jossakin on maa...")
15. T'Mershi Duween  1:31  (instrumental)
16. The Dog Breath Variations  1:38  (instrumental)
17. Uncle Meat  2:28 (instrumental)
18. Building a Girl  1:00  (instrumental)
19. Montana (Whipping Floss)  10:15  (spoken: "Say that again, please? 'Whipping Post'? Oh sorry, we don't know that one. Anything else?" sung: "I might be moving to -- Hold it! Hold it!")
20. Big Swifty  2:16  (instrumental with band names at end)

Issues:  ZFT reissue  Zappa Records ZR 3878
           Original issue Rykodisc RCD 10563/64

Transcriptions: none.


HERE'S THE DEAL: A fine concert by many fans' favorite Zappa band.

RATINGS: ****

DOWNLOAD THESE: Satumaa, Montana (Whipping Floss)

DIFFERENCES BETWEEN THE ZFT CD REISSUE AND PREVIOUS CD REISSUES: The original Rykodisc pressing of this CD was sourced from a 1988 Sony 1630 digital master tape. This tape was copied in 1993 under FZ's supervision and issued as part of the 1995 Ryko CD reissue series. The content and mix of the 1988 and 1993 masters are identical. The 1993 1630 digital master was issued again in 2012 by the ZFT.

Zappa CD number: 53

Broadway The Hard Way (October 1988)

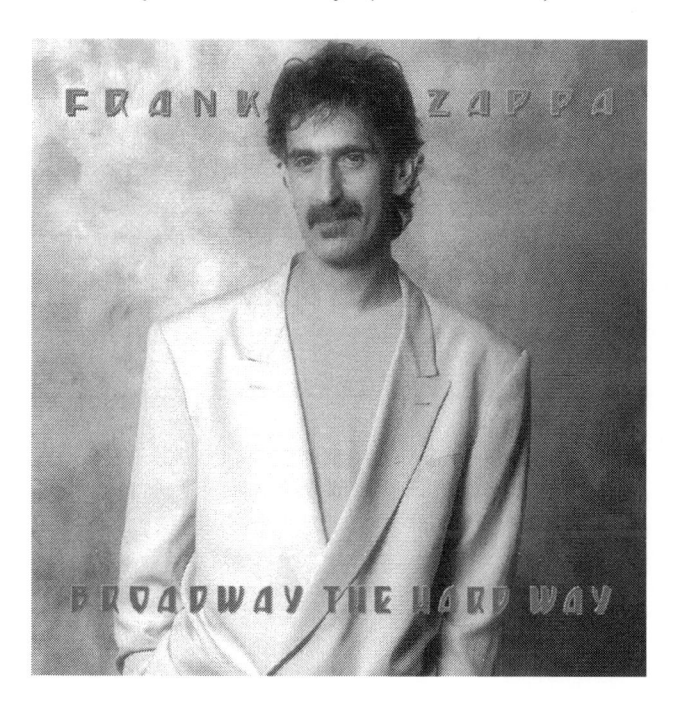

Performers:

Frank Zappa (lead guitar/vocal)
Ike Willis (guitar/vocal)
Mike Keneally (guitar/synth/vocal)
Bobby Martin (keyboards/vocal)
Ed Mann (percussion)
Walt Fowler (trumpet)
Bruce Fowler (trombone)
Paul Carman (alto sax)
Albert Wing (tenor sax)
Kurt McGettrick (baritone sax)
Scott Thunes (bass)
Chad Wackerman (drums)
Eric Buxton (guest vocalist)


All selections recorded live by the UMRK Mobile, February-June, 1988
Earliest dates per song is indexed

February 9, 1988 Warner Theatre, Washington DC
February 12, 1988 Tower Theater, Upper Darby, PA

February 13, 1988 Tower Theater, Upper Darby, PA
February 14, 1988 Tower Theater, Upper Darby, PA
February 17, 1988 Bushnell Memorial Hall, Hartford
February 25, 1988 Syria Mosque, Pittsburgh
February 26, 1988 Royal Oak Music Theatre, Detroit, Michigan

March 1, 1988 Frauenthal Auditorium, Muskegon, Michigan
March 3, 1988 Auditorium Theatre, Chicago
March 4, 1988  Auditorium Theatre, Chicago
March 5, 1988 Music Hall, Cleveland, Ohio
March 9, 1988, Shea's Theater, Buffalo
March 11, 1988 War Memorial Auditorium, Rochester, NY
March 15, 1988 Cumberland County Civic Center, Portland


March 16, 1988 Civic Center, Providence
March 17, 1988  Broome County Arena, Binghamton, NY
March 20, 1988 Rothman Center, Teaneck, New Jersey
March 25, 1988 Nassau Coliseum, Uniondale, NY

April 19, 1988 Wembley Arena, London, UK
April 25, 1988 Falkoner Teatret, Copenhagen, Denmark
April 26, 1988 Olympen, Lund, Sweden

May 8, 1988 Stadthalle, Vienna, Austria
May 9, 1988 Rudi-Sedlmeyer Sporthalle, Munich, Germany
May 23, 1988 Hall Tivoli, Strasbourg, France
May 24, 1988 Beethovensaal, Liederhalle, Stuttgart, Germany

June 9, 1988 Palasport, Genoa, Italy

1. Elvis Has Just Left The Building 2:24   ("Elvis has just left the building, those are his footprints, right there")  May 24 and June 9, 1988
2. Planet Of The Baritone Women 2:48   ("On the Planet of the Baritone Women") February 9 and 12, and March 5, 1988
3. Any Kind Of Pain 5:42  (spoken: "Broadway The Hard Way, ladies and gentlemen!" sung: "You are the girl")  February 9 and 12, March 5, and April 25, 1988
4. Dickie's Such An Asshole 5:45  (spoken: "Alright. CNN ran a story last week about this new product that has been developed for our prison system." sung: "One 'n one is eleven!") February 9 and 12, March 5, March 17, April 26, and May 23, 1988
5. When The Lie's So Big 3:38  (spoken: "Pinch it good! You know, that *confinement loaf* is real good stuff" sung: "They got lies so big")  February 9 and March 5, 1988
6. Rhymin' Man 3:50   ("Rhymin' Man, tall and tan") May 9, 1988
7. Promiscuous 2:02   ("The Surgeon General, Doctor Koop") February 26, 1988
8. The Untouchables (Riddle/Zappa) 2:26   ("Rico! Youngblood! Wake up!")  March 16, 1988
9. Why Don't You Like Me? 2:57   ("Why don't you like me?") February 13, 17, 25, and March 3, 1988

10. Bacon Fat (Williams/Brown/Zappa) 1:29   ("While I was down in W.D.C.") March 1, 1988
11. Stolen Moments (Nelson) 2:58   March 1 and 3, 1988
12. Murder By Numbers (Summers/Sting) 5:37   (spoken: "Now, this afternoon on my way down the elevator we stopped at the lobby" sung: "Once that you've decided on a killing")  March 3, 1988
13. Jezebel Boy 2:27   ("Jezebel Boy!") February 13, 1988
14. Outside Now 7:49   ("These executives have plooked the fuck out of me")  April 19 and June 9, 1988
15. Hot Plate Heaven At The Green Hotel 6:40   ("I used to have a job")  May 8 and 9, 1988
16. What Kind Of Girl? 3:16   ("What's a girl like you, doin' in a motel like this")  March 1 and 4, 1988
17. Jesus Thinks You're A Jerk 9:16   ("There's an ugly little weasel 'bout three-foot nine")  February 9, 13, 14, and 26, March 9, 11, 15, 16, 20, 25, and April 19, 1988

Issues:   ZFT reissue  Zappa Records ZR3879
          Original issue Barking Pumpkin D1 74218 (LP), Ryko RCD 40096
          Rykodisc reissue Ryko RCD 10552


Transcriptions: none.

HERE'S THE DEAL: One of Zappa's last albums of (mostly) new songs prepared by him (for new material, only The *Yellow Shark* [no. 62] and *Civilization Phaze III* [no. 63] would follow; the rest of his CDs were renditions of previously released songs and compositions). Also, this is the first of several CDs for which Zappa painstakingly used many recordings from the 1988 tour to produce composites and mash-ups.

RATINGS: ****

DOWNLOAD THESE:  Elvis Has Just Left The Building, Dickie's Such An Asshole, Hot Plate Heaven At The Green Hotel

DIFFERENCES BETWEEN THE ZFT CD REISSUE AND PREVIOUS CD REISSUES: The original Rykodisc pressing of this CD was sourced from a 1988 Sony 1630 digital master tape. This tape was copied in 1993 under FZ's supervision and issued as part of the 1995 Ryko CD reissue series. The content and mix of the 1988 and 1993 masters are identical. The 1993 1630 digital master was issued again in 2012 by the ZFT.

Zappa CD number: 54

You Can't Do That On Stage Anymore Vol. 3

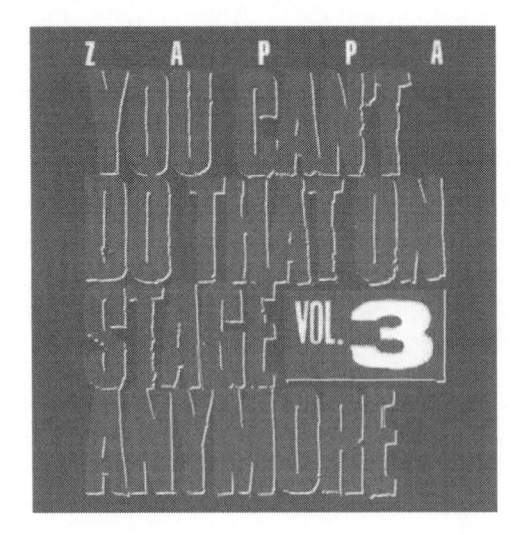

Performers:

December 10, 1971 - London, England
Frank Zappa (guitar/vocals)
Mark Volman (vocal)
Howard Kaylan (vocal)
Jim Pons (bass)
Don Preston (keyboards/electronics)
Ian Underwood (keyboards/alto sax)
Aynsley Dunbar (drums)

December 12, 1973, Hollywood, CA
Frank Zappa (lead guitar/vocal)
Napoleon Murphy Brock (sax/vocal)
George Duke (keyboard/vocal)
Ruth Underwood (percussion)
Tom Fowler (bass)
Chester Thompson (drums)
Ralph Humphrey (drums)


February 3, 1976 Tokyo NOT 1975 Tokyo
Frank Zappa (guitar)

Napoleon Murphy Brock (sax)
Andre Lewis (keyboards)
Roy Estrada (bass)
Terry Bozzio (drums)

October 31, 1981, New York City
June 1982 Cap D'Agde, France
July 1982, Balzano, Italy
July 14, 1982 Palermo, Sicily NOT July 12, 1982
Frank Zappa (lead guitar/vocal)
Ray White (guitar/vocal)
Steve Vai (stunt guitar)
Tommy Mars (keyboards/vocal)
Bobby Martin (keyboards/sax/vocals)
Ed Mann (percussion)
Scott Thunes (bass)
Chad Wackerman (drums)

August 26, 1984 NOT July 1984 - New York City
November 23, 1984, Chicago
December 17, 1984 Seattle
December 23, 1984, Los Angeles
Frank Zappa (lead guitar/vocal)
Ike Willis (guitar/vocal)
Ray White (guitar/vocal)
Alan Zavod (keyboards)
Bobby Martin (keyboards/sax/vocals)
Scott Thunes (bass)
Chad Wackerman (drums)


Disc 1:

1. Sharleena 8:54 (spoken: "Okay, ladies and gentlemen, my son, Dweezil" sung: "Battlestar Galactica?") December 23, 1984
2. Bamboozled By Love/ Owner of a Lonely Heart  6:06  ("Bamboozled by love...") November 23, 1984
3. Lucille Has Messed My Mind Up  2:52  ("Lucille has messed my mind up...")  November 23, 1984
4. Advance Romance (1984)  6:56  ("No more credit from the liquor store")  November 23, 1984
5. Bobby Brown Goes Down 2:44  (spoken: "A real hologram, I mean, not real, but almost a real hologram"  sung: "Hey there people I'm Bobby Brown...") December 17, 1984
6. Keep It Greasy  3:30   (spoken: "Hi-ho, Silver, away!"  sung: "Keep it greasy so it will go down easy"  December 17, 1984
7. Honey, Don't You Want A Man Like Me? 4:16  ("Honey honey, hey, baby don't you want a man like me?") August 26, 1984 NOT July 1984
8. In France 3:01 ("We're playing in a tent, it's payin' the rent") November 23, 1984

9. Drowning Witch  9:22  ("The ship is arriving too late, to save a drowning witch") July 1982 (Balzano, Italy) and December 17, 1984
10. Ride My Face To Chicago 4:22 ("Ride my face to Chicago") November 23, 1984
11. Carol, You Fool 4:06 ("You was a fool, oh Carol, you fool") November 23, 1984
12. Chana In De Bushwop  4:52  ("Chana In de bushwop, in de bushwop") November 23, 1984
13. Joe's Garage  2:20  ("It wasn't very large")  November 23, 1984
14. Why Does It Hurt When I Pee? 3:06 ("This is dedicated to the two guys in the crew who went to see the doctor today" sung: "Why does it hurt when I pee?") November 23, 1984

Disc 2:

15. Dickie's Such An Asshole  10:08 (spoken: "Okay, hold your applause for one second." sung: "One and one is eleven...") December 12, 1973
16. Hands With A Hammer  3:18  (Terry Bozzio drum solo)  February 3, 1976, Tokyo NOT 1975 (month unknown), Tokyo
17. Zoot Allures 6:09  1975 (month unknown), instrumental, February 3, 1976 (NOT 1975 [month unknown] Tokyo) and June 1982 France
18.  Society Pages 2:33  ("You're the old lady, from the society pages.") October 31, 1981
19. I'm A Beautiful Guy 1:55  ("I'm a beautiful guy...")  October 31, 1981
20. Beauty Knows No Pain  2:55  ("Beauty knows no pain...") October 31, 1981
21. Charlie's Enormous Mouth 3:40  ("Charlie's enormous mouth, well, it's all right")  October 31, 1981
22. Cocaine Decisions 3:14  (spoken: "Drop a line now " sung: "Cocaine decisions, you are a person with a snow job")  November 23, 1984, and July 12, 1982
23. Nig Biz  4:59  ("I signed on the line, for seven long years") July 12, 1982.
24. King Kong  24:32  (instrumental)  December 10, 1971 and June 1982
25. Cosmik Debris  5:13  ("The mystery man came over, said 'I'm out of sight'") December 17, 1984

Issues:    ZFT reissue:  Zappa Records ZR 3880
           Original issue:    Rykodisc RCD 10085/86


Transcriptions: None

HERE'S THE DEAL: Most of Disc One comes from a November 23, 1984, Chicago concert, while Disc Two has a mixture of recordings from the mid-1970s and the early 1980s.

RATINGS: ***1/2

DOWNLOAD THESE: Ride My Face To Chicago

DIFFERENCES BETWEEN THE ZFT CD REISSUE AND PREVIOUS CD REISSUES: The original Rykodisc pressing of this CD was sourced from a 1989 Sony 1630 digital master tape. This tape was copied in 1993 under FZ's supervision and issued as part of the 1995 Ryko CD reissue series. The content and mix of the 1989 and 1993 masters are identical. The 1993 1630 digital master was issued again in 2012 by the ZFT.

Zappa CD number: 55

The Best Band You Never Heard In Your Life (April 1991)

Performers:

Frank Zappa (lead guitar/vocal)
Ike Willis (guitar/vocal)
Mike Keneally (guitar/synth/vocal)
Bobby Martin (keyboards/vocal)
Ed Mann (percussion, vibes, marimba, electronic percussion)
Walt Fowler (trumpet, flugelhorn)
Bruce Fowler (trombone)
Paul Carman (soprano, alto, and baritone saxophones)
Albert Wing (tenor sax)
Kurt McGettrick (baritone and bass saxophone, contrabass clarinet)
Scott Thunes (bass, minimoog)
Chad Wackerman (drums, electronic percussion)


All selections recorded live by the UMRK Mobile, February-June, 1988
Earliest dates per song is indexed


February 14, 1988  Tower Theater, Upper Darby, PA
February 23, 1988 Mid Hudson Civic Center, Poughkeepsie, NY
February 25, 1988  Syria Mosque, Pittsburgh
February 28, 1988, Royal Oak Music Theatre, Detroit, Michigan

March 17, 1988  Broome County Arena, Binghamton, NY
March 19, 1988,  Memorial Hall, Allentown, Pennsylvania
March 20, 1988  Rothman Center, Teaneck, New Jersey
March 21, 1988, Landmark Theater, Syracuse, NY

April 16, 1988, Brighton Centre, Brighton, UK
April 18, 1988,  Wembley Arena, London, UK
April 19, 1988, Wembley Arena, London, UK
April 22, 1988, Carl-Diem-Halle, Würzburg, Germany


May 3, 1988, The Ahoy, Rotterdam, Netherlands
May 8, 1988, Stadthalle, Vienna, Austria
May 9, 1988, Rudi-Sedlmeyer Sporthalle, Munich, Germany
May 18, 1988  Le Zenith, Montpellier, France
May 23, 1988 Hall Tivoli, Strasbourg, France
May 24, 1988  Beethovensaal, Liederhalle, Stuttgart, Germany
May 26, 1988, Stadthalle, Fuerth, Germany
May 28, 1988, Sporthalle, Linz, Austria


June 5, 1988  Palasport, Modena, Italy
June 6, 1988, Palasport, Florence, Italy




01. Heavy Duty Judy 6:04 ("Hello! Boy, got y'all JAMMED in here, don't dey?")  April 22 and May 3, 1988
02. Ring Of Fire (Merle Kilgore and June Carter) 2:00 ("Love is a burning thing ") April 22, 1988
03. Cosmik Debris 4:32 ("The Mystery Man came over") April 22, 1988
04. Find Her Finer 2:42 ("Find her finer, sneak up behind her")  May 9, 1988
05. Who Needs The Peace Corps? 2:40 ("What's there to live for?") April 22 and May 9, 1988
06. I Left My Heart In San Francisco (George C. Cory, Jr. and Douglas Cross)  0:36 ("I left my heart, way down in San Francisco") April 22, 1988
07. Zomby Woof 5:41 ("Three hundred years ago ")  March 19 and May 9, 1988
08. Bolero (Maurice Ravel)  5:19  May 3, 1988
09. Zoot Allures 7:07  April 16, 1988
10. Mr. Green Genes 3:40 ("Eat your greens")  May 23, 1988
11. Florentine Pogen 7:11 ("She was the daughter of a wealthy Florentine Pogen") May 23 and June 6, 1988
12. Andy 5:51 ("Is there anything good inside of you") May 26, 1988
13. Inca Roads 8:19 ("Did a vehicle come from somewhere out there") April 22 and May 8, 1988
14. Sofa #1 2:49  May 24, 1988
15. Purple Haze (Jimi Hendrix)  2:27 ("Purple haze, all in my brain")  May 28, 1988

16. Sunshine Of Your Love (Peter Brown, Jack Bruce and Eric Clapton) 2:30 ("Isaac Hayes, Gabby Hayes" "It's gettin' near dark ")  May 28, 1988
17. Let's Move To Cleveland 5:51  May 18 and June 5, 1988
18. When Irish Eyes Are Smiling (Ernest Ball, George Graff and Chancey Olcott) 0:46 ("Happy Saint Pattie's day, now! ")  March 17, 1988
19. "Godfather Part II" Theme (Nino Rota)  0:30  March 17, 1988
20. A Few Moments With Brother A. West (Brother A. West and FZ) 4:01 ("Thank you very much, Mr. Zappa. Ah, I'm very pleased to be here on behalf of the Administration")  February 14, 1988
21. The Torture Never Stops Part One 5:20 ("Flies all green 'n buzzin' in his dungeon of despair")  April 19 and 22, 1988
22. Theme From "Bonanza"  (Ray Evans and Jay Livingstone) 0:28 ("And speaking of torture, how about this ugly sonofabitch?") April 19, 1988
23. Lonesome Cowboy Burt (Swaggart Version) 4:54 ("My name is Swaggart, I am an asshole")  February 25, 1988
24. The Torture Never Stops Part Two 10:47 ("Flies all green 'n buzzin' in his dungeon of despair") March 20, 1988
25. More Trouble Every Day (Swaggart Version) 5:28 ("Well I'm about to get sick, from watchin' my TV")  February 23, 1988
26. Penguin In Bondage (Swaggart Version) 5:05 ("She's just like a Penguin in Bondage, boy")  February 23, 1988
27. The Eric Dolphy Memorial Barbecue 9:18 ("It's hot") February 28, March 21, and May 8, 1988
28. Stairway To Heaven (Jimmy Page and Robert Plant)  9:20 ("There's a lady who's sure all that glitters is gold")   May 8, June 6, and April 18, 1988

Issues:    ZFT reissue   Zappa Records ZR 3881
           Original issue Barking Pumpkin D2 74233
           Rykodisc reissue Ryko RCD 10553/54


Transcriptions: none.

HERE'S THE DEAL: An intensively-edited post mortem of the 1988 touring band. Equal helpings of religious satire and musical virtuosity, which then blend together in Zappa's arrangement of Led Zeppelin's juggernaut, "Stairway to Heaven." As some fans have promoted, this may well be the last great album that Zappa recorded with his touring band.

RATINGS: *****

DOWNLOAD THESE: Stairway To Heaven

DIFFERENCES BETWEEN THE ZFT CD REISSUE AND PREVIOUS CD REISSUES: The original Rykodisc pressing of this CD was sourced from a 1990 Sony 1630 digital master tape. This tape was copied in 1993 under FZ's supervision and issued as part of the 1995 Ryko CD reissue series. The content and mix of the 1990 and 1993 masters are identical. The 1993 1630 digital master was issued again in 2012 by the ZFT.

Zappa CD number: 56

You Can't Do That On Stage Anymore Vol. 4

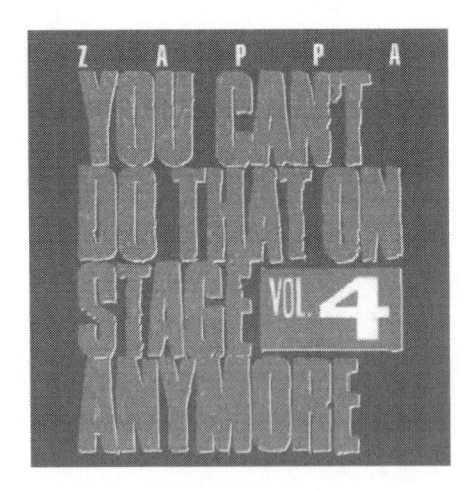

Performers:

February 13, 1969 (NOT Spring 1969) Bronx NY
February 14, 1969, New York City
February 21, 1969 Fillmore East, New York City
Frank Zappa (lead guitar/vocal)
Lowell George (guitar/vocal)
Roy Estrada (bass/vocal)
Don Preston (keyboard/electronics)
Buzz Gardner (trumpet)
Ian Underwood (alto sax)
Bunk Gardner (tenor sax)
Motorhead Sherwood (baritone sax)
Jimmy Carl Black (drums)
Arthur Dyer Tripp III (drums)
Dave Samuels (guest, vibes on Feb. 14)

December 8-12, 1973 (NOT November 1973), Los Angeles
Frank Zappa (lead guitar/vocal)
Napoleon Murphy Brock (sax/vocal)
George Duke (keyboard/vocal)
Ruth Underwood (percussion)
Bruce Fowler (trombone)`
Tom Fowler (bass)
Chester Thompson (drums)
Ralph Humphrey (drums)

November 8 (NOT winter) 1974 Passaic, New Jersey
Frank Zappa (lead guitar/vocal)
Napoleon Murphy Brock (sax/vocal)
George Duke (keyboard/vocal)
Ruth Underwood (percussion)
Tom Fowler (bass)
Chester Thompson (drums)

May 21, 1975, Austin TX NOT Winter 1976
Frank Zappa (lead guitar/vocal)
Captain Beefheart (harmonica/vocals)
Napoleon Murphy Brock (sax/vocal)
George Duke (keyboards)
Bruce Fowler (trombone)
Denny Walley (slide guitar)
Tom Fowler (bass)
Terry Bozzio (drums)

February 18, 1979, London
Frank Zappa (lead guitar/vocal)
Ike Willis (lead vocal)
Denny Walley (slide guitar/vocals)
Warren Cucurrullo (guitar)
Tommy Mars (keyboards)
Peter Wolf (keyboards)
Ed Mann (percussion)
Arthur Barrow (keyboards/bass)
Vinnie Colaiuta (drums)

October 28, 1978 New York City
October 31, 1978 New York City
Frank Zappa (lead guitar/vocal)
Denny Walley (slide guitar/vocals)
Tommy Mars (keyboards)
Peter Wolf (keyboards)
Ed Mann (percussion)
Patrick O'Hearn (bass/vocals)
Arthur Barrow (keyboards/bass)
Vinnie Colaiuta (drums)

May 8, 1980 New York City
Frank Zappa (lead guitar/vocal)
Ike Willis (guitar/vocal)
Ray White (guitar/vocal)
Tommy Mars (keyboards)
Arthur Barrow (keyboards/bass)

David Logeman (drums)

June 22, 1982 Metz, France
June 26, 1982 Munich, West Germany
July 8, 1982  Pistoia, Italy
July 9, 1982 Rome, Italy
Frank Zappa (lead guitar/vocal)
Ray White (guitar/vocal)
Steve Vai (stunt guitar)
Tommy Mars (keyboards/vocal)
Bobby Martin (keyboards/sax/vocals)
Ed Mann (percussion)
Scott Thunes (bass)
Chad Wackerman (drums)

August 24, 1984 Detroit
September 24-25, 1984, London
October 28, 1984 (NOT November 1984) Amherst MA
November 10, 1984 Upper Day, PA NOT November 1984  Philadelphia
December 1, 1984 St. Petersburg FL
December 18, 1984 (NOT November 1984) Vancouver
December 20 (NOT November) 1984 Portland OR
December 23, 1984, Hollywood, CA
Frank Zappa (lead guitar/vocal)
Ike Willis (guitar/vocal)
Ray White (guitar/vocal)
Alan Zavod (keyboards)
Bobby Martin (keyboards/sax/vocals)
Scott Thunes (bass)
Chad Wackerman (drums)
Archie Shepp (guest on October 28, 1984, tenor sax)

May 13,1988 Bilbao, Spain
May 19, 1988 Grenoble, France
Frank Zappa (lead guitar)
Ike Willis (guitar)
Mike Kenneally (guitar/synth)
Bobby Martin (keyboards)
Ed Mann (percussion)
Walt Fowler (trumpet)
Bruce Fowler (trombone)
Paul Carman (alto sax)
Albert Wing (tenor sax)
Kurt McGettrick (baritone sax)
Scott Thunes (bass)

Chad Wackerman (drums)

Song titles  Duration  (first line)  Date of source recording(s)
Notes: Dates verified through Frank Zappa Gig List, Zappa Wiki Jawaka, and Scott Parker's *Hungry Freaks, Daddy*

Disc 1:

1. Little Rubber Girl 2:57   (spoken: "Thank you. Okay, sit down, some more raw unbridled buffoonery... " introduction: "A year ago today, was when you went away..." sung: "I don't need you, I don't want you..." October 31, 1978 NOT October 31, 1979
2. Stick Together 2:04    ("This is a song about the union, friends...") December 18, 1984 NOT November 1984
3. My Guitar Wants To Kill Your Mama 3:20  ("You know, your mama and your daddy...")   December 23, 1984
4. Willie the Pimp  ("I'm a little pimp with the hair gassed back...") 2:07   December 23, 1984
5. Montana  5:43 ("I might be moving to Montana soon...")   December 8-12, 1973 (NOT November 1973) and December 23, 1984
6. Brown Moses  2:38  ("What wickedness is this...")   December 23, 1984
7. The Evil Prince  7:13  ("Well well well, now, dis de nasty sucker dat be respondable fo de enwhiffment o de origumal potium...") September 24-25, 1984
8. Approximate  1:49  (instrumental)  July 8, 1982  Pistoia, Italy
9. Love of My Life Mudd Club Version 1:58  ("Love of the my life, I love you so...") May 8, 1980  New York City
10. Let's Move to Cleveland Solos (1984) 7:11  (instrumental)  October 28, 1984 (NOT November 1984) Amherst MA
11. You Call That Music? 4:07  (instrumental)   February 14, 1969
12.  Pound for a Brown Solos (1978)  6:30  (instrumental)   October 28, 1978 NOT October 31, 1979
13. The Black Page (1984)  5:15  (instrumental)   December 18, 1984 NOT November 1984
14. Take Me Out To The Ball Game  3:02  (spoken: "Alright, welcome and good evening to the baseball game..")    May 13,1988 Bilbao, Spain
15. Filthy Habits  5:40  (instrumental)  May 13,1988 Bilbao, Spain
16. The Torture Never Stops Original Version 9:15  ("Flies all green and buzzing...")  May 21, 1975, Austin TX  NOT 1976 Austin TX


Disc 2:

17. Church Chat  2:00  ("You know, today the church is in a terrible state...")   June 22, 1982 Metz, France
18. Stevie's Spanking 10:51 ("His name is Stevie Vai...")    July 9, 1982 Rome, Italy
19. Outside Now  6:10  ("These executives have plooked the fuck out of me...")  November 1984  Philadelphia (Note: Zappa did not perform in Philadelphia in 1984)
20. Disco Boy 3:00  ("Disco boy, run to the toilet, comb your hair...") June 26, 1982 Munich
21. Teen-Age Wind  1:54   ("I got to be free, free as the wind...")   June 26, 1982 Munich

22. Truck Driver Divorce 4:47 ("Truck driver divorce, it's very sad...") December 20 (NOT November) 1984 Portland OR and September 24-25, 1984 London
23. Florentine Pogen 5:10 ("She was the daughter of a wealthy Florentine Pogen...") February 18, 1979
24. Tiny Sick Tears 4:30 ("You know, sometimes in the middle of the night, you get to feeling uptight...") February 1969 (NOT Spring 1969) Bronx NY
25. Smell My Beard 4:30 ("Now the sound that you hear in the background right now is the sound caused by George Duke agitating two metal insignias...") November 8 (NOT winter) 1974 Passaic, New Jersey
26. The Booger Man 2:47 ("White juice on his beard, the booger man, get down...") November 8 (NOT winter) 1974 Passaic, New Jersey
27. Carolina Hard Core Ecstasy 6:28 ("I could have swore her hair was made of rayon...") December 20 (NOT November) 1984 Portland OR
28. Are You Upset? 1:29 (spoken [to screaming audience member]: "Shh, shhh, are you upset?") 21 February 1969 Fillmore East
29. Little Girl of Mine 1:41 ("Oh little girl of mine..") August 24, 1984 Detroit and December 1, 1984 St. Petersburg FL
30. The Closer You Are ("The closer you are...") 2:05 August 24, 1984 Detroit and December 1, 1984 St. Petersburg FL
31. Johnny Darling 0:52 ("And she said, Johnny darling...") August 24, 1984 Detroit and December 1, 1984 St. Petersburg FL
32. No, No Cherry 1:26 ("Well I found out baby you told me a great big lie...") August 24, 1984 Detroit and December 1, 1984 St. Petersburg FL
33. The Man From Utopia 1:16 ("Well this is the story of a man who lived in Pistoria...) July 8, 1982 Pistoia, Italy
34. Mary Lou 2:14 ("I'm gonna tell you a story about Mary Lou...") July 8, 1982 Pistoia, Italy

Issues: ZFT reissue   Zappa Records ZR 3882
         Original issue  Rykodisc 10087

Transcriptions:  none.

HERE'S THE DEAL: More mementos from Zappa's touring bands. Unlike Volume 1, here Zappa includes some bits from 1988.

RATINGS: ****


DOWNLOAD THESE:  The Torture Never Stops Original Version (1975)


DIFFERENCES BETWEEN THE ZFT CD REISSUE AND PREVIOUS CD REISSUES: The original Rykodisc pressing of this CD was sourced from a 1991 Sony 1630 digital master tape. This tape was copied in 1993 under FZ's supervision and issued as part of the 1995 Ryko CD reissue series. The content and mix of the 1991 and 1993 masters are identical. The 1993 1630 digital master was issued again in 2012 by the ZFT.

Zappa CD number: 57

Make A Jazz Noise Here  (June 1991)

Performers:

Frank Zappa (lead guitar/vocal)
Ike Willis (guitar/vocal)
Mike Keneally (guitar/synth/vocal)
Bobby Martin (keyboards/vocal)
Ed Mann (percussion, vibes, marimba, electronic percussion)
Walt Fowler (trumpet, flugelhorn)
Bruce Fowler (trombone)
Paul Carman (soprano, alto, and baritone saxophones)
Albert Wing (tenor sax)
Kurt McGettrick (baritone and bass saxophone, contrabass clarinet)
Scott Thunes (bass, minimoog)
Chad Wackerman (drums, electronic percussion)


All selections recorded live by the UMRK Mobile, February-June, 1988
Earliest dates per song is indexed

February 9, 1988 Warner Theatre, Washington, DC
February 10, 1988 Warner Theatre, Washington, DC
February 12, 1988 Tower Theater, Upper Darby, PA

February 20, 1988 Orpheum Theater, Boston, MA
February 23, 1988 Mid Hudson Civic Center, Poughkeepsie, NY
February 25, 1988 Syria Mosque, Pittsburgh, PA
February 26, 1988 Royal Oak Music Theatre, Detroit, Michigan

March 5, 1988 Music Hall, Cleveland, Ohio
March 12, 1988 Memorial Auditorium, Burlington, VT
March 13, 1988  Civic Center, Springfield, MA
March 19, 1988 Memorial Hall, Allentown, PA

April 14, 1988 Sporthalle, Cologne, Germany
April 16, 1988 Brighton Centre, Brighton, UK
April 18, 1988  Wembley Arena, London, UK
April 19, 1988 Wembley Arena, London, UK
April 24, 1988 Stadthalle, Bremen, Germany
April 26, 1988 Olympen, Lund, Sweden

May 3, 1988  The Ahoy, Rotterdam, Netherlands
May 4, 1988 The Ahoy, Rotterdam, Netherlands
May 8, 1988 Stadthalle, Vienna, Austria
May 9, 1988  Rudi-Sedlmeyer Sporthalle, Munich, Germany
May 13, 1988 Pabellón de los Deportes de La Casilla, Bilbao, Spain
May 15, 1988 Prado de San Sebastián, Seville, Spain
May 19, 1988 Le Summum, Grenoble, France
May 24, 1988 Beethovensaal, Liederhalle, Stuttgart, Germany
May 25, 1988  Rosengarten/Mozartsaal, Mannheim, Germany
May 28, 1988 Sporthalle, Linz, Austria

June 3, 1988 Palasport, Turin, Italy
June 5, 1988 Palasport, Modena, Italy
June 6, 1988  Palasport, Florence, Italy
June 7, 1988 PalaEur, Rome, Italy




01. Stinkfoot 7:39 (spoken: "Okay, thank you, thank you, thank you!" sung: "In the dark where all the fevers grow") February 20 and 23, and May 4, 1988
02. When Yuppies Go To Hell 13:28 ("Goin' to hell! Goin' to hell!") (0:00 - 3:03 from "Dessicated," 3:03 - 11:22 and 12:55 - 13:28 from "Pound For A Brown")  February 9, March 12, April 14, 16, 24, and May 28, 1988
03. Fire And Chains 5:04 ("Woaaaaaa-aaaaaah! SATAN?")  (Pound For A Brown) February 9, 1988
04. Let's Make The Water Turn Black 1:36 May 3, 1988
05. Harry, You're A Beast 0:47 May 3, 1988
06. The Orange County Lumber Truck 0:41 May 3, 1988
07. Oh No 4:43 ("Oh no, I don't believe it") April 19 and May 3, 1988

08. Theme From Lumpy Gravy 1:11 May 3, 1988
09. Eat That Question 1:54  June 7, 1988
10. Black Napkins 6:56 May 8, 1988
11. Big Swifty 11:12 ("Aye, aye, aye, everybody! Aye! Make a jazz noise here!")  April 18, May 3 and 9, 1988
12. King Kong 13:04 ("You know, you know that reminds me of a real sad story") February 26, March 5, and May 9, 1988
13. Star Wars Won't Work 3:40  ("Star Wars won't work")    May 24, 1988


Disc 2:

14. The Black Page (New Age Version) 6:45  February 12, May 19, and June 5, 1988
15. T'Mershi Duween 1:42 ("Ron, Ron, Ron") May 24, 1988
16. Dupree's Paradise 8:34  May 24 and 25, and June 5, 1988
17. City Of Tiny Lights 8:01 ("City of tiny lites, don't you wanna go")  June 5, 1988
18. Royal March From "L'Histoire Du Soldat" (Igor Stravinsky)  0:59 February 25, 1988 (probably)
19. Theme From The Bartok Piano Concerto #3  (Béla Bartók) 0:43  March 13, 1988
20. Sinister Footwear 2nd mvt. 6:39  February 10, March 19, May 3 and 25, 1988
21. Stevie's Spanking 4:25 ("His name is Stevie Vai")  March 19, 1988
22. Alien Orifice 4:15  May 25 and June 3, 1988
23. Cruisin' For Burgers 8:27 ("I must be free, my fake I.D.") April 26 and May 4, 1988
24. Advance Romance 7:43 ("No more credit from the liquor store") March 12, May 13, and June 6, 1988
25. Strictly Genteel (FZ, horn arrangement: Kurt McGettrick) 6:36  May 15, 1988

Issues:    ZFT reissue Zappa Records ZR 3883
           Original issue  Barking Pumpkin D2 74234
           Rykodisc reissue Ryko RCD 10555/56

Transcriptions: none.

HERE'S THE DEAL: More of the 1988 band at work.  In addition to the classics by Bartok and Stravinsky, there are lots by the 20th century Zappa (not the 18th century one).


RATINGS: ****


DOWNLOAD THESE:  When Yuppies Go To Hell and Fire and Chains

Zappa CD number: 58

You Can't Do That On Stage Anymore Vol. 5

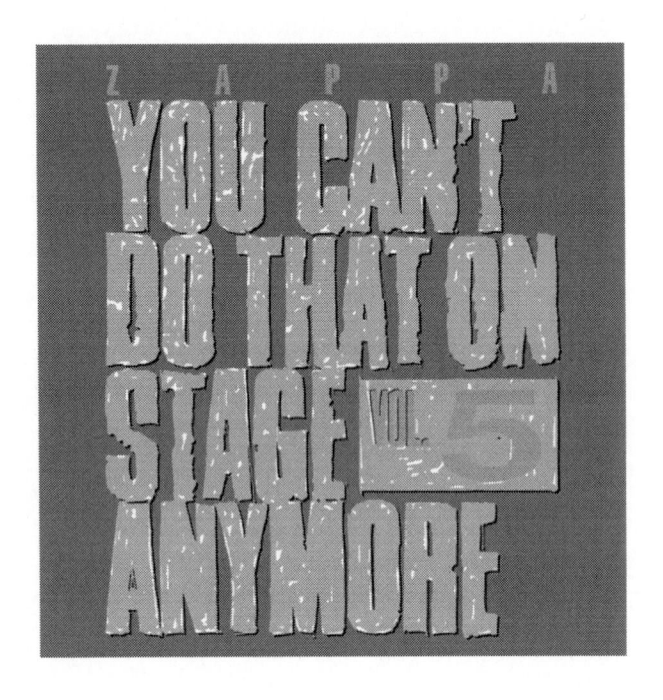

Performers:

"1965 Fillmore West"  (NOTE: actually recorded June 25, 1966, Fillmore, San Francisco)
Frank Zappa (lead guitar/vocal)
Elliot Ingber (rhythm guitar)
Ray Collins (tambourine/vocals)
Roy Estrada (bass/vocal)
Jimmy Carl Black (drums)

October 1, 1967, Copenhagen
Frank Zappa (lead guitar/vocal)
Ray Collins (tambourine/vocals)
Roy Estrada (bass/vocal)
Don Preston (keyboard/electronics)
Ian Underwood (alto sax)
Bunk Gardner (tenor sax)
Motorhead Sherwood (baritone sax)
Jimmy Carl Black (drums)
Billy Mundi (drums)

July 23, 1968, L.A. Whisky
Frank Zappa (lead guitar/vocal)
Ray Collins (tambourine/vocals)
Roy Estrada (bass/vocal)
Don Preston (keyboard/electronics)
Ian Underwood (alto sax)
Bunk Gardner (tenor sax)
Motorhead Sherwood (baritone sax)
Jimmy Carl Black (drums)
Arthur Dyer Tripp III (drums)

1969 A&R NYC
1969 Greyhound tour bus
February 7 or 8, 1969 Miami Thee Image
February 7 or 8, 1969 Miami Criterion
February 13, 1969 - The Bronx, New York City
February 14, 1969, New York City
March 1969, Providence
July 8,1969 Boston Ark
September 10,1969 Sunset Hollywood
Frank Zappa (lead guitar/vocal)
Lowell George (guitar/vocal)
Roy Estrada (bass/vocal)
Don Preston (keyboard/electronics)
Buzz Gardner (trumpet)
Ian Underwood (alto sax)
Bunk Gardner (tenor sax)
Motorhead Sherwood (baritone sax)
Jimmy Carl Black (drums)
Arthur Dyer Tripp III (drums)

June 6, 1969
Frank Zappa (lead guitar/vocal)
Lowell George (guitar/vocal)
Roy Estrada (bass/vocal)
Don Preston (keyboard/electronics)
Buzz Gardner (trumpet)
Ian Underwood (alto sax)
Bunk Gardner (tenor sax)
Motorhead Sherwood (baritone sax)
Jimmy Carl Black (drums)
Arthur Dyer Tripp III (drums)
Noel Redding (dance stylings)
Dick Barber (rubber chicken)
Kanzus J. Kanzus ("biological masterpiece")

June 11, 1982 Frankfurt, West Germany
June 26, 1982 Munich, West Germany
July 1, 1982 Geneva
July 3, 1982 Balzano, Italy
Frank Zappa (lead guitar/vocal)
Ray White (guitar/vocal)
Steve Vai (stunt guitar)
Tommy Mars (keyboards/vocal)
Bobby Martin (keyboards/sax/vocals)
Ed Mann (percussion)
Scott Thunes (bass)
Chad Wackerman (drums)

Disc 1:

1. The Downtown Talent Scout 4:01 ("the kids are freaking out...")   1965 Fillmore West
2. Charles Ives 4:37 (instrumental)   February 14, 1969
3. Here Lies Love (Martin and Dobard)  2:44  ("Here lies love...") February 14, 1969
4. Piano/Drum Duet 1:57  (instrumental)  July 8, 1969 Boston
5. Mozart Ballet  (W.A. Mozart) 4:05  (spoken: "While the well-disciplined Ian Underwood plays selected fragments from Mozart's piano sonata in B-flat...") June 6, 1969
6. Chocolate Halvah (Zappa/George/Estrada) 3:25 ("... ahhh, chocolate halvah...") February 7 or 8, 1969 Miami Thee Image
7. JCB and Kansas on the Bus #1  (Kanzus/Black/Kunc/Barber) 1:03  (spoken: "Hands up!")  1969 Greyhound tour bus
8. Run Home Slow: Main Title Theme  1:16 (instrumental) February 14, 1969, New York City
9. The Little March 1:20  (instrumental)  February 14, 1969, New York City
10. Right There  (Zappa/Estrada)  5:10 (shrieked: "Oh God, stop! Oh God, oh God!")  February 7 or 8, 1969 Miami Criterion
11. Where Is Johnny Velvet? 0:48  (spoken: "Would you like to come up here and sing with us?") February 13, 1969 - The Bronx, New York City
12. Return of the Hunch-Back Duke (instrumental)  1:44  February 13, 1969 - The Bronx, New York City
13. Trouble Every Day  4:06  ("Well I'm about to get sick from watching my tv...")  February 13, 1969 - The Bronx, New York City
14. Proto-Minimalism  1:41 (instrumental)   February 14, 1969, New York City
15. JCB and Kansas on the Bus #2  (Kanzus/Black/Kunc/Barber) 1:06 ("My name's Ken...")  1969 Greyhound
16. My Head? (Mothers of Invention) 1:22 (spoken: "I gotta fart son," "See my head here, see my head? My head?!...") September 10, 1969 Sunset Hollywood
17. Meow 1:23  (instrumental) July 23, 1968, L.A. Whisky
18. Baked-Bean Boogie 3:26  (instrumental) July 8, 1969 Boston Ark
19. Where's Our Equipment?  2:29 (instrumental) October 1, 1967, Copenhagen
20. FZ/JCB Drum Duet 4:26  (instrumental) February 14, 1969, New York City
21. No Waiting For the Peanuts To Dissolve  4:45  February 7 or 8,1969 Miami Thee Image

22. A Game of Cards (Zappa/Sherwood/Tripp/I. Underwood) 0:44 (spoken "They're really getting professional now in the dressing room...") March 1969, Providence
23. Underground Freak-Out Music 3:51 (spoken: "This is underground psychedelic acid-rock freak-out music...") February 7 or 8,1969 Miami Thee Image
24. German Lunch (Mothers of Invention) 6:43 (spoken: [cash register bell, cashier: "Thank You"] "May I see your papers please?...") February 7 or 8,1969 Miami Criterion
25. My Guitar Wants To Kill Your Mama 2:11 ("You know, your mama, and your daddy...") 1969 A&R NYC

Disc 2:

All titles on Disc 2 from 1982 concerts at Geneva, Munich, Balzano, Frankfurt (no more specific song/location information known)

26. Easy Meat 7:38 ("This girl is easy meat...")
27. Dead Girls of London (Zappa/Shankar) 2:29 ("Can you see what they are, do you hear what they say...")
28. Shall We Take Ourselves Seriously? 1:44 ("Mike Schiller says, his life is a mess..")
29. What's New In Baltimore? 5:03 ("Hey, what's new in Baltimore...")
30. Moggio 2:29 (instrumental)
31. Dancin' Fool 3:12 ("Don't know much about dancing...")
32. RDNZL 7:58 (instrumental)
33. Advance Romance 7:01 ("No more credit from the liquor store...")
34. City of Tiny Lites 10:38 ("City of tiny lites, don't you want to go?...")
35. A Pound for a Brown (on the Bus) 8:38 (instrumental)
36. Doreen 1:58 ("Doreen, don't make me wait 'till tomorrow...")
37. The Black Page 9:56
38. Geneva Farewell 1:38 ("Okay, if you throw anything else on the stage, this concert is over.")

Issues: ZFT reissue   Zappa Records ZR 3884
        Original issue    Rykodisc RCD 10569/70

Transcriptions: None

HERE'S THE DEAL: Disc One is devoted to hi-jinks with the 1969 Mothers of Invention, and Disc Two presents the 1982 Steve Vai-era band. More than the other *Stage* volumes, this volume has a documentary feel.

RATINGS: ***1/2

DOWNLOAD THESE: Charles Ives, Dead Girls of London


DIFFERENCES BETWEEN THE ZFT CD REISSUE AND PREVIOUS CD REISSUES: None. All CD issues of this title are sourced from the original 1992 Sony 1630 digital master tape.

Zappa CD number: 59

You Can't Do That On Stage Anymore Vol. 6

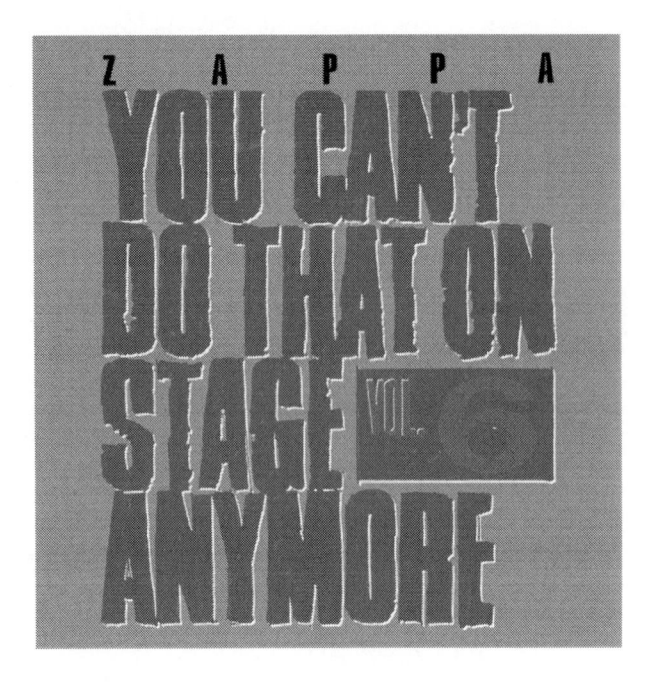

Performers:

"September 1970, FL" (Note: Zappa may not have performed in Florida that month; he played two concerts in October 1970.)
Frank Zappa (guitar/vocals)
Mark Volman (vocal)
Howard Kaylan (vocal)
Jeff Simmons (bass)
George Duke (keyboards)
Ian Underwood (keyboards/alto sax)
Aynsley Dunbar (drums)

June 1971, NYC Fillmore East
Frank Zappa (guitar/vocals)
Mark Volman (vocal)
Howard Kaylan (vocal)
Jim Pons (bass)
Bob Harris (keyboards)
Ian Underwood (keyboards/alto sax)
Aynsley Dunbar (drums)

August 7, 1971, Los Angeles
Frank Zappa (guitar/vocals)
Mark Volman (vocal)
Howard Kaylan (vocal)
Jim Pons (bass)
Don Preston (keyboards)
Ian Underwood (keyboards/alto sax)
Aynsley Dunbar (drums)
Jimmy Carl Black (guest vocal)

June 25, 1973, Sydney, Australia
Frank Zappa (lead guitar/vocal)
Jean-Luc Ponty (violin)
George Duke (keyboard/vocal)
Ian Underwood (woodwinds)
Ruth Underwood (percussion)
Bruce Fowler (trombone)
Tom Fowler (bass)
Ralph Humphrey (drums)

November 3,1975 Philadelphia
Frank Zappa (lead guitar/vocal)
Ray White (guitar/vocal)
Bianca Thornton (keyboards/vocal)
Patrick O'Hearn (bass)
Terry Bozzio (drums)

February 29, 1976, Copenhagen, Denmark
Frank Zappa (guitar)
Napoleon Murphy Brock (sax)
Andre Lewis (keyboards)
Roy Estrada (bass)
Terry Bozzio (drums)

December 29, 1976 New York City
Frank Zappa (lead guitar/vocal)
Ray White (guitar/vocal)
Eddie Jobson (keyboards)
Ruth Underwood (percussion)
Patrick O'Hearn (bass)
Terry Bozzio (drums)
Michael Brecker (tenor sax solo)
Randy Brecker (trumpet)
Lou Marini (alto sax)
Ronnie Kuber (baritone sax0
Tom Malone (trombone)

January 25, 1977 Nuremberg, West Germany
October 31, 1977 NYC
Frank Zappa (lead guitar/vocal)
Adrian Belew (guitar/vocal)
Tommy Mars (keyboards)
Peter Wolf (keyboards)
Ed Mann (percussion)
Patrick O'Hearn (bass)
Terry Bozzio (drums)

October 31, 1978, New York
Frank Zappa (lead guitar/vocal)
L. Shankar (electric violin)
Denny Walley (slide guitar/vocals)
Warren Cucurrullo (guitar)
Tommy Mars (keyboards)
Peter Wolf (keyboards)
Ed Mann (percussion)
Arthur Barrow (keyboards/bass)
Patrick O'Hearn (bass)
Vinnie Colaiuta (drums)

February 18, 1979 London
Frank Zappa (lead guitar/vocal)
Ike Willis (lead vocal)
Denny Walley (slide guitar/vocals)
Warren Cucurrullo (guitar)
Tommy Mars (keyboards)
Peter Wolf (keyboards)
Ed Mann (percussion)
Arthur Barrow (keyboards/bass)
Vinnie Colaiuta (drums)

November 16, 1980 Madison WI
December 3, 1980 Salt Lake City
December 11, 1980 Santa Monica
Frank Zappa (lead guitar/vocal)
Ike Willis (guitar/vocal)
Ray White (guitar/vocal)
Steve Vai (stunt guitar)
Tommy Mars (keyboards/vocal)
Bob Harris (keyboards/sax/vocals)
Scott Thunes (bass)
Chad Wackerman (drums)

August 26, 1984 NOT July 1984 - New York City
November 23, 1984, Chicago
December 23, 1984, Los Angeles
Frank Zappa (lead guitar/vocal)
Ike Willis (guitar/vocal)
Ray White (guitar/vocal)
Alan Zavod (keyboards)
Bobby Martin (keyboards/sax/vocals)
Scott Thunes (bass)
Chad Wackerman (drums)

February 12, 1988, Upper Darby PA
March 3-4 1988, Chicago
March 23, 1988 Towson MD
June 9,1988 Genoa
Frank Zappa (lead guitar)
Ike Willis (guitar)
Mike Kenneally (guitar/synth)
Bobby Martin (keyboards)
Ed Mann (percussion)
Walt Fowler (trumpet)
Bruce Fowler (trombone)
Paul Carman (alto sax)
Albert Wing (tenor sax)
Kurt McGettrick (baritone sax)
Scott Thunes (bass)
Chad Wackerman (drums)


1. The M.O.I Anti-Smut Loyalty Oath 3:01  (spoken: "Okay, listen this is very important, okay?... I, do hereby solemnly swear...")  September 1970
2. The Poodle Lecture  5:02  (spoken: "In the beginning God made the light...") October 31, 1977 NYC
3. Dirty Love  2:39  ("Give me your dirty love...") February 18, 1979 London
4. Magic Fingers 2:21 ("Ooh, the way you love me baby...")  December 11, 1980 Santa Monica
5. The Madison Panty-Sniffing Festival 2:44  (spoken: "Well it's contest time, ladies and gentlemen...")  November 16, 1980 Madison WI
6. Honey, Don't You Want A Man Like Me?  4:01  ("Honey honey hey, baby don't you want a man like me?...") March 23, 1988 Towson MD
7. Father O'Blivion  2:21  (spoken: "Ladies and gentlemen, making his first Sydney appearance, or maybe his second Sydney appearance..." chanted "Father Vivian O'Blivion resplendent in his frock..." )  June 25, 1973 Sydney, Australia NOT 1972
8. Is That Guy Kidding Or What?  4:02  (spoken: "Alright, see that, that's what you call a new song..." )  October 31, 1977 NYC

9. I'm So Cute  1:39  ("Feelin' sorry, feelin' sad, so many ugly people, I feel bad...")  December 11, 1980 Santa Monica
10. White Person  2:07  ("Golf shoes... Sport shirt... White Person...")  January 25, 1977, Nuernberg, West Germany
11. Lonely Person Devices  (spoken: "Has anyone ever seen Ms. Pinky?")  3:13  February 29, 1976, Copenhagen, Denmark
12. Ms. Pinky  2:00 ("I got a girl with a little rubber head...")   December 11, 1980 Santa Monica
13. Shove It Right In  6:45  ("She painted up her face..." )  June 1971, NYC Fillmore East
14. Wind Up Working In A Gas Station  2:32  ("This here song might offend you some, if it does it's because you're dumb...")  November 3, 1975 Philadelphia
15. Make A Sex Noise  3:09 (spoken: "Now ladies and gentlemen, we don't normally do this but just because this is St. Patrick's Day...")  March 23, 1988 Towson MD
16.  Tracy Is A Snob  3:54 (instrumental)  December 3, 1980 Salt Lake City
17. I Have Been In You  5:04  ("I have been in you..." )  October 31, 1978, New York
18. Emperor of Ohio  1:31  ("Hail Caesar!...") December 3, 1980 Salt Lake City
19. Dinah-Moe Humm 3:16 ("Couldn't say where she's comin' from, but I just met a lady named Dinah-Moe Humm...")  November 23, 1984, Chicago
20. He's So Gay  2:34  ("He's so gay, he's so very, very gay...") August 26, 1984 NOT July 1984 - New York City
21. Camarillo Brillo  3:09  ("She had that camarillo brillo..") November 23, 1984, Chicago
22. Muffin Man 2:25 ("You thought he was a man, but he was a muffin...") November 23, 1984, Chicago
23. NYC Halloween Audience  0:46  (spoken: "What, I'm supposed to kiss her?...") (?)  October 31, 1978, New York City?
24. The Illinois Enema Bandit  8:04 ("The Illinois enema bandit...") December 23, 1984, Los Angeles
25.  Thirteen  (Zappa/Shankar)  6:08 (spoken: "This little number is in thirteen..."; instrumental) October 31, 1978, New York City
26. Lobster Girl (O'Hearn/Colaiuta) 2:20  (instrumental) October 31, 1978, New York City
27. Black Napkins  5:21  (instrumental)    December 29, 1976  New York City
28. We're Turning Again  4:56  ("Turn turn, turn turn, we're turning again...") March 23, 1988 Towson MD
29. Alien Orifice  4:16  (instrumental)  October 31, 1978, New York City
30. Catholic Girls  4:04    ("Well, Catholic girls, with the tiny little mustache...")   Winter 1988   Philadelphia
31. Crew Slut  5:33 ("Hey hey hey all you girls in these industrial towns...")   March 3 or 4, 1988   Chicago
32. Tryin' To Grow A Chin  3:33 ("Hey! I'm only 14, sickly and thin...")   October 31, 1977 NYC
33. Take Your Clothes Off When You Dance 3:46  (instrumental performance) October 31, 1978, New York City
34. Lisa's Life Story (Zappa/Popeil) 3:05 (spoken: "Hello! My name is Lisa Popeil...") December 11, 1980 Santa Monica
35. Lonesome Cowboy Nando  5:15  ("My name is Nando, I'm a Marine biologist...")  August 7, 1971, Los Angeles  and summer 1988 Genoa

36. 200 Motels Finale  3:43  ("They're gonna clear out the studio...") August 7, 1971, Los Angeles
37. Strictly Genteel  7:07  (instrumental performance) October 31, 1978, New York City


Issues:   ZFT reissue   Zappa Records ZR 3885
          Original issue   Rykodisc 10571/72


Transcriptions: None

HERE'S THE DEAL: Various bits and rarities from the 1970s and -80s. Zappa brings the *Stage* series to a definite close with live performances of the last two numbers of *200 Motels* (no. 13).

RATINGS: ****

DOWNLOAD THESE: White Person, Thirteen, Lisa's Life Story

DIFFERENCES BETWEEN THE ZFT CD REISSUE AND PREVIOUS CD REISSUES: None. All CD issues of this title are sourced from the original 1992 Sony 1630 digital master tape.

Zappa CD number: 60

Playground Psychotics   (November 1992)

Performers:

On all tracks:

Frank Zappa (voice, guitar)
Mark Volman (voice)
Howard Kaylan (voice)
Aynsley Dunbar (voice, drums)
Ian Underwood (keyboards, alto sax)

Also on Field Recordings (September, 1970-February, 1971):

Jeff Simmons (voice, bass)
George Duke (voice, keyboards)
Martin Lickert (voice)
Dick Barber (voice)
Roelof Kiers (voice)

Also on Fillmore East, NYC (June 5-6, 1971):

Jim Pons (bass, vocal)
Bob Harris (wurlitzer)
Don Preston (keyboards, electronics)

John Lennon (guitar, vocal)
Yoko Ono (bag, vocal)

Also on Pauley Pavilion, UCLA, California (August 7, 1971) and Rainbow Theatre, London, UK (December 10, 1971):

Jim Pons (bass, vocal)
Don Preston (keyboards, electronics)


Disc 1:


**A TYPICAL DAY ON THE ROAD, PART 1**
1. Here Comes The Gear, Lads 1:00  ("Here comes the gear, lads! ")  c. September 17, 1970
2. The Living Garbage Truck 1:20  ("Bruce Bissell . . . ") Vancouver, BC, Canada  September 19, 1970
3. A Typical Sound Check 1:19  (". . . find out where . . .")
4. "This Is Neat" 0:23  ("This is neat! ")
5. The Motel Lobby 1:21  ("Sure, man, and I'll go until two and I'm gonna be in there supporting 'em") Spokane, WA September 17, 1970
6. Getting Stewed 0:55  ("Yes, ladies and gentlemen, coming to you direct from high atop the Konrad Adenauer Inn")  Spokane, WA September 17, 1970
7. The Motel Room 0:29  ("Leaving in fifty minutes, Frank.") prob. Portland, OR September 21, 1970
8. "Don't Take Me Down" 1:11 ("Not duke, not queen, but king")
9. The Dressing Room 0:24 ("Big John Mazmanian! ")
10. Learning "Penis Dimension" 2:02 ("Hi, friends. Now just be honest about it, friends and neighbors.")
11. "You There, With The Hard On!" 0:25   ("You, you there with the hard-on! ") Buffalo, NY October 23, 1970 NOT  c. November, 1970
12. Zanti Serenade 2:40  Rainbow Theatre, London, UK December 10, 1971
13. Divan 1:46  ("Ballen von Zirkon") Pauley Pavilion, UCLA, California August 7, 1971
14. Sleeping In A Jar 1:30  Rainbow Theatre, London, UK December 10, 1971
15. "Don't Eat There" 2:26  ("Are you having breakfast for lunch?")  Rainbow Theatre, London, UK December 10, 1971
16. Brixton Still Life 2:59  Rainbow Theatre, London, UK December 10, 1971
17. Super Grease 1:39   ("Poor baby!") Fillmore East, NYC  June 5-6, 1971
18. Wonderful Wino 4:52   ("Bringing in the sheaves")  Rainbow Theatre, London, UK December 10, 1971
19. Sharleena 4:23  ("I'm cryin'") Rainbow Theatre, London, UK December 10, 1971
20. Cruisin' For Burgers 2:53  ("Me! I must be free") Rainbow Theatre, London, UK December 10, 1971
21. Diptheria Blues 6:19   ("Back about a hundred years ago") Tully Gymnasium, Florida State University October 9, 1970
22. Well 4:43  ("You know I love you, baby, please don't go, well, well ") Fillmore East, NYC  June 6, 1971 (late show)

23. Say Please 0:57  ("Please! Say please!") June 6, 1971 (late show)
24. Aaawk 2:59  June 6, 1971 (late show)
25. Scumbag 5:53  ("Scum Bag, Scum Bag") June 6, 1971 (late show)
26. A Small Eternity With Yoko Ono 6:07  June 6, 1971 (late show)

Disc 2:

**A TYPICAL DAY ON THE ROAD, PART 2**
27. Beer Shampoo 1:39   ("That's the kind of guy")
28. Champagne Lecture 4:29  ("You know, a lotsa people don't bother about their friends in the VEGETABLE KINGDOM")
29. Childish Perversions 1:31 ("Oh, still drinks it, man")
30. Playground Psychotics 1:08 ("Put that mike down, Frank, it's obscene ")
31. The Mudshark Interview 2:39 ("What's your name? I'm Martin Tickman ")
32. "There's No Lust In Jazz" 0:55 ("Okay, is it just about time, you guy? What d'you say? ")
33. Botulism On The Hoof 0:47 ("Whoa, that's really great! Botulism on the hoof! ")
34. You Got Your Armies 0:10  ("Let me tell you right now, man: You got your armies") Fillmore West, San Francisco, CA November, 1970
35. The Spew King 0:24  ("I think the big problem, Ian, is that you've sort of gotta go "HOO-HAA!" as you do it") Edmonton, Alberta, Canada  September 19, 1970
36. I'm Doomed 0:25   ("We gotta do two shows tonight? ")
37. Status Back Baby 2:49  ("Of course we'll send the penguin through the flaming hoop tonight! ") Fillmore East, NYC  June 5-6, 1971
38. The London Cab Tape 1:24  ("Fuckin' guy has flipped out, man!")  London, UK  c. November 29, 1970
39. Concentration Moon, Part One 1:20  ("Concentration Moon, over the camp in the valley")  Fillmore East, NYC  June 5-6, 1971
40. The Sanzini Brothers 1:33   ("The Sanzini Brothers!") Fillmore East, NYC  June 5-6, 1971
41. "It's A Good Thing We Get Paid To Do This" 2:45  ("It's a good thing we get paid to do this") Kensington Palace Hotel, January 18, 1971
42. Concentration Moon, Part Two 2:04  ("Carl Sanzini will now join in on the second verse of "Concentration Moon"! ") Fillmore East, NYC  June 5-6, 1971
43. Mom and Dad 3:16   ("Mama! Mama! Someone said they made some noise")  Fillmore East, NYC  June 5-6, 1971
44. Intro To Music For Low Budget Orchestra 1:32   ("Ready, Marge?") Fillmore East, NYC  June 5-6, 1971
45. Billy The Mountain 30:25  Fillmore East, NYC  ("BILLY the Mountain") June 5-6, 1971

**THE TRUE STORY OF 200 MOTELS**
46. He's Watching Us 1:21   ("It's him, he's watching us!")  Kensington Palace Hotel, January 18, 1971
47. If You're Not A Professional Actor 0:23 ("If you're not a professional actor")

48. He's Right 0:14  ("Howard . . . he's right! Ha ha ha!") Kensington Palace Hotel, January 18, 1971

49. Going For The Money 0:12  ("Smurf mee! ") Fillmore West, San Francisco, CA November, 1970

50. Jeff Quits 1:33  ("This is what I joined for. This I don't think is pertinent.") Kensington Palace Hotel, January 19, 1971

51. A Bunch Of Adventures 0:56  ("From the point that Jeff Simmons quit the group we've had a bunch of adventures trying to find somebody to replace him")

52. Martin Lickert's Story 0:39 ("I just went out to get some cigarettes for him one day ")

53. A Great Guy 0:30 ("Well, the character I play is a great guy")

54. Bad Acting 0:10 ("Ever since you left the jazz world to seek fame and fortune in the rock and roll industry")

55. The Worst Reviews 0:20 ("From *200 Motels* he expects the worst reviews of any movie ever put out")

56. A Version Of Himself 1:02 ("I play a version of myself as Frank sees me")

57. I Could Be A Star Now 0:36 ("What do you do? You join the Mothers and you end up working for Zappa!")

Issues:   ZFT reissue  Zappa Records ZR 3886
          Original issue  Barking Pumpkin D2 74244
          Rykodisc reissue  Ryko RCD 10557/58


Transcriptions: none.


HERE'S THE DEAL: An audio documentary of the 1970-1971 "Vaudeville" band with former Turtles members Howard Kaylan, Mark Volman and Jim Pons. Until the video *The True Story of 200 Motels* is reissued on DVD, disc 2 is just about the only available "behind the scenes" material for *200 Motels* (no. 13). Also, The Mothers' set with ex-Beatle John Lennon and Yoko Ono brings about a memorably searing version of The Olympics' "Well."


RATINGS: ***1/2


DOWNLOAD THESE: Well (with John Lennon)


DIFFERENCES BETWEEN THE ZFT CD REISSUE AND PREVIOUS CD REISSUES: None. All CD issues of this title are sourced from the original 1992 Sony 1630 digital master tape.

Zappa CD number: 61

Ahead of Their Time   (March 1993)

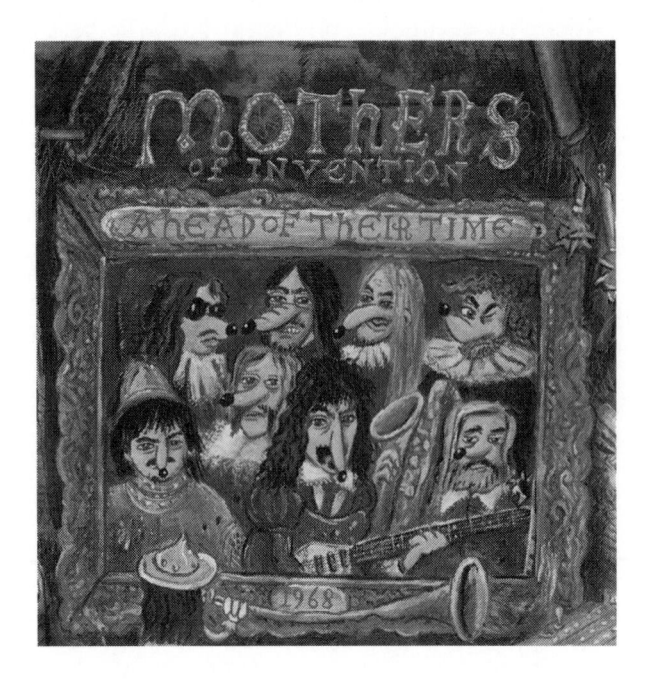

Performers:

Frank Zappa (guitar and vocals)
Ian Underwood (alto sax and piano)
Bunk Gardner (tenor sax and clarinet)
Euclid James Motorhead Sherwood (baritone sax and tambourine)
Roy Estrada (bass and vocals)
Don Preston  (electric piano and odd noises)
Arthur Dyer Tripp III (drums and percussion)
Jimmy Carl Black  (drums)
Members of the BBC Symphony Orchestra


Recorded at Royal Festival Hall, London, UK, October 25, 1968


1. Prologue 3:07
2. Progress? (Preston/Underwood/Gardner/Tripp/Sherwood/FZ) 4:44   ("Donnie" "Hey, put that down")
3. Like It Or Not 2:21

4. The Jimmy Carl Black Philosophy Lesson (Black/FZ) 2:01  ("At this very moment Jimmy Carl Black, the Indian of the group, is approaching the stage")
5. Holding The Group Back (Estrada/Underwood/FZ) 2:00  ("Then, from out of the corner from the stage, comes Roy Ralph Estrada")
6. Holiday In Berlin 0:56  ("Poo-lah, Poo-la-ah poo-lah")
7. The Rejected Mexican Pope Leaves The Stage 2:55  ("The rejected Mexican pope leaves the stage.")
8. Undaunted, The Band Plays On 4:34  ("Meanwhile, the snack enters the mind of Dom DeWild.")
9. Agency Man 3:17  ("Sell us a president, agency man")
10. Epilogue 1:52
11. King Kong 8:13
12. Help, I'm A Rock 1:38
13. Transylvania Boogie 3:07
14. Pound For A Brown 6:50
15. Sleeping In A Jar 2:24
16. Let's Make The Water Turn Black 1:51
17. Harry, You're A Beast 0:53
18. The Orange County Lumber Truck (Part I) 0:47
19. Oh No 3:22
20. The Orange County Lumber Truck (Part II) 10:40

Issues:   ZFT reissue Zappa Records ZR 3887
          Original issue  Barking Pumpkin D2 74246
          Rykodisc reissue  Ryko RCD 10559


Transcriptions: none

HERE'S THE DEAL: Zappa's edition of his 1968 London concert at Royal Festival Hall. The first half consists of a musical skit about a few "progressive" members leaving the Mothers, and the second half is a medley that culminates in "The Orange County Lumber Truck." Portions of this concert was used previously in *Weasels Ripped My Flesh,* the second Mystery Disc in *Old Masters* volume 2, and the video *Uncle Meat*. Although Zappa thought this concert was "above average," he gets a relentless pulse from the Mothers during his guitar solo during "The Orange County Lumber Truck."

RATINGS: ***1/2

DOWNLOAD THESE: Agency Man, Orange County Lumber Truck Part I / Oh No / Orange County Lumber Truck Part II.

DIFFERENCES BETWEEN THE ZFT CD REISSUE AND PREVIOUS CD REISSUES: None. All CD issues of this title are sourced from the original 1992 Sony 1630 digital master tape.

Zappa CD number: 62

The Yellow Shark   (October 1993)

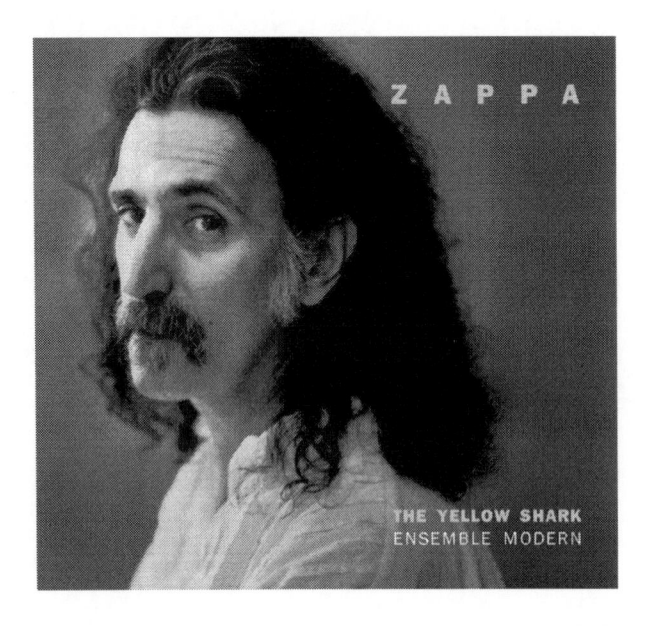

Performers:

Frank Zappa (composer)
Ensemble Modern
Peter Rundel (conductor)

All titles recorded during Ensemble Modern performances in September, 1992: 17-19 (Alte Oper Frankfurt), 22-23 (Philharmonie Berlin), and 26-28 (Wiener Konzerthaus)

1. Intro 1:43  ("Thank you. Thank you. Thank you, thank you, thank you and thank you.")
2. Dog Breath Variations 2:06
3. Uncle Meat 3:24
4. Outrage At Valdez 3:27
5. Times Beach II 7:30
6. III Revised 1:44
7. The Girl In The Magnesium Dress 4:33
8. Be-Bop Tango 3:43
9. Ruth Is Sleeping 6:06
10. None Of The Above 2:06
11. Pentagon Afternoon 2:27
12. Questi Cazzi Di Piccione 3:02
13. Times Beach III 4:25
14. Food Gathering In Post-Industrial America, 1992 2:48 ("Food Gathering In Post-Industrial America, 1992.") September 17, 1992

15. Welcome To The United States 6:41 ("Ladies and gentlemen, here he goes, Peter Rundel, he seems to be disgusted.") September 19, 1992
16. Pound For A Brown 2:12
17. Exercise #4 1:37
18. Get Whitey 7:00
19. G-Spot Tornado 5:17

Issues:    ZFT reissue  Zappa Records ZR 3888
             Original issue  Barking Pumpkin R2 71600
             Rykodisc reissue  Ryko RCD 40560

Scores:

"Outrage at Valdez," "Get Whitey," and "G-Spot Tornado" are available as rental only from Schott Music.

"The Girl in the Magnesium Dress" (piano part only) was published in *Zappa!* (a special issue from the publishers of *Keyboard* and *Guitar Player* magazines, 1992), pp. 66-72.

HERE'S THE DEAL: Zappa's last public hurrah. The Ensemble Modern was truly, as Zappa appraised them, "an ensemble of soloists." It inspired his best classical music scores, and it unleashed his creepiest musical moments since "The Torture Never Stops" (see *Zoot Allures*, no. 22).

RATINGS: *****

DOWNLOAD THESE: The Girl in the Magnesium Dress, Ruth Is Sleeping, Welcome to the United States.

DIFFERENCES BETWEEN THE ZFT CD REISSUE AND PREVIOUS CD REISSUES: None. All CD issues of this title are sourced from the original 1993 Sony 1630 digital master tape.

Zappa CD number: 63

Civilization Phase III (December 1994)

Performers:

Frank Zappa (composer, Synclavier direction)
Ensemble Modern

1967 VOICES:
Spider Barbour
All-Night John (Kilgore)
Frank Zappa
Euclid James "Motorhead" Sherwood [a.k.a. Larry Fanoga]
Roy Estrada
Louis "The Turkey" Cuneo
Monica
Gilly Townley
Unknown Girl #1 (Beckie)
Unknown Girl #2 (Maxine)

1991 VOICES (*):
Moon Unit Zappa
Michael Rappaport
Ali N. Askin
Catherine Milliken
Walt Fowler
Todd Yvega

Michael Svoboda
Michael Gross
William Forman
Uwe Dierksen
Stefan Dohr
Daryl Smith
Franck Ollu
Hermann Kretzschmar
Dweezil Zappa


1967 dialog recorded at Apostolic Studio, New York City, NY

1991 dialog and chamber group pieces recorded at UMRK, Hollywood, CA

1991 full ensemble recordings recorded at "Joe's Garage," North Hollywood, CA

1992 Synclavier material and all final mixes engineered by Spencer Chrislu at UMRK, Hollywood


**ACT ONE**
1. "This Is Phaze III" 0:47    ("This is Phaze III.")
2. Put A Motor In Yourself 5:13
3. "Oh-Umm" 0:50    ("Ohh. Umm. Hmm. ")
4. They Made Me Eat It 1:48    ("What's it like when . . . when they play the piano?")
5. Reagan At Bitburg 5:39
6. "A Very Nice Body" 1:00    ("Yes . . ." "I kind of miss him ")
7. Navanax 1:40
8. "How The Pigs' Music Works" 1:49    ("I think I can explain about about how the pigs' music works")
9. Xmas Values 5:31
10. "Dark Water!" 0:23    ("D-a-a-a-a-r-r-r-k W-a-a-a-t-e-r-r-r")
11. Amnerika 3:03
12. "Have You Heard Their Band?" 0:38    ("Have you ever heard their band?")
13. Religious Superstition 0:43    ("That's religious superstition. ")
14. "Saliva Can Only Take So Much" 0:27    ("Saliva can only take so much. ")
15. Buffalo Voice 5:12    ("Buffalo voice!")
16. "Someplace Else Right Now" 0:32    ("I'd like to be . . . someplace else right now.")
17. Get A Life 2:20
18. "A Kayak (On Snow)" 0:28    ("A kayak . . . on snow . . . a mountain")
19. N-Lite 18:00

## ACT TWO
20. "I Wish Motorhead Would Come Back" 0:14   ("Ah, I wish Motorhead would come back.")
21. Secular Humanism 2:41
22. "Attack! Attack! Attack!" 1:24   ("RAAAH! ATTACK! ATTACK!")
23. I Was In A Drum 3:38
24. "A Different Octave" 0:57   ("We are . . . actually the same note, but . . .")
25. "This Ain't CNN" 3:20   ("I bin grad nei' kimma, und do hob I g'sehn") *
26. "The Pigs' Music" 1:17   ("Tonight you guys are going to try and figure out the pigs' music")
27. A Pig With Wings 2:52
28. "This Is All Wrong" 1:42   ("This is all wrong.") *
29. Hot and Putrid 0:29   ("The hotter the sound is, the more putrid it smells.") *
30. "Flowing Inside-Out" 0:46   ("Flowing inside out creates neutral energy.")
31. "I Had A Dream About That" 0:27   ("I had a dream about that once")
32. Gross Man 2:54   ("GROSS MAN! ")
33. "A Tunnel Into Muck" 0:21   ("Maybe the kayak is just a big worm ")
34. Why Not? 2:18   ("Then we can sell them ladders")
35. "Put A Little Motor In 'Em" 0:50   ("We're gonna put a little motor in 'em ") *
36. "You're Just Insultin' Me, Aren't You!" 2:13   ("You're just insulting me, aren't you?") *
37. "Cold Light Generation" 0:44   ("You know as well as I do that cold light generation depends on your state of health and energy") *
38. Dio Fa 8:18
39. "That Would Be The End Of That" 0:35   ("We can get our strength up by making some music")
40. Beat The Reaper 15:23
41. Waffenspiel 4:04

Issues:  Barking Pumpkin UMRK 01


Transcriptions: none.


HERE'S THE DEAL: Zappa's final masterpiece. He returns to the soundscape of "Lumpy Gravy," which after 25 years now seems bleak. Within such a stark context, pieces like "Amnerika" take on an austere beauty.

RATINGS: *****

DOWNLOAD THESE: Amnerika, Beat the Reaper, Waffenspiel.

NOTE: This title was issued on CD by Barking Pumpkin Records in 1994, through the Zappa family's mail order company Barfko-Swill. As of this writing, the original pressing is no longer in print and this title and has not been reissued in any form.

Zappa CD number: 64

The Lost Episodes  (February 1996)

Performers:

Frank Zappa (vocals, drums, guitar) all tracks
Wayne Lyles (voice) track 1
Terry Wimberly (voice) track 1
Elwood Jr. Madeo (voice) track 1
Don Van Vliet (vocals)  track 2, 8, 20, 21, 22
Bobby Zappa (rhythm guitar)  track 2
Ronnie Williams (vocal) tracks 3, 5
Kenny Williams (vocal) track 4
Malcolm McNab (trumpet)  track 6
Peter Arcaro (trumpet, brass section conductor)  track 6
Philip Barnett (oboe, English horn)  track 6
Barry (woodwinds section conductor)  track 6
Danny Helferin (piano)  track 7
Chuck Foster (trumpet) track 7, 9, 11
Tony Rodriguez (Tony Rodriquenz) (alto sax) track 7
Caronga Ward (bass) track 7
Chuck Grove (Chuck Glave) (drums) track 7
Alex Snouffer (guitar?) track 8
Janschi (bass) track 8
Vic Mortensen (drums)   track 8
Ron Myers (trombone) track 9, 11, 13
Chick Carter (flute, tenor sax, baritone sax)  track 9, 11, 13
Don Christlieb (oboe) track 9, 11, 13
Pete Christlieb (tenor sax) track 9, 11, 13
Chuck Domanico (bass) track 9, 11, 13
John Guerin (drums ) track 9, 11, 13, 28
Ray Collins (lead and background vocals) tracks 10, 12
Paul Buff (fuzz bass, organ, percussion)  tracks 10, 12
Dick Kunc (voice) track 15
Art Tripp (marimba, vibes)  tracks 16, 17
Don Preston (keyboards) tracks 16, 17

195

Jimmy Carl Black (drums) tracks 16, 17
Patrolman LaFamine (voice) track 18
Dick Barber (snorks) track 19
Winged Eel Fingerling (Elliot Ingber) (slide guitar) track 21
Drumbo (John French) (drums)  track 21
Ricky Lancelotti (vocal) track 23
Erroneous (bass) track 23
Aynsley Dunbar (drums) tracks 23, 30
Ian Underwood (saxophone) tracks 23, 25, 27, 28, 30
Bruce Fowler (trombone) track 23
Sal Marquez (trumpet) track 23
George Duke (keyboard) tracks 23, 24, 25, 27
Ruth Underwood (percussion) tracks 24, 25, 27
Bruce Fowler (trombone) tracks 24, 25, 27
Tom Fowler (bass) tracks 24, 25, 27
Chester Thompson (drums) track 24
Ralph Humphrey (drums) tracks 24, 25, 27
Jean-Luc Ponty (violin) tracks 25, 27
Don "Sugar Cane" Harris (violin) tracks 28, 30
Tommy Mars (keyboards, vocals)  track 29
Arthur Barrow (bass)  track 29
Vinnie Colaiuta (drums)  track 29
Terry Bozzio (vocals)  track 29
Dale Bozzio (vocals)  track 29
Ray White (vocals)  track 29
Ike Willis (vocals)  track 29
Max Bennett (bass) tracks tracks 28, 30

1. The Blackouts 0:22  ("So, uh, I'd just like to tell you about a little incident at Shrine Auditorium.")  1958
2. Lost In A Whirlpool (Van Vliet/FZ) 2:46  ("Well, I'm lost in a whirlpool") December 1958-January 1959, Antelope Valley Jr. College, Lancaster, CA
3. Ronnie Sings? 1:05  ("What key do you wanna do it in?") 1961-1962 Ontario, California
4. Kenny's Booger Story 0:33  ("Afore of it, wh-while I was away in boarding school lived with Ronnie by the name of Dwight uh, Bement.") 1961-1962 Ontario, California
5. Ronnie's Booger Story 1:16  ("We lived in a little room, man.") 1961-1962 Ontario, California
6. Mount St. Mary's Concert Excerpt 2:28  ("The next piece that we're going to play . . . Maybe I should tell you what we were doing . . .") May 19, 1963  Mount St. Mary's College, LA
7. Take Your Clothes Off When You Dance 3:51   Pal Recording Studio, Cucamonga, CA January, 1964
8. Tiger Roach (Van Vliet/FZ) 2:20  ("This album is not available to the public.")  Pal Recording Studio, Cucamonga, CA  late 1964
9. Run Home Slow Theme 1:25 Art Laboe's Original Sound Studios, LA c. 1964
10. Fountain Of Love (FZ/Collins) 2:08  ("It was September, the leaves were gold ")  Pal Recording Studio, Cucamonga, CA March 1963

11. Run Home Cues, #2 0:28 Art Laboe's Original Sound Studios, LA c. 1964
12. Any Way The Wind Blows 2:14 ("Any way the wind blows") Pal Recording Studio, Cucamonga, CA late 1964
13. Run Home Cues, #3 0:11 Art Laboe's Original Sound Studios, LA c. 1964
14. Charva 1:59 ("Charva, I loved you, I loved you through and through") Studio Z, Cucamonga, CA, 1964
15. The Dick Kunc Story 0:46 ("I started out in Florida uh, producing a record at a studio") Apostolic Studios, NYC, October, 1967-February, 1968
16. Wedding Dress Song (Trad., arr. by FZ) 1:14 Apostolic Studios, NYC, October, 1967-February, 1968
17. Handsome Cabin Boy (Trad., arr. by FZ) 1:21 Apostolic Studios, NYC, October, 1967-February, 1968
18. Cops and Buns 2:36 ("Now, we don't come up here because we feel like walkin' four flights at three o'clock in the morning.") Apostolic Studios, NYC, October, 1967-February, 1968
19. The Big Squeeze 0:43 Mayfair Studios, NYC, August-September, 1967
20. I'm A Band Leader 1:14 ("I'm a band leader.") 1969
21. Alley Cat (Van Vliet/FZ) 2:47 ("You may find me, baby") Zappa basement, 1969
22. The Grand Wazoo 2:12 ("You might think my hat is funny, but I don't.") 1969
23. Wonderful Wino (FZ/Simmons) 2:47 ("L.A. in the summer of '69") Paramount Studios, LA Spring 1972 with overdubs 1973
24. Kung Fu 1:06 Bolic Sound, Inglewood, late 1973-early 1974
25. RDNZL 3:49 Whitney Studios, Glendale, CA April 4, 1973
26. Basement Music #1 3:46 1978
27. Inca Roads 3:42 Whitney Studios, Glendale CA, April 3, 1973
28. Lil' Clanton Shuffle 4:47 Hot Rats Sessions, August-September, 1969
29. I Don't Wanna Get Drafted 3:24 ("Hello! Anybody home? Special Delivery.") Ocean Way Recorders, Hollywood February, 1980
30. Sharleena 11:54 ("I would be so delighted!") The Record Plant, LA, CA March 4 and 11, 1970

Issues:  ZFT reissue Zappa Records ZR 3889
         Original issue Rykodisc RCD 40573

Transcriptions: none.


HERE'S THE DEAL: Some snippets from Zappa's earliest recordings. Various figures in Zappa lore are heard here, such the real-life Kenny and Ronnie (of "Let's Make The Water Turn Black" notoriety), and the cop who busted a late-night *Uncle Meat*-era recording session. The 1980 single "I Don't Wanna Get Drafted" is finally included on an album.

RATINGS: ***1/2

DOWNLOAD THESE: Cops and Buns, Wonderful Wino, I Don't Wanna Get Drafted

DIFFERENCES BETWEEN THE ZFT CD REISSUE AND PREVIOUS CD REISSUES: None. All CD issues of this title are sourced from the original 1993 Sony 1630 digital master tape.

Zappa CD number: 65

Lather  (September 1996)

Performers:

Frank Zappa (vocals, guitars, bass, percussion)
George Duke (keyboards)
Bruce Fowler (brass)
James "Bird Legs" Youmans (bass)
Ruth Underwood (percussion)
Chester Thompson (drums)
Patrick O'Hearn (voice, bass)
Terry Bozzio (voice, drums)
André Lewis (keyboards)
Roy Estrada (bass)
Ray White (guitar)
Eddie Jobson (violin, keyboards)
Davey Moire (voice)
Jim Gordon (drums)
Tom Fowler (bass)
Ralph Humphrey (drums)
Ricky Lancelotti (vocals)
David Samuels (timpani, vibes)
Randy Brecker (trumpet)
Mike Brecker (tenor sax, flute)

Lou Marini (alto sax, flute)
Ronnie Cuber (baritone sax, clarinet)
Tom Malone (trombone, trumpet, piccolo)
Don Pardo (sophisticated narration)
Max Bennett (bass)
Don Brewer (bongos)
Dave Parlato (bass)
The Abnuceals Emuukha Electric Orchestra


1. Re-gyptian Strut 4:36  December, 1974
2. Naval Aviation In Art? 1:32  Royce Hall, UCLA, September 18-19, 1975
3. A Little Green Rosetta 2:48  ("A little green rosetta") January-February, 1975 and February 3, 1976
4. Duck Duck Goose 3:01  Hammersmith Odeon, London, UK, February 17, 1977
5. Down In De Dew 2:57  September 1972, 1975
6. For The Young Sophisticate 3:14  ("Baby baby why you cryin'") March 19, 1973
7. Tryin' To Grow A Chin 3:26  ("Yes! I'm only fourteen, sickly 'n thin ") January-February, 1977
8. Broken Hearts Are For Assholes 4:40  ("Come on! Hey! Do you know what you are? You're an asshole! Hey!") Hammersmith Odeon, London, UK, February 16, 1977
9. The Legend Of The Illinois Enema Bandit 12:43  (spoken: "And now folks, it's time for Don Pardo to deliver our special Illinois Enema Bandit-type announcement." sung: "The Illinois Enema Bandit ")  The Palladium, NYC, December 29, 1976
10. Lemme Take You To The Beach 2:46  ("Lemme take you to the beach") August-September, 1969, with overdubs c. 1976
11. Revised Music For Guitar and Low Budget Orchestra 7:36  January-February, 1975 and Royce Hall, UCLA, September 18-19, 1975
12. RDNZL 8:14 December, 1974
13. Honey, Don't You Want A Man Like Me? 4:56  ("Honey honey, hey, baby don't you want a man like me ")  The Palladium, NYC, December 26-29, 1976
14. The Black Page #1 1:57  The Palladium, NYC, December 28, 1976
15. Big Leg Emma 2:11  ("There's a big dilemma, 'bout my Big Leg Emma") The Palladium, NYC, December 28, 1976
16. Punky's Whips 11:06  (spoken: "In today's rapidly changing world..." sung: "I can't stand the way he pouts")  The Palladium, NYC, December 26, 27, 28 and 29, 1976
17. Flambé 2:05  December, 1974 with overdub c. 1976
18. The Purple Lagoon 16:22  The Palladium, NYC, December 28 and 29, 1976
19. Pedro's Dowry 7:45   Royce Hall, UCLA, September 18-19, 1975
20. Läther 3:50  The Palladium, NYC, December 27 and 29, 1976
21. Spider Of Destiny 2:40 December, 1974
22. Duke Of Orchestral Prunes 4:21   Royce Hall, UCLA, September 18-19, 1975
23. Filthy Habits 7:12  c. May-June, 1976
24. Titties 'n Beer 5:23  ("It was the blackest night") The Palladium, NYC December 29, 1976
25. The Ocean Is The Ultimate Solution 8:32  c. 1976
26. The Adventures of Greggery Peccary 21:00  ("The adventures of GREGGERY PECCARY!") Royce Hall, UCLA, September 18-19, 1975

Additional tracks on 1996 CD set:

27. Regyptian Strut (1993) (4:42)  December, 1974
28. Leather Goods (6:01)  Hammersmith Odeon, London, UK February 17, 1977
29. Revenge Of The Knick Knack People (2:25) date unknown (indexed as c.1976)
30. Time Is Money (3:05)  Caribou Studios, Nederland, Colorado December, 1974

Issues:   ZFT reissue Zappa Records ZR 3893
          Original issue Rykodisc RCD 10574/76

Scores: The chamber version of "Pedro's Dowry" is available for rental only from Schott Music.

HERE'S THE DEAL: Zappa's mid-1970s opus in the track sequence and mix he preferred, before the pieces were parceled out for *Sleep Dirt*, *Studio Tan*, and *Orchestral Favorites* (no. 24, 25, and 27). Had this been released in 1977, it would have heralded the creative phase for *Sheik Yerbouti* (no. 26) and *Joe's Garage* (nos. 28-29).

RATINGS: *****

DOWNLOAD THESE: Re-gyptian Strut, Naval Aviation in Art, A Little Green Rosetta.

DIFFERENCES BETWEEN THE ZFT CD REISSUE AND PREVIOUS CD REISSUES: The bonus tracks present on the original 1996 Rykodisc CD issue of this album were removed for the 2012 ZFT reissue. The source for both CD issues is a 1996 digital master tape produced under the auspices of the ZFT.

Zappa CD number: 66

Frank Zappa Plays The Music of Frank Zappa (October 1996)

Performers:

Frank Zappa (lead guitar on all tracks)

For tracks 1-3:
Terry Bozzio (drums)
Napoleon Murphy Brock (vocals)
Norma Bell (vocals)
André Lewis (keyboards)
Roy Estrada (bass)

For track 4:
Chester Thompson (drums)
Tom Fowler (bass)
Napoleon Murphy Brock (tenor sax and vocals)
George Duke (keyboards and vocals)

For track 5:
Terry Bozzio (drums)
Dave Parlato (bass)
Ruth Underwood (marimba)
Lou Anne Neill (harp)

For track 6:
Terry Bozzio (drums)
Patrick O'Hearn (bass)
Tommy Mars (keyboards)
Peter Wolf (keyboards)
Ed Mann (percussion)
Adrian Belew (rhythm guitar)

For track 7:
Vinnie Colaiuta (drums)
Arthur Barrow (bass)
Peter Wolf (keyboards)
Ed Mann (percussion)
Warren Cuccurullo (rhythm guitar)

1. Black Napkins 7:10 ("Thank you! Now this is a, this is an instrumental song, it's a tender, slow-moving ballad sort of a song")  Ljubljana, Yugoslavia, November 22, 1975
2. Black Napkins "Zoot Allures" Album Version 4:15  Kosei Nenkin Kaikan, Osaka, Japan February 3, 1976
3. Zoot Allures 15:45  Nihon Seinenkan, Tokyo, Japan February 5, 1976
4. Merely A Blues In A 7:26 ("Alright, look here folks: We're gonna play another song for ya, but, uh . . .")  Palais des Sports, Paris, France, September 27, 1974
5. Zoot Allures "Zoot Allures" Album Version 4:05  Kosei Nenkin Kaikan, Osaka, Japan February 3, 1976
6. Watermelon In Easter Hay 6:41 Rhein-Neckar Stadion, Eppelheim, Germany February 24, 1978
7. Watermelon In Easter Hay "Joe's Garage" Album Version 8:42  April 1979

Issues:  Barking Pumpkin UMRK 02

Transcriptions: none.

HERE'S THE DEAL: A family tribute to Zappa, presenting the album versions and earliest tape recordings of three of his signature guitar solos.

RATINGS: ***

DOWNLOAD THESE: The early versions of Black Napkins, Zoot Allures, and Watermelon in Easter Hay.

NOTE: This title was issued on CD by Barking Pumpkin Records in 1996, through the Zappa family's mail order company Barfko-Swill. As of this writing, the original pressing is still in print and available from Barfko.

Zappa CD number: 67

Have I Offended Someone? (April 1997)

Performers:

For the previously unreleased tracks:

Frank Zappa (lead guitar and vocal)
Ray White (rhythm guitar and vocal)
Ike Willis (rhythm guitar and vocal)
Bobby Martin (keyboards, sax and vocal)
Allan Zavod (keyboards)
Scott Thunes (bass)
Chad Wackerman (drums)

For the previously released and remixed tracks, the collective personnel:

Frank Zappa (lead guitar, lead vocals)

Arthur Barrow (bass)
Adrian Belew (rhythm guitar, vocals)
Jimmy Carl Black (voice)
Dale Bozzio (vocals)

Terry Bozzio (drums, vocals)
Mike Brecker (tenor sax, flute)
Randy Brecker (trumpet)
Napoleon M. Brock (background vocals [?])
Vinnie Colaiuta (drums, combustible vapors)
Ronnie Cuber (baritone sax, clarinet)
Warren Cuccurullo (rhythm guitar, vocals)
George Duke (keyboards and synthesizer)
Roy Estrada (bg. vocal)
Tom Fowler (bass)
Bob Harris (vocals)
Ralph Humphrey (drums)
Eddie Jobson (keyboards, violin, vocals)
André Lewis (background vocals)
Al Malkin (vocals)
Tom Malone (trombone, trumpet, piccolo)
Ed Mann (percussion, vocals)
Lou Marini (alto sax, flute)
Sal Marquez (vocals)
Tommy Mars (keyboards, vocals)
Bobby Martin (keyboards, voice, harmonica solo)
Davey Moire (background vocals)
Patrick O'Hearn (bass, vocals)
Sparkie Parker (bg. vocal)
David Samuels (timpani, vibes)
Randy Thornton (background vocals)
Scott Thunes (bass)
Tina Turner, Debbie and Lynn (The Ikettes) (backing vocals)
Ruth Underwood (percussion, synthesizer)
Steve Vai (written guitar parts)
Kin Vassy (vocals)
Chad Wackerman (drums [including overdubs])
Denny Walley (slide guitar, vocals)
Johnny "Guitar" Watson (lead vocal)
Ray White (vocals)
Ike Willis (vocals)
Peter Wolf (keyboards, butter)
Moon Zappa (vocal)
Allan Zavod (keyboard)

Tracks 9 and 12 were previously unreleased; remaining tracks previously issued and drawn from *Over-Nite Sensation* (no.17), *Zoot Allures* (no.22), *Zappa In New York* (no.23), *Sheik Yerbouti* (no.26), *Joe's Garage* Act I (no.28), *Tinsel Town Rebellion* (no.30), *You Are What You Is* (no.34), *Ship Arriving Too Late To Save A Drowning Witch* (no.35), *The Man From Utopia* (no.36), *Them Or Us* (no.40), *Thing-Fish* (no. 41), *Frank Zappa Meets The Mothers of Prevention* (no.44).

1. Bobby Brown Goes Down 2:43 ("Hey there, people, I'm Bobby Brown") from Sheik Yerbouti
2. Disco Boy 4:23 ("Disco Boy") from Zoot Allures
3. Goblin Girl 4:19 ("Hob-noblin, wit de goblin") from You Are What You Is
4. In France 3:30 ("We're playin' in a tent, it's payin' the rent") from Them Or Us
5. He's So Gay 2:45 ("He's so gay, He's very very gay") from Thing-Fish
6. SEX 3:44 ("What's the thing that they's talkin' about everywhere? SEX") from The Man From Utopia
7. Titties 'n Beer (alternate edit) 4:37 ("It was the blackest night, there was no moon in sight") from Zappa in New York December 29, 1976
8. We're Turning Again 4:56 ("Turn turn, Turn turn, We're turning again") from Frank Zappa Meets The Mothers of Prevention
9. Dumb All Over (previously unreleased live performance) 5:43 ("Whoever we are, wherever we're from") The Pier, NYC, August 25, 1984
10. Catholic Girls 3:51 ("Catholic Girls, with a tiny little mustache") from Joe's Garage Act I
11. Dinah-Moe Humm 7:14 ("I couldn't say where she's coming' from, but I just met a lady named Dinah-Moe Humm") from Over-Nite Sensation
12. Tinsel Town Rebellion (previously unreleased live performance) 4:24 ("From *Madam Wong's* to *Starwood* to the *Whiskey* on the Strip") The Pier, NYC, August 26, 1984
13. Valley Girl (FZ/Moon Zappa) 4:50 ("Valley Girl, she's a Valley Girl") from Ship Arriving Too Late To Save A Drowning Witch
14. Jewish Princess 3:15 ("I want a nasty little Jewish Princess") from Sheik Yerbouti
15. Yo Cats (FZ/Mariano) 3:32 ("Yo cats, yo yo") from Frank Zappa Meets The Mothers of Prevention


Issues:   ZFT reissue  Zappa Records ZR 3890
          Original issue  Rykodisc RCD 10577

Transcriptions: none.

HERE'S THE DEAL: A basic collection of the spicy stuff, hot 'cha!

RATINGS: ***

DOWNLOAD THESE: Dumb All Over, Tinsel Town Rebellion

DIFFERENCES BETWEEN THE ZFT CD REISSUE AND PREVIOUS CD REISSUES: None. All CD issues of this title are sourced from the original 1993 Sony 1630 digital master tape.

Zappa CD number: 68

Mystery Disc (September 1998)

Performers:

1964 (tr.1-2)

Frank Zappa (guitar)
Chuck Foster (trumpet)
Ron Myers (trombone)
Chick Carter (flute, tenor sax, baritone sax)
Don Christlieb (oboe)
Pete Christlieb (tenor sax)
Chuck Domanico (bass)
John Guerin (drums)

1963-65 (tr. 3-13)

Frank Zappa (guitar)
Don Van Vliet (vocals)
Laurie Stone (vocals)
Ray Collins (vocals)
Bob Narciso (vocals)
Cora (vocals)
Euclid James Motorhead Sherwood (tenor sax, acoustic guitar)

Johnny Franklin (bass)
Toby (drums)
Vic Mortensen (drums)
Alex Snouffer (guitar?)
Les Papp (drums)
Paul Woods (bass)
Bobby Saldana (bass)
Doug Moon (rhythm acoustic guitar)

1965-1969 (tr.14-35)

Frank Zappa (guitar)
Ray Collins (vocals, tambourine)
Elliot Ingber (rhythm guitar)
Lowell George (guitar/vocals)
Roy Estrada (bass/vocals)
Don Preston (keyboards/electronics)
Ian Underwood (keyboards/alto sax)
Buzz Gardner (trumpet)
Bunk Gardner (tenor sax)
Euclid James Motorhead Sherwood (baritone sax)
Jimmy Carl Black (drums)
Art Tripp (drums)
Bill Graham (announcement)
Annie Zannas (voice)
Cynthia Dobson (voice)


1. Theme from "Run Home Slow" 1:23 1964, Art Laboe's Original Sound Studios, Los Angeles
2. Original Duke Of Prunes 1:17 1964, Art Laboe's Original Sound Studios, Los Angeles
3. Opening Night at "Studio Z" (Collage) 1:34 ("Oh, I smoked a Pall Mall, yes, I did, oh, yeah") Studio Z, Cucamonga, CA, August 1, 1964
4. The Village Inn 1:17 ("Ladies and gentlemen, do you like the band?") The Village Inn and Barbecue, Sun Village, CA, early 1965
5. Steal Away (Hughes) 3:43 ("I've got to see you") The Village Inn and Barbecue, Sun Village, CA, early 1965
6. I Was A Teen-Age Malt Shop 1:10 ("I was a Teen-age Malt Shop! Ha ha!") Studio Z, Cucamonga, CA, late 1964
7. The Birth of Captain Beefheart 0:18 ("Hello, there, kids, it's your old friend Captain Beefheart!") Studio Z, Cucamonga, CA, late 1964
8. Metal Man Has Won His Wings 3:06 ("Wheet! Wheet wheet!") Pal Recording Studio, Cucamonga, CA, late 1964
9. Power Trio from The Saints 'n Sinners 0:34 The Saints 'N Sinners, Ontario, CA, 1964
10. Bossa Nova Pervertamento 2:15 Studio Z, Cucamonga, CA March 25, 1965

11. Excerpt from The Uncle Frankie Show 0:40  ("Here's another thing that you can do on the piano, if you have one around.")  Studio Z, Cucamonga, CA c. Halloween, 1964

12. Charva 2:01   ("Charva, I loved you, I loved you through and through") Studio Z, Cucamonga, CA,  1964

13. Speed-Freak Boogie 4:14  Pal Recording Studio, Cucamonga, CA, January, 1963

14. Original Mothers at The Broadside (Pomona) 0:55 The Broadside, Pomona, c. May, 1965

15. Party Scene from "Mondo Hollywood" 1:54 c.1965

16. Original Mothers Rehearsal 0:22  ("Oh, rock, rock!") Seward St. Studio, Los Angeles, CA early 1966

17. How Could I Be Such A Fool? 1:49  ("When I won your love, I was very glad") Seward St. Studio, Los Angeles, CA
early 1966

18. Band introductions at The Fillmore West 1:10  ("Like to introduce the band") Fillmore Auditorium, San Francisco, CA, June 24-25, 1966

19. Plastic People (Berry/FZ)  1:58  ("Plastic people, you gotta go ") Fillmore Auditorium, San Francisco, CA, June 24-25, 1966

20. Original Mothers at Fillmore East 0:50  Fillmore East, NYC, April 19, 1968

21. Harry, You're A Beast 0:30 Royal Festival Hall, London, UK, October 25, 1968

22. Don Interrupts 4:39  ("Donnie!" "Hey, put that down!") Royal Festival Hall, London, UK, October 25, 1968

23. Piece One 2:26 Royal Festival Hall, London, UK, October 25, 1968

24. Jim/Roy 4:04  ("What's goin' on here? I thought we were gonna play a Rock and Roll concert.") Royal Festival Hall, London, UK, October 25, 1968

25. Piece Two 6:59  ("TWO, THREE, FOUR, ONE") Royal Festival Hall, London, UK, October 25, 1968

26. Agency Man 3:25  ("Sell us a president, agency man") Royal Festival Hall, London, UK, October 25, 1968

27. Agency Man (Studio Version) 3:27  ("Sell us a president, agency man") Apostolic Studios, NYC, December, 1967-February, 1968

28. Lecture from Festival Hall Show 0:21  ("Mothers Of Invention have spent many long hours in rehearsal") Royal Festival Hall, London, UK, October 25, 1968

29. Wedding Dress Song/The Handsome Cabin Boy 2:36  Apostolic Studios, NYC, December, 1967-February, 1968

30. Skweezit Skweezit Skweezit 2:57  ("Oh God, Oh God, Oh God, Oh God, Oh God, Oh, Oh, Oh") The Ballroom, Stratford, Connecticut  February 16, 1969

31. The Story of Willie The Pimp 1:33  ("'Son-of-a-bitch, you did this one, you did that one,' he told me.") New York City, August 1969

32. Black Beauty 5:23  Thee Image, Miami, Florida February 7-9, 1969

33. Chucha 2:47  ("Chucha, why won't you accept my proposal?")  Criteria Studios, Miami, Florida February 1969

34. Mothers at KPFK 3:26  ("I'd like to dedicate an ode to Joe Lattanzi") KPFK Studios, LA Early 1968

35. Harmonica Fun 0:41  ("Play the harmonica . . . ")  Criteria Studios, Miami, Florida February 1969

Issues:          ZFT reissue   Zappa Records ZR 3891
Original issue   Barking Pumpkin BPR 7777-6, from The Old Masters Box One, (1985), and Barking Pumpkin BPR 8888-8, from The Old Masters Box Two, (1986)
Rykodisc reissue    Rykodisc RCD 10580

Transcriptions: none.

HERE'S THE DEAL: The CD version of the two "Mystery Discs" that Zappa compiled for the first two *Old Masters* box sets (nos. 43 and 46). The only LPs tracks not on the CD are those on the "Big Leg Emma"/"Why Don'cha Do Right?" single for MGM-Verve, which are included on the CD version of *Absolutely Free* (no. 2).

RATINGS: ****

DOWNLOAD THESE: Theme from "Run Home Slow," Original Duke Of Prunes, Wedding Dress Song/The Handsome Cabin Boy, Skweezit Skweezit Skweezit, Chucha

DIFFERENCES BETWEEN THE ZFT CD REISSUE AND PREVIOUS CD REISSUES: None. All CD issues of this title are sourced from a 1998 digital master tape produced under the auspices of the ZFT.

Zappa CD number: 69

Everything Is Healing Nicely (December 1999)

Performers:

Frank Zappa (guitar)
Ensemble Modern
L. Shankar (violin)
Claudia Sack (violin)
Ellen Wegner (harp)

All songs recorded at Joe's Garage Studio and UMRK, July, 1991

1. Library Card 7:42 ("Weist scho i hab naufgeschaut und da ist's ganz dunkel")
2. This Is A Test 1:35
3. Jolly Good Fellow 4:34
4. Roland's Big Event/Strat Vindaloo 5:56
5. Master Ringo 3:35 ("Dear *PFIQ*, Since you printed my question and photo in issue #29, *PFIQ*, I have received many letters")
6. T'Mershi Duween 2:30
7. Nap Time 8:02 ("Ai mite no, nochi no kokoro ni")
8. 9/8 Objects 3:06
9. Naked City 8:42
10. Whitey (Prototype) 1:12
11. Amnerika Goes Home 3:00
12. None Of The Above (Revised and Previsited) 8:38

13. Wonderful Tattoo! 10:01 ("Dear Jim and *PFI*, enclosed are photos of my cock")

Issues: Barking Pumpkin UMRK 03

Transcriptions: None.

HERE'S THE DEAL: Zappa's first recording sessions with the Ensemble Moderne. Even though they are just getting to know each other, they produce some music too good to leave unreleased. Caution, though: some of it is in the same vein as "The Torture Never Stops."

RATINGS: \*\*\*\*

DOWNLOAD THESE: Master Ringo, Amerika Goes Home, Wonderful Tattoo!

NOTE: This title was issued on CD by Barking Pumpkin Records in 1999, through the Zappa family's mail order company Barfko-Swill. As of this writing, the original pressing is still in print and available from Barfko.

Zappa CD number: 70

FZ:OZ   (August 2002)

**ZAPPA**
approximately 25 years 13 months and a bunch of days ago
played the Hordern Pavilion in Sydney AUSTRALIA on 20 January 1976.

Performers:

Frank Zappa (guitar, vocals)
Napoleon Murphy Brock (tenor sax, vocals)
André Lewis (keyboards, vocals)
Roy Estrada (bass, vocals)
Terry Bozzio (drums, vocals)
Norman Gunston (harmonica)


Mostly from Hordern Pavilion, Sydney, Australia, January 20, 1976 except for two songs indicated with respective dates

1. Hordern Intro (Incan Art Vamp) 3:10 ("Good evening, ladies and gentlemen, welcome to The Mothers Of Invention Extravaganza for Sydney, Australia, 1976")
2. Stink-Foot 6:35 ("In the dark, where all the fevers grow")
3. The Poodle Lecture 3:05 ("In the beginning GOD made 'the light.' ")
4. Dirty Love 3:13 ("Give me your dirty love")
5. Filthy Habits 6:18
6. How Could I Be Such A Fool? 3:27 ("When I won your love I was very glad") first half recorded Tokyo, Japan February 5, 1976
7. I Ain't Got No Heart 2:26 ("Ain't got no heart, no no")
8. I'm Not Satisfied 1:54 ("Got no place to go")
9. Black Napkins 11:57 ("Thank you! . . . This is called "Black Napkins")

10. Advance Romance 11:17 ("No more credit from the liquor store")
11. The Illinois Enema Bandit 8:45 (spoken: "Ah, thank you very much, Ladies and Gentlemen, let's get this feedback under control" "For the past 10 years in a town just outside of Chicago" sung: "The Illinois Enema Bandit")
12. Wind Up Workin' In A Gas Station 4:14 ("This here song might offend you some")
13. The Torture Never Stops 7:12 ("Flies all green 'n buzzin' in his dungeon of despair")
14. Canard Toujours 3:22
15. Kaiser Rolls 3:17 ("This is a story, tell it quick as I can")
16. Find Her Finer 3:48 ("Find her finer, sneak up behind her")
17. Carolina Hard-Core Ecstasy 6:12 ("I coulda swore her hair was made of rayon")
18. Lonely Little Girl 2:39 ("You're a lonely little girl")
19. Take Your Clothes Off When You Dance 2:02 ("There will come a time when everybody who is lonely will be free")
20. What's The Ugliest Part Of Your Body? 1:07 ("What's the ugliest (OWW!) of your body?")
21. Chunga's Revenge 15:41
22. Zoot Allures 12:50
23. Keep It Greasy 4:40 ("Keep it greasey so it'll go down easy")
24. Dinah-Moe Humm 6:54 ("I couldn't say where she's coming' from")
25. Camarillo Brillo 3:58 ("She had that Camarillo brillo")
26. Muffin Man 3:41 ("Girl, you thought he was a man but he was a muffin")
27. Kaiser Rolls (Du Jour) 3:00 ("This is a story, tell it quick as I can") January 6, 1976 rehearsal

Issues: Vaulternative VR 2002-1

Transcriptions: none.

HERE'S THE DEAL: A concert Down Under with Zappa's band in transition, retaining Napoleon Murphy Brock and Roy Estrada and taking up Terry Bozzio.


RATINGS: ****


DOWNLOAD THESE: Zoot Allures


NOTE: This title was issued on CD by Vaulternative Records in 2002, through the Zappa family's mail order company Barfko-Swill. As of this writing, the original pressing is still in print and available from Barfko.

Zappa CD number: 71

Halloween   (February 2003)

**FRANK ZAPPA**

**HALLOWEEN**

Performers:

Frank Zappa (lead guitar/vocal)
Denny Walley (guitar/vocals)
Tommy Mars (keyboards/vocals)
Peter Wolf (keyboards)
Ed Mann (percussion)
Arthur Barrow (bass)
Patrick O'Hearn (bass)
Vinnie Colaiuta (drums)
L. Shankar (electric violin)
Mark Simone (voice)
Alan Rubin (trumpet)
Tom Malone (trombone)
Lew Del Gatto (alto sax)
Lou Marini (tenor sax)
Howard Johnson (baritone sax)

1. NYC Audience 1:17   The Palladium, NYC, October 31, 1978
2. Ancient Armaments 8:23  ("Awright. This is it. This is the Big One. Happy Halloween everybody!")  The Palladium, NYC, October 31, 1978
3. Dancin' Fool 4:35  ("One, two, three, four! I don't know much about dancin', that's why I got this song")   The Palladium, NYC, October 31, 1978
4. Easy Meat 6:03  ("This girl is easy meat")The Palladium, NYC, October 27, 1978 (late show)
5. Magic Fingers 2:33  ("Ooh, the way you love me, lady, I get so hard now I could die")  The Palladium, NYC, October 27 (both shows) and 31, 1978
6. Don't Eat The Yellow Snow 2:24  ("Dreamed I was an Eskimo")  The Palladium, NYC, October 31, 1978
7. Conehead 4:02  ("Conehead . . . she ain't really dumb")  The Palladium, NYC, October 28, 1978 (early show)
8. "Zeets" 2:58  The Palladium, NYC, October 31, 1978
9. Stink-Foot 8:51  ("In the dark where all the fevers grow")    The Palladium, NYC, October 31, 1978
10. Dinah-Moe Humm 5:27  ("One, two, three, four! I couldn't say where she's coming' from,")  The Palladium, NYC, October 27, 1978 (early show)
11. Camarillo Brillo 3:14  (spoken: "The name of this song is "Camarillo Brillo." One, two, three, four!" sung: "She had that Camarillo brillo")  The Palladium, NYC, October 27, 1978 (early show)
12. Muffin Man 3:32  ("That's right, "Muffin Man"! Girl, you thought he was a man but he was a muffin")  October 27, 1978 (early show)
13. Black Napkins (The Deathless Horsie) 16:56  The Palladium, NYC, October 31, 1978
Additional titles:
14. Suicide Chump (Video) 9:31  ("You say there ain't no use in livin'")  Capitol Theatre, Passaic, NJ October 13, 1978 (late show)
15. Dancin' Fool (Video) 3:48  (spoken: "Tonight we'd like to do a song about an important social problem: Disco." sung: "I don't know much about dancin', that's why I got this song")  Saturday Night Live, NYC October 21, 1978
16. Radio Interview 9:41  WPIX, NYC October 30, 1978

Issues:  Vaulternative/DTS 1101

Transcriptions: none.

HERE'S THE DEAL: High-end audio presentation of selections from Zappa's 1978 Halloween shows.

RATINGS: ****

DOWNLOAD THESE: Downloads not available.

NOTE: This title was issued as a DVD-Audio disc by Vaulternative Records in 2003, through the Zappa family's mail order company Barfko-Swill. As of this writing, the original pressing is no longer in print and this title and has not been reissued in any form.

Zappa CD number: 72

Joe's Corsage

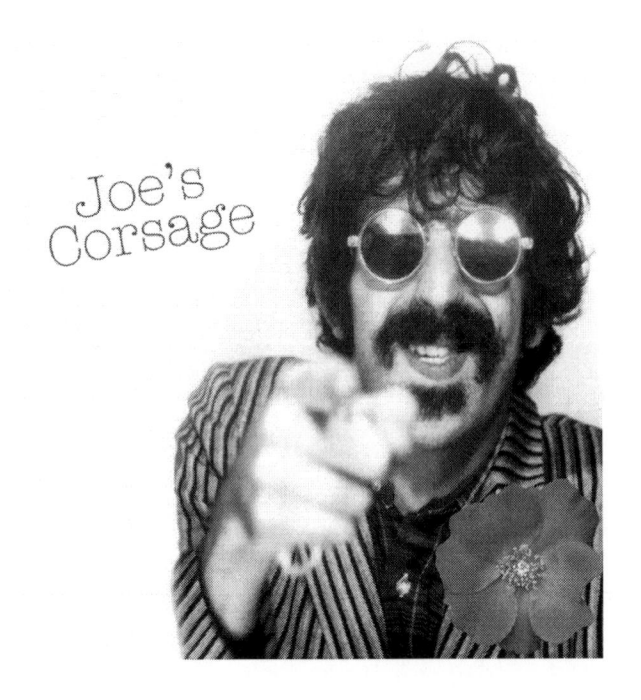

Performers:

Frank Zappa (guitar, vocals)
Ray Collins (vocals, tambourine)
Henry Vestine (guitar) (1965 studio recordings only)
Roy Estrada (bass)
Jimmy Black (drums)

1. "pretty pat" 0:33  ("Who came up with the name "Mothers of Invention"?") 1967 interview
2. Motherly Love 2:21  ("What you need is … Motherly love") 1965 studio
3. Plastic People 3:05  ("Plastic people") 1965 studio
4. Anyway The Wind Blows 2:55  ("Any way the wind blows") 1965 studio
5. I Ain't Got No Heart 3:50  (spoken: "Okay, ready?" "Okay, yeah." sung: "Ain't got no heart") 1965 studio
6. "The Phone Call"/My Babe (Hatfield/Medley) 4:06  (interviewer: "How did the group get together?" sung "I'm talkin' 'bout my baby")  1965 live prob. The Broadside, Pomona, CA
7. Wedding Dress Song/Handsome Cabin Boy (Trad.) 1:02 1965 live prob. The Broadside, Pomona, CA
8. Hitch Hike (Gaye/Paul/Stevenson) 2:54  ("Well, I'm goin' to Chicago")  1965 live prob. The Broadside, Pomona, CA
9. I'm So Happy I Could Cry 2:43  ("Going back again to see that girl")  c.1965-66, studio

10. Go Cry On Somebody Else's Shoulder (Zappa/Collins) 3:29 ("A year ago today") c.1965-66, studio
11. How Could I Be Such A Fool? 3:00 ("When I won your love") c.1965-66, studio
12. "We Made Our Reputation Doing It That Way…" 5:34 ("The story of music of the Mothers is the story of a combination of what I knew about music") 1967 interview


Issues: Vaulternative VR 20041


Transcriptions: none


HERE'S THE DEAL: Some of Zappa's earliest recordings with newly christened Mothers, with guitarist Henry Vestine before he left to help form the band Canned Heat.


RATINGS: ***1/2


DOWNLOAD THESE: Hitch Hike


NOTE: This title was issued on CD by Vaulternative Records in 2004, through the Zappa family's mail order company Barfko-Swill. As of this writing, the original pressing is still in print and available from Barfko.

Zappa CD number: 73

Joe's Domage  (October 2004)

Performers:

Frank Zappa (guitar, voice)
Tony Duran (guitar, vocals)
Ian Underwood (organ)
Sal Marquez (trumpet)
Malcolm McNab (trumpet)
Ken Shroyer (trombone)
Tony Ortega (baritone sax)
Alex Dmochowski (bass, vocals)
Aynsley Dunbar (drums)


1. When it's perfect... 3:18  ("just so I can hear the song again... One two one two three")
2. The New Brown Clouds 2:44  ("One, two, three four")
3. Frog Song 17:23  ("Kenny, remember that part on that Frog Song?")
4. It Just Might Be A One Shot Deal 1:57  ("One, two, three, four . . . You can be scared when it gets too real")
5. The ending line... 3:12  ("This, excuse me, the ending line. ")
6. Blessed Relief/The New Brown Clouds 5:03  ("I'd like to go back to-- to this thing one time")
7. It Ain't Real So What's The Deal 13:14  ("One, two, one, two, three, four . . . And, it will fall down")
8. Think It Over (some)/Think It Over (some more) 5:20  ("If something gets in your way, Just THINK IT Over")

9. Another Whole Melodic Section 1:53
10. When it feels natural... 1:27  ("Anyway, that's quite a bit of, uh, drawing.")

Issues:  Vaulternative VR 20042


Transcriptions: none.


HERE'S THE DEAL: A rare set of rehearsal recordings made while Zappa was recovering from his near-fatal 1971 injuries.


RATINGS: ***1/2


DOWNLOAD THESE: It Ain't Real So What's The Deal


NOTE: This title was issued on CD by Vaulternative Records in 2004, through the Zappa family's mail order company Barfko-Swill. As of this writing, the original pressing is still in print and available from Barfko.

Zappa CD number: 74

QuAUDIOPHILIAc (September 2004)

Performers:

Frank Zappa (guitar, vocals, conducting)

Ben Manilla (interviewer)
Napoleon Murphy Brock (vocals)
Randy Thornton (vocals)
Adrian Belew (guitar)
Tommy Mars (keyboards, vocals)
Peter Wolf (keyboards)
Patrick O'Hearn (bass)
Terry Bozzio (drums, vocals)
Ed Mann (percussion)
David Ocker (clarinets)
André Lewis (keyboards)
Roy Estrada (bass)
Ian Underwood (keyboards)
Max Bennett (bass)
Aynsley Dunbar (drums)
George Duke (keyboards, screams)

Tom Fowler (bass)
Chester Thompson (drums)
Don Preston (keyboards)
Sal Marquez (trumpets, flugel horn)
Bill Byers (trombone, baritone horn)
Ken Shroyer (trombone, baritone horn)
Mike Altschul (piccolo, bass flute, bass clarinet, tenor and baritone sax)
Alex Dmochowski (bass)

The Abnuceals Emuukha Electric Orchestra

1. Naval Aviation In Art? 1:34 Royce Hall, UCLA, September 18-19, 1975
2. Lumpy Gravy 1:05 Royce Hall, UCLA, September 18, 1975
3. Rollo 6:00 Royce Hall, UCLA, September 18, 1975
4. Drooling Midrange Accountants On Easter Hay 2:15 March 1978 (music) November 17, 1981 (interview)
5. Wild Love 4:07 Hammersmith Odeon, London, UK, February 28, 1978
6. Ship Ahoy 5:47 Kosei Nenkin Kaikan, Osaka, Japan, February 3, 1976
7. Chunga Basement 11:48 Zappa home basement, March 1, 1970
8. Venusian Time Bandits 1:54 Festhalle Mustermesse, Basel, Switzerland October 1, 1974 (early show)
9. Waka/Jawaka 13:23 April-May 1972
10. Basement Music #2 2:43 April 30, 1978


Issues: Barking Pumpkin/DTS 1125


Transcriptions: none.

HERE'S THE DEAL: More high-end audio, mostly of instrumental compositions.


RATINGS: ****


DOWNLOAD THESE: Downloads not available.


NOTE: This title was issued as a DVD-Audio disc by Barking Pumpkin Records in 2004, through the Zappa family's mail order company Barfko-Swill. As of this writing, the original pressing is no longer in print and this title and has not been reissued in any form.

Zappa CD number: 75

Joe's XMASage  (December 2005)

Performers (collective):

Frank Zappa (voice, vocals, guitar, drums, piano)
Kay Sherman (voice)
Ray Collins (voice)
Al Surratt (voice)
Mr. Clean (lead vocals)
Paul Buff (electric piano, bass)
Les Papp (drums)
Paul Woods (bass)
Gene (guest guitar)
Floyd (vocals)
Bobby Saldana (bass)


1. Mormon Xmas Dance Report 1:51 ("My husband, Frank, had a very interesting gig tonight") December 1962
2. Prelude To "The Purse" 2:24 ("I don't know that I'm on, but I don't get the sound of that chair") 1963
3. Mr. Clean (Alternate Mix) 2:04 ("All you fine young honeys")  Pal Recording Studio, Cucamonga, CA, June, 1963

4. Why Don'tcha Do Me Right? 5:01 (spoken: "Right away. Now what I say . . ." sung: "Why don'tcha do me right")  Pal Recording Studio, Cucamonga, CA, summer 1963
5. The Muthers/Power Trio 3:15 ("Thank you, Lou. Hey, we're gonna have a little show time now") The Saints 'N Sinners, Ontario, CA,  1964
6. The Purse 11:38 ("Oh, jeez. Beech-Nut Spearmint Gum")  1963
7. The Moon Will Never Be The Same 1:10  [c.Fall 1964?]
8. GTR Trio 11:21 ("Quiet, so I can tune up.")  Studio Z, Cucamonga, CA, March 25, 1965
9. Suckit Rockit 4:11 ("This is Paul Jackets, and tonight we're interviewing a very interesting guest.")  1963
10. Mousie's First Xmas 0:56 [c.Fall 1964?]
11. The Uncle Frankie Show 11:42  ("Once again, the *Jewitt, Klopfenstein and Things* program takes great pride in presenting to you") Studio Z, Cucamonga, CA ca. October 1964

Issues:  Vaulternative VR 20051

Transcriptions: none.

HERE'S THE DEAL: Early material from the Cucamonga/Studio Z era.

RATINGS: ***1/2

DOWNLOAD THESE: GTR Trio, The Uncle Frankie Show.

NOTE: This title was issued on CD by Vaulternative Records in 2005, through the Zappa family's mail order company Barfko-Swill. As of this writing, the original pressing is still in print and available from Barfko.

Zappa CD number: 76

Imaginary Diseases (January 2006)

Performers:

Frank Zappa (conductor, guitar)
Tony Duran (slide guitar)
Malcolm McNab (trumpet)
Gary Barone (trumpet, flügelhorn)
Tom Malone (trumpet, trombone, tuba, piccolo, saxophone)
Bruce Fowler (trombone)
Glenn Ferris (trombone)
Earle Dumler (oboe, saxophone, sarrusophone)
Dave Parlato (bass)
Jim Gordon (drums)

1. Oddients 1:13 Forum, Montreal, Quebec, Canada, October 27, 1972
2. Rollo 3:21  Irvine Auditorium, University Of Pennsylvania, Philadelphia, PA, November 10, 1972 (early show)
3. Been To Kansas City In A Minor 10:15 Cowtown Ballroom, Kansas City, MO, December 2, 1972 (late show)
4. Father O'Blivion 16:02 ("Okay. The name of this song is "Father Oblivion" and it has a tango in the middle of it.")  [October 27, 1972 - December 15, 1972]
5. D.C. Boogie 13:27  ("Let's make this a democratic process--how would you like to have this song end?")  DAR Constitution Hall, Washington, DC, November 11, 1972 (early show)
6. Imaginary Diseases 9:45  Palace Theatre, Waterbury, CT November 1, 1972
7. Montreal 9:11  Forum, Montreal, Quebec, Canada, October 27, 1972

Issues: Zappa Records ZR 20001

Transcriptions: none.

HERE'S THE DEAL: A set of recordings from Zappa's "Petit Wazoo" tour from Fall 1972.

RATINGS: ****

DOWNLOAD THESE: D.C. Boogie, Imaginary Diseases.

NOTE: This title was issued on CD by Zappa Records in 2006, through the Zappa family's mail order company Barfko-Swill. As of this writing, the original pressing is still in print and available from Barfko. The source for this release was an analog master tape prepared in 1973 by FZ.

Zappa CD number: 77

The MOFO Project/Object  (December 2006)

**FRANK ZAPPA**

**the MOFO project/object**


Performers:

The Mothers of Invention:
Frank Zappa (guitar, vocals)
Ray Collins (lead vocalist, harmonica, percussion)
Jim Black (drums, vocals)
Roy Estrada (bass, vocals)
Elliot Ingber (guitar)

"The Mothers' Auxiliary":
Gene Estes (percussion)
Eugene Di Novi (piano)
Neil Le Vang (guitar)
John Rotella (clarinet, saxophone)
Kurt Reher (cello)
Raymond Kelley (cello)
Paul Bergstrom (cello)
Emmet Sargeant (cello)
Joseph Saxon (cello)
Edwin Beach (cello)
Arthur Maebe (French horn, tuba)
George Price (French horn)
John Johnson (tuba?)
Carol Kaye (12-string guitar)
Virgil Evans (trumpet)
David Wells (trombone)
Kenneth Watson (percussion)

Plas Johnson (sax, flute)
Roy Caton (copyist)
Carl Franzoni (voice)
Vito (voice)
Kim Fowley (hyophone)
Benjamin Barrett (contractor)
David Anderle
Motorhead Sherwood (noises)
Mac Rebenack "Dr. John" (piano)
Paul Butterfield
Les McCann (piano)
Jeannie Vassoir (voice of Suzy Creamcheese)

Tom Wilson (producer)


All tracks recorded March 9-12, 1966, Sunset-Highland Studios of T.T.G, Los Angeles CA unless noted


Disc 1:

1. Hungry Freaks, Daddy 3:27 ("Mr. America, walk on by your schools that do not teach")
2. I Ain't Got No Heart 2:30 ("Ain't got no heart, I ain't got no heart to give away")
3. Who Are The Brain Police? 3:22 ("What will you do if we let you go home?")
4. Go Cry On Somebody Else's Shoulder 3:31 (Zappa/Collins) (spoken: "A year ago today, was when you went away") (sung: "Go cry, on somebody else's shoulder")
5. Motherly Love 2:45 ("Motherly love, motherly love")
6. How Could I Be Such A Fool 2:12 ("When I won your love, I was very glad")
7. Wowie Zowie 2:45 ("Wowie zowie, your love's a treat")
8. You Didn't Try To Call Me 3:17 ("You didn't try to call to me")
9. Any Way The Wind Blows 2:52 ("Any way the wind blows...")
10. I'm Not Satisfied 2:37 ("Got no place to go")
11. You're Probably Wondering Why I'm Here 3:37 ("You're probably wondering why I'm here")
12. Trouble Every Day 6:16 ("Well I'm about to get upset, from watching my T.V.")
13. Help, I'm A Rock (I. Okay to Tap Dance II. In memoriam Edgar Varese III. It Can't Happen Here) 8:37 (I. "Help I'm a rock, help I'm a rock" III. "It can't happen here, it can't happen here")
14. The Return of the Son of Monster Magnet (Unfinished ballet in two tableaux: I. Ritual Dance of the Child Killer II. Nullis Pretti [No Commercial Potential]) (spoken: "Suzy?" "Yes?" "Suzy Creamcheese?" "Yes?")

Disc 2:

15. Hungry Freaks, Daddy - Vocal Overdub Take 1 3:47  (*"Angry Freaks," take one.*")
16. Anyway The Wind Blows - Vocal Overdub 2:54  ("Any way the wind blows, Is-a fine with me")
17. Go Cry On Somebody Else's Shoulder - Vocal Overdub Take 2 3:48  ("A year ago today, Was when you went away")
18. I Ain't Got No Heart - Vocal Overdub Master Take 2:37  ("Ain't got no heart")
19. Motherly Love - Vocal Overdub Master Takes 3:09  ("Motherly love")
20. I'm Not Satisfied - 2nd Vocal Overdub Master, Take 2 (Rough Mix) 2:38  ("Got no place to go")
21. You're Probably Wondering Why I'm Here - Vocal Overdub Take 1 (Incomplete)/Take 2 (Incomplete) 1:58  (""You're Probably Wondering Why I'm Here," vocal overdub, take one")
22. You're Probably Wondering Why I'm Here - Basic Tracks 3:40
23. Who Are The Brain Police? - Basic Tracks 3:42
24. How Could I Be Such A Fool? - Basic Tracks 2:24  ("One! One, two, three, one, two, three")
25. Anyway The Wind Blows - Basic Tracks 2:48
26. Go Cry On Somebody Else's Shoulder - Basic Tracks 3:43
27. I Ain't Got No Heart - Basic Tracks 2:36
28. You Didn't Try To Call Me - Basic Tracks 3:00
29. Trouble Every Day - Basic Tracks 7:11  ("Well I'm about to get sick from watchin' my TV")
30. Help, I'm A Rock - FZ Edit 5:48  ("Help, I'm a rock")
31. Who Are The Brain Police? (Section B) - Alternate Take 1:15  ("Okay? Rolling, two.")
32. Groupie Bang Bang 3:51  (spoken: "Rolling? This is . . ." take proper: "She's my groupie bang bang")
33. Hold On To Your Small Tiny Horsies... 2:08  ("Creamcheese")

Disc 3:

34. Objects 4:32
35. Freak Trim (Kim Outs A Big Idea) 5:14
36. Percussion Insert Session Snoop 3:18
37. Freak Out Drum Track w/ Timp. and Lion 4:04
38. Percussion Object 1 and 2 6:01
39. Lion Roar and Drums From Freak Out! 5:36
40. Vito Rocks The Floor (Greek Out!) 6:09
41. "Low Budget Rock and Roll Band" 2:14  ("Ladies and gentlemen, attention, please. I'd really like to thank you for coming up here to this, uh, musical thing")
42. Suzy Creamcheese (What's Got Into You?) 5:49  ("Frank, who is Suzy Creamcheese?")  KBEY-FM, Kansas City, MO, October 22, 1971
43. Motherly Love 3:12  (spoken: "The word "beautiful" is used erroneously, but these are very beautiful people. The Mothers." sung: "Whatcha need is Motherly love")  Fillmore Auditorium, San Francisco, LA June 25, 1966
44. You Didn't Try To Call Me 4:06  ("You didn't try to call me")  Fillmore Auditorium, San Francisco, LA June 25, 1966

45. I'm Not Satisfied 2:53 ("Got no place to go") Fillmore Auditorium, San Francisco, LA June 25, 1966
46. Hungry Freaks, Daddy 3:37 ("Mister America, walk on by") Fillmore Auditorium, San Francisco, LA June 25, 1966
47. Go Cry On Somebody Else's Shoulder 2:31 ("A year ago today, was when you went away") Fillmore Auditorium, San Francisco, LA June 25, 1966

Disc 4:

48. Wowie Zowie 3:02
49. Who Are The Brain Police? (Section A, C, B) 4:32 ("One, two, three, one, two, three . . .Who Are The Brain Police?", Section C, take one.")
50. Hungry Freaks, Daddy 3:37 ("Take two.")
51. Cream Cheese (Work Part) 8:18 ("One of the major songs on that album was the Watts Riot song, "Trouble Every Day."")
52. Trouble Every Day 2:39 ("Well I'm about to get sick, from watchin' my TV")
53. It Can't Happen Here (Mothermania Version) 3:19 ("It can't happen here")
54. "Psychedelic Music" 2:34 ("Well, you see, at the time *Freak Out!* came out, there was no such thing as psychedelic music") Mixed Media, Detroit, MI November 13, 1967
55. "MGM" 1:54 ("When they first heard us, we were working at a club in Hollywood called the Whisky à Go-Go") Mixed Media, Detroit, MI November 13, 1967
56. "Dope Fiend Music" 2:06 ("There's a story that, um, during one of your recording sessions") WRVR, New York City, NY, Summer, 1967
57. "How We Made It Sound That Way" 5:08 ("") WDET, Detroit, MI, November 13, 1967
58. "Poop Rock" 0:46 ("What do you think about the, uh, current state of rock and roll") WRVR, New York City, NY, Summer, 1967
59. "Machinery" 1:00 ("They do know that we exist in Europe.") WRVR, New York City, NY, Summer, 1967
60. "Psychedelic Upholstery" 1:44 ("What do you think's gonna be next, after psychedelic?") Mixed Media, Detroit, MI November 13, 1967
61. "Psychedelic Money" 1:34 ("Somebody approached me with an interesting question about, uh, the title of the first album, *Freak Out!*") WRVR, New York City, NY, Summer, 1967
62. Who Are The Brain Police? 3:39 ("What will you do if we let you go home")
63. Any Way The Wind Blows 2:58 ("Any way the wind blows, is-a fine with me")
64. Hungry Freaks, Daddy 3:33 ("Mister America, walk on by")
65. "The 'Original' Group" 1:29 ("It existed as a group called the Soul Giants") Interview with Nigel Leigh for BBC Late Show, UMRK, LA, March, 1993
66. "Necessity" 1:18 ("They were originally just called The Mothers") Interview with Nigel Leigh for BBC Late Show, UMRK, LA, March, 1993
67. "Union Scale" 1:47 ("The Whisky was the home base for Johnny Rivers") Interview with Nigel Leigh for BBC Late Show, UMRK, LA, March, 1993
68. "25 Hundred Signing Fee" 1:12 ("The guy who came to see us, who was the staff producer at Verve, Tom Wilson, had other priorities") Interview with Nigel Leigh for BBC Late Show, UMRK, LA, March, 1993
69. "Tom Wilson" 0:33 ("What was it like working with Tom Wilson?") MTV interview, 1986

70. "My Pet Theory" 2:18  ("The '60s was really stupid.")   MTV interview, 1986
71. "There Is No Need" 0:43  ("As a man with a sense of history")   Playboy Magazine interview, UMRK, March 8, 1986

Issues:  Zappa Records ZR 20004


Transcriptions and lead sheets:

Piano/vocal arrangements of "How Could I Be Such A Fool" and "I'm Not Satisfied" may be in *The Frank Zappa Songbook* volume 1 (Los Angeles: Frank Zappa Music; Astoria NY: Big 3, 1973; reprinted in Cologne and Frankfurt, West Germany: Amsco/Melodie der Welt, 1982).

Inquiries about the lead-sheet collection for *Freak Out!* may be made in writing to Zappa's music publishing firm Munchkin Music at <munchkinmusic@zappa.com> .


HERE'S THE DEAL: A deluxe 4-CD historical package of the 1966 *Freak Out!* Sessions, including a stereo remastering of the finished album.

RATINGS: *****

DOWNLOAD THESE: Groupie Bang Bang, Lion Roar and Drums From Freak Out!, Vito Rocks The Floor (Greek Out!), the five live tracks from the Fillmore recorded June 25, 1966.


NOTE: This title was issued on CD by Zappa Records in 2006, through the Zappa family's mail order company Barfko-Swill. As of this writing, the original pressing is still in print and available from Barfko.

Zappa CD number: 78

The MOFO Project/Object (fazedooh) (December 2006)

Performers:

The Mothers of Invention:
Frank Zappa (guitar, vocals)
Ray Collins (lead vocalist, harmonica, percussion)
Jim Black (drums, vocals)
Roy Estrada (bass, vocals)
Elliot Ingber (guitar)

"The Mothers' Auxiliary":
Gene Estes (percussion)
Eugene Di Novi (piano)
Neil Le Vang (guitar)
John Rotella (clarinet, saxophone)
Kurt Reher (cello)
Raymond Kelley (cello)
Paul Bergstrom (cello)
Emmet Sargeant (cello)
Joseph Saxon (cello)
Edwin Beach (cello)
Arthur Maebe (French horn, tuba)
George Price (French horn)
John Johnson (tuba?)
Carol Kaye (12-string guitar)
Virgil Evans (trumpet)
David Wells (trombone)
Kenneth Watson (percussion)
Plas Johnson (sax, flute)

Roy Caton (copyist)
Carl Franzoni (voice)
Vito (voice)
Kim Fowley (hyophone)
Benjamin Barrett (contractor)
David Anderle
Motorhead Sherwood (noises)
Mac Rebenack "Dr. John" (piano)
Paul Butterfield
Les McCann (piano)
Jeannie Vassoir (voice of Suzy Creamcheese)

Tom Wilson (producer)

All tracks recorded March 9-12, 1966, Sunset-Highland Studios of T.T.G, Los Angeles CA unless noted

Disc 1:

1. Hungry Freaks, Daddy 3:27 ("Mr. America, walk on by your schools that do not teach")
2. I Ain't Got No Heart  2:30  ("Ain't got no heart, I ain't got no heart to give away")
3. Who Are The Brain Police?  3:22 ("What will you do if we let you go home?")
4. Go Cry On Somebody Else's Shoulder 3:31 (Zappa/Collins)  (spoken: "A year ago today, was when you went away") (sung: "Go cry, on somebody else's shoulder")
5. Motherly Love 2:45 ("Motherly love, motherly love")
6. How Could I Be Such A Fool 2:12 ("When I won your love, I was very glad")
7. Wowie Zowie 2:45  ("Wowie zowie, your love's a treat")
8. You Didn't Try To Call Me  3:17 ("You didn't try to call to me")
9. Any Way The Wind Blows  2:52  ("Any way the wind blows...")
10. I'm Not Satisfied  2:37  ("Got no place to go")
11. You're Probably Wondering Why I'm Here  3:37  ("You're probably wondering why I'm here")
12. Trouble Every Day 6:16 ("Well I'm about to get upset, from watching my T.V.")
13. Help, I'm A Rock  (I. Okay to Tap Dance  II. In memoriam Edgar Varese  III. It Can't Happen Here) 8:37 (I. "Help I'm a rock, help I'm a rock" III. "It can't happen here, it can't happen here")
14. The Return of the Son of Monster Magnet (Unfinished ballet in two tableaux: I. Ritual Dance of the Child Killer II. Nullis Pretti [No Commercial Potential]) (spoken: "Suzy?" "Yes?" "Suzy Creamcheese?" "Yes?")

Disc 2:

15. Trouble Every Day - Basic Tracks 7:11  ("Well I'm about to get sick from watchin' my TV")
16. Who Are The Brain Police? - Basic Tracks 3:42
17. I Ain't Got No Heart - Vocal Overdub Master Take 2:37  ("Ain't got no heart")
18. You Didn't Try To Call Me - Basic Tracks 3:00

19. How Could I Be Such A Fool? - Basic Tracks 2:24  ("One! One, two, three, one, two, three")
20. Any Way The Wind Blows 2:58  ("Any way the wind blows, is-a fine with me")
21. Go Cry On Somebody Else's Shoulder - Vocal Overdub Take 2 3:48  ("A year ago today, Was when you went away")
22. Motherly Love - Vocal Overdub Master Takes 3:09  ("Motherly love")
23. "Tom Wilson" 0:33  ("What was it like working with Tom Wilson?") MTV interview, 1986
24. "My Pet Theory" 2:18  ("The '60s was really stupid.")  MTV interview, 1986
25. Hungry Freaks, Daddy - Vocal Overdub Take 1 3:47  ("*"Angry Freaks," take one.*")
26. Help, I'm A Rock - FZ Edit 5:48  ("Help, I'm a rock")
27. It Can't Happen Here (Mothermania Version) 3:19  ("It can't happen here")
28. Freak Out Drum Track w/ Timp. and Lion 4:04
29. Watts Riot Demo / Fillmore Sequence 2:07 ("Well I'm about to get sick from watchin' my TV") 1965-66 demo of "Trouble Every Day, with excerpts of "You Didn't Try To Call Me" and "Go Cry On Somebody Else's Shoulder" from Fillmore Auditorium, San Francisco, CA, June 25, 1966
30. Freak Out Zilofone 2:42 ("Zilofone")
31. "Low Budget Rock and Roll Band" 2:14  ("Ladies and gentlemen, attention, please. I'd really like to thank you for coming up here to this, uh, musical thing")

Issues:   Zappa Records ZR 20005

Transcriptions and lead sheets:

Piano/vocal arrangements of "How Could I Be Such A Fool" and "I'm Not Satisfied" may be in *The Frank Zappa Songbook* volume 1 (Los Angeles: Frank Zappa Music; Astoria NY: Big 3, 1973; reprinted in Cologne and Frankfurt, West Germany: Amsco/Melodie der Welt, 1982).

Inquiries about the lead-sheet collection for *Freak Out!* may be made in writing to Zappa's music publishing firm Munchkin Music at <munchkinmusic@zappa.com> .

HERE'S THE DEAL: An improved stereo remastering of the debut album *Freak Out!* (no. 1), with contextual material. While this 2-CD set is a budget edition of the 4-CD collection (no. 79), it does have some moments unavailable on the larger set and elsewhere (see Download These).

RATINGS: ****

DOWNLOAD THESE: Who Are The Brain Police? - Basic Tracks, How Could I Be Such A Fool? - Basic Tracks, Help, I'm A Rock - FZ Edit, Watts Riot Demo / Fillmore Sequence, Freak Out Zilofone

NOTE: This title was issued on CD by Zappa Records in 2006, through the Zappa family's mail order company Barfko-Swill. As of this writing, the original pressing is still in print and available from Barfko.

Zappa CD number: 79

Trance-Fusion   (October 2006)

Performers:

The Palladium, NYC, October 28, 1977 (early show)
Frank Zappa (lead guitar)
Adrian Belew (guitar)
Tommy Mars (keyboards)
Peter Wolf (keyboards)
Ed Mann (percussion)
Patrick O'Hearn (bass)
Terry Bozzio (drums)

Rhein-Neckarhalle, Eppelheim, Germany, March 21, 1979
Frank Zappa (lead guitar)
Ike Willis (guitar)
Denny Walley (slide guitar)
Warren Cuccurullo (guitar)
Tommy Mars (keyboards)
Peter Wolf (keyboards)
Ed Mann (percussion)
Arthur Barrow (bass)
Vinnie Colaiuta (drums)

The Pier, NYC, August 25, 1984
Civic Center, Providence, Rhode Island, October 26, 1984
Orpheum Theater, Memphis, Tennessee, December 4, 1984
Paramount Theatre, Seattle, Washington, December 17, 1984 (late show)
Frank Zappa (lead guitar)

Ray White (rhythm guitar)
Ike Willis (rhythm guitar)
Bobby Martin (keyboards, sax)
Allan Zavod (keyboards)
Scott Thunes (bass)
Chad Wackerman (drums)

Memorial Hall, Allentown, Pennsylvania, March 19, 1988
Brighton Centre, Brighton, UK, April 16, 1988
Wembley Arena, London, UK, April 19, 1988
Johanneshovs Isstadion, Stockholm, May 1, 1988
Stadthalle, Vienna, Austria, May 8, 1988
Rudi-Sedlmeyer Sporthalle, Munich, Germany, May 9, 1988
Liederhalle, Stuttgart, Germany, May 24, 1988,
Palasport, Genoa, Italy, June 9, 1988
Frank Zappa (lead guitar)
Dweezil Zappa (lead guitar)  (April 19 and May 9 only)
Ike Willis (guitar)
Mike Keneally (guitar/synth)
Bobby Martin (keyboards)
Ed Mann (percussion)
Walt Fowler (trumpet)
Bruce Fowler (trombone)
Paul Carman (alto sax)
Albert Wing (tenor sax)
Kurt McGettrick (baritone sax)
Scott Thunes (bass)
Chad Wackerman (drums)

1. Chunga's Revenge 7:01  April 19, 1988
2. Bowling On Charen 5:03 (Wild Love)  October 28, 1977 (early show)
3. Good Lobna 1:39 (Let's Move To Cleveland)  December 4, 1984
4. A Cold Dark Matter 3:31 (Inca Roads)  March 19, 1988
5. Butter Or Cannons 3:24 (Let's Move To Cleveland)  August 25, 1984
6. Ask Dr. Stupid 3:20 (Easy Meat)  March 21, 1979
7. Scratch and Sniff 3:56 (City Of Tiny Lights)  April 16, 1988
8. Trance-Fusion 4:19 (Marque-Son's Chicken)  May 24, 1988
9. Gorgo 2:41 (The Torture Never Stops)  May 1, 1988
10. Diplodocus 3:22 (King Kong)  October 26, 1984
11. Soul Polka 3:17 (Oh No)  March 19, 1988
12. For Giuseppe Franco 3:48 (Hot-Plate Heaven At The Green Hotel)  December 17, 1984 (late show)
13. After Dinner Smoker 4:45 (The Torture Never Stops) June 9, 1988
14. Light Is All That Matters 3:46 (Let's Move To Cleveland)  December 17, 1984 (late show)
15. Finding Higgs' Boson 3:41 (Hot-Plate Heaven At The Green Hotel)  May 8, 1988
16. Bavarian Sunset 4:00 (I Am The Walrus )  May 9, 1988

Issues: Zappa Records ZR 20002

Transcriptions: none.

HERE'S THE DEAL: A third collection of guitar solos selected by Zappa before his death, this time drawn mostly from his 1988 tour.

RATINGS: ***

DOWNLOAD THESE: Chunga's Revenge, After Dinner Smoker

NOTE: This title was issued on CD by Zappa Records in 2006, through the Zappa family's mail order company Barfko-Swill. As of this writing, the original pressing is still in print and available from Barfko. The source for this release was a Sony 1630 master tape prepared in 1993 by FZ.

Zappa CD number: 80

Buffalo (April 2007)

Performers:

Frank Zappa (lead guitar and vocals)
Steve Vai (stunt guitar and background vocals)
Ray White (vocals and rhythm guitar)
Ike Willis (vocals and rhythm guitar)
Tommy Mars (keyboards and vocals)
Bob Harris (keyboards, trumpet and high vocals)
Arthur Barrow (bass and vocals)
Vinnie Colaiuta (drums, vocals)

All titles recorded at the Memorial Auditorium, Buffalo, NY, October 25, 1980

1. Chunga's Revenge 8:34 ("Hi! Welcome to the show tonight, ladies and gentlemen.")
2. You Are What You Is 4:12 ("Do you know what you are? ")
3. Mudd Club 3:02 (*And here we are, at the Mudd Club, y'all* ")
4. The Meek Shall Inherit Nothing 3:21 ("While you WORK THE WALL ")
5. Cosmik Debris 3:50 ("The Mystery Man came over")
6. Keep It Greasy 2:58 ("Keep it greasey so it'll go down easy")
7. Tinsel Town Rebellion 4:19 ("Thank you! This is a song about the punk bands that come from Los Angeles.")
8. Buffalo Drowning Witch 2:44 ("There is a ship arriving too late")

9. Honey, Don't You Want A Man Like Me? 4:36 ("Honey honey, hey, baby don't you want a man like me")
10. Pick Me, I'm Clean 10:15 ("Why not come over?")
11. Dead Girls Of London 3:02 ("Can you see what they are")
12. Shall We Take Ourselves Seriously? 1:36 ("Mike Scheller says his life is a mess")
13. City Of Tiny Lites 9:58 ("City of tiny lites")
14. Easy Meat 9:26 ("This girl is easy meat")
15. Ain't Got No Heart 2:00 ("Ain't got no heart")
16. The Torture Never Stops 23:36 ("Flies all green 'n buzzin' in his dungeon of despair")
17. Broken Hearts Are For Assholes 3:39 ("*Hey! Do you know what you are?*")
18. I'm So Cute 1:38 ("Feelin' sorry, feelin' sad ")
19. Andy 8:14 ("Is there anything good inside of you")
20. Joe's Garage 2:12 ("It wasn't very large")
21. Dancing Fool 3:36 ("I don't know much about dancin'")
22. The "Real World" Thematic Extrapolations 8:53 ("You know, you've heard those lines so many times. ")
23. Stick It Out 5:36 ("Fick mich, du miserabler Hurensohn")
24. I Don't Wanna Get Drafted 2:48 ("Special Delivery.")
25. Bobby Brown 2:42 ("Hey there, people, I'm Bobby Brown")
26. Ms Pinky 3:48 ("I got a girl with a little rubber head")

Issues: Vaulternative VR 2007-1

Transcriptions: none

HERE'S THE DEAL: A concert from the same tour that brought us *Tinsel Town Rebellion*, with an early version of "Ship Arriving Too Late To Save A Drowning Witch."

RATINGS: \*\*\*\*

DOWNLOAD THESE: Buffalo Drowning Witch

NOTE: This title was issued on CD by Vaulternative Records in 2007, through the Zappa family's mail order company Barfko-Swill. As of this writing, the original pressing is still in print and available from Barfko.

Zappa CD number: 81

The Dub Room Special! (August 2007)

Performers:

KCET, Los Angeles, August 27, 1974
Frank Zappa (guitar, percussion, vocals)
Napoleon Murphy Brock (sax, vocals)
George Duke (keyboards, finger cymbals, tambourine, vocals)
Ruth Underwood (percussion)
Tom Fowler (bass)
Chester Thompson (drums)
Mort Libov (vocals) (uncredited)

The Palladium, NYC, October 31, 1981
Frank Zappa (lead guitar, vocals)
Ray White (guitar, vocals)
Steve Vai (stunt guitar, vocals)
Tommy Mars (keyboards, vocals)
Robert Martin (keyboards, vocals)
Ed Mann (percussion, vocals)
Scott Thunes (bass, vocals)
Chad Wackerman (drums)

1. A Token Of My Extreme (Vamp) 2:29 ("What the? Heh heh heh") August 27, 1974
2. Stevie's Spanking 5:54 ("His name is Stevie Vai") October 31, 1981
3. The Dog Breath Variations 1:42 August 27, 1974
4. Uncle Meat 2:16 August 27, 1974
5. Stink-Foot 3:58 ("Ahem. In the dark Where all the fevers grow") August 27, 1974
6. Easy Meat 6:51 ("This girl is easy meat") October 31, 1981
7. Montana 4:24 ("I might be movin' to Montana soon") August 27, 1974
8. Inca Roads 9:46 ("Did a vehicle come from somewhere out there") August 27, 1974
9. Room Service 9:15 ("Hello? Is this room service?") August 27, 1974
10. Cosmik Debris 7:44 ("The Mystery Man came over") August 27, 1974
11. Florentine Pogen 10:13 ("She was the daughter of a wealthy Florentine Pogen") August 27, 1974

Issues: Zappa Records ZR 20006


Transcriptions: none.


HERE'S THE DEAL: Zappa's mid-1980s edit of selections from the 1974 KCET television taping session with two excerpts from his 1981 Halloween concert. This issue is related to the DVD presentation of the *Dub Room Special* videotape that Zappa sold in the mid-1980s through his mail-order company.


RATINGS: ***1/2


DOWNLOAD THESE: Stevie's Spanking, Easy Meat (see no. 97 for suggestions from the 1974 KCET recordings).


NOTE: This title was issued on CD by Zappa Records in 2007, through the Zappa family's mail order company Barfko-Swill. As of this writing, the original pressing is still in print and available from Barfko. The source for this release was an analog master tape prepared in 1982 by FZ.

Zappa CD number: 82

Wazoo (October 2007)

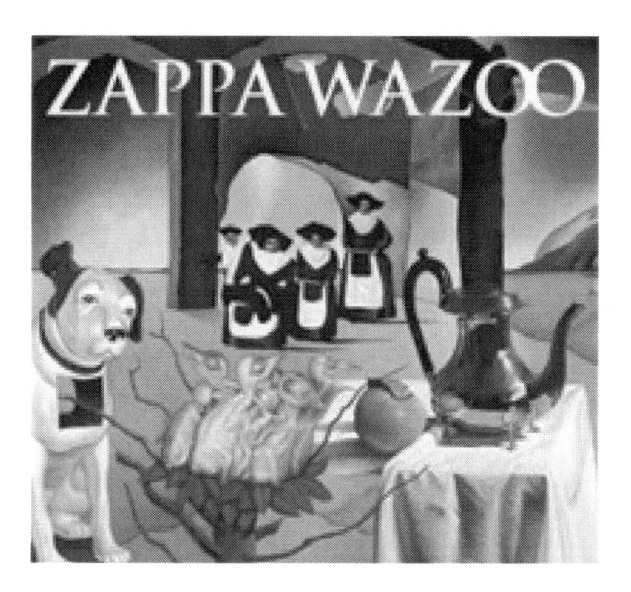

Performers:

Frank Zappa (guitar and white stick with cork handle)
Tony Duran (slide guitar)
Ian Underwood (piano and synthesizer)
Dave Parlato (bass)
Jerry Kessler (electric cello)
Jim Gordon (electric drums)
Mike Altschul (piccolo, bass clarinet and other winds)
Jay Migliori (flute, tenor sax and other winds)
Earle Dumler (oboe, contrabass sarrusophone and other winds)
Ray Reed (clarinet, tenor sax and other winds)
Charles Owens (soprano sax, alto sax and other winds)
Joann McNab (bassoon)
Malcolm McNab (trumpet in D)
Sal Marquez (trumpet in Bb)
Tom Malone (trumpet in Bb, also tuba)
Glenn Ferris (trombone and euphonium)
Kenny Shroyer (trombone and baritone horn)
Bruce Fowler (trombone of the upper atmosphere)
Tom Raney (vibes and electric percussion)
Ruth Underwood (marimba and electric percussion)

All titles recorded Boston Music Hall, Boston, MA, September 24, 1972

1. Intro Intros 3:19  ("Well, here we are in Boston, ladies and gentlemen. ")
2. The Grand Wazoo (Think It Over) 17:21  ("Thank you. Thank you very much. Thank you very, very, very much. I'd like to tell you a little bit about this here band. ")
3. Approximate 13:35
4. Big Swifty 11:49
5. "Ulterior Motive" 3:19  ("Thank you. How's the sound balance out there? ")
6. The Adventures Of Greggery Peccary:
     Movement I 4:50
7. Movement II 9:07
8. Movement III 12:33  ("Circular breathing.")
9. Movement IV - The New Brown Clouds 6:07
10. Penis Dimension 3:35
11. Variant I Processional March 3:28

Issues:  Vaulternative VR 2007-2

Transcriptions: none

HERE'S THE DEAL: A rare concert recording from Zappa's brief big-band tour in the fall of 1972.

RATINGS: ****

DOWNLOAD THESE: Grand Wazoo, Approximate, Big Swifty

NOTE: This title was issued on CD by Vaulternative Records in 2007, through the Zappa family's mail order company Barfko-Swill. As of this writing, the original pressing is still in print and available from Barfko.

Zappa CD number: 83

One-Shot Deal (June 2008)

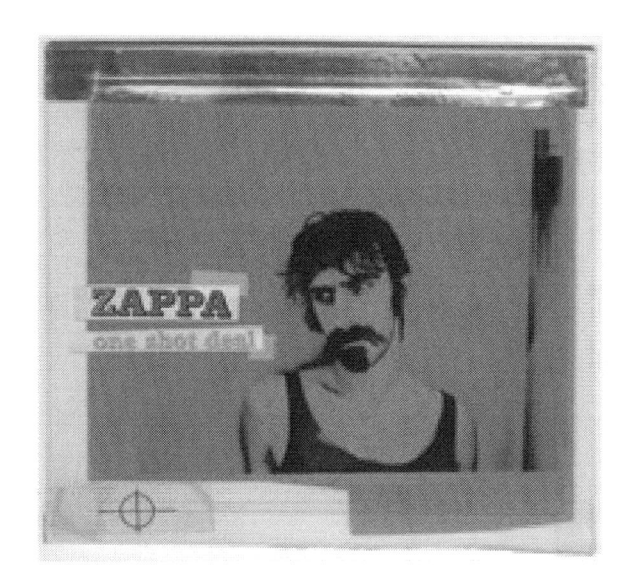

Performers:

DAR Constitution Hall, Washington, DC
November 11, 1972 (early show)
Frank Zappa  (conductor, guitar)
Tony Duran  (slide guitar)
Malcolm McNab  (trumpet)
Gary Barone  (trumpet (solo))
Tom Malone  (trumpet, trombone, tuba, piccolo, saxophone)
Bruce Fowler  (trombone)
Glenn Ferris  (trombone)
Earle Dumler  (oboe, saxophone, sarrusophone)
Dave Parlato  (bass)
Jim Gordon  (drums, steel drums)

Hordern Pavilion, Sydney, Australia
June 25, 1973
Frank Zappa (guitar, vocals)
Sal Marquez  (trumpet, vocals)
Jean-Luc Ponty  (violin)
George Duke  (keyboards, vocals)
Ian Underwood  (woodwinds, synthesizer)
Ruth Underwood (percussion)
Bruce Fowler (trombone)
Tom Fowler (bass)
Ralph Humphrey (drums)

Capitol Theatre, Passaic, New Jersey, November 8, 1974 (late show)
Palais des Sports, Paris, France, September 26, 1974
Frank Zappa (guitar, vocals)
Napoleon Murphy Brock (vocals, saxophone)
George Duke (keyboards, vocals)
Ruth Underwood (percussion)
Tom Fowler (bass)
Chester Thompson (drums)

Royce Hall, UCLA
September 18, 1975
The Abnuceals Emuukha Electric Orchestra

Rhein-Neckar Stadion, Eppelheim, Germany
February 24, 1978
Frank Zappa (lead guitar)
Adrian Belew (guitar)
Tommy Mars (keyboards)
Peter Wolf (keyboards)
Ed Mann (percussion)
Patrick O'Hearn (bass)
Terry Bozzio (drums)

Rhein-Neckarhalle, Eppelheim, Germany
March 21, 1979
Frank Zappa (lead guitar)
Warren Cuccurullo (guitar)
Denny Walley (guitar, background vocal)
Ike Willis (background vocal)
Tommy Mars (keyboards)
Peter Wolf (keyboards)
Ed Mann (percussion)
Arthur Barrow (bass)
Vinnie Colaiuta (drums)

The Palladium, NYC
October 31, 1981 (late show)
Frank Zappa (guitar, vocals)
Ray White (vocals, guitar)
Steve Vai (guitar)
Tommy Mars (keyboards)
Bobby Martin (keyboards, vocals)
Ed Mann (percussion)
Scott Thunes (bass)
Chad Wackerman (drums)

1. Bathtub Man (Brock/Duke/FZ) 5:43 ("Ah, look, you know they tried to tell me") September 26, 1974
2. Space Boogers 1:24 November 8, 1974 (late show)
3. Hermitage 2:00 September 18, 1975
4. Trudgin' Across The Tundra 4:01 November 11, 1972 (early show)
5. Occam's Razor 9:11 March 21, 1979
6. Heidelberg 4:46 February 24, 1978
7. The Illinois Enema Bandit 9:27 ("The Illinois Enema Bandit") October 31, 1981 (late show)
8. Australian Yellow Snow 12:26 (intro: "*No, no, don't eat it*" sung: "Dreamed I was an Eskimo") June 25, 1973
9. Rollo 2:57 September 18, 1975

Issues: Zappa Records ZR 20007

Transcriptions: none.

HERE'S THE DEAL: A hodgepodge of Zappa tracks, some as storyteller, some as guitarist, some as conductor.

RATINGS: ***1/2

DOWNLOAD THESE: Bathtub Man, Occam's Razor

NOTE: This title was issued on CD by Zappa Records in 2008, through the Zappa family's mail order company Barfko-Swill. As of this writing, the original pressing is still in print and available from Barfko.

Zappa CD number: 84

Joe's Menage  (September 2008)

Performers:

Frank Zappa (guitar, vocals)
Norma Jean Bell (alto sax, vocals)
Napoleon Murphy Brock (tenor sax, vocals)
André Lewis (keyboards, vocals)
Roy Estrada (bass, vocals)
Terry Bozzio (drums, vocals)

All tracks recorded at William and Mary Hall, College Of William and Mary, Williamsburg, VA, November 1, 1975


1. Honey, Don't You Want A Man Like Me? 3:57 (spoken: "Now this is a new song--you haven't heard this one before." sung: "Honey honey, hey, baby don't you want a man like me")
2. The Illinois Enema Bandit 8:42 (spoken: "And now, ladies and gentlemen, we bring you direct from the front page of the *Police Gazette* a true story"   sung: "The Illinois Enema Bandit")
3. Carolina Hard-Core Ecstasy 6:02 ("I coulda swore her hair was made of rayon")
4. Lonely Little Girl 2:46 ("You're a lonely little girl")

5. Take Your Clothes Off When You Dance 2:10 ("There will come a time when everybody who is lonely will be free")
6. What's The Ugliest Part Of Your Body? 1:16 ("What's the ugliest (OWW!) of your body?")
7. Chunga's Revenge 14:18 ("Hey yeah, yeah, some folks know about it")
8. Zoot Allures 6:41

Issues: Vaulternative Records VR 20081

Transcriptions: none.

HERE'S THE DEAL: A rare live recording of the Zappa band during the brief period when it included singer/saxophonist Norma Jean Bell.

RATINGS: ***1/2

DOWNLOAD THESE: Take Your Clothes When You Dance, What's the Ugliest Part of Your Body

NOTE: This title was issued on CD by Vaulternative Records in 2006, through the Zappa family's mail order company Barfko-Swill. As of this writing, the original pressing is still in print and available from Barfko.

Zappa CD number: 85

Lumpy Money  (January 2009)

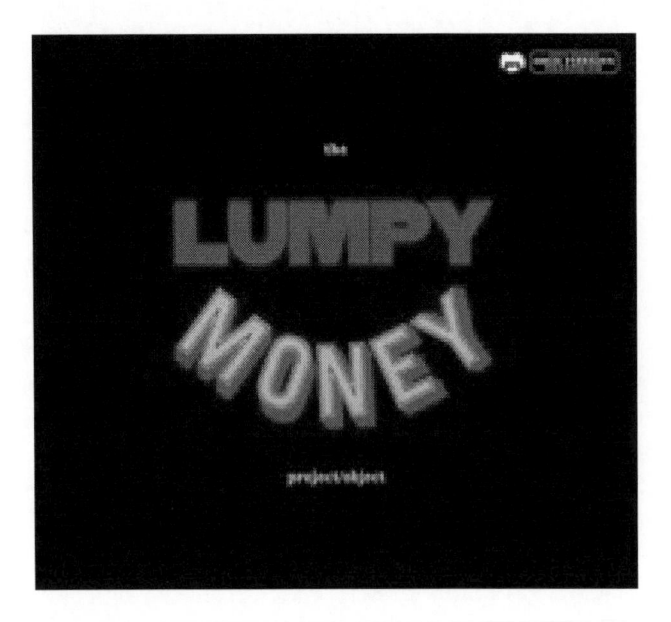

Performers:

1967 Lumpy Gravy sessions:
Frank Zappa (composer, conductor)
Abnuceals Emuukha Electric Symphony Orchestra and Chorus
selected members:
Shelly Manne (drums)
Victor Feldman (percussion)
Bunk Gardner (woodwinds)
Louie The Turkey (chorus speaker)
Ronnie Williams  (chorus speaker)
Dick Barber
Roy Estrada
Motorhead Sherwood
Pumpkin (Gail Zappa)
Jimmy Carl Black

1967 We're Only In It For The Money sessions:
Frank Zappa (guitar, piano, lead vocals, weirdness and editing)
Billy Mundi (drums, vocal)
Roy Estrada (bass, vocals)
Jimmy Carl Black (drums, trumpet, vocals)
Ian Underwood (piano, woodwinds)
Suzy Creamcheese (telephone)

Dick Barber (snorks)
Gary Kellgren (engineer, whispering)
Eric Clapton (spoken exclamation)
Sid Sharp (orchestra conductor)
(Note: performing personnel from the Mothers verified from www.zappa.com)

1984 Overdub sessions:
Ike Willis (vocals)
Ray White (vocals)
Arthur Barrow (bass)
Chad Wackerman (drums)

Disc 1:

(Tracks 1-9):
Lumpy Gravy (Primordial)
FZ's Original Orchestral Edit for Capitol Records.
Orchestral music at Capitol Studios, Hollywood, February 13 and March 14-16, 1967.

1. I Sink Trap 2:45
2. II Gum Joy 3:44
3. III Up and Down 1:52
4. IV Local Butcher 2:36
5. V Gypsy Airs 1:41
6. VI Hunchy Punchy 2:06
7. VII Foamy Soaky 2:34
8. VIII Let's Eat Out 1:49
9. IX Teen-Age Grand Finale 3:30

(Tracks 10-28):
We're Only In It For The Money
1968 mono mix, produced by Frank Zappa, created by him with with Dick Kunc in 1968.
Recorded August-September 1967, Mayfair Studios, New York City, and October 1967, Apostolic Studios, New York City.

10. Are You Hung Up? 1:24 ("Are you, Are you hung up? Are you hung up?")
11. Who Needs The Peace Corps? 2:34 ("What's there to live for? Who needs the peace corps?")
12. Concentration Moon 2:22 ("Concentration Moon, over the camp in the valley")
13. Mom and Dad 2:16 ("Mama! Mama! Someone said they made some noise")
14. Telephone Conversation 0:48 ("Well, operator? Hold for a minute, please")
15. Bow Tie Daddy 0:33 ("Bow tie daddy, don't you blow your top")
16. Harry, You're A Beast 1:21 ("I'm gonna tell you the way it is ")
17. What's The Ugliest Part Of Your Body? 1:03 ("What's the ugliest part of your body?")
18. Absolutely Free 3:24 (spoken: "I don't do publicity balling for you anymore" "The first word in this song is 'discorporate.' It means 'to leave your body.'" sung: "Discorporate and come with me")
19. Flower Punk 3:03 ("Hey punk, where you goin' with that flower in your hand?")

20. Hot Poop 0:26
21. Nasal Retentive Calliope Music 2:02  (spoken: "Oh my God" "Beautiful! God! It's God! I see God!")
22. Let's Make The Water Turn Black 2:01 ("Now believe me when I tell you that my song is really true")
23. The Idiot Bastard Son 3:18 ("The idiot bastard son")
24. Lonely Little Girl 1:09 ("You're a lonely little girl")
25. Take Your Clothes Off When You Dance 1:32 ("There will come a time when everybody Who is lonely will be free to sing and dance and love")
26. What's The Ugliest Part Of Your Body? (Reprise) 1:02 ("What's the ugliest part of your body?")
27. Mother People 2:26 ("We are the other people")
28. The Chrome Plated Megaphone Of Destiny 6:25


Disc 2:
(Tracks 29-30)
Lumpy Gravy
1984 UMRK Remix

Orchestral music at Capitol Studios, Hollywood, February 13 and March 14-16, 1967.
People inside the piano recorded at Apostolic Studios, NYC, October, 1967.
Overdubs at UMRK, L.A., CA in 1984

29. Lumpy Gravy - Part One 15:57 ("The way I see it, Barry, this should be a very dynamite show.")
30. Lumpy Gravy - Part Two 17:15  (*"Buh-bah-bahdn"* "Oh!" "There it went again.")

(Tracks 31-49)
We're Only In It For The Money  © 1968 (P) 1986 ZFT
1984 UMRK Remix, originally released on CD, 1986
Recorded August-September 1967, Mayfair Studios, New York City, and October 1967, Apostolic Studios, New York City.
Overdubs at UMRK, L.A., CA in 1984

31. Are You Hung Up? 1:24 ("Are you, Are you hung up? Are you hung up?")
32. Who Needs The Peace Corps? 2:34  ("What's there to live for? Who needs the peace corps?")
33. Concentration Moon 2:22 ("Concentration Moon, over the camp in the valley")
34. Mom and Dad 2:16 ("Mama! Mama! Someone said they made some noise")
35. Telephone Conversation 0:48 ("Well,  operator? Hold for a minute, please")
36. Bow Tie Daddy 0:33 ("Bow tie daddy, don't you blow your top")
37. Harry, You're A Beast 1:21 ("I'm gonna tell you the way it is ")
38. What's The Ugliest Part Of Your Body? 1:03 ("What's the ugliest part of your body?")
39. Absolutely Free 3:24 (spoken: "I don't do publicity balling for you anymore" "The first word in this song is 'discorporate.' It means 'to leave your body.'" sung: "Discorporate and come with me")
40. Flower Punk 3:03 ("Hey punk, where you goin' with that flower in your hand?")

41. Hot Poop 0:26
42. Nasal Retentive Calliope Music 2:02 (spoken: "Oh my God" "Beautiful! God! It's God! I see God!")
43. Let's Make The Water Turn Black 2:01 ("Now believe me when I tell you that my song is really true")
44. The Idiot Bastard Son 3:18 ("The idiot bastard son")
45. Lonely Little Girl 1:09 ("You're a lonely little girl")
46. Take Your Clothes Off When You Dance 1:32 ("There will come a time when everybody Who is lonely will be free to sing and dance and love")
47. What's The Ugliest Part Of Your Body? (Reprise) 1:02 ("What's the ugliest part of your body?")
48. Mother People 2:26 ("We are the other people")
49. The Chrome Plated Megaphone Of Destiny 6:25

Disc 3:

(Tracks 50-78)
Additional and supplementary recordings
Recording dates indicated for each item

50. How Did That Get In Here? 25:01  13 February 1967 at Capitol
51. Lumpy Gravy "Shuffle" :30   ("John Cage's work has had an influence on *Lumpy Gravy*")  21 February 1969 at The New School, NYC
52. Dense Slight 1:42  ("Light, is just a vibration of the note, too.") 14 March 1967 at Capitol.
53. Unit 3A, Take 3 2:24  ("Sid, you'll have to get on the mike.")  14 March 1967 at Capitol.
54. Unit 2, Take 9 1:10  ("Unit 2, take 9. The timp can play a little heavier out there.")  14 March 1967 at Capitol.
55. Section 8, Take 22 2:39  ("22. One, two, three, four")  14 March 1967 at Capitol.
56. "My Favorite Album" :59   ("I think that's probably one of the rarest Mothers albums too")  22 October 1971, KBEY- FM, Kansas City.
57. Unit 9 :41  14 March 1967 at Capitol.
58. N. Double A, AA :55   ("Well, somebody called me anyway and I— Here I am")  14 March 1967 at Capitol.
59. Theme From Lumpy Gravy  [© 1991] 1:56   Recorded and mixed by FZ at Studio Z, Cucamonga, circa 1964.
60. "What The Fuck's Wrong With Her?" 1:07   ("Good Lord!") West Village Apt. NYC, working on Lumpy Gravy, late 1967.
61. Intelligent Design 1:11 ("Right now I have two hit records on the charts, but it has not made me any money")  Recorded at Mayfair, August-September 1967.
62. Lonely Little Girl (Original Composition - Take 24) 3:35  Recorded at Mayfair, August-September 1967.
63. "That Problem With Absolutely Free" :30   ("Have a new album called *We're Only In It For The Money*")  Interview, Mixed Media, Detroit, 13 November 1967.
64. Absolutely Free (Instrumental) 3:59   Recorded at Mayfair, August-September 1967.
65. Harry, You're A Beast (Instrumental) 1:16   Recorded at Mayfair, August-September 1967.

66. What's The Ugliest Part of Your Body? (Reprise/Instrumental) 2:01   Recorded at Mayfair, August-September 1967.
67. Creationism 1:11   Recorded during the "Money" sessions, Mayfair, 6 September 1967.
68. Idiot Bastard Snoop :47   ("Like, you know, you know what is it") Mayfair Studios August-September 1967.
69. The Idiot Bastard Son (Instrumental) 2:48   Recorded at Mayfair, August-September 1967.
70. "What's Happening Of The Universe" 1:37   ("On the, on the *We're*— on the *We're Only In It For The Money* album you take a lot of [...] of the hippies") Interview with David Silver, Boston, 1969.
71. "The World Will Be A Far Happier Place" :21   ("The essence of it is that, uhm, that if, if we get enough kids in America playing guitar all the same way")   Recorded at Mayfair, August-September 1967.
72. Lonely Little Girl (Instrumental) 1:26   Recorded at Mayfair, August-September 1967.
73. Mom and Dad (Instrumental) 2:16   Recorded at Mayfair, August-September 1967.
74. Who Needs The Peace Corps? (Instrumental) 2:51  Recorded at Mayfair, August-September 1967.
75. "Really Little Voice" 2:28   ("Hey, kids, let's have a hootenanny!") Recorded at Mayfair, August-September 1967.
76. Take Your Clothes Off When You Dance (Instrumental) 1:24   Recorded at Mayfair, August-September 1967.
77. Lonely Little Girl - The  Single 2:45   ("You're a lonely little girl")   Recorded at Mayfair, August-September 1967.
78. "In Conclusion" :25   ("Yeah, I do have some last words, let me— I would like to say something in conclusion.")  Recorded at Mayfair, August-September 1967.


Issues:  Zappa Records  ZR 20008

Transcriptions:  Piano/vocal arrangements of "Mom and Dad," "Absolutely Free," "Let's Make The Water Turn Black," "The Idiot Bastard Son," and "Mother People"  were published in *The Frank Zappa Songbook* volume 1 (Los Angeles: Frank Zappa Music; Astoria NY: Big 3, 1973; reprinted in Cologne and Frankfurt, West Germany: Amsco/Melodie der Welt, 1982).

HERE'S THE DEAL: A documentary set devoted to the *Lumpy Gravy/We're Only In It For The Money* (nos. 3-4). It contains the 1980s revisions of both albums, the 1967 mono mix of *Money* for MGM-Verve release, and the original 1967 version of *Lumpy Gravy* as submitted to Capitol Records.

RATINGS: *****

DOWNLOAD THESE: Lumpy Gravy (Primordial) (Capitol Records version) part I-IX.


NOTE: This title was issued on CD by Zappa Records in 2009, through the Zappa family's mail order company Barfko-Swill. As of this writing, the original pressing is still in print and available from Barfko.

Zappa CD number: 86

Philly '76 (December 2009)

Performers:

Frank Zappa (guitar, vocals)
Bianca Odin (vocals, keyboards)
Ray White (vocals, rhythm guitar, cowbell)
Eddie Jobson (keyboards, violin)
Patrick O'Hearn (bass, vocals)
Terry Bozzio (drums, vocals)

All tracks recorded at Spectrum Theater, Philadelphia, PA, October 29, 1976

1. The Purple Lagoon 3:36   ("Hello! Well, good evening, ladies and gentlemen.")
2. Stink-Foot 5:53   ("In the dark where all the fevers grow")
3. The Poodle Lecture 3:49   ("In the beginning GOD made 'the light.'")
4. Dirty Love 3:37   ("Give me your dirty love")
5. Wind Up Workin' In A Gas Station 2:32   ("This here song might offend you some")
6. Tryin' To Grow A Chin 4:02   ("Yes! I'm only fourteen, sickly 'n thin ")
7. The Torture Never Stops 13:32   ("Flies all green 'n buzzin' in his dungeon of despair")
8. City Of Tiny Lites 7:47   ("City of tiny lites")
9. You Didn't Try To Call Me 6:32   ("You didn't try to call me")
10. Manx Needs Women 1:45

11. Chrissy Puked Twice 6:49 ("It was the darkest night, there was no moon in sight ") (aka Titties and Beer)
12. Black Napkins 18:58 ("Awright! Now we have a song for lovers only.")
13. Advance Romance 13:56 ("No more credit at the liquor store")
14. Honey, Don't You Want A Man Like Me? 4:09 ("Honey honey, hey, baby don't you want a man like me")
15. Rudy Wants To Buy Yez A Drink 2:20 ("And here he comes . . . Hi and howdy doody")
16. Would You Go All The Way? 2:04 ("Remember Freddie and Jo?")
17. Daddy, Daddy, Daddy 2:05 ("She's such a dignified lady")
18. What Kind Of Girl Do You Think We Are? 4:58 ("What's a girl like you doin' in a place like this?")
19. Dinah-Moe Humm 8:10 ("I couldn't say where she's coming' from")
20. Stranded In The Jungle (Johnson/Smith) 6:32 (spoken "The name of this song is "Stranded In The Jungle."" sung: "I crashed in the jungle while trying to keep a date")
21. Find Her Finer 3:18 ("Find her finer, sneak up behind her")
22. Camarillo Brillo 4:04 ("She had that Camarillo brillo")
23. Muffin Man 6:55 ("Girl, you thought he was a man but he was a muffin")


Issues: Vaulternative Records VR 20091

Transcriptions: none.

HERE'S THE DEAL: A rare and complete concert from the 1976 tour with singer/keyboardist "Lady Bianca" Odin.

RATINGS: ****1/2

DOWNLOAD THESE: Stink-Foot, Wind Up Workin' In A Gas Station, Black Napkins


NOTE: This title was issued on CD by Vaulternative Records in 2009, through the Zappa family's mail order company Barfko-Swill. As of this writing, the original pressing is still in print and available from Barfko.

Zappa CD number: 87

Greasy Love Songs  (April 2010)

Performers:

Frank Zappa (lead guitar, vocals)
Jimmy Carl Black (drums)
Ray Collins (lead vocals)
Roy Estrada (electric bass, vocals)
Bunk Gardner (tenor and alto saxophones)
Don Preston (keyboards)
Motorhead Sherwood (baritone saxophone, tambourine)
Arthur Dyer Tripp III (drums)
Ian Underwood (keyboards, tenor and alto saxophones)


All tracks recorded Apostolic Studios, NYC December, 1967-February, 1968  unless noted otherwise.

1. Cheap Thrills 2:23 ("Darling, darling, please hear my plea")
2. Love Of My Life 3:10 ("Love of my life, I love you so")
3. How Could I Be Such A Fool 3:35 ("When I won your love, I was very glad")
4. Deseri 2:07 ("When I'm dancing with Deseri")
5. I'm Not Satisfied 4:03 ("Got no place to go, No love left for me to give")
6. Jelly Roll Gum Drop 2:20 ("Jelly Roll Gum Drop, got my eyes on you")
7. Anything 3:04  ("For you, I could do anything")
8. Later That Night 3:06  ("You surely must be trying to break this heart of mine")
9. You Didn't Try To Call Me 3:57 ("You didn't try to call me, why didn't you try?")
10. Fountain Of Love 3:01 ("It was September, the leaves were gold")

11. No. No. No. 2:29 ("Boppa dooayyydoo, boppa dooayyydoo")
12. Anyway The Wind Blows 2:58  ("Any way the wind blows, is fine with me")
13. Stuff Up The Cracks 4:35  ("If you decide to leave me, it's all over")
14. Jelly Roll Gum Drop (Alternate Mix - Mono) 2:18 ("Jelly Roll Gum Drop, got my eyes on you")
15. No. No. No. (Long Version) 3:06 ("Boppa dooayyydoo, boppa dooayyydoo")
16. Stuff Up The Cracks (Alternate Mix) 6:05 ("If you decide to leave me, it's all over") Recorded at Mayfair Studios, 24 July 1967.
17. "Serious Fan Mail" 5:11 ("We released a single from the album *Ruben & The Jets*—a song called "Deseri."") Segments/Excerpts: FZ Lecture with Q & A at The New School, NYC, 21 Feb. 1969 / Interview at WMEX with Warren Duffy, Boston, 31 Jan 1969.
18. Valerie (C. Lewis/B. Robinson, BMI) (Alternate version) 3:03  ("Although you don't love me no more") Mayfair Studios, 21 July 1967.
19. Jelly Roll Gum Drop (Single Version) 2:24  ("Jelly Roll Gum Drop, got my eyes on you")
20. "Secret Greasing"  3:36  ("some of the great sounds from out of the past. It's time actually for an unofficial commercial.") November 27, 1968. KPPC in Pasadena CA with Les Carter.
21. Love Of My Life 2:06  ("Love of my life, I love you so") April, 1963 Zappa, Collins, and Mary Gonzales, with Paul Buff, Studio Z, Cucamonga CA.

Issues: Zappa Records ZR20010


Transcriptions: Piano/vocal arrangements of "How Could I Be Such A Fool" and "I'm Not Satisfied" may be in *The Frank Zappa Songbook* volume 1 (Los Angeles: Frank Zappa Music; Astoria NY: Big 3, 1973; reprinted in Cologne and Frankfurt, West Germany: Amsco/Melodie der Welt, 1982).


HERE'S THE DEAL: The original mix of the early album *Cruising With Ruben and the Jets* with its "lewd pulsating rhythms" intact (Zappa had removed them for his CD release [no. 5]), with additional Mothers of Invention era doo-wop.

RATINGS: *****

DOWNLOAD THESE: Cheap Thrills, How Could I Be Such A Fool, I'm Not Satisified, Fountain of Love, Stuff Up The Cracks

NOTE: This title was issued on CD by Zappa Records in 2010, through the Zappa family's mail order company Barfko-Swill. As of this writing, the original pressing is still in print and available from Barfko.

Zappa CD number: 88

Congress Shall Make No Law (September 2010)

Performers:

Frank Zappa (public addresses, spoken word, music composition and performance)

Track 1 recorded U.S. Congressional Committee on Commerce, Science and Transportation, Washington DC, September 19, 1985; track 2 Maryland State Legislature February 14, 1986; all other tracks are undated but for chronological indexing will be filed as 1985.

Song titles  Duration  (first line)  year of source recording(s)
1. Congress Shall Make No Law 32:46  (*"CONGRESS SHALL MAKE NO LAW . . . "*)
2. Perhaps in Maryland 10:45  ("Thank you, Chairman Miller, members of the Senate Judicial Proceedings Committee")
3. thou shalt have no other gods before Me 2:56  ("Well, uh, my opinion is that it's probably the worst thing that has happened to songwriters") ca. 1985
4. thou shalt not make unto thee any graven image - any likeness of anything in heaven above, nor in the earth beneath, nor ?n the water under the earth 2:31  ("Well, it's as simple as this: the PMRC goes to the record industry")
5. thou shalt not take the name of the Lord thy God in vain 2:26  ("It's always been a business issue")
6. thou shalt keep holy the Sabbath day 2:05  ("There are artists who do not write their own material")
7. thou shalt honor thy father and thy mother 2:21  ("Well, I'll give you the best example of why such a panel is a pure fiction and a pure fantasy")
8. thou shalt not Kill 2:06  ("You always see the future by looking backwards, okay?")

9. thou shalt not commit adultery 0:55 ("Look, nobody in his right mind believes for a minute that an artist makes more money than the record company")
10. thou shalt not steal 0:39 ("I have a feeling that it's all bought and sold")
11. thou shalt not bear false witness against thy neighbor 1:48 ("Well, to the record industry it means a little bit more hope for their bill")
12. thou shalt not covet the house of thy neighbor, the wife of thy neighbor, nor his male servant, nor his female servant, nor his ass, nor anything that belongs to thy neighbor 1:13 ("Here's that thing about the FCC")
13. Reagan at Bitburg some more 1:10

Issues: Zappa Records ZR 20011

Transcriptions: none

HERE'S THE DEAL: Zappa's complete testimonies at the U.S. Sentate (1985) and the Maryland State Legislature (1986), with additional Zappa comments (verbal and musical).

RATINGS: ***1/2

DOWNLOAD THESE: Congress Shall Make No Law.

NOTE: This title was issued on CD by Zappa Records in 2010, through the Zappa family's mail order company Barfko-Swill. As of this writing, the original pressing is still in print and available from Barfko.

Zappa CD number: 89

Hammersmith Odeon  (November 2010)

Performers:

Frank Zappa (lead guitar and vocals)
Adrian Belew (guitar and vocals)
Tommy Mars (keyboards and vocals)
Peter Wolf (keyboards)
Ed Mann (percussion)
Patrick O'Hearn (bass and vocals)
Terry Bozzio (drums and vocals)


1. Convocation/The Purple Lagoon 2:18 ("Good evening, ladies and gentlemen. Welcome to show #4 de la London, England")  January 27, 1978
2. Dancin' Fool 3:43 ("I don't know much about dancin' ")  January 27, 1978
3. Peaches En Regalia 2:36  February 28, 1978
4. The Torture Never Stops 13:52 ("Flies all green 'n buzzin' in his dungeon of despair")  February 28, 1978
5. Tryin' To Grow A Chin 3:37 ("Hey! I'm only fourteen, sickly 'n thin ")  February 28, 1978
6. City Of Tiny Lites 7:01 ("City of tiny lites ")  February 28, 1978
7. Baby Snakes 1:54 ("Baby Snakes")  February 28, 1978
8. Pound For A Brown 20:39 ("Hail Caesar!")  February 28, 1978
9. I Have Been In You 13:55 (spoken: "Alright. It's romance time, ladies and gentlemen"  sung: "I have been in you, baby")  January 26, 1978
10. Flakes 6:39 ("Flakes! Flakes!")  February 28, 1978
11. Broken Hearts Are For Assholes 3:54 (*Hey! Do you know what you are?*")  February 28, 1978
12. Punky's Whips 10:26 (spoken: "In today's rapidly changing world, rock groups appear every 14 or 15 minutes" sung: "I can't stand the way he pouts")  January 26, 1978
13. Titties 'N Beer 4:49 ("It was the blackest night")  January 26, 1978

14. Audience Participation 3:32 ("Alright. This is it. This is Audience Participation Time")   January 26, 1978
15. The Black Page #2 2:49    January 26, 1978
16. Jones Crusher 3:01 ("My baby's got Jones crushin' love ")    January 25, 1978
17. The Little House I Used To Live In 7:13    January 25, 1978
18. Dong Work For Yuda 2:56 ("Dong work for Yuda")    January 25, 1978
19. Bobby Brown 4:54 (spoken: "The tragic story of the three assholes" sung: "Hey there, people, I'm Bobby Brown")    January 26, 1978
20. Envelopes  2:16 ("You are, are my desire ")    January 26, 1978
21. Terry Firma (Bozzio) 4:10  January 26, 1978
22. Disco Boy  6:43 ("Disco Boy")    January 26, 1978
23. King Kong  10:10 February 28, 1978
24. Watermelon In Easter Hay [Prequel]  3:55   January 27, 1978
25. Dinah-Moe Humm 6:10 (spoken: "Let's play 'Doctor.'" sung: "I couldn't say where she's coming' from")   January 26, 1978
26. Camarillo Brillo 3:23 (spoken: "One, two, three, four!" sung: "She had that Camarillo brillo")   January 26, 1978
27. Muffin Man 6:18 ("Girl, you thought he was a man")    January 26, 1978
28. Black Napkins 5:16    January 25, 1978
29. San Ber'dino  5:54  ("Lives in Mojave in a Winnebago")    January 25, 1978

Issues:  Vaulternative Records VR 20101

Transcriptions: none.


HERE'S THE DEAL: A composite concert of the 1978 band (with Adrian Belew and Terry Bozzio) drawn from its Hammersmith Odeon concerts.

RATINGS: ****

DOWNLOAD THESE: I Have Been In You, Terry Firma

NOTE: This title was issued on CD by Vaulternative Records in 2010, through the Zappa family's mail order company Barfko-Swill. As of this writing, the original pressing is out of print and has not been reissued in any form.

Zappa CD number: 90

Feeding The Monkies At Ma Mansion (September 2011)

Performers:

Frank Zappa (Synclavier)
Moon Zappa (vocals)

All titles recorded at the UMRK, LA, CA, circa 1986

1. Feeding The Monkies at Ma Maison 20:12
2. Buffalo Voice 11:34 ("Buffalo voice!")
3. Secular Humaism 6:37
4. Worms From Hell 5:31
5. Samba Funk 11:29

Issues: Zappa Records ZR20012

Transcriptions: none.

HERE'S THE DEAL: Synclavier compositions executed sometime around the time of *Jazz From Hell* (1986).

RATINGS: ***1/2

DOWNLOAD THESE: Worms from Hell.

NOTE: This title was issued on CD by Zappa Records in 2011, through the Zappa family's mail order company Barfko-Swill. As of this writing, the original pressing is still in print and available from Barfko. The source for this title is a Sony 1630 digital master tape assembled by FZ in 1986.

Zappa CD number: 91

Carnegie Hall (November 2011)

Performers:

(Tracks 1-7)
The Persuasions

(Tracks 8-34)
The Mothers:
Frank Zappa (lead guitar, vocals)
Mark Volman (vocals, percussion)
Howard Kaylan (vocals)
Ian Underwood (keyboards, alto sax)
Don Preston (keyboards, gong)
Jim Pons (bass, vocals)
Aynsley Dunbar (drums )

All titles recorded October 11, 1971, Carnegie Hall, NYC

Disc 1:

The Persuasions:

1. I Just Can't Work No Longer (Curtis Mayfield, Jerry Butler) 2:32

2. Working All The Live Long Day/ Chain Gang (Trad./Sam Cooke) 2:20
3. Medley #1 tt 7:28
4. Pieces of A Man (Jerry Galen Foster, Wilburn Rice) 2:53
5. Buffalo Soldier (David Barnes, Margaret Ann Lewis, Mira Ann Smith) 4:33
6. Medley #2 tt 2:36
7. Medley #3 tt 3:14

Zappa:

8. Hello (to FOH)/ Ready?! (to the BAND) 1:03  ("Hello?")
9. Call Any Vegetable 10:36  (spoken: "This is a song about vegetables. They keep you regular, they're real good for you." sung: "Call any vegetable")
10. Anyway The Wind Blows 4:00  ("Any way the wind blows")
11. Magdalena* (Zappa/Kaylan) 6:08  (spoken: "Here's a little story I learned upstream in prison, Folsom Prison, 1968. Hey!" sung: "There was a man")
12. Dog Breath 5:41  ("Primer mi carucha (Chevy '39)")

Disc 2:

13. Peaches En Regalia 4:24  ("Thank you very much. We'll play another conglomerate item for you now")
14. Tears Began To Fall 2:32  ("Tears began to fall")
15. Shove It Right In 6:32  ("She painted up her face")
16. King Kong 30:25
17. 200 MOTELS Finale 3:41  ("We'd like to play something from our new movie.")
18.. Who Are The Brain Police? 7:08  ("What will you do if we let you go home")

Disc 3:

19. Auspicious Occasion 2:45  ("Hello? Welcome to Carnegie Hall, ladies and gentlemen.")
20. DIVAN (20-24):   Once Upon A Time 5:40  ("We will translate, as we go along, some of the more important facets of this particular piece")
21. Sofa #1 3:11  ("Ich bin der Himmel ")
22. Magic Pig 1:43  ("Ein Licht scheint vom Himmel herab")
23. Stick It Out 4:54  ("Fick mich, du miserabler Hurensohn")
24. Divan Ends Here 4:17  ("Sheets of fire, ladies and gentlemen, sheets of fire.")
25. Pound For A Brown 6:03
26. Sleeping In A Jar 2:46
27. Wonderful Wino* (Zappa/Simmons) 5:46  ("Bringing in the sheaves ")
28. Sharleena 4:52  ("I'm cryin'")
29. Cruising For Burgers 3:17  ("I (My ay ay ay ay) Must be free")

Disc 4:

30. Billy The Mountain - Part 1  28:33  ("Well, the next . . . Relax, ladies and gentlemen . . . I'll tell you what you're going to hear, that's "Billy The Mountain."")
31. Billy The Mountain - the Carnegie solos  13:31
32.. Billy The Mountain - Part 2  5:37  ("Fly to New York!")
33. The $600 Mud Shark Prelude  1:27  ("I'd like to tell you something. I'd like to play an encore for you.")
34. The Mud Shark  13:35  ("The mating call of the adult male Mud Shark")

Issues:  Vaulternative Records VR2011-1

Transcriptions: none

HERE'S THE DEAL: Zappa's Carnegie Hall concert, presented here complete with the Persuasions' opening act.

RATINGS: ****

DOWNLOAD THESE: Magdalena, Wonderful Wino, Sharleena

NOTE: This title was issued on CD by Zappa Records in 2011, through the Zappa family's mail order company Barfko-Swill. As of this writing, the original pressing is still in print and available from Barfko.

Zappa CD number: 92

The Road Tapes, Venue #1 (October 2012)

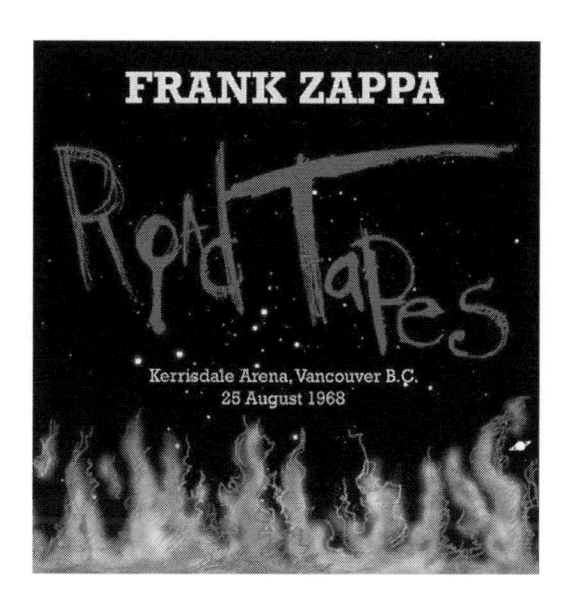

Performers:

Frank Zappa (guitar, vocals)
Don Preston (keyboards)
Ian Underwood (keyboards, woodwinds)
Bunk Gardner (woodwinds, voice)
Motorhead Sherwood (baritone sax, tambourine, harmonica)
Roy Estrada (bass, vocals)
Jimmy Carl Black (drums, vocals)
Art Tripp III (drums, percussion)

All titles recorded Kerrisdale Arena, Vancouver, B.C., Canada, August 25, 1968

1. The Importance Of An Earnest Attempt (By Hand) 3:44 ("and then we'll proceed to make an earnest attempt to rock out for you")
2. Help, I'm A Rock ("Help, I'm a rock!")
3. Transylvania Boogie 9:30
4. Flopsmash Musics 4:50
5. Hungry Freaks, Daddy 3:59 ("Mister America walk on by")
6. The Orange County Lumber Truck 20:57 ("We'd like to perform for you now a tune known to the civilized world as "The Orange County Lumber Truck"")
7. The Rewards Of A Career In Music 3:29 ("I'd like to tell you about the first time I went down to take some piano lessons from the lady on the corner")
8. Trouble Every Day 5:08 ("Well I'm about to get sick from watchin' my TV")

9. Shortly: Suite Exists Of Holiday In Berlin Full Blown 9:29 ("Okay. We're gonna do another brief re-tuning")
10. Pound For A Brown 3:13
11. Sleeping In A Jar 3:23
12. Oh, In The Sky 2:42 ("Oh, in the sky")
13. Octandre* 7:40 ("We'll play you our special number.")
14. King Kong 10:17 ("We would like to play for you 'The Legend Of King Kong.'")

Issues: Vaulternative Records VR 20122

Transcriptions: none.

HERE'S THE DEAL: A vintage Mothers of Invention concert. It contains the only version released to date of "Oh, In The Sky," the doo-wop feature number for Roy Estrada.

RATINGS: ****

DOWNLOAD THESE: Oh, In The Sky.


NOTE: This title was issued on CD by Zappa Records in 2012, through the Zappa family's mail order company Barfko-Swill. As of this writing, the original pressing is still in print and available from Barfko.

Zappa CD number: 93

Understanding America (October 2012)

Performers:

All titles previously released, except for "Porn Wars Deluxe," which is a reworking of "Porn Wars" (see *Frank Zappa Meets the Mothers of Prevention*, no. 44). For personnel and their indexing points, see the entries for the source albums.

Song titles  Duration  (first line)  title of source album

1. Hungry Freaks, Daddy 3:28  ("Mister America walk on by") *Freak Out!*
2. Plastic People 3:42  (spoken: "Ladies and gentlemen, the President of the United States!" sung: "Plastic people, oh baby now, you're such a drag") *Absolutely Free*
3. Mom and Dad   2:17  ("Mama! Mama!") *We're Only In It For The Money*
4. It Can't Happen Here  3:07  ("It can't happen here") *Freak Out!*
5. Who Are The Brain Police?  3:33  ("What will you do if we let you go home") *Freak Out!*
6. Who Needs The Peace Corps?   2:35  ("What's there to live for?") *We're Only In It For The Money*
7. Brown Shoes Don't Make It    7:29  ("Brown shoes don't make it") *Absolutely Free*
8. Concentration Moon 2:17  ("Concentration Moon") *We're Only In It For The Money*
9. Trouble Every Day 5:08  ("Well I'm about to get sick") *Freak Out!*
10. You're Probably Wondering Why I'm Here  3:36  ("You're probably wondering why I'm here") *Freak Out!*

11. We're Turning Again  4:55  ("Turn turn, Turn turn, We're turning again")  *Frank Zappa Meets the Mothers of Prevention*
12. Road Ladies 4:08  ("Don't it ever get lonesome?")  *Chunga's Revenge*
13. What Kind Of Girl Do You Think We Are? 4:33  ("What's a girl like you doin' in a place like this")  *Fillmore East - June 1971*
14. Camarillo Brillo 3:53  ("She had that Camarillo brillo")  *Over-nite Sensation*
15. Find Her Finer 3:34  ("Find her finer, sneak up behind her")  *Zoot Allures*
16. Dinah-Moe Humm   6:02  ("I couldn't say where she's coming' from")   *Over-nite Sensation*
17. Disco Boy   4:19  ("Disco Boy")  *Zoot Allures*
18. 200 Years Old  4:30  ("I was sitting in a breakfast room in Allentown, Pennsylvania ")  *Bongo Fury*
19. I'm The Slime 2:35  ("I am gross and perverted")   *Over-nite Sensation*
20. Be In My Video 3:37  ("Be in my video")  *Them Or Us*
21. I Don't Even Care   3:48  ("Would ya b'lieve it")   *Frank Zappa Meets the Mothers of Prevention*
22. Can't Afford No Shoes 2:38  ("Have you heard the news?") *One Size Fits All*
23. Heavenly Bank Account 3:16  ("He's got twenty million dollars ")  *You Are What You Is*
24. Cocaine Decisions 2:52  ("Cocaine decisions")  *The Man From Utopia*
25. Dumb All Over  4:03  ("Whoever we are ")  *You Are What You Is*
26. Promiscuous 2:03  ("The Surgeon General, Doctor Koop")  *Broadway The Hard Way*
27. Thing-Fish Intro 2:56  ("Once upon a time, musta been 'round October")  *Thing-Fish*
28. The Central Scrutinizer 2:50  ("This is the CENTRAL SCRUTINIZER")  *Joe's Garage Act 1*
29. Porn Wars Deluxe 25:51  ("The reason for this hearing is not to promote any legislation.")   *Frank Zappa Meets the Mothers of Prevention*
30. Tinsel Town Rebellion 3:43  ("From *Madam Wong's* to *Starwood*")  *Tinsel Town Rebellion*
31. Jesus Thinks You're A Jerk 9:18  ("There's an ugly little weasel 'bout three-foot nine")  *Broadway The Hard Way*

Issues:  Zappa Record ZR 3892

Transcriptions: none.

HERE'S THE DEAL: Thematic compilation exploring American conventions and mores.

RATINGS: ***1/2

DOWNLOAD THESE: Porn Wars Deluxe

NOTE: This title was issued on CD by Zappa Records in 2012, and was the only title made available in mainstream record stores as it was the sole "new" title released as part of the ZFT's deal with UMe. It remains in print as of this writing. The source was a digital master tape compiled in 1993 by FZ, consisting mainly of tracks previously released on the first round of Rykodisc/Barking Pumpkin catalog CD issues, utilizing the mixes prepared for those releases. The exception to this is a greatly extended version of "Porn Wars," which is exclusive to this compilation.

Zappa CD number: 94

Finer Moments (December 2012)

Performers:

Mayfair Studios, NYC, August-September, 1967
Dick Barber (snorks)
Frank Zappa (all instruments)

Sunset Sound, LA September, 1968 [c. March-April, 1968?]
Frank Zappa (conductor, performer)
Arthur Dyer Tripp III (percussion)

Criteria Studios, Miami, Florida c. February, 1969
McMillin Theater, Columbia University, NYC February 14, 1969
The Ballroom, Stratford, Connecticut, February 16, 1969
Royal Albert Hall, London, UK June 6, 1969
The Ark, Boston July 8, 1969
Frank Zappa (guitar)
Roy Estrada (bass)
Don Preston (keyboards)
Ian Underwood (woodwinds, acoustic piano)
Buzz Gardner (trumpet)
Bunk Gardner (woodwinds)
Motorhead Sherwood (baritone sax)
Jimmy Carl Black (drums)
Arthur Dyer Tripp III (drums, percussion)
Lowell George (guitar; February 1969 only)

Auditorium Theatre, Chicago, IL May 21, 1971
Frank Zappa (guitar)
Mark Volman and Howard Kaylan (tambourines, cowbell)
Jim Pons (bass)

Bob Harris (keyboards)
Ian Underwood (alto sax)
Aynsley Dunbar (drums)

Carnegie Hall, NYC, NY
October 11, 1971
Frank Zappa (guitar)
Ian Underwood (keyboards)
Don Preston (keyboards, Minimoog)
Jim Pons (bass)
Aynsley Dunbar (drums)

Zappa Basement, 1972
Frank Zappa (performance, engineer)

1. Intro 1:19 ("Hello, boys and girls.") June 6, 1969
2. Sleazette 3:32 June 6, 1969
3. Mozart Piano Sonata in B flat 6:20 ("Okay, now, the entertaining part of this section.") June 6, 1969
4. The Walking Zombie Music 3:22 (*He came on a Saturday afternoon from Manchester*) June 6, 1969
5. The Old Curiosity Shoppe 7:08 May 21, 1971
6. You Never Know Who Your Friends Are 2:19 ("Play the harmonica . . . Chíngale a tu madre") c. February, 1969
7. Uncle Rhebus 17:43 July 8, 1969
8. Music from "The Big Squeeze" 0:41 August-September, 1967
9. Enigmas 1 Thru 5 8:14 September, 1968 [c. March-April, 1968?]
10. Pumped And Waxed 4:18 1972
11. "There Is No Heaven From Where Slogans Go To Die" 4:36 February 14, 1969
12. Squeeze It, Squeeze It, Squeeze It 3:20 ("Oh God, Oh God, Oh God, Oh God, Oh God, Oh, Oh, Oh") February 16, 1969
13. The Subcutaneous Peril 19:38 October 11, 1971

Issues: Zappa Records/UMe ZR3894

Transcriptions: none.

HERE'S THE DEAL: Various bits from the Mothers of Inventions and the so-called "Vaudeville Band."

RATINGS: ***1/2

DOWNLOAD THESE: Uncle Rhebus, The Subcutaneous Peril.

NOTE: This title was issued on CD by Zappa Records in 2012, through the Zappa family's mail order company Barfko-Swill. As of this writing, the original pressing is still in print and available from Barfko.

Zappa CD number: 95

Baby Snakes: The Compleat Soundtrack (December 21, 2012)

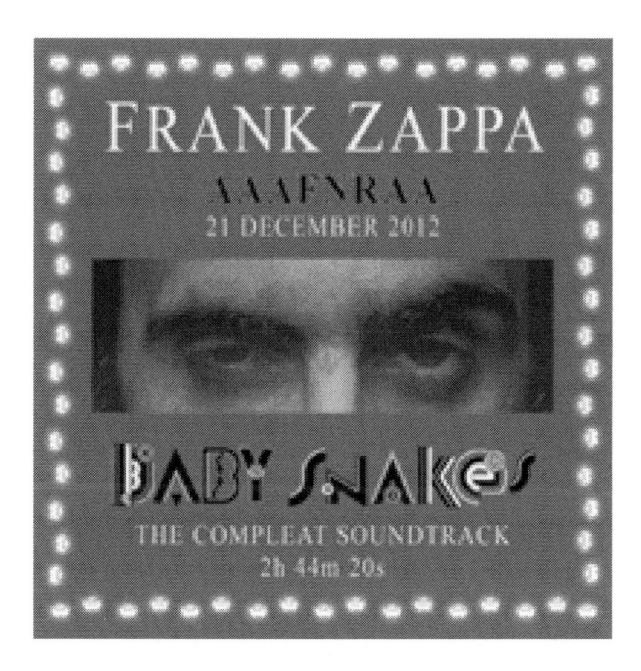

Performers:

New York Palladium, Halloween 1977
Frank Zappa (guitars, vocals)
Terry Bozzio (drums, vocals)
Roy Estrada (bass)
Adrian Belew (guitar, some vocals)
Ed Mann (percussion)
Patrick O'Hearn (bass)
Peter Wolf (keyboards)
Tommy Mars (keyboards)
and
New York's Finest Crazy Persons

1. Baby Snakes Rehearsal 2:11 ("Heh heh heh ye-yes!" "L-l-l-l-l-l . . ." [snippet of "Baby Snakes":] " Baby. . " [Zappa speaking:] "Rolling, Kerry? No-no, don't do it.")
2. "This Is the Show They Never See" 5:52 (spoken: "What do you say we all go out and have a dinner")
3. Baby Snakes - The Song 2:04 (spoken: "I told you the first time I met you . . . you remember that, what I said?" sung: "Baby Snakes")

4. Bruce Bickford/"Disco Outfreakage"  6:15   (spoken "I think my first animation was with cars runnin' over the tops of hills.")
5. The Poodle Lecture  5:04   ("In the beginning God made 'the light.'")
6. "She Said"/ City Of Tiny Lites  10:28   (spoken "She said" "Hi, uh, I'd like to say a few words about Warner Brothers." sung: "City of tiny lites")
7. New York's Finest Crazy Persons  1:56   (spoken: "Zappa is the best guitarist in the city, in the world.")
8. "The Way The Air Smells..."/Flakes  4:01   (spoken: "My name is Bill Harrington, I do the keyboards on stage left" sung: "I'm a moron 'n this is my wife" )
9. Pound Bass and Keyboards Solo  6:36
10. "In You" Rap/ Dedication  6:47   (spoken: "How did you like that one?"  sung: "I have been in you, baby")
11. Managua/Police Car/Drum Solo  9:45   ("Ay, ay, ay, ay, ay. Oy! Oh- oh, oh!")
12. Disco Boy  4:02   ("Disco Boy")
13. "Give People Somewhere To X-Scape Thru"  6:26   ("And when the, when the dis-, disco or something as obtuse as that could link up with . . .")
14. King Kong/Roy's Halloween Gas Mask  9:01
15. Bobby Brown Goes Down   3:43   (spoken: "The name of this song is "Bobby Brown Goes Down" sung: "Hey there, people, I'm Bobby Brown")
16. Conehead/ "All You Need To Know"  5:32   (spoken: "Watch me now, because the name of this song is 'Conehead'" )
17. I'm So Cute/ "Entertainment All The Way"   5:15   (spoken: "Aw, I knew you'd be surprised . . ."   sung: "Feelin' sorry, feelin' sad")
18. Titties 'N' Beer  6:19   ("It was the BLACKEST NIGHT!")
19. Audience Participation/The Dance Contest  6:36   (spoken: "Alright! You know what time it is, don't you?")
20. The Black Page 2   2:55  ("The name of this song is 'The Black Page #2.' One, two, three, four!")
21. Jones Crusher   2:53   ("My baby's got Jones-crushin' love")
22. Broken Hearts Are For Assholes  3:50   (spoken: "Hey! Do you know what you are? You're an asshole! An ASSHOLE!" sung:  "Some of you might not agree")
23. Punky's Whips    12:10   (spoken: "In today's rapidly changing world rock groups appear every fifteen minutes")
24. "Thank You"/ Dinah Moe-Humm  7:19   (spoken: "Alright . . . I wanna tell you one more time, I wanna thank you, because I really appreciate this"   sung: "I couldn't say where she's comin' from, but I just met a lady named Dinah-Moe Humm")
25. Camarillo Brillo 3:26   (spoken: "One, two, three, four!"  sung: "She had that Camarillo brillo")
26. Muffin Man  4:59   ("Girl, you thought he was a man, but he was a muffin")
27. San Ber'dino  5:02   (spoken: "The name of this song is 'San Bernardino'"  sung: "She lives in Mojave in a Winnebago")
28. Black Napkins  7:54
29. New York's Finest Crazy Persons 2   4:09   (sung: "and bust his balls. Hey! You know what!")
30. "Good Night"  1:22   (spoken: "Good night! Okay . . .")

Issues: Zappa Records download in the AAAFNRAA series

Transcriptions: none.

HERE'S THE DEAL: Every sound as heard in the *Baby Snakes* movie, direct from its soundtrack.

RATINGS: ****

DOWNLOAD THESE: All (it's a download-only release, anyway).

NOTE: This title was issued on CD by Zappa Records in 2012, as a digital download made available through the Zappa family's mail order company Barfko-Swill. It is the only exclusively digital download to be given a "core" release number status by the ZFT. It consists of the complete audio track to the 1979 FZ film *Baby Snakes* in its entirety.

Zappa CD number: 96

Road Tapes #2: Helsinki 1973

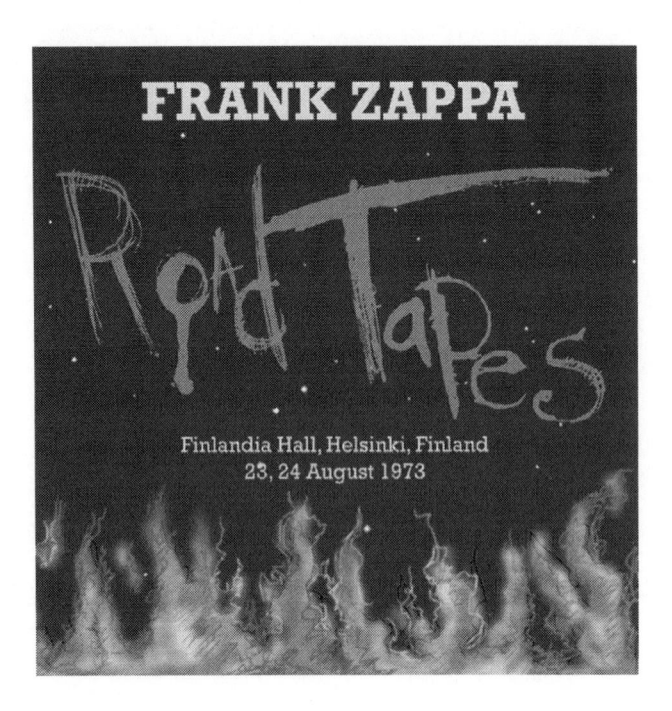

Performers:

Finlandia-talo, Helsinki, Finland
August 23 (early show)*, 23 (late show)#, and 24, 1973
Frank Zappa (guitar, vocals)
Jean-Luc Ponty (violin)
George Duke (keyboards, vocals)
Ian Underwood (woodwinds, synthesizer)
Ruth Underwood (percussion)
Bruce Fowler (trombone)
Tom Fowler (bass)
Ralph Humphrey (drums)

1. Introcious 5:18 (spoken: "Hello. Before we start, I'd like to introduce the members of the group to you and have them play a little bit, so that we know everything works.")
2. The Eric Dolphy Memorial Barbecue 1:08
3. Kung Fu 1:11
4. Penguin In Bondage 4:07 ("She's just like a Penguin in Bondage, boy.")
5. * Exercise #4 1:58
6. * Dog Breath 1:36
7. * The Dog Breath Variations 1:30

8.     * Uncle Meat 2:27
9.     * RDNZL 6:17
10. Montana 7:03 (spoken: "Right. This is a song, folks, about dental floss. That's that string that you put between your teeth to get the corn pieces out.")
11. Your Teeth And Your Shoulders And Sometimes Your Foot Goes Like This . . . /Pojama Prelude 10:14 (spoken: "The name of this song is "Dupree's Paradise," and it features a piano introduction and some other stuff by Mr. George Duke.") (sung: "Some folks are hot, and some folks are not")
12. Dupree's Paradise 15:55
13. * All Skate/Dun-Dun-Dun (The Finnish Hit Single) 14:10 (spoken: "Well, I think what we're gonna do right now is make something up. One time only. For this audience here. Ian will start it.")
14. Village Of The Sun 5:40 (spoken: "Thank you! Okay, we have sort of a rock and roll song for you now." (sung: "Goin' back home To the Village of the Sun")
15. Echidna's Arf (Of You) 4:22
16. Don't You Ever Wash That Thing? 9:56 (spoken: "Thank you! Thank you. Ralph Humphrey on duck call, ladies and gentlemen, Ralph Humphrey!")
17.     # Big Swifty 12:58
18.     # Farther O'Blivion 22:54 (spoken: "We're gonna play another instrumental event for you. This is called "Farther Oblivion."") (sung: "Psychedelic music is here to stay. Everybody sing along!")
19.     * Brown Shoes Don't Make It 7:33 ("One, two, one, two, three . . ." "Brown shoes Don't make it")

Issues: Vaulternative Records 2013

Transcriptions: none.

HERE'S THE DEAL: An early concert with a fan favorite of the Zappa bands and Jean-Luc Ponty.


RATINGS: ****


DOWNLOAD THESE: All Skate/Dun-Dun-Dun (The Finnish Hit Single).


NOTE: This title was issued on CD by Zappa Records in 2013, through the Zappa family's mail order company Barfko-Swill. As of this writing, the original pressing is still in print and available from Barfko.

Zappa CD number: 97

A Token Of His Extreme

Performers:

Frank Zappa (vocals and guitars)
Ruth Underwood (percussion)
Napoleon Murphy Brock (tenor sax, lead vocals and exotic dancing)
Tom Fowler (bass and snap)
Chester Thompson (drums and gorilla)
George Duke (keyboards and finger cymbals)

KCET television studios, Los Angeles
August 27, 1974

1. The Dog Breath Variations/Uncle Meat 4:02
2. Montana 6:44 ("I might be movin' to Montana soon")
3. Earl Of Duke 5:49 ("That is the sound of a very short cymbal. It's a finger cymbal.")
4. Florentine Pogen 11:08 ("She was the daughter of a wealthy Florentine Pogen")
5. Stink-Foot 3:58 ("Well . . . Ahem. In the dark Where all the fevers grow")
6. Pygmy Twylyte 7:47 ("Green hocker croakin' In the Pygmy Twylyte")
7. Room Service 12:12 ("Honey, honey Honey, honey Honey, honey Honey, honey Why don't you sharpen it then!")
8. Inca Roads 9:51 ("Did a vehicle, come from somewhere out there")

9.  Oh No/Son Of Orange County 7:10 ("One, two, three, four . . ." ("Oh no I don't believe it")
10. More Trouble Every Day 7:17 ("Well I'm about to get sick, from watchin' my TV")
11. A Token Of My Extreme 1:25   (spoken: "Ladies and gentlemen, this is the end of our program. We wanna thank you very much for coming down to the studio, helping us out with it.")


Issues:   Zappa Records ZR20015

Transcriptions: none.

HERE'S THE DEAL: The soundtrack to the fullest edit of the oft-used KCET television taping. Portions of a previous edit was issued as *The Dub Room Special!* (see no. 81).


RATINGS: ****


DOWNLOAD THESE: The Dog Breath Variations/Uncle Meat, Pygmy Twylyte


NOTE: This title was issued on CD by Zappa Records in 2013, through the Zappa family's mail order company Barfko-Swill. As of this writing, the original pressing is still in print and available from Barfko. The source for this release was an analog master tape prepared for vinyl release by FZ in 1974.

Zappa CD number: 98

Joe's Camouflage (January 30, 2014)

# Frank Zappa

## Joe's Camouflage

Performers:

Frank Zappa (guitar and vocals)
Denny Walley (slide guitar and vocals)
Robert "Frog" Camerena (vocals and guitar)
Novi Novog (viola, keyboards and vocals)
Napoleon Murphy Brock (vocals, sax and keyboards)
Roy Estrada (bass and vocals)
Terry Bozzio (drums)

All tracks recorded at various rehearsals, August and September, 1975

1. Phyniox (Take 1) 2:29 August 25, 1975
2. T'Mershi Duween 2:28 ("Doodle-oodle-oodle-oodle-it") August 25, 1975
3. Reeny Ra 4:13 ("Hoy hoy roy dala data.") August 25, 1975
4. "Who Do You Think You Are?" 1:39 ("Let me get a phase sound") August 25, 1975
5. "Slack 'Em All Down" 1:26 ("You know how to do it?") early September, 1975
6. Honey, Don't You Want A Man Like Me? 4:16 ("Honey, honey, hey") early September, 1975
7. The Illinois Enema Bandit 6:27 ("The Illinois Enema Bandit") August 25, 1975

8.	Sleep Dirt – In Rehearsal 1:08 early September, 1975
9.	Black Napkins 8:12  August 25, 1975
10.	Take Your Clothes Off When You Dance 1:55 ("There will come a time when everybody") August 25, 1975
11.	Denny and Froggy Relate 0:31  ("I'm The Slime?") early September, 1975
12.	"Choose Your Foot" 1:20  ("Choose your foot!") early September, 1975
13.	Any Downers? 6:11    ("Just popped a couple") August 25, 1975
14.	Phyniox (Take 2) 4:18  ("Can you put some of the guitar in Terr's monitor?") August 25, 1975
15.	"I Heard A Note!" 1:20   ("Come on in") early September, 1975

Issues:  Vaulternative Records VR 20132

Transcriptions: none.

HERE'S THE DEAL: Rehearsals with a less-remembered Zappa lineup including Denny Walley, Robert "Frog" Camerena, and Novi Novog.

RATINGS: ***1/2

DOWNLOAD THESE: Phyniox (Take 2)

NOTE: This title was issued on CD by Zappa Records in 2014, through the Zappa family's mail order company Barfko-Swill. As of this writing, the original pressing is still in print and available from Barfko.

Zappa CD number: 99

Roxy By Proxy (March 13, 2014)

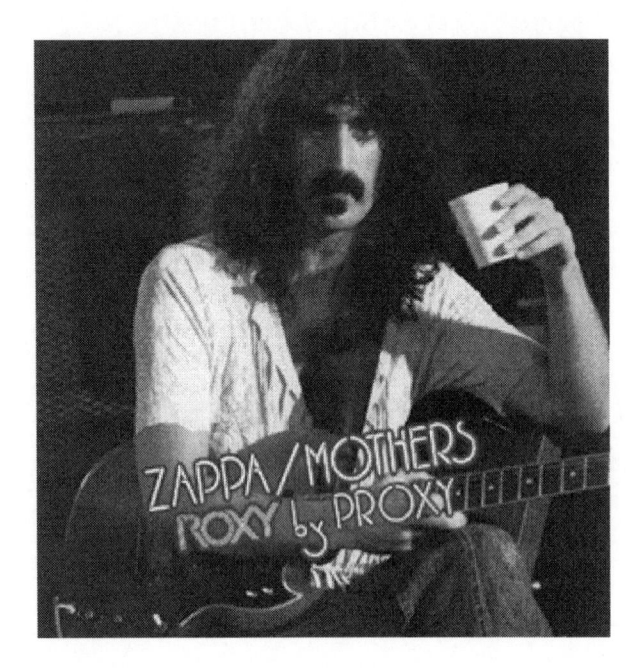

Performers:

Frank Zappa (guitars and vocals)
Napoleon Murphy Brock (tenor sax, flute, vocals)
George Duke (keyboards, vocals)
Bruce Fowler (trombone)
Ruth Underwood (percussion)
Tom Fowler (bass)
Ralph Humphrey (drums)
Chester Thompson (drums)

All tracks recorded the Roxy, Los Angeles, CA, December 8-10, 1973

01.     "Carved In The Rock" 3:30 ("Hello, folks!")
02.     Inca Roads 8:21  (spoken: "That's right, honey"  sung: "Did a vehicle come from somewhere out there")
03.     Penguin In Bondage 5:52  ("She's just like a penguin in bondage, boy.")
04.     T'Mershi Duween" 1:55
05.     Dog Breath Variations/Uncle Meat 4:13
06.     RDNZL 5:27 (Spoken: "Thank you")
07.     Village Of The Sun 3:21  (Goin' back home")
08.     Echidna's Arf (Of You) 4:00 ("Ooh well, oh")
09.     Don't You Ever Wash That Thing? 6:59 (Ladies and gentlemen, watch Ruth!")

10.     Cheepnis--Percussion 3:53  ("Ruth Underwood, Ralph Humphrey, Chester Thompson")
11.     Cheepnis 3:35    ("I ate a hot dog")
12.     Dupree's Paradise 15:12  ("I'd like to thank you very much for coming to the concert tonight")
13.     King Kong/Chunga's Revenge/Mr. Green Genes 9:13    ("Alright, we're gonna play "King Kong" for you")


Issues:  Zappa Records ZR 20016

Transcriptions: none.



HERE'S THE DEAL: Additional music from the string of dates that produced the live album *Roxy and Elsewhere* (no.19).



RATINGS: ****



DOWNLOAD THESE: King Kong/Chunga's Revenge/Mr. Green Genes


NOTE: This title was issued on CD by Zappa Records in 2014, through the Zappa family's mail order company Barfko-Swill. As of this writing, the original pressing is still in print and available from Barfko.

Zappa CD number: 100

Dance Me This (release projected for June 2015)

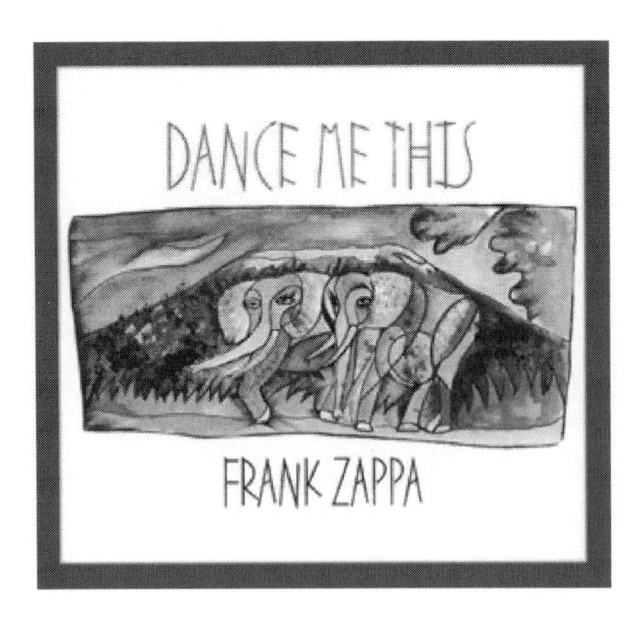

Performers:

Frank Zappa (Synclavier)

All titles recorded at the UMRK, LA, CA, circa 1991-1993; track titles taken from a photograph of a 1994 advance cassette-tape copy.

1. Dance Me This
2. Pachuco Gavotte
3. Wolf Harbor Movement I
4. Wolf Harbor Movement II
5. Wolf Harbor Movement III
6. Wolf Harbor Movement IV
7. Wolf Harbor Movement V
8. Goat Polo
9. Rykoniki
10. Piano
11. Calculus

Issues: Zappa Records

Transcriptions: none.

HERE'S THE DEAL: Synclavier compositions executed sometime around 1991-1993; with *The Yellow Shark* (no.62) and *Civilization Phaze III* (no. 63), these tracks are among Zappa's last creations.

RATINGS: ***1/2

DOWNLOAD THESE: Dance Me This, Calculus.

NOTE: The release through the Zappa family's mail order company Barfko-Swill of this title for June 1, 2015 was announced by Zappa Records in April 2015.

Name Index

Numerical references are for the Zappa Family Trust numbered entries as used in the Catalogue section.

Abnuceals Emuukha Electric Symphony Orchestra    3, 65, 71, 83, 85
Altschul, Mike    15, 16, 27, 74, 82
Anderle, David    1, 77, 78,
Anderson, Jay    5, 41, 87
Arcaro, Peter    64
Askin, Ali N.    63

Barber, Dick    3, 4, 19, 58, 60, 64, 85, 94
Barbour, Spider    63
Barker, Sharkie  see Sparkie Barker    22, 67, 93
Barker, Sparkie    22, 67
Barking Pumpkin Digital Gratification Consort    39, 42
Barnett, Philip    64
Barone, Gary    76, 83
Barrett, Benjamin    1, 77, 78,
Barrow, Arthur    4, 5, 28, 29, 30, 31, 32, 33, 34, 36, 40, 41, 50, 51, 56, 59, 64, 66, 67, 71, 79, 80, 83, 85 93,
Barry    64
Bassoli, Massimo    6
BBC Symphony Orchestra    61
Beach, Edwin V.    1, 77, 78,
Beckie    63
Beefheart, Captain    8, 20, 21, 22, 27, 64, 68, 93,
Belew, Adrian    26, 37, 51, 59, 66, 67, 74, 79, 83, 89, 95
Bell, Norma    66, 84
Bennett, Max    8, 11, 24, 64, 65, 74
Bergamo, John    23
Bergstrom, Paul    1, 77, 78,
Bikel, Theodore    13
Black, Jimmy Carl    1, 2, 3, 4, 5, 6, 7, 9, 10, 13, 34, 51, 56, 58, 59, 61, 64, 67, 68, 72, 77, 78, , 85, 87, 92, 93, 94
Bloodshot Rollin' Red see Captain Beefheart    20
Boulez, Pierre    39
Bozzio, Dale    28, 29, 41, 64, 67
Bozzio, Terry    21, 22, 23, 25, 26, 27, 32, 37, 41, 51, 54, 57, 59, 64, 65, 66, 67, 70, 74, 79, 83, 84, 86, 89, 93, 95, 98
Brecker, Michael    22, 59, 65, 67
Brecker, Randy    22, 59, 65, 67
Brewer, Don    24, 65
Brock, Napoleon Murphy    18, 19, 20, 21, 22, 26, 40, 41, 51, 52, 54, 57, 59, 66, 67, 70, 74, 81, 83, 84, 93, 97, 98, 99
Bruce, Jack    18

Bryn-Julson, Phyllis   13
Buff, Paul   64, 75, 87
Butterfield, Paul   1, 77, 78,
Buxton, Eric   53
Byers, Bill   15, 16, 74

Caldwell-McNab, Jo-Ann   16
Camarena, Robert "Frog"   18, 19, 21, 98
Carman, Paul   53, 55, 56, 57, 59, 79, 93,
Carter, Chick   64, 68
Carter, Les   87
Caton, Roy   1, 77, 78,
Christlieb, Don   64, 68
Christlieb, Pete   64, 68
Chunky   16
Clapton, Eric   4, 85
Clement, Lee   16
Colaiuta, Vinnie   28, 29, 30, 31, 32, 33, 36, 50, 51, 56, 59, 64, 66, 67, 71, 79, 80, 83, 93
Collins, Ray   1, 2, 5, 6, 7, 10, 18, 58, 64, 68, 72, 75, 77, 78, 87 93,
Cora   68
Cowen, Creg   30
Creamcheese, Suzy   4, 85
Cuber, Ronnie   23, 65, 67
Cucurullo, Warren   28, 29, 30, 31, 32, 33, 50, 51, 56, 59, 66, 67, 79, 83, 93

De Furia, Steve   41
Debbie see Wilson, Debbie   17, 18, 19end
Del Gatto, Lew   71
Di Novi, Eugene   1, 93, 77, 78,
Dierksen, Uwe   63
Dmochowski, Alexander "Alex" aka Erroneous   15, 16, 18, 73, 74
Dobson, Cynthia   68
Dohr, Stefan   63
Domanico, Chuck   64, 68
Dr. John   1, 77, 78,
Dubow, Bobby   27
Duffy, Warren   87
Duke, David   27
Duke, George   11, 13, 15, 16, 17, 18, 19, 20, 21, 24, 25, 40, 51, 52, 54, 56, 59, 60, 64, 65, 66, 67, 74, 81, 83, 93, 96, 97, 99
Dumler, Earl   16, 27, 76, 82, 83, 93,
Dunbar, Aynsley   11, 12, 13, 14, 15, 16, 18, 51, 54, 59, 60, 64, 73, 74, 91, 94
Duran, Tony   15, 16, 18, 73, 76, 82, 83

Ensemble Intercontemporain   39
Ensemble Moderne   62, 63, 69

Erroneous   15, 16, 64
Estes, Alan   16
Estes, Gene   1, 93, 77, 78,
Estrada, Roy   1, 2, 3, 4, 5, 6, 7, 9, 10, 22, 32, 35, 36, 37, 40, 51, 54, 56, 58, 59, 61, 63, 65, 66, 67, 68, 70, 72, 74, 77, 78, 84, 85, 87, 92, 93, 94, 95, 98
Evans, Virgil   1, 77, 78,

Fegy, Dick   36
Feldman, Victor   3, 85
Ferguson, Janet   9, 15, 16end
Ferris, Glenn   76, 82, 83
Fielder, Jim   2, 7, 93,
Floyd   75
Forman, William   63
Foster, Chuck   64, 68
Fowler, Bruce   17, 18, 19, 21, 25, 27, 53, 55, 56, 57, 59, 64, 65, 76, 79, 82, 83, 93, 96, 99
Fowler, Tom   17, 18, 19, 20, 21, 51, 52, 54, 56, 59, 64, 65, 66, 67, 74, 81, 83, 93, 96, 97, 99
Fowler, Walt   19, 53, 55, 56, 57, 59, 63, 79, 93,
Fowley, Kim   1, 77, 78,
Franklin, Johnny   68
Franzoni, Carl   1, 77, 78,
French, John   64

Gardner, Bunk   2, 3, 5, 6, 7, 9, 10, 51, 56, 58, 61, 68, 85, 87, 92, 93, 94
Gardner, Buzz   9, 10, 51, 56, 58, 68, 94
Gene   75
George, Lowell   8, 9, 10, 51, 56, 58, 68, 94
Glover, Susie   18
Goldsmith, Pamela   27
Gonzales, Mary   87
Gordon, Jim   18, 65, 76, 82, 83
Graham, Bill   68
Gross, Michael   63
Grove, Chuck   64
Guerin, John   8, 11, 18, 64, 68
Guevara, Ruben Ladron de   18, 19, 22, 93,
Gunston, Norman   70

Harris, Bob   12, 30, 31, 32, 33, 34, 35, 36, 41, 59, 60, 67, 80, 93, 94
Harris, Sugarcane   8, 9, 10, 11, 18, 64
Harris, Thana   25, 40
Helferin, Danny   64
Hollie, Jeff   28, 29,
Hormel, Geordie   29
Howarth, Elgar   13
Hughes, Dana   27

Humphrey, Paul   8
Humphrey, Ralph    17, 18, 19, 24, 51, 54, 56, 59, 64, 65, 67, 83 93, 96, 99

Ingber, Elliot    1, 7, 19, 58, 64, 68, 77, 78, 93,
Isaak, Barbara    29

Jackson, Fred    16
Janschi    64
Jeff see Hollie, Jeff    28, 29,
Jobson, Eddie    23, 24, 32, 59, 65, 67, 86
Johnson, Howard    71
Johnson, John    1, 77, 78,
Johnson, Plas    1, 77, 78,

Kanzus, Kanzus J.    58
Kaye, Carol    1, 77, 78,
Kaylan, Howard    11, 12, 13, 14, 51, 54, 59, 60, 91, 93, 94
Kelley, Raymond    1, 77, 78,
Kellgren, Gary    4, 85 93,
Kenneally, Mike    53,  55, 56, 57, 59, 79, 93,
Kessler, Jerry    27, 82
Kiers, Roelof    60
Kilgore, All-Night John    63
Kleinow, Sneaky Pete    15
Komanoff, Ruth    see Underwood, Ruth
Kretzschmar, Hermann    63
Krystall, Marty    36
Kuber, Ronnie    59
Kunc, Dick    64

LaFamine, patrolman    64
Lancelotti, Ricky    17, 64, 65
Lang, Mike    27
Le Vang, Neil    1, 93, 77, 78,
Lennon, John    60
Lewis, Andre    22, 26, 32, 54, 59, 65, 66, 67, 70, 74, 84, 93,
Libov, Mort    81
Lickert, Martin    60
Logeman, David    30, 34, 51, 56, 93,
London Symphony Orchestra    38, 48,
Louie the Turkey    3, 63, 85
Lyles, Wayne    64
Lynn see Sims, Linda    17, 18, 19end

Madeo, Elwood Jr    64
Maebe, Arthur    1, 77, 78,

Malkin, Al   28, 29, 67
Malone, Tom   23, 59, 65, 67, 71, 76, 82, 83
Manilla, Ben   74
Mann, Ed   23, 26, 28, 29, 30, 31, 32, 33, 34, 35, 36, 37, 38, 40, 41, 44, 50, 51, 53, 54, 55, 57, 58, 59, 66, 67, 71, 74, 79, 81, 83, 89 93, 95
Manne, Shelly   3, 85
Marginal Chagrin see Dumler, Earle   28, 29,
Marini, Lou   23, 59, 65, 67, 71
Marquez, Sal   15, 16, 17, 18, 64, 67, 73, 74, 82, 83, 93,
Mars, Tommy   26, 28, 29, 30, 31, 32, 33, 34, 35, 36, 37, 40, 41, 44, 50, 51, 54, 56, 58, 59, 64, 66, 67, 71, 74, 79, 80, 81, 83, 89, 93, 95
Martin, Bobby   35, 36, 40, 44, 50, 51, 53, 54, 55, 56, 57, 58, 59, 67, 79, 81, 83, 93,
Maxine   63
McCann, Les   1, 77, 78,
McGettrick, Kurt   53, 55, 56, 57,59, 79, 93,
McNab, JoAnn   82
McNab, Malcom   64
McNabb, Kerry   18
McNabb, Malcolm   16, 27, 73, 76, 82, 83
Migliori, Jay   82
Milliken, Catherine   63
Moire, Davey   22, 24, 26, 65, 67, 93,
Monica   63
Moon, Doug   68
Morgan, Tommy   27
Mortensen, Vic   64, 68
Mr. Clean   75
Mundi, Billy   2, 4, 6, 7, 19, 58, 85 93,
Myers, Ron   64, 68

Nagano, Kent   38, 48,
Narciso, Bob   68
Neill, Lu Ann   22, 23, 66
Novog, Novi   98

O'Hearn, Patrick   23, 25, 26, 29, 30, 32, 35, 37, 40, 51, 56, 59, 65, 66, 67, 71, 74, 79, 83, 86, 89, 95
Ocker, David   26, 34, 38, 41, 42, 74
Odin, Bianca   86
Ollu, Franck   63
Ono, Yoko   60
Ortega, Fred   16, 73
Otis, Shuggy   8
Owens, Charles   82

Papp, Les   68, 75
Pardo, Don   23, 65
Parents Music Resource Center   44
Parlato, Dave   22, 25, 27, 65, 66, 76, 82, 83
Perellis, Marty   27
Persuasions, The   91
Peskin, Joel   15, 16end
Peterson, Kris   15
PMRC (Parents Music Resource Center)   44
Pons, Jim   12, 13, 14, 51, 54, 59, 60, 91, 93, 94
Ponty, Jean-Luc   8, 17, 18, 33, 59, 64, 83, 93, 96
Popeil, Lisa   35
Preston, Don   2, 5, 6, 7, 10, 12, 14, 15, 16, 19, 51, 54, 56, 58, 59, 60, 61, 64, 68, 74, 87, 91, 92, 93, 94
Price, George   1, 77, 78,

Raney, Tom   82
Rappaport, Ilene aka Chunky   16
Rappaport, Michael   63
Rebenack, Mac "Dr. John"   1, 77, 78,
Redding, Noel   58
Reed, Ray   27, 82
Reher, Kurt   1, 77, 78,
Richards, Emil   27
Rodriquez, Tony   64
Rotella, John   1, 16, 77, 78,
Royal Philharmonic Orchestra   13
Rubin, Alan   71
Rundel, Peter   62

Sack, Claudia   69
Saldana, Bobby   68, 75
Samuels, Dave   23, 56, 65, 67
Sargeant, Emmet   1, 77, 78,
Saxon, Joseph   1, 77, 78,
Selico, Ron   8
Shankar, L.   59, 69, 71
Sharp, Sid   4, 85
Shepp, Archie   56
Sherman, Kay   75
Sherwood, Euclid Motorhead   1, 3, 5, 6, 9, 10, 34, 51, 56, 58, 61, 63, 68, 77, 78, 85, 87, 92, 94
Shostak, David   27
Shroyer, Ken   15, 16, 73, 74, 82
Simmons, Jeff   11, 15, 19, 51, 59, 60, 93,
Simone, Mark   71
Sims, Linda   17, 18, 19end

Smith, Daryl   63
Snouffer, Alex   64, 68
Steward, Craig   28, 29, 34 93,
Stone, Laurie   68
Stumuk   28, 29,
Surratt, Al   75
Svoboda, Michael   63

Tack, Ernie   16
Thompson, Chester   19, 20, 21, 24, 25, 51, 52, 54, 56, 65, 66, 74, 81, 83, 93, 97, 99
Thornton, Bianca   59
Thornton, Randy   26, 67, 74
Thunes, Scott   35, 36, 40, 41, 44, 45, 50, 51, 53, 54, 55, 56, 57, 58, 59, 67, 79, 81, 83, 93,
Toby   68
Top Score Singer   13
Townley, Gilley   63
Tripp, Arthur Dyer   5, 6, 9, 10, 51, 56, 58, 61, 64, 68, 87, 92, 94
Turner, Tina   17, 67, 93,

Underwood, Ian   4, 5, 6, 7, 8, 9, 10, 11, 12, 13, 14, 17, 18, 51, 54, 56, 58, 59, 60, 61, 64, 67, 68, 73, 74, 82, 83, 85, 87, 91, 92, 93, 94, 96
Underwood, Ruth   6, 13, 17, 18, 19, 20, 22, 23, 24, 25, 51, 52, 54, 56, 59, 64, 65, 66, 81, 82, 83, 93, 96, 97, 99

Vai, Steve   30, 31, 32, 33, 34, 35, 36, 40, 41, 44, 50, 51, 54, 56, 58, 59, 67, 80, 81, 83 93,
Van Asch, David   13
Vassoir, Jeanne   1, 77, 78, 93,
Vassy, Kin   17, 67, 93,
Vestine, Henry   72
Vito   1, 77, 78,
Vliet, Donnie see Captain Beefheart   22
Volman, Mark   11, 12, 13, 14, 51, 54, 59, 60, 91, 93, 94

Wackerman, Chad   4, 5, 25, 35, 36, 38, 40, 41, 44, 45, 50, 51, 53, 54, 55, 56, 57, 58, 59, 67, 79, 81, 83, 85 93,
Walker, Nelcy   6
Walley, Denny   21, 28, 29, 30, 31, 32, 33, 34, 50, 51, 56, 59, 67, 71, 79, 83, 93, 98
Ward, Caronga   64
Watson, Johnny "Guitar"   20, 40, 41, 44, 93,
Watson, Kenneth   1, 77, 78,
Watts, Ernie   16
Wegener, Ellen   69
Wells, David   1, 77, 78,
White, Ray   23, 30, 31, 32, 33, 34, 35, 36, 40, 41, 44, 45, 50, 51, 54, 56, 58, 59, 64, 65, 67, 79, 80, 81, 83, 86, 93,
Wild, Chuck   41

Williams, John   13
Williams, Kenny   64
Williams, Ronnie   3, 64
Willis, Ike   28, 29, 30, 31, 32, 33, 34, 35, 36, 40, 41, 44, 45, 50, 51, 53, 55, 56, 57, 59, 64, 67, 79, 80, 83, 85, 93,
Wilson, Debbie   17, 18, 19end
Wilson, Tom   1, 2, 77, 78,
Wimberly, Terry   64
Wing, Albert   53, 55, 56, 57, 59, 79, 93,
Wittenberg, John   27
Wolf, Peter   26, 28, 29, 30, 31, 32, 33, 37, 50, 51, 56, 59, 66, 67, 71, 74, 79, 83, 89, 95
Wood, Lauren aka Chunky   16
Woods, Paul   68, 75

Youman, James   20, 24, 25, 65 93,
Yvega, Todd   63

Zannas, Annie   68
Zappa, Ahmet   34
Zappa, Bobby   64
Zappa, Dweezil   40, 45, 63, 79
Zappa, Frank   1-100
Zappa, Gail   3, 85
Zappa, Moon Unit   34, 35, 63, 67, 90
Zarubica, Pamela   6
Zavod, Alan   45, 50, 51, 54, 56, 59, 67, 79
Zimmitti, Bob   16

END OF NAME INDEX

Title/First Line Index

UPPER CASE titles are for album titles

**Boldface** titles are for song titles

Regular upper and lower case text are for first lines of songs.

Numerical references are for the Zappa Family Trust numbered entries as used in the Catalogue section.

Individual song listings are for album number and track number. For example, the song "A Cold Dark Matter" will have the reference 79.04, which signifies album number 79 (Trance-Fusion) and track 4.


200 MOTELS 13
**200 Motels Finale** 59.36, 91.17
**200 Years Old** 21.05, 93.18
**25 Hundred Signing Fee** 77.68
300 years ago, I thought I might get some sleep... 51.18
**9/8 Objects** 69.08


**A Cold Dark Matter** 79.04
**A Different Octave** 63.24
**A Few Moments With Brother A. West** 55.20
A kayak . . . on snow . . . a mountain 63.18
**A Kayak (On Snow)** 63.18
A little green rosetta 29.10, 65.03
A lot of people don't bother about their friends in the vegetable kingdom 2.07
A moon beam through the prune, in June 2.02, 7.03
**A Nun Suit Painted On Some Old Boxes** 13.26
**A Pig With Wings** 63.27
**A Pound for a Brown (on the Bus)** 58.35
A real hologram, I mean, not real, but almost a real hologram 54.05
A TOKEN OF HIS EXTREME 97
**A Token of My Extreme** 29.01, 52.01, 81.01, 97.11
**A Tunnel Into Muck** 63.33
**A Very Nice Body** 63.06
**A Vicious Circle** 3.17
A year ago today, was when you went away 1.04, 56.01, 72.10, 77.04, 77.17, 77.47, 78.04, 78.21
Ahhh, chocolate halvah 58.06
**Aaawk** 60.24

Aavan meren tuolla puolen jossakin on maa... 52.14
ABSOLUTELY FREE (album) 2
**Absolutely Free** (song) 4.09, 85.18 85.39, 85.64
Absolutely Free ("1st in a series of underground oratorios") 2.01-07
Advance Romance 21.07, 50.11, 54.04, 57.24, 58.33, 70.10, 86.13
**Adventures of Greggery Peccary, The** 24.01, 65.26, 82.06-09
**Aerobics In Bondage** 44.04
Afore of it, wh-while I was away in boarding school lived with Ronnie by the name of Dwight uh,    Bement. 64.04
**After Dinner Smoker** 79.13
**Agency Man** 61.09, 68.26, 68.27
Ah, I wish Motorhead would come back. 63.20
Ah, look, you know they tried to tell me 83.01
Ah, tengo na minchia tanta 6.24
Ah, thank you very much, Ladies and Gentlemen, let's get this feedback under control 70.11
Ah! I know the perfect thing to accompany this man's trumpet 6.07
AHEAD OF THEIR TIME 61
Ahem. In the dark Where all the fevers grow 81.05
Ai mite no, nochi no kokoro ni 69.07
Ain't got no heart 1.02, 30.05, 70.07, 72.05, 77.02, 77.18, 78.02, 78.17, 80.15
Ain't got no heart, no no 70.07
**Ain't Got No Heart** (see also **I Ain't Got No Heart**) 80.15
**Air, The** 6.20
**Alien Orifice** 44.06, 59.29, 57.22
**All Skate**  96.13
All you fine young honeys 75.03
**All You Need To Know**    95.16
**Alley Cat** 64.21
**Almost Chinese** 3.07
Almost Chinese, huh? 3.07
Alright. CNN ran a story last week about this new product that has been developed for our prison system 53.04
Alright . . . I wanna tell you one more time, I wanna thank you, because I really appreciate this  95.24
Alright. It's romance time, ladies and gentlemen 89.09
Alright, look here folks: We're gonna play another song for ya, but, uh ... 66.04
Alright! Now we have a song for lovers only 86.12
Alright, see that, that's what you call a new song... 59.08
Alright. This is it. This is "Audience Participation Time" 89.14
Alright. This is it. This is the Big One. Happy Halloween everybody! 71.02
Alright, welcome and good evening to the baseball game…   56.14
Alright, we're gonna play "King Kong" for you   99.13
Alright! You know what time it is, don't you?   95.19
Although you don't love me no more 87.18
Although you don't want me no more 9.09
**Amen** 3.15

**America Drinks** 2.10
**America Drinks and Goes Home** 2.15, 7.11
**Amnerika** 63.11
**Amnerika Goes Home** 69.11
**Amnesia Vivace** 2.03
**Ancient Armaments** 71.02
And all around, at the side of the grave 34.10
And bust his balls  95.29
And here he comes . . . Hi and howdy doody 86.15
And here we are, at the Mudd Club, y'all 34.13, 41.08, 80.03
And if his dick is a monster 12.04
And if these words you do not heed, your pocketbook just kinda might recede 34.16
And if with these words, you do not heed... 51.25
And in your dreams, you can see yourself 19.08
And now folks, it's time for Don Pardo 23.06, 65.09
And now, ladies and gentlemen, we bring you direct from the front page of the Police Gazette a true story 84.02
And she said, Johnny darling... 56.31
And speaking of torture, how about this ugly sonofabitch? 55.22
And then we'll proceed to make an earnest attempt to rock out for you 92.01
And when the, when the dis-, disco or something as obtuse as that could link up with  95.13
And you'll be my duchess, my Duchess of Prunes 2.04
And, it will fall down 73.07
**Andy** 20.08, 55.12, 80.19
"Angry Freaks," take one 77.15, 78.25
**Another Pickup** 3.11
Another Whole Melodic Section 73.09
**Any Downers?** 34.10, 98.13
**Any Kind Of Pain** 53.03
**Any Way The Wind Blows** 1.09, 64.12, 77.09, 77.63, 78.09, 78.20
Any way the wind blows 1.09, 5.12, 64.12, 72.04, 77.09, 77.16, 77.25, 77.63, 78.09, 78.20, 87.12, 91.10
**Anything** 5.07, 87.07
Anything you say, master! Take me, I'm yours! 41.18
**Anyway The Wind Blows**  (see **Any Way The Wind Blows**)
**Anyway The Wind Blows - Basic Tracks** 77.25
**Anyway The Wind Blows - Vocal Overdub** 77.16
Anyway, that's quite a bit of, uh, drawing 73.10
APOSTROPHE (') (album) 18
**Apostrophe'** (song) 18.07
**Approximate** 23.15, 52.12, 56.08, 82.03
Are we movin' too slow? 18.08
Are you having breakfast for lunch? 60.15
**Are You Hung Up?** 4.01, 85.10, 85.31
**Are You Upset?** 56.28
Are you with me on this, people? 21.08

Are you, are you hung up? Are you hung up? 4.01, 85.10, 85.31
**Artificial Rhonda** 41.14
As a man with a sense of history 77.71
**Ask Dr. Stupid** 79.06
At Saint Alfonzo's Pancake Breakfast 18.03
**At The Gas Station** 3.10
At this very moment Jimmy Carl Black, the Indian of the group, is approaching the stage 61.04
At this very moment on stage we have drummer A playing in ⅞ 10.04
**Attack! Attack! Attack!** 63.22
**Audience Participation** 89.14, 95.19
**Auspicious Occasion** 91.19
**Australian Yellow Snow** 83.08
Aw, I knew you'd be surprised 95.17
Awright - see Alright
Ay, ay, ay, ay, ay. Oy! Oh- oh, oh! 95.11
**Aybe Sea** 9.07
Aye, aye, aye, everybody! Aye! Make a jazz noise here! 57.11

**Babbette** 51.11
Baby baby why you cryin' 30.03, 65.06
BABY SNAKES (album) 37
BABY SNAKES: THE COMPLEAT SOUNDTRACK 95
**Baby Snakes (song)** 26.12, 37.01, 89.07, 95.03
Baby snakes 26.12, 37.01, 89.07, 95.03
**Baby Snakes Rehearsal 95.01**
**Baby, Take Your Teeth Out** 40.08
Baby take your teeth out 40.08
Back about a hundred years ago 60.21
**Bacon Fat** 53.1
**Bad Acting** 60.54
**Baked-Bean Boogie** 58.18
Ballen von Zirkon 60.13
**Bamboozled By Love** 30.13, 54.02
Bamboozled by love 30.13, 54.02
**Band introductions at The Fillmore West** 68.18
**Bartok: Piano Concerto #3** 57.19
**Basement Music #1** 64.26
**Basement Music #2** 74.10
**Bathtub Man** 83.01
Battlestar Galactica? 54.01
**Bavarian Sunset** 79.16
**Be In My Video** 40.11, 51.21, 93.20
Be in my video, darling, every night 40.11, 51.21, 93.20
**Be-Bop Tango (Of The Old Jazzmen's Church)** 19.10, 62.08
**Beat It With Your Fist** 33.01
**Beat The Reaper** 63.40

**Beauty Knows No Pain** 34.08, 54.20
Beauty knows no pain 34.08, 54.20
**Been To Kansas City In A Minor** 76.03
**Beer Shampoo** 60.27
Before we start, I'd like to introduce the members of the group to you and have them play a little bit, so that we know everything works 96.01
**Beltway Bandits** 47.02
Big John Mazmanian! 60.09
**Big Leg Emma** 2.08, 23.11, 65.15
**Big Squeeze** 64.19, 94.08
**Big Swifty** 15.01, 51.13, 52.20, 57.11, 82.04, 96.17
**Billy The Mountain** 14.01, 60.45, 91.30, 91.32
BILLY the Mountain 60.45
**Billy The Mountain - Part 1** 91.30
**Billy The Mountain - Part 2** 91.32
**Billy The Mountain - the Carnegie solos** 91.31
Billy The Mountain! Billy The Mountain! 14.01
**Birth of Captain Beefheart** 68.07
**Bit Of Nostalgia** 3.04
Bit of nostalgia for the old folks! 3.04
Bizarre 6.10
**Black Beauty** 68.32
**Black Napkins** 22.02, 32.07, 57.10, 59.27, 66.01, 66.02, 70.09, 71.13, 86.12, 89.28, 95.28, 98.09
**Black Napkins "Zoot Allures" Album Version** 66.02
**Black Page, The** 40.12, 50.02, 50.16, 50.27, 56.13, 57.14, 58.37
**Black Page, The (New Age Version)** 57.14
**Black Page #1** 23.10, 65.14
**Black Page #2** 23.13, 37.03, 95.20
**Black Page Drum Solo** 23.10
**Blackouts** 64.01
**Blessed Relief** 16.05
**Blessed Relief/The New Brown Clouds** 73.06
**Blue Light** 30.10
**Bob In Dacron** 48.02
**Bobby Brown Goes Down** 26.09, 54.05, 67.01, 80.25, 89.19, 95.15
**Bogus Pomp** 27.05, 48.01
**Bolero** 55.08
**Bonanza** 55.22
BONGO FURY 21
Boppa dooayyydoo, boppa dooayyydoo 5.11, 87.11, 87.15
**Bored Out 90 Over** 3.06
**Bossa Nova Pervertamento** 68.10
**Botulism On The Hoof** 60.33
BOULEZ CONDUCTS ZAPPA: THE PERFECT STRANGER 39
**Bow Tie Daddy** 4.06, 85.15, 85.36
Bow tie daddy, don't you blow your top 4.06, 85.15, 85.36

**Bowling On Charen** 79.02
Boy! WORK THE WALL! 41.09
**Briefcase Boogie** 41.18
Bringing in the sheaves 60.18, 91.27
**Brixton Still Life** 60.16
**Broadside (Pomona)** 68.14
BROADWAY THE HARD WAY 53
Broadway The Hard Way, ladies and gentlemen! 53.03
**Broken Hearts Are For Assholes** 26.03, 65.08, 80.17, 89.11, 95.22
Broth reminds me of nuns 13.33
Brown Moses 41.19, 56.06
**Brown Shoes Don't Make It** 2.14, 7.01, 30.14, 93.07, 96.19
Brown shoes, don't make it 2.14, 7.01, 30.14, 93.07, 96.19
**Bruce Bickford/"Disco Outfreakage"** 95.04
Bruce Bissell 60.02
BUFFALO 80
**Buffalo Drowning Witch** 80.08
**Buffalo Soldier** (Persuasions) 91.05
**Buffalo Voice** 63.15, 90.02
Buffalo voice! 63.15, 90.02
Buh-bah-bahdn Oh! There it went again 3.13, 85.3
**Building a Girl** 52.18
**Bunch Of Adventures** 60.51
BURNT WEENY SANDWICH 9
**But Who Was Fulcanelli?** 50.20
**Butter Or Cannons** 79.05
**Bwana Dik** 12.04

**Calculus** 100.11
**Call Any Vegetable** 2.05, 7.04,14.02, 91.09
Call any vegetable 2.05, 7.04,14.02, 91.09
**Camarillo Brillo** 17.01, 59.21, 70.25, 71.11, 86.22, 89.26, 93.14, 95.25
Can I ask some of anybody here, has anyone seen me puke onstage? 51.01
Can you put some of the guitar in Terry's monitor? 98.14
Can you see what they are, do you hear what they say 58.27, 80.11
**Can't Afford No Shoes** 20.02, 93.22
**Canadian Customs** 50.3
**Canard Du Jour** 33.06
**Canard Toujours** 70.14
**Canarsie** 32.03
Carl Sanzini will now join in on the second verse of "Concentration Moon"! 60.42
CARNEGIE HALL 91
**Carol, You Fool** 54.11
**Carolina Hard Core Ecstasy** 21.02, 56.27, 70.17, 84.03
**Carved in the Rock** 99.01
**Catholic Girls** 28.03, 59.30, 67.10

Catholic Girls! With a tiny little mustache 28.03, 59.30, 67.10
Cause round things are... are boring 3.21
**Centerville** 13.13
Centerville: A real nice place to raise your kids up 13.13
**Central Scrutinizer** 28.01, 93.28
**Chalk Pie** 50.05
**Champagne Lecture** 60.28
**Chana In De Bushwop** 54.12
Chana In de bushwop, in de bushwop 54.12
**Charles Ives** 58.02
**Charlie's Enormous Mouth** 34.09, 54.21
Charlie's enormous mouth, well, it's all right 34.09, 54.21
**Charva** 64.14, 68.12
Charva, I loved you, I loved you through and through 64.14, 68.12
**Cheap Thrills** 5.01, 87.01
**Cheepnis** 19.07, 52.11, 99.10, 99.11
Cheepnis. Let me tell you something, do you like monster movies? 19.07
**Cheepnis—Percussion** 99.10
**Childish Perversions** 60.29
Chíngale a tu madre 94.06
**Chocolate Halvah** 58.06
**Choose Your Foot** 98.12
Choose your foot! 98.12
**Chrissy Puked Twice** 86.11
**Chrome Plated Megaphone Of Destiny, The** 4.19, 85.28, 85.49
**Chucha** 68.33
Chucha, why won't you accept my proposal? 68.33
**Chunga Basement** 74.07
CHUNGA'S REVENGE 11
**Chunga's Revenge** 11.07, 33.03, 70.21, 79.01, 80.01, 84.07, 99.13
**Church Chat** 56.17
Circular breathing 82.08
**City Of Tiny Lights [Lites]** 26.14, 32.01, 50.10, 50.13, 50.28, 57.17, 58.34, 79.07, 86.08, 80.13, 89.06, 95.06
City of tiny lites, don't you wanna go 26.14, 32.01, 50.10, 50.13, 50.28, 57.17, 58.34, 79.07, 86.08, 80.13, 89.06, 95.06
CIVILIZATION PHASE III 63
**Clap, The** 11.08
**Cletus Awreetus-Awrightus** 16.03
**Closer You Are, The** 40.01
**Clowns On Velvet** 41.10
**Cocaine Decisions** 36.01, 54.22, 93.24
Cocaine decisions, you are a person with a snow job 36.01, 54.22, 93.24
Cock-sucker Sammy, get your mother fuckin' mammy 45.07
**Cock-Suckers' Ball** 45.07
**Cold Dark Matter, A** 79.04

**Cold Light Generation** 63.37
Come on in   98.15
Come on Ruth, come on, aw come on Ruth, sing along, aw come on Ruth sing along with me. 52.12
Come on! Hey! Do you know what you are? You're an asshole! Hey! 65.08
**Coming Soon!** (0:31) 13.37, 13.35
**Concentration Moon** 4.03, 60.39, 85.12, 85.33, 93.08
Concentration Moon, over the camp in the valley 4.03, 60.39, 85.12, 85.33
**Concentration Moon, Part One** 60.39
**Concentration Moon, Part Two** 60.42
**Conehead** 31.01, 34.11, 71.07, 95.16
Conehead . . . she ain't really dumb 34.11, 71.07
CONGRESS SHALL MAKE NO LAW 88
**Congress Shall Make No Law** 88.01
Congress shall make no law 88.01
**Convocation/The Purple Lagoon** 89.01
**Cops and Buns** 64.18
**Cosmik Debris** 18.05, 54.25, 55.03, 80.05, 81.10
Couldn't say where she's comin' from, but I just met a lady named Dinah-Moe Humm... 59.19
**Crab-Grass Baby** 41.15
**Cream Cheese (Work Part)** 77.51
**Creamcheese** 77.33
**Creationism** 85.67
**Crew Slut** 28.04, 59.31
**Cruisin' For Burgers** 6.22, 23.02, 57.23, 60.20, 91.29
CRUISING WITH RUBEN & THE JETS 5
CRUISING WITH RUBEN & THE JETS revised 5
**Cucamonga** 21.06
Cucuroo carucha Chevy '39 6.05


**D.C. Boogie** 76.05
**Daddy, Daddy, Daddy** 13.23, 86.17
**Damp Ankles** 47.06
**Dance Contest** 30.09, 95.19
DANCE ME THIS  100
**Dance Me This** 100.01
**Dance Of The Just Plain Folks** 13.06
**Dance Of The Rock and Roll Interviewers** 13.03
**Dancin' Fool (Dancing Fool)** 26.15, 58.31, 71.03, 71.15, 80.21, 89.02
**Dangerous Kitchen, The** 36.06, 51.23
**Dark Water** 63.10
D-a-a-a-a-r-r-r-k W-a-a-a-t-e-r-r-r 63.10
Darling, darling, please hear my plea 5.01, 87.01
De white boy troubles 41.16
**Dead Girls Of London** 58.27, 80.11
Dear Jim and PFI, enclosed are photos of my cock 69.13

Dear PFIQ: Since you printed my question and photo in issue #29 69.05
**Deathless Horsie, The** 32.05, 51.22
**Debra Kadabra** 21.01
Debra Kadabra, say she's a witch 21.01
Dee . . . dee bah dam . . . 6.18
**Denny and Froggy Relate** 98.11
**Dense Slight** 85.52
**Dental Hygiene Dilemma** 13.21
**Deseri** 5.04, 87.04
**Dew On The Newts We Got** 13.29
Dew, on the newts we got 13.29
**Dick Kunc Story** 64.15
**Dickie's Such An Asshole** 53.04, 54.15
Did a vehicle come from somewhere out there 20.01, 52.03, 55.13, 81.08, 97.08, 99.02
**Didja Get Any Onya?** 10.01
**Different Octave, A** 63.24
**Dinah-Moe Humm** 17.06, 37.06, 59.19, 67.11, 70.24, 71.10, 86.19, 89.25, 93.16, 95.24
**Dio Fa** 63.38
**Diplodocus** 79.10
**Diptheria Blues** 60.21
Direct, directly from my heart to you 10.02
**Directly From My Heart To You** 10.02
**Dirty Love** 17.03, 59.03, 70.04, 86.04
**Disco Boy** 22.09, 37.05, 56.20, 67.02, 89.22, 93.17, 95.12
Disco boy, run to the toilet, comb your hair 22.09, 37.05, 56.20, 67.02, 89.22, 93.17, 95.12
**Disco Outfreakage** 95.04
Discorporate and come with me 4.09, 85.18, 85.39
**Diseases of the Band** 51.06
**Divan** 60.13
**Divan Ends Here** 91.24
**Do Not Pass Go** 50.04
**Do Not Try This At Home** 50.27
Do you know what you are? You are what you is 34.12, 80.02
**Do You Like My New Car** 12.07
Does anybody here know where Palmdale is 19.04
DOES HUMOR BELONG IN MUSIC 45
**Does This Kind of Life Look Interesting To You?** 13.22
Does this kind of life look interesting to you? 13.22
**Dog Breath, In The Year Of The Plague** 6.05 14.05, 91.12, 96.06
**Dog Breath Variations, The** 6.08, 52.16, 62.02, 81.03, 96.07, 97.01, 99.05
**Don Interrupts** 68.22
**Don't Eat The Yellow Snow** 18.01
Don't it ever get lonesome 11.02, 93.12
Don't look OB'DEWLLA! It's too horrible! 41.14
**Don't You Ever Wash That Thing?** 19.06, 96.16, 99.09
**Don't Eat The Yellow Snow** 51.14, 71.06

**Don't Eat There** 60.15
Don't know much about dancing... 58.31 (see also "I don't know much about dancin'")
**Don't Take Me Down** 60.08
**Don't You Ever Wash That Thing?** 52.07
Don't you tell me "No," Babbette... 51.11
**Dong Work For Yuda** 29.04, 89.18
Dong work for Yuda 89.18
Donnie - Hey, put that down 61.02, 68.22
Doodle-oodle-oodle-oodle-it 98.02
**Dope Fiend Music** 77.56
**Doreen** 34.03, 58.36
Doreen, don't make me wait 'till tomorrow... 34.03, 58.36
**Down In De Dew** 65.05
**Drafted Again** 34.20
Dreamed I was an Eskimo 18.01, 51.14, 71.06, 83.08
**Dressing Room** 60.09
**Drooling Midrange Accountants On Easter Hay** 74.04
Drop a line now 54.22
**Drop Dead** 41.21
**Drowning Witch** 35.04, 47.07, 50.04, 50.12, 50.20, 54.09
**Drums Are Too Noisy** 3.19
Drums are too noisy, 'n you've got no corners to hide in! 3.19
DUB ROOM SPECIAL 81
**Duck Duck Goose** 65.04
**Duke Of Orchestral Prunes** 27.04, 65.22
**Dumb All Over** 34.15, 51.24, 67.09, 93.25
**Dummy Up** 19.03
**Dun-Dun-Dun** 96.13
**Duodenum** 3.02
**Dupree's Paradise** 39.04, 52.13, 57.16, 96.12, 99.12
**Dwarf Nebula Processional March and Dwarf Nebula** 10.07

**Earl of Duke** 97.03
**Easy Meat** 30.02, 31.02, 50.18, 71.04, 79.06, 81.06, 58.26, 80.14
**Eat That Question** 16.04, 57.09
Eat your greens 6.17, 55.10
**Echidna's Arf (Of You)** 19.05, 52.06, 96.15, 99.08
**Eddie, Are You Kidding?** 14.03
Eddie, are you kidding? I've seen you on my TV 14.03
Ein Licht scheint vom Himmel herab 91.22
**Electric Aunt Jemima** 6.12
Electric Aunt Jemina, goddess of love 6.12
**Elvis Has Just Left The Building** 53.01
Elvis has just left the building, those are his footprints, right there 53.01
**Emperor of Ohio** 59.18
**Ending Line, The** 73.05

**Enigmas 1 Thru 5** 94.09
**Entertainment All The Way** 95.17
**Envelopes** 35.05, 38.03, 89.20
**Envelops The Bath Tub** 3.21
**Epilogue** 61.10
**Eric Dolphy Memorial Barbecue** 10.06, 55.27, 96.02
**Evelyn, A Modified Dog** 20.06
Evelyn, a modified dog 20.06
Ever since you left the jazz world to seek fame and fortune in the rock and roll industry 60.54
Everybody sing 11.04
EVERYTHING IS HEALING NICELY 69
**Evil Prince** 41.06
**Excentrifugal Forz** 18.06
**Excerpt from The Uncle Frankie Show** 68.11
**Exercise #4** 62.17, 96.05

**Father O'Blivion** 18.04, 59.07
Father Vivian O'Blivion resplendent in his frock 18.04, 59.07
**Farther O'Blivion** 76.04, 96.18
FEEDING THE MONKIES AT MA MANSION 90
**Feeding The Monkies at Ma Maison** 90.01
Feelin' sorry, feelin' sad, so many ugly people, I feel bad... 26.04, 59.09, 80.18, 95.17
**Fembot In A Wet T-Shirt** 28.05
**Few Moments With Brother A. West, A** 55.20
Fick mich, du miserabler Hurensohn 29.02, 80.23, 91.23
**Fifty-Fifty** 17.04
FILLMORE EAST - JUNE 1971 12
**Filthy Habits** 25.01, 56.15, 65.23, 70.05
**Find Her Finer** 22.05, 55.04, 70.16, 86.21, 93.15
Find her finer, sneak up behind her 22.05, 55.04, 70.16, 86.21, 93.15
Find out where 60.03
**Finding Higgs' Boson** 79.15
**Fine Girl** 30.01, 51.17
FINER MOMENTS 94
**Finnish Hit Single** 96.13
**Fire And Chains** 57.03
**five-five-FIVE** 31.01
**Flakes** 26.02, 89.10, 95.08
Flakes! Flakes! Flakes! Flakes! 26.02, 89.10
**Flambay** 25.02
**Flambé** 65.17
Flies all green 'n buzzin' in his dungeon of despair 22.03, 23.14, 41.05, 51.16, 55.21, 55.24, 56.16, 70.13, 80.16, 86.07, 89.04
**Flopsmash Musics** 92.04
**Florentine Pogen** 20.05, 55.11, 56.23, 81.11, 97.04
**Florida Airport Tape** 51.01

**Flower Punk** 4.10, 85.19, 85.40
**Flowing Inside-Out** 63.30
Flowing inside out creates neutral energy. 63.30
Fly to New York! 91.32
**Foamy Soaky** 85.07
**Food Gathering In Post-Industrial America, 1992** 62.14
**For Calvin (And His Next Two Hitch-Hikers)** 16.01
**For Duane** 50.21
**For Giuseppe Franco** 79.12
For the past 10 years in a town just outside of Chicago 70.11
**For The Young Sophisticate** 30.03, 65.06
For you, I could do anything 5.07, 87.07
**Fountain Of Love** 5.10, 64.10, 87.10
FRANCESCO ZAPPA 42
FRANK ZAPPA MEETS THE MOTHERS OF PREVENTION 44
FRANK ZAPPA PLAYS THE MUSIC OF FRANK ZAPPA 66
**Frank Zappa's 200 Motels** 13.38
Frank, who is Suzy Creamcheese? 77.42
**Freak Out Drum Track w/ Timp. and Lion** 77.37, 78.28
**Freak Out Zilofone** 78.30
FREAK OUT! 1
**Freak Trim (Kim Outs A Big Idea)** 77.35
**Friendly Little Finger** 22.06
**Frog Song** 73.03
**Frogs With Dirty Little Lips** 40.13
Frogs with dirty little lips 40.13
From 200 Motels he expects the worst reviews of any movie ever put out 60.55
From Madam Wong's to Starwood to the Whiskey on the Strip 30.11, 45.02, 67.12, 93.30
From the point that Jeff Simmons quit the group, we've had a bunch of adventures trying to find somebody to replace him 60.51
Fuckin' guy has flipped out, man! 60.38
Fuzzy dice and bongos, fuzzy dice 6.11
FZ:OZ 70
**FZ/JCB Drum Due**t 58.20


**G-Spot Tornado** 47.05, 62.19
Galoot co-log-nuh! 41.04
**Galoot Up-Date** 41.04
**Game of Cards** 58.22
**Gee, I Like Your Pants** 32.02
**Geneva Farewell** 58.38
**German Lunch** 58.24
**Get A Life** 63.17
**Get a Little** 10.05
Get on your feet an' do the funky Alfonzo! 18.04

**Get Whitey** 62.18
**Getting Stewed** 60.06
**Girl In The Magnesium Dress, The** 39.03, 62.07
**Girl Wants To Fix Him Some Broth, The** 13.31
Girl, you thought he was a man but he was a muffin 21.09, 70.26, 71.12, 86.23, 89.27, 95.26
**Girl's Dream** 13.32
Give me your dirty love 17.03, 59.03, 70.04, 86.04
**Give People Somewhere To X-Scape Thru** 95.13
**Go Cry on Somebody's Else Shoulder** 1.04, 72.10, 77.04, 77.17, 77.26, 77.47, 78.04, 78.21, 78.29
Go cry, on somebody else's shoulder 1.04, 77.04, 78.04
**GOA** 50.22
**Goat Polo** 100.08
**Goblin Girl** 34.04, 67.03
**God Bless America (Live at the Whisky A Go Go)** 6.14
God bless America, land that I love 6.14
**Godfather Part II** 55.19
Goin' back home to the village of the sun... 52.05, 96.14, 99.07
Goin' to hell! Goin' to hell! 57.02
Going back again to see that girl 72.09
**Going For The Money** 60.49
Going to El Monte Legion Stadium 6.05
**Golf shoes... Sport shirt... White Person...** 59.10
Good evening, ladies and gentlemen, welcome to The Mothers Of Invention Extravaganza for Sydney, Australia, 1976 70.01
Good evening, ladies and gentlemen. Welcome to show #4 de la London, England 89.01
**Good Lobna** 79.03
**Good Lord** 85.60
**Good Night** 95.30
Good night! Okay 95.30
**Gorgo** 79.09
Got no place to go, no love left for me to give 1.10, 5.05, 70.08, 77.10, 77.20, 77.45, 78.10, 87.05
GRAND WAZOO, THE 16
**Grand Wazoo, The** 16.02 64.22
**Grand Wazoo (Think It Over)** 82.02
GREASY LOVE SONGS 87
**Great Guy** 60.53
Green hocker croakin' in the Pygmy Twylyt 19.02, 52.08, 97.06
**Gross Man** 63.32
GROSS MAN! 63.32
**Groupie Bang Bang** 77.32
**Groupie Routine** 51.09
Grrr... Arf arf arf ar-ar-ar-ar-ar! Teeth out there, and ready to attack 'em 3.14
**GTR Trio** 75.08
GUITAR 50

**Gum Joy** 85.02
**Gumbo Variations, The** 8.05
**Gypsy Airs** 85.05


**H.R. 2911** 44.1
Hail Caesar!... 59.18, 89.08
**Half A Dozen Provocative Squats** 13.16
HALLOWEEN 71
HAMMERSMITH ODEON 89
Hands up! 58.07
**Hands With A Hammer** 54.16
**Handsome Cabin Boy, The** 64.17, 68.29, 72.07
Happy Saint Pattie's day, now! 55.18
**Happy Together** 12.08
**Harder Than Your Husband** 34.02
**Harmonica Fun** 68.35
**Harry and Rhonda** 41.03
**Harry-As-A-Boy** 41.11
HARRY, this is not DREAM GIRLS 41.03
**Harry, You're A Beast** 4.07, 51.08, 57.05, 61.17, 68.21, 85.16, 85.37, 85.65
HARRY! HARRY, is that YOU as a BOY? 41.11
Has anyone ever seen Ms. Pinky? 59.11
Have a new album called We're Only In It For The Money 85.63
HAVE I OFFENDED SOMEONE? 67
Have you ever heard their band? 63.12
Have you heard the news? 20.02, 93.22
**Have You Heard Their Band?** 63.12
He came on a Saturday afternoon from Manchester 94.04
He used to be very kind in his own crude way 25.02
**He Used To Cut The Grass** 29.07
He's got twenty million dollars 93.23
**He's So Gay** 41.12, 59.20, 67.05
He's so gay, he's very very gay 41.12, 59.20, 67.05,
**He's Right** 60.48
**He's Watching Us** 60.46
**Heavenly Bank Account** 34.16, 51.25, 93.23
**Heavy Duty Judy** 31.06, 55.01
Heh heh heh ye-yes!   95.01
**Heidelberg** 83.06
Hello? 91.08
Hello, anybody home? Special Delivery. 64.29
Hello. Before we start, I'd like to introduce the members of the group to you and have them play a little bit, so that we know everything works  96.01
Hello! Boy, got y'all JAMMED in here, don't dey? 55.01
Hello, boys and girls 94.01
Hello, folks  99.01

Hello, is this room service? 81.09
Hello! My name is Lisa Popeil  59.34
Hello, ready?!  91.08
Hello, teenage America, my name is Suzy Creemcheese 6.02
Hello, there, kids, it's your old friend Captain Beefheart! 68.07
Hello there, welcome to the show. No, we're not going to play 'Cheepnis' 30.06
Hello? Welcome to Carnegie Hall, ladies and gentlemen. 91.19
Hello! Well, good evening, ladies and gentlemen 86.01
**Help I'm A Rock** 1.13,  61.12, 77.13, 77.30, 78.13, 78.26, 92.02
Help I'm a rock, help I'm a rock 1.13, 77.13, 77.30, 78.13, 78.26, 92.02
**Here Comes The Gear, Lads** 60.01
Here comes the gear, lads! 60.01
**Here Lies Love** 58.03
Here lies love  58.03
Here's a little story I learned upstream in prison, Folsom Prison, 1968. Hey! 91.11
Here's another thing that you can do on the piano, if you have one around 68.11
Here's that thing about the FCC 88.12
**Hermitage** 83.03
Hey! Do you know what you are? 80.17, 89.11, 95.22
Hey! Ha! Ooh! There was a man, a little ole man 14.04
Hey Hey Hey all you girls in these industrial towns 28.04, 59.31
Hey! I'm only fourteen, sickly 'n thin 26.13, 59.32, 89.05
Hey punk, where you goin' with that flower in your hand? 4.10, 85.19, 85.40
Hey there people I'm Bobby Brown    26.09, 54.05, 67.01, 80.25, 89.19, 95.15
Hey yeah, yeah, some folks know about it 84.07
Hey, kids, let's have a hootenanny! 85.75
Hey, now, hey! Hey! Do you know what you are? 26.03
Hey, this is for all the Republicans in the audience! 45.07
Hey, what's new in Baltimore... 45.06, 58.29
Hey, who are these dudes? Are you a boy, or a girl 13.12
Hi and howdy doody, I'm the union man 11.09
Hi-ho, Silver, away! 54.06
Hi, friends. Now just be honest about it, friends and neighbors 60.10
Hi, uh, I'd like to say a few words about Warner Brothers  95.06
Hi! Welcome to the show tonight, ladies and gentlemen 80.01
His name is Stevie Vai 40.07, 56.18, 57.21, 81.02
**Hitch Hike** 72.08
Hmmm! Dat quite a massive improve'lence, dah-lin'! 41.13
Hob-noblin, wit de goblin 34.04, 67.03
**Hog Heaven** 31.02
**Hold On To Your Small Tiny Horsies** 77.33
**Holding The Group Back** 61.05
**Holiday In Berlin** 61.06
**Holiday In Berlin Full Blown** 9.06, 92.09
**Honey, Don't You Want A Man Like Me?** 23.05, 54.07, 59.06, 65.13, 80.09, 84.01, 86.14, 98.06

Honey honey, hey, baby don't you want a man like me? 23.05, 54.07, 59.06, 65.13, 80.09, 84.01, 86.14, 98.06
Honey, honey Honey, honey Honey, honey Honey, honey Why don't you sharpen it then  97.07
Honey, honey 52.09
**Hordern Intro (Incan Art Vamp)** 70.01
**Hot and Putrid** 63.29
**Hot Plate Heaven at the Green Hotel** 45.05, 50.14, 53.15, 79.12, 79.15
**Hot Poop** 4.11, 85.20, 85.41
HOT RATS 8
**Hotel Atlanta Incidentals** 50.14
**How Could I Be Such A Fool?** 1.06, 5.03, 68.17, 70.06, 72.11, 77.06, 77.24, 78.06, 78.19, 87.03
**How Did That Get In Here?** 85.50
How did the group get together? 72.06
How did you like that one?  95.10
How long? How long? 13.02
**How The Pigs' Music Works** 63.08
**How We Made It Sound That Way** 77.57
Howard . . . he's right! Ha ha ha! 60.48
Howdy folks. Alright, here's the deal, this is our last show here in London... 51.06
Hoy hoy roy dala data   98.03
**Hunchy Punchy** 85.06
**Hungry Freaks, Daddy** 1.01, 7.10, 77.01, 77.15, 77.46, 77.50, 77.64, 78.01, 78.25, 92.05, 93.01


**I Ain't Got No Heart** 1.02, 30.05, 70.07, 72.05, 77.02, 77.18, 77.27, 78.02, 78.17
I am gross and perverted 17.02, 23.07, 93.19
I am the heaven 20.09, 40.03
**I Am The Walrus** 79.16
I ate a hot dog, it tasted real good... 19.07, 52.11, 99.11
I been run down, Lord, 'n I been lied to 40.14, 45.10
I bin grad nei' kimma, und do hob I g'sehn 63.25
I can't stand the way he pouts 23.04, 37.07, 65.16
I can't see you, but I know you are out there  51.10
**I Come From Nowhere** 35.03
I come from nowhere 35.03
**I Could Be A Star Now** 60.57
I could have swore her hair was made of rayon...
I coulda swore her hair was made of rayon 21.02, 56.27, 70.17, 84.03
I couldn't say where she's coming' from, but I just met a lady named Dinah-Moe Humm 17.06, 37.06, 67.11, 70.24, 71.10, 86.19, 89.25, 93.16, 95.24
I crashed in the jungle while trying to keep a date 86.2
I don't do publicity balling for you anymore 4.09, 85.18, 85.39
**I Don't Even Care** 44.01, 93.21
**I Don't Know If I Can Go Through This Again** 3.12
I don't know much about dancin', that's why I got this song 26.15, 71.03, 71.15, 80.21, 89.02
I don't know that I'm on, but I don't get the sound of that chair 75.02

I don't need you, I don't want you  56.01
**I Don't Wanna Get Drafted** 64.29, 80.24
I don't wanna get drafted 34.20
I got a big dilemma, about my Big Leg Emma, uh huh 2.08
I got a girl with a little rubber head 22.04, 41.14, 59.12, 80.26
I got to be free, free as the wind... 56.21
I gotta fart son -- See my head here, see my head? My head?!... 58.16
**I Had A Dream About That** 63.31
I had a dream about that once 63.31
I have a feeling that it's all bought and sold 88.1
**I Have Been In You**  26.01, 59.17, 89.09
I have been in you 59.17
I have been in you, baby 89.09, 95.10
**I Heard A Note**   98.15
**I Just Can't Work No Longer** (Persuasions) 91.01
I just went out to get some cigarettes for him one day 60.52
I keep switching girls all the time 3.08
I knew you'd be surprised  95.17
I know the perfect thing to accompany this man's trumpet 6.07
**I Left My Heart In San Francisco** 55.06
I left my heart, way down in San Francisco 55.06
I mean, really. Really! I mean, you guys, what can I say, you guys are my favorite band. You gotta tell me something, are you here in Hollywood long? 51.09
I might be movin' to Montana soon 17.07, 56.05, 81.07, 96.10, 97.02
I might be moving to -- Hold it! Hold it! 52.19
I must be free 6.22, 23.02, 57.23, 91.29
I (My ay ay ay ay) must be free 91.29
I play a version of myself as Frank sees me 60.56
**I Promise Not To Come In Your Mouth** 23.03
I say WPLJ, really taste good to me 9.01
I say WPLJ, won't you take a drink with me 45.08
I signed on the line, for seven long years 54.23
I started out in Florida uh, producing a record at a studio 64.15
I think I can explain about about how the pigs' music works 63.08
I think my first animation was with cars runnin' over the tops of hills  95.04
I think that's probably one of the rarest Mothers albums too 85.56
I think the big problem, Ian, is that you've sort of gotta go "HOO-HAA!" as you do it 60.35
I think what we're gonna do right now is make something up   96.13
I told you the first time I met you  95.03
I tried to find how my heart could be so blind, dear 2.1, 2.15, 7.11
I used to have a job 45.05, 53.15
I used to watch him eat 6.25
I wanna tell you one more time, I wanna thank you, because I really appreciate this  95.24
I want a nasty little Jewish Princess 26.16, 67.14
**I Was A Teen-Age Malt Shop** 68.06

I was a Teen-age Malt Shop! Ha ha! 68.06
**I Was In A Drum** 63.23
I was sitting in a breakfast room in Allentown, Pennsylvania 21.05, 93.18
**I Wish Motorhead Would Come Back** 63.20
I worked in a cheesy newspaper company for a while but that was terrible 3.10
I would be so delighted! 64.30
I would go to Orlando if you would let me on your plane 51.21
I, do hereby solemnly swear... 59.01
I'd like to be . . . someplace else right now. 63.16
I'd like to dedicate an ode to Joe Lattanzi 68.34
I'd like to go back to-- to this thing one time 73.06
I'd like to say a few words about Warner Brothers   95.06
I'd like to tell you about the first time I went down to take some piano lessons from the lady on the corner 92.07
I'd like to tell you something. I'd like to play an encore for you. 91.33
**I'm A Band Leader** 64.20
I'm a band leader. 64.20
**I'm A Beautiful Guy** 34.07, 54.19
I'm a beautiful guy... 54.19
I'm a little pimp with my hair gassed back 8.02, 56.04
I'm a moron 'n this is my wife  95.08
I'm cryin', I'm cryin', cryin' for Sharleena 11.10, 40.04, 60.19, 91.28
**I'm Doomed** 60.36
I'm gonna tell you a story about Mary Lou... 56.34
I'm gonna tell you the way it is 4.07, 85.16, 85.37
I'm gross and perverted... 51.12
I'm losin' status at the high school 2.11
**I'm Not Satisfied** 1.10,  5.05,  0.08, 77.10, 77.20, 77.45, 78.10, 87.05
I'm only 14, sickly and thin... 51.07
I'm out at last 29.07
**I'm So Cute** 26.04, 59.09, 80.18, 95.17
**I'm So Happy I Could Cry** 72.09
**I'm Stealing The Towels** 13.20
I'm stealing the towels 13.20
I'm talkin' 'bout my baby 72.06
**I'm The Slime** 17.02, 23.07, 51.12, 93.19
I'm The Slime? 98.11
I've got to see you 68.05
**Ian Underwood Whips It Out** 6.16
**Ich bin den Himmel** 51.03, 91.21
**Idiot Bastard Snoop** 85.68
**Idiot Bastard Son, The**  52.10, 85.69
**If Only She Woulda** 34.19
If something gets in your way, just THINK IT Over 73.08
If the froggy come up a--with his satchel in his hand 15.03
**If We'd All Been Living In California** 6.19

If you decide to leave me, it's all over 5.13, 87.13, 87.16
**If You're Not A Professional Actor** 60.47
If you're not a professional actor 60.47
**Igor's Boogie, Phase One** 9.02
**Igor's Boogie, Phase Two** 9.05
**III Revised** 62.06
**Illinois Enema Bandit, The** 23.06, 31.07, 59.24, 70.11, 83.07, 84.02, 98.07
IMAGINARY DISEASES 76
**Imaginary Diseases** 76.06
Imagine me and you, I do 12.08
**Importance Of An Earnest Attempt (By Hand)** 92.01
**In Conclusion** 85.78
**In France** 40.02, 54.08, 67.04
**In Memoriam Edgar Varese** 1.13, 77.13, 78.13
In the beginning GOD made 'the light.' 59.02, 70.03, 86.03, 95.05
In the dark where all the fevers grow 18.09, 52.02, 57.01, 70.02, 71.09, 81.05, 86.02, 97.05
In today's rapidly changing world rock groups appear every fifteen minutes 23.04, 37.07, 65.16, 89.12, 95.23
**"In You" Rap/ Dedication** 95.10
**In-A-Gadda-Stravinsky** 50.06
**Inca Roads** 20.01, 31.03, 32.02, 32.06, 33.02, 50.26, 52.03, 55.13, 64.27, 79.04, 81.08, 97.07, 99.02
**Intelligent Design** 85.61
**Intro** 62.01, 94.01
**Intro Intros** 82.01
**Intro Rap/Baby Snakes** 37.01
**Intro To Music For Low Budget Orchestra** 60.44
**Introcious** 96.01
**Invocation And Ritual Dance Of The Young Pumpkin** 2.06
**Is That All There Is?** 50.31
**Is That Guy Kidding Or What?** 59.08
Is there anything good inside of you 20.08. 55.12, 80.19
Isaac Hayes, Gabby Hayes 55.16
**It Ain't Necessarily The Saint James Infirmary** 50.32
**It Ain't Real So What's The Deal** 73.07
**It Can't Happen Here** 1.13, 7.06, 77.13, 77.53, 78.13, 78.27, 93.04
It can't happen here, it can't happen here 1.13, 7.06, 77.13, 77.53, 78.13, 78.27, 93.04
It existed as a group called the Soul Giants 77.65
**It Just Might Be A One Shot Deal** 15.03, 73.04
**It Must Be A Camel** 8.06
It was September, the leaves were gold 5.10, 64.10, 87.10
It was the blackest night, there was no moon in sight 23.01, 37.02, 65.24, 67.07, 89.13, 95.18
It was the darkest night, there was no moon in sight 86.11
It wasn't very large 28.02, 54.13, 80.20
**It's A Good Thing We Get Paid To Do This** 60.41
It's a good thing we get paid to do this 60.41

It's a miserable Friday night 34.01
It's about all of the sunshine here in Finland... 52.01
It's always been a business issue 88.05
**It's From Kansas** 3.05
It's gettin' near dark 55.16
It's him, he's watching us! 60.46
It's hot 55.27
It's the middle of the night 6.09


**Janet's Big Dance Number** 13.15
**Jazz Discharge Party Hats** 36.09
JAZZ FROM HELL 47
**Jazz From Hell** 47.04
**JCB and Kansas on the Bus #1** 58.07
**JCB and Kansas on the Bus #2** 58.15
**Jeff Quits** 60.5
**Jelly Roll Gum Drop** 5.06, 87.06, 87.14, 87.19
Jelly Roll Gum Drop, got my eyes on you 5.06, 87.06, 87.14, 87.19
**Jesus Thinks You're A Jerk** 53.17, 93.31
JESUS, that was terrific! 41.21
**Jewish Princess** 26.16, 67.14
**Jezebel Boy** 53.13
Jezebel Boy! 53.13
**Jim and Tammy's Upper Room** 50.11
**Jim/Roy** 68.24
**Jimmy Carl Black Philosophy Lesson** 61.04
Jingle bells, Jingle bells, Jingle all the way 41.18
JOE'S CAMOUFLAGE 98
JOE'S CORSAGE 72
JOE'S DOMAGE 73
**Joe's Garage** 28.02, 54.13, 80.20
JOE'S GARAGE ACT I 28
JOE'S GARAGE ACTS II AND III 29
JOE'S MENAGE 84
JOE'S XMASAGE 75
John Cage's work has had an influence on Lumpy Gravy 85.51
**Johnny Darling** 56.31
**Jolly Good Fellow** 69.03
**Jones Crusher** 26.05, 37.04, 89.16, 95.21
**Jonestown** 39.07
**Jumbo Go Away** 34.18
Jumbo, go away 34.18
JUST ANOTHER BAND FROM L.A. 14
**Just One More Time** 3.16
Just popped a couple 98.14
Just so I can hear the song again 73.01

**Kaiser Rolls** 70.15
**Kaiser Rolls (Du Jour)** 70.27
**Kangaroos** 3.20
**Kayak (On Snow), A** 63.18
**Keep It Greasey** 29.05, 54.06, 70.23, 80.06
Keep it greasey so it'll go down easy 29.05, 54.06, 70.23, 80.06
Kenny, remember that part on that Frog Song 73.03
**Kenny's Booger Story** 64.04
**King Kong** 3.18, 6.26, 50.15, 50.25, 54.24, 57.12, 61.11, 79.10, 89.23, 91.16, 92.14, 95.14, 99.13
**Kung Fu** 64.24, 96.03

L.A. in the summer of '69 22.07, 64.23
**L'Histoire Du Soldat** 57.18
La la la la la la la 9.09
La la lala la la lala lah lah 2.03
**Lad Searches The Night For His Newts, The** 13.30
Ladies and gentlemen, attention, please. I'd really like to thank you for coming up here to this, uh, musical thing 77.41, 78.31
Ladies and gentlemen, do you like the band? 68.04
Ladies and gentlemen, here he goes, Peter Rundel, he seems to be disgusted. 62.15
Ladies and gentlemen, making his first Sydney appearance, or maybe his second Sydney appearance... 59.07
Ladies and gentlemen, the name of this song, seeing as we are confronted with a partial, how shall we say, language barrier here, we don't want to press the issue too much... 52.13
Ladies and gentlemen, the President of the United States! 2.01, 7.09, 93.02
Ladies and gentlemen, this is the end of our program. 97.11
Ladies and gentlemen, watch Ruth! 19.06, 99.10
Ladies and gentlemen! 13.01
**Later That Night** 5.08, 87.08
**Latex Solar Beef** 12.05
LATHER 65
**Läther** 65.20
**Learning "Penis Dimension"** 60.10
**Leather Goods** 65.28
Leaving in fifty minutes, Frank. 60.07
**Lecture from Festival Hall Show** 68.28
**Legend Of The Golden Arches, The** 6.06
**Legend Of The Illinois Enema Bandit, The** 65.09
**Lemme Take You To The Beach** 24.03, 65.10
Lemme take you to the beach 24.03, 65.10
Let me get a phase sound 98.04

Let me tell you right now, man: You got your armies 60.34
**Let's Eat Out** 85.08
Let's Make The Water Turn Black 4.13, 51.08, 57.04, 61.16, 85.22, 85.43
Let's make this a democratic process--how would you like to have this song end? 76.05
**Let's Move To Cleveland** 45.09, 50.03, 50.06, 50.09, 50.17, 50.22, 50.30, 50.31, 55.17, 56.10, 79.03, 79.05, 79.14
Let's move to Cleveland 45.09
Let's play "Doctor." 89.25
**L'Histoire Du Soldat (Stravinsky): Royal March** 57.18
**Library Card** 69.01
**Light Is All That Matters** 79.14
Light, is just a vibration of the note, too 85.52
**Like It Or Not** 61.03
Like to introduce the band 68.18
Like, you know, you know what is it 85.68
**Lil' Clanton Shuffle** 64.28
**Lion Roar and Drums From Freak Out!** 77.39
**Lisa's Life Story** 59.34
Listen carefully, spider of destiny 25.03
**Little Beige Sambo** 44.03
**Little Green Rosetta, A** 29.10, 65.03
**Little Green Scratchy Sweaters and Courduroy Ponce** 13.33
**Little House I Used To Live In** 12.01, 89.17
**Little March, The** 58.09
**Little Rubber Girl** 56.01
**Little Umbrellas** 8.04
**Lives in Mojave in a Winnebago** 89.29
**Living Garbage Truck** 60.02
**Lobster Girl** 59.26
**Local Butcher** 85.04
**London Cab Tape** 60.38
LONDON SYMPHONY ORCHESTRA VOL.1 38
LONDON SYMPHONY ORCHESTRA VOL.2 48
**Lonely Little Girl** 4.15, 70.18, 84.04, 85.24, 85.45, 85.62, 85.72, 85.77
**Lonely Person Devices** 59.11
**Lonesome Cowboy Burt** 13.09
**Lonesome Cowboy Burt (Swaggart Version)** 55.23
**Lonesome Cowboy Nando** 59.35
**Lonesome Electric Turkey** 12.09
Look, nobody in his right mind believes for a minute that an artist makes more money than the record company 88.09
Looks to me like something funny is goin' on around here 28.05
Lord, have mercy on the people of England 13.34
LOST EPISODES, THE 64
**Lost In A Whirlpool** 64.02
**Louie Louie (At the Royal Albert Hall in London)** 6.07

Love is a burning thing 55.02
**Love Of My Life** 5.02, 30.04, 56.09, 87.02, 87.21
**Love of My Life Mudd Club Version** 56.09
Love of my life, I love you so  5.02, 30.04, 56.09, 87.02, 87.21
**Love Story** 39.05
**Low Budget Rock and Roll Band** 77.41, 78.31
**Lucille Has Messed My Mind Up** 28.08, 54.03
Lucille has messed my mind up 28.08, 54.03
**Lucy's Seduction of A Bored Violinist and Postlude** 13.19
**Luigi and The Wise Guys** 36.10
LUMPY GRAVY 3, 85
**Lumpy Gravy** 74.02
**Lumpy Gravy - Part One** 85.29
**Lumpy Gravy - Part Two** 85.30
**Lumpy Gravy "Shuffle"** 85.51
**Lumpy Gravy Part One** 3.01-12, 85.29
**Lumpy Gravy Part Two** 3.13-22, 85.30
LUMPY MONEY 85


**M.O.I Anti-Smut Loyalty Oath** 59.01
**Machinery** 77.59
**Madison Panty-Sniffing Festival** 59.05
**Magdalena** 14.04, 91.11
**Magic Fingers** 13.27, 13.39, 59.04, 71.05
**Magic Pig** 91.22
MAKE A JAZZ NOISE HERE 57
Make a jazz noise here! 57.11
**Make A Sex Noise** 59.15
Mama! Mama! Someone said they made some noise 4.04, 60.43, 85.13, 85.34,  93.03
**Mammy Anthem** 51.04
**Mammy Nuns** 41.02
**Man From Utopia Meets Mary Lou, The** 36.07
**Man With The Woman Head** 21.08
Man! This stuff is great! 13.21
**Managua/Police Car/Drum Solo**   95.11
**Manx Needs Women** 23.09, 86.10
Many well-dressed people in several locations 26.17
**Marque-Son's Chicken** 40.09, 79.08
**Martin Lickert's Story** 60.52
**Mary Lou** 56.34
**Massaggio Galore** 47.08
**Massive Improve'lence** 41.13
**Master Ringo** 69.05
Maybe the kayak is just a big worm 63.33
Maybe you should stay with yo' mama 26.18
Maybe you thought I was the Packard Goose 29.08

Me! I must be free 60.20
Meanwhile, the snack enters the mind of Dom DeWild 61.08
**Medley #1 (Persuasions)** 91.03
**Medley #2 (Persuasions)** 91.06
**Medley #3 (Persuasions)** 91.07
**Meek Shall Inherit Nothing, The** 34.14, 41.09, 80.04
**Meow** 58.17
**Merely A Blues In A** 66.04
**Metal Man Has Won His Wings** 68.08
**MGM** 77.55
Mike Scheller says his life is a mess 58.28, 80.12
Mister America walk on by your schools that do not teach  1.01, 7.10, 77.01, 77.46, 77.64, 78.01, 92.05, 93.01
**Mo' n Herb's Vacation** 38.04
**Moggio 36.11, 58.30**
**Mom and Dad**  4.04, 60.43, 85.13, 85.34, 85.73, 93.03
**Mondo Hollywood** 68.15
**Montana** 17.07, 52.19, 56.05,  81.07, 96.10, 97.02
**Montana (Whipping Floss)** 52.19
**Montreal** 76.07
Moo-ahhh, moo-ahhh, moo-ahhh! 10.01
**Moon Will Never Be The Same, The** 75.07
**More Trouble Every Day** 19.09, 97.10
**More Trouble Every Day (Swaggart Version)** 55.25
**Mormon Xmas Dance Report** 75.01
**Motel Lobby** 60.05
**Motel Room** 60.07
Mother People 4.18, 7.02, 85.27, 85.48
**Motherly Love** 1.05,  72.02, 77.05,  77.19, 77.43, 78.05,  78.22
Motherly love, motherly love 1.05, 77.05, 77.19, 78.05, 78.22
MOTHERMANIA 7
**Mothers at KPFK** 68.34
Mothers Of Invention have spent many long hours in rehearsal 68.28
**Motorhead's Midnight Ranch** 13.28
**Mount St. Mary's Concert Excerpt** 64.06
**Mousie's First Xmas** 75.1
**Move It Or Park It** 50.16
**Mozart Ballet** 58.05
**Mozart Piano Sonata in B flat** 58.05, 94.03
Mr. America, walk on by your schools that do not teach see Mister America
**Mr. Clean** 75.03
**Mr. Green Genes** 6.17, 55.10, 99.13
**Ms. Pinky** 22.04, 59.12, 80.26
**Mud Shark** 12.02, 91.34
Mud shark 12.02
Mud shark, mud shark, you could hear the steam baby 12.05

**Mudd Club** 34.13, 41.08, 80.03
**Mudshark Interview** 60.31
**Muffin Man** 21.09, 59.22, 70.26, 71.12, 86.23, 89.27, 95.26
**Murder By Numbers** 53.12
**Music from "The Big Squeeze"** 94.08
**Muthers/Power Trio** 75.05
My baby's got Jones crushin' love 26.05, 37.04, 89.16, 95.21
My dandruff is loose 17.04
**My Favorite Album** 85.56
**My Guitar Wants To Kill Your Mama** 10.08, 56.03, 58.25
**My Head?** 58.16
My husband, Frank, had a very interesting gig tonight 75.01
My name is Bill Harrington 95.08
My name is Burtram, I am a redneck 13.09
My name is Ian Underwood 6.16
My name is Nando, I'm a Marine biologist... 59.35, 59.35
My name is Swaggart, I am an asshole 55.23
My name's Ken... 58.15
**My Pet Theory** 77.70, 78.24
**Mysterioso** 13.17
MYSTERY DISC 68
**Mystery Roach** 13.02


**N-Lite** 63.19
**N. Double A, AA** 85.58
**Naked City** 69.09
**Nancy and Mary Music** 11.04
**Nanook Rubs It** 18.02
**Nap Time** 69.07
**Nasal Retentive Calliope Music** 4.12, 85.21, 85.42
**Naval Aviation In Art?** 27.03, 39.02, 65.02, 74.01
**Navanax** 63.07
**Necessity** 77.66
**New Brown Clouds** 73.02
**New York's Finest Crazy Persons** 95.07
**New York's Finest Crazy Persons 2** 95.29
**Nig Biz** 54.23
**Night School** 47.01
**9/8 [nine-eight] Objects** 69.08
**Nine Types Of Industrial Pollution** 6.03
**No Commercial Potential** 1.14, 77.14, 78.14
No more credit from the liquor store 21.07, 54.04, 57.24, 58.33, 70.10, 86.13
**No No No** 5.11, 87.11, 87.15
**No Not Now** 35.01, 41.17
No not now 35.01
**No Waiting For the Peanuts To Dissolve** 58.21

316

No, Jeff 13.21
**No, No Cherry** 56.32
No, no, don't eat it 83.08
**None Of The Above** 62.10
**None Of The Above (Revised and Previsited)** 69.12
Not duke, not queen, but king 60.08
Now believe me when I tell you that my song is really true 4.13, 85.22, 85.43
Now if you still want to get your name in magazines 6.19
Now ladies and gentlemen, we don't normally do this but just because this is St. Patrick's Day.. 59.15
Now the sound that you hear in the background right now is the sound caused by George Duke agitating two metal insignias... 56.25
Now this is a new song--you haven't heard this one before 84.01
**Now You See It--Now You Don't** 30.08
Now, dis nasty sucker is de respondable party fo de en-whiffment 41.05
Now, this afternoon on my way down the elevator we stopped at the lobby 53.12
Now, we don't come up here because we feel like walkin' four flights at three o'clock in the morning. 64.18
**Nullis Prettis** 1.14, 77.14, 78.14
**Nun Suit Painted On Some Old Boxes, A** 13.26
**NYC Audience** 71.01
**NYC Halloween Audience** 59.23


**Objects** 77.34
**Occam's Razor** 83.05
**Ocean Is The Ultimate Solution, The** 25.07, 65.25
**Octandre** 92.13
**Oddients** 76.01
Of course we'll send the penguin through the flaming hoop tonight! 60.37
Oh God, Oh God, Oh God, Oh God, Oh God, Oh, Oh, Oh 68.30, 94.12
Oh God, stop! Oh God, oh God! 58.10
Oh, I smoked a Pall Mall 68.03
**Oh, In The Sky** 92.12
Oh, in the sky 92.12
Oh, jeez. Beech-Nut Spearmint Gum 75.06
Oh little girl of mine.. 56.29
Oh my God! Beautiful! God! It's God! I see God! 4.12, 85.20, 85.41
**Oh No** 3.03, 10.09, 51.20, 57.07, 61.19, 79.11, 97.09
**Oh No Again** 3.09
Oh no I don't believe it 10.09, 57.07, 97.09
Oh-oh! Wait a minute! What? 41.19
Oh, rock, rock! 68.16
Oh, still drinks it, man 60.29
**Oh-Umm** 63.03
Ohh. Umm. Hmm. 63.03
Oh yeah! That's just fine! Come on boys! Just one more time! 3.16

Okay, hold your applause for one second 54.15

Okay, if you throw anything else on the stage, this concert is over. 58.38

Okay, is it just about time, you guy? What d'you say? 60.32

Okay, ladies and gentlemen, my son, Dweezil 54.01

Okay, listen this is very important, okay? 59.01

Okay? Now if you still want to get your name in magazines 6.19

Okay, now, the entertaining part of this section 94.02

Okay, ready? Okay, yeah. 72.05

Okay? Rolling, two 77.31

Okay, thank you, thank you, thank you! 57.01

Okay. The name of this song is "Farther Oblivion" and it has a tango in the middle of it. 76.04

**Okay To Tap Dance** 1.13, 77.13, 78.13

Okay, we're gonna do another brief re-tuning 92.09

Okay, we have sort of a rock and roll song for you now 96.14

**Old Curiosity Shoppe** 94.05

OLD MASTERS BOX 1 43

OLD MASTERS BOX 2 46

OLD MASTERS BOX 3 49

**On The Bus** 28.06

**On the Planet of the Baritone Women** 53.02

On the, on the We're— on the We're Only In It For The Money album you take a lot of [...] of the hippies 85.70

Once again, the Jewitt, Klopfenstein and Things program takes great pride in presenting to you 75.11

**Once Again, Without The Net** 50.09

Once that you've decided on a killing 53.12

**Once Upon A Time** 51.02, 91.20

Once upon a time, it was in Albuquerque, New Mexico 36.09

Once upon a time, musta been 'round October, few years back 41.01, 93.27

Once upon a time, way back a long time ago... 51.02

One 'n one is eleven! 53.04, 54.15

**One Man, One Vote** 44.02

One of the major songs on that album was the Watts Riot song, "Trouble Every Day." 77.51

ONE SHOT DEAL 83

ONE SIZE FITS ALL 20

One of the things that I like best about playing in New York 30.09

One! One, two, three, one, two, three 77.24

One! One, two, three, one, two, three 78.19

One, two, one, two, three . . . Brown shoes don't make it 96.19

One, two, one, two, three, four . . . And, it will fall down 73.07

One, two, three, four 73.02, 85.55, 89.26, 95.25

One, two, three, four! I couldn't say where she's coming' from 71.10

One, two, three, four! I don't know much about dancin', that's why I got this song 71.03

One, two, three, four . . . Oh no I don't believe it" 97.09

One, two, three, four . . . You can be scared when it gets too real 73.04

One, two, three, one, two, three . . .Who Are The Brain Police?", Section C, take one 77.49

Ooh yeah, she was a fine girl... 51.17
Ooh, the way you love me baby... 59.04
Ooh, the way you love me, lady, I get so hard now I could die 13.27, 13.39, 71.05
Ooh well, oh   99.08
Ooo-ooo, do you like my new car? 13.23
**Opening Night at "Studio Z"** 68.03
**Opus 1, no. 1-6** 42.01-11
**Opus 4, nos. 1-4** 42.12-17
**Orange County Lumber Truck** 10.10, 51.08, 57.06, 92.06
ORCHESTRAL FAVORITES 27
**Original Duke Of Prunes** 68.02
**Original Group, The** 77.65
**Original Mothers at Fillmore East** 68.2
**Original Mothers at The Broadside (Pomona)** 68.14
**Original Mothers Rehearsal** 68.16
**Orrin Hatch On Skis** 50.19
**Our Bizarre Relationship** 6.10
**Out in Cucamonga** 21.06
**Outrage At Valdez** 62.04
**Outside Now** 29.06, 50.10, 53.14, 56.19
**Outside Now (Original Solo)** 50.10
**Outside Now Again** 39.06
OVER-NITE SENSATION 17
**Overture To A Holiday In Berlin** 9.03
Ow ow ow ow, rundee rundee rundee dinny wop wop 6.12
**Owner of a Lonely Heart** 54.02


**Pachuco Gavotte** 100.02
**Packard Goose** 29.08
**Panty Rap** 30.06
**Party Scene from "Mondo Hollywood"** 68.15
**Peaches En Regalia** 8.01, 12.10, 89.03, 91.13
**Peaches III** 30.15
**Pedro's Dowry** 27.02, 38.02, 65.19
**Penguin In Bondage** 19.01, 45.04, 96.04, 99.03
**Penguin In Bondage (Swaggart Version)** 55.26
**Penis Dimension** 13.24, 82.10
Penis dimension 13.24
**Pentagon Afternoon** 62.11
**Percussion Insert Session Snoop** 77.36
**Percussion Object 1 and 2** 77.38
**Perfect Stranger** 39.01
**Perhaps in Maryland** 88.02
PHILLY '76 86
**Phyniox** 98.01, 98.14

319

**Piano** 100.10
**Piano/Drum Duet** 58.04
**Pick Me, I'm Clean** 30.12, 80.10
**Piece One** 68.23
**Piece Two** 68.25
**Pieces of A Man (Persuasions)** 91.04
**Pig With Wings, A** 63.27
Pinch it good! You know, that confinement loaf is real good stuff 53.05
**Pink Napkins** 32.07
**Pinocchio's Furniture** 33.03
**Planet Of My Dreams** 40.10
**Planet Of The Baritone Women** 53.02
**Plastic People 2**.01, 7.09, 51.15, 68.19, 72.03, 93.02
Plastic people 72.03
Plastic people, oh baby now, you're such a drag 2.01, 7.09, 93.02
Plastic people, you gotta go 51.15, 68.19
Play the harmonica 68.35, 94.06
PLAYGROUND PSYCHOTICS 60
**Playground Psychotics** 60.30
Please! Say please! 60.23
**Po-Jama People** 20.04
**Pojama Prelude** 96.11
**Police Car/Drum Solo** 95.11
Poo-lah, Poo-la-ah poo-lah 61.06
**Poodle Lecture, The** 59.02, 70.03, 86.03, 95.05
**Poofter's Froth Wyoming Plans Ahead** 21.04
Poofter's Froth, Wyoming 21.04
**Poop Rock** 77.58
Poor baby! 60.17
**Porn Wars** 44.09
**Porn Wars Deluxe** 93.29
**Pound Bass and Keyboards Solo** 95.09
**Pound For A Brown, A** 6.15, 23.08, 33.04, 50.24, 50.32, 61.14, 62.16, 89.08, 91.25, 92.10
**Pound for a Brown Solos** 56.12
**Power Trio from The Saints 'n Sinners** 68.09
**Prelude To "The Purse"** 75.02
**Prelude To King Kong** 6.13
**Prelude to the Afternoon of a Sexually Aroused Gas Mask** 10.03
**"pretty pat"** 72.01
Primer mi carucha, Chevy '39 14.05, 91.12
**Progress?** 61.02
**Project X** 6.21
**Prologue** 41.01, 61.01
**Promiscuous** 53.07, 93.26
**Proto-Minimalism** 58.14
**Psychedelic Money** 77.61

**Psychedelic Music** 77.54
Psychedelic music is here to stay 96.18
**Psychedelic Upholstery** 77.60
**Pumped And Waxed** 94.10
**Punky's Whips** 23.04, 37.07, 65.16, 89.12, 95.23
**Purple Haze** 55.15
Purple haze, all in my brain 55.15
**Purple Lagoon** 65.18, 86.01, 89.01
**Purple Lagoon/Approximate** 23.15
**Purse, The** 75.06
**Put A Little Motor In 'Em** 63.35
**Put A Motor In Yourself** 63.02
Put that mike down, Frank, it's obscene 60.30
**Pygmy Twylyte** 19.02, 52.08, 97.06


QuAUDIOPHILIAc 74
**Questi Cazzi Di Piccione** 62.12
Quiet, so I can tune up 75.08


Raah! Attack! Attack! 63.22
**Radio Interview** 71.16
**Radio Is Broken, The** 36.04
Ralph Humphrey on duck call 96.16
**Rat Tomago** 26.07
**RDNZL** 24.04, 52.04, 58.32, 64.25, 65.12, 96.09, 99.06
**Re-gyptian Strut** 65.01
**Ready, Marge?** 60.44
**Reagan At Bitburg** 63.05
**Reagan at Bitburg some more** 88.13
**Real World Thematic Extrapolations** 80.22
**Really Little Voice** 85.75
**Redneck Eats** 13.12
**REDUNZL** 24.04
**Reeny Ra** 98.03
**Regyptian Strut** 25.04
**Regyptian Strut (1993)** 65.27
**Rejected Mexican Pope Leaves The Stage, The** 61.07
**Religious Superstition** 63.13
**Remember Freddie and Jo?** 11.06, 86.16
**Republicans** 50.03
**Return of the Hunch-Back Duke** 58.12
**Return of the Son of Monster Magnet, The** 1.14, 77.14, 78.14
RETURN OF THE SON OF SHUT AND PLAY YER GUITAR 33
**Return Of The Son Of Shut Up 'N Play Yer Guitar** 33.02
**Revenge Of The Knick Knack People** 65.29
**Revised Music For Guitar And Low-Budget Orchestra** 24.02, 65.11

**Rewards Of A Career In Music** 92.07
RHONDA, that EVIL PRINCE 41.06
**Rhymin' Man** 53.06
Rhymin' Man, tall and tan 53.06
Rico! Youngblood! Wake up! 53.08
**Ride My Face To Chicago** 50.19, 54.10
Ride my face to Chicago 54.10
Right. This is a song, folks, about dental floss. 96.10
Right away. Now what I say 75.04
Right now I have two hit records on the charts, but it has not made me any money 85.61
**Right There** 58.10
**Ring Of Fire** 55.02
**Ritual Dance of the Child Killer** 1.14, 77.14, 78.14
**Road Ladies** 11.02, 93.12
ROAD TAPES VENUE 1  92
ROAD TAPES VENUE 2  96
**Roland's Big Event/Strat Vindaloo** 69.04
Rolling? This is 77.32
Rolling, Kerry? No-no, don't do it.  95.01
**Rollo** 74.03, 76.02, 83.09
Ron, Ron, Ron 57.15
**Ronnie Sings?** 64.03
**Ronnie's Booger Story 64.05**
**Room Service** 52.09, 81.09, 96.07
ROXY AND ELSEWHERE 19
ROXY BY PROXY  99
**Roy's Halloween Gas Mask**  95.14
**Royal March From "L'Histoire Du Soldat"** 57.18
**Rubber Shirt** 26.1
**Rudy Wants To Buy Yez A Drink** 11.09, 86.15
**Run Home Cues, #2** 64.11
**Run Home Cues, #3** 64.13
**Run Home Slow Theme**  58.08, 64.09, 68.01
**Run Home Slow: Main Title Theme** 58.08
**Ruth Is Sleeping** 62.09
**Ruthie-Ruthie** 51.10
Ruthie-Ruthie, where did you go? 51.10
**Rykoniki**  100.09

**Sad Jane** 38.01
**Saliva Can Only Take So Much** 63.14
Saliva can only take so much. 63.14
**Sam With The Showing Scalp Flat Top** 21.03
Sam with the showing scalp flat top 21.03
**Samba Funk** 90.05
**San Ber'dino** 20.07, 89.29, 95.27
**Sanzini Brothers** 60.40

**Satumaa (Finnish Tango)** 52.14
**Say Please** 60.23
Say that again, please? "Whipping Post"? Oh sorry, we don't know that one. Anything else? 52.19
**Scratch and Sniff** 79.07
**Scrutinizer Postlude** 28.09
Scum Bag, Scum Bag 60.25
**Scumbag** 60.25
**Sealed Tuna Bolero** 13.08
**Secret Greasing** 87.2
**Section 8, Take 22** 85.55
**Secular Humanism** 63.21, 90.03
Sell us a president, agency man 61.09, 68.26, 68.27
**Semi-Fraudulent/Direct-From-Hollywood Overture** 13.01
**Serious Fan Mail** 87.17
**Sex** 36.02, 67.06
**Sexual Harassment In The Workplace** 50.01
Shall We Take Ourselves Seriously? 58.28, 80.12
**Sharleena** 11.10, 40.04, 50.23, 54.01, 60.19, 64.30, 91.28
She chooses all the clothes 13.18,
She had that Camarillo brillo 17.01, 59.21, 70.25, 71.11, 86.22, 89.26, 93.14, 95.25
She lives in Mojave in a Winnebago 20.07, 95.27
**She Painted Up Her Face** 13.14
She painted up her face 13.14, 13.16, 59.13, 91.15
**She Said**    95.06
She said    95.06
She was the daughter of a wealthy Florentine Pogen 20.05, 55.11, 56.23, 81.11, 97.04
She's just like a Penguin in Bondage, boy 45.04,  55.26, 96.04, 99.03
She's my groupie bang bang 77.32
She's only seventeen 35.06
She's such a dignified lady 86.17
Sheets of fire, ladies and gentlemen, sheets of fire. 91.24
SHEIK YERBOUTI 26
**Sheik Yerbouti Tango** 26.11
Shh, shhh, are you upset? 56.28
**Ship Ahoy** 32.04, 74.06
SHIP ARRIVING TOO LATE TO SAVE A DROWNING WITCH 35
**Shortly (suite)** 92.09
**Shove It Right In** 13.18, 59.13, 91.15
SHUT AND PLAY YER GUITAR 31
SHUT AND PLAY YER GUITAR SOME MORE 32
**Shut Up 'N Play Yer Guitar** 31.03
**Shut Up 'N Play Yer Guitar Some More** 32.06
Sid, you'll have to get on the mike 85.53
**Sinister Footwear** 34.05
**Sinister Footwear 2nd mvt.** 57.20

**Sinister Footwear II** 40.05
**Sink Trap** 85.01
**Skweezit Skweezit Skweezit** 68.30
**Slack 'Em All Down** 98.05
**Sleazette** 94.02
SLEEP DIRT 25
**Sleep Dirt** 25.06, 98.08
**Sleeping In A Jar** 6.09, 60.14, 61.15, 91.26, 92.11
**Small Eternity With Yoko Ono** 60.26
**Smell My Beard** 56.25
Smurf mee! 60.49
So, uh, I'd just like to tell you about a little incident at Shrine Auditorium. 64.01
**Society Pages** 34.06, 54.18
**Sofa** 23.12
**Sofa # [No.] 1** 20.03, 20.09, 51.03, 55.14, 91.21
**Sofa #2** 51.28
**Soft-Sell Conclusion** 2.07
Some folks are hot, and some folks are not 96.11
Some of the great sounds from out of the past 87.20
Some of you may know that the tango 19.10
Some of you might not agree 26.03, 95.22
Some people's hot, some people's cold 20.04
Some take THE BIBLE for what it's worth 41.09
Somebody approached me with an interesting question about, uh, the title of the first album, Freak Out! 77.61
**Someplace Else Right Now** 63.16
**Son Of Mr. Green Genes** 8.03
**Son Of Orange County** 19.08, 97.09
**Son Of Suzy Creamcheese** 2.13
Son-of-a-bitch, you did this one, you did that one 68.31
**Soul Polka** 79.11
**Soup 'N Old Clothes** 31.07
**Space Boogers** 83.02
Special delivery . . . registered mail . . . 34.20
**Special Delivery** 80.24
**Speed-Freak Boogie** 68.13
**Spew King** 60.35
**Spider Of Destiny** 25.03, 65.21
**Squeeze It, Squeeze It, Squeeze It** 94.12
**St. Alfonzo's Pancake Breakfast** 18.03
**St. Etienne** 47.07
**Stairway To Heaven** 55.28
**Star Wars Won't Work** 57.13
Star Wars won't work 57.13
**Status Back Baby** 2.11, 60.37
**Steal Away** 68.05

**Stevie's Spanking** 40.07, 56.18, 57.21, 81.02
**Stick It Out** 29.02, 80.23, 91.23
**Stick Together** 36.08, 56.02
**Stink-Foot [Stinkfoot]** 18.09, 52.02, 57.01, 70.02, 71.09, 81.05, 86.02, 97.05
**Stolen Moments** 53.11
**Story of Willie The Pimp** 68.31
Straighten up in dat chair and pay ATTENTIUM 41.07
**Stranded In The Jungle** 86.20
**Strat Vindaloo** 69.04
**Stravinsky, L'Histoire Du Soldat: Royal March** 57.18
**Strictly Genteel (The Finale)** 13.34, 27.01, 48.03, 57.25, 59.37
Stroke me pompadour 41.15
**Stucco Homes** 33.05
STUDIO TAN 24
**Stuff Up The Cracks** 5.13, 87.13, 87.16
**Subcutaneous Peril** 94.13
**Suckit Rockit** 75.09
**Suicide Chump** 34.17, 51.26, 71.14
**Sunrise Redeemer** 50.17
Sunrise, get up in the mornin' 19.03
**Sunshine Of Your Love** 55.16
**Super Grease** 60.17
Sure, man, and I'll go until two and I'm gonna be in there supporting 'em 60.05
**Suzy Creamcheese (What's Got Into You?)** 77.42
Suzy Creamcheese, oh mama now, what's got into you? 2.13
Suzy? Yes? Suzy Creamcheese? Yes? 1.14, 77.14, 78.14
**Swans? What Swans?** 50.24
**Sweet Leilani** 51.19
"Sweet Leilani," in A. Just pretend it was 30 years ago... 51.19
**Switching Girls** 3.08
**Sy Borg** 29.03
Sy Borg, gimme dat, gimme dat 29.03
**Systems Of Edges** 50.26


**T'Mershi Duween** 52.15, 57.15, 69.06, 98.02, 99.04
**Take Me Out To The Ball Game** 56.14
Take two 77.5
**Take Your Clothes Off** 3.22
**Take Your Clothes Off When You Dance** 4.16, 59.33, 64.07, 84.05, 85.25, 85.46, 85.76, 98.10
**Take Your Clothes Off When You Dance 2** 70.19
**Tears Began To Fall** 12.11, 91.14
Tears began to fall 12.11, 91.14
**Teen-Age Grand Finale** 85.09
**Teen-age Prostitute** 35.06
**Teen-Age Wind** 34.01, 56.21

**Telephone Conversation** 4.05, 85.14, 85.35
**Tell Me You Love Me** 11.05, 30.07, 51.27
Tell me you love me  11.05, 30.07, 51.27
**Tengo Na Minchia Tanta** 6.24
**Terry Firma** 89.21
Thank you; Brian, I could use a little bit more monitor 19.01
Thank you, Chairman Miller, members of the Senate Judicial Proceedings Committee 88.02
**Thank You / Dinah Moe Humm** 95.24
Thank you, good night 9.09
Thank you. How's the sound balance out there? 82.05
Thank you, Lou. Hey, we're gonna have a little show time now 75.05
Thank You -- May I see your papers please?... 58.24
Thank you! Now this is a, this is an instrumental song, it's a tender, slow-moving ballad sort of a song 66.01
Thank you. Okay, sit down, some more raw unbridled buffoonery... 56.01
Thank you! Okay, we have sort of a rock and roll song for you now  96.14
Thank you! Thank you. Ralph Humphrey on duck call    96.16
Thank you ...thank you very much ...awright, does anybody here know where Palmdale is 19.04
Thank you! This is a song about the punk bands that come from Los Angeles 80.07
Thank you! . . . This is called "Black Napkins" 70.09
Thank you very much, Mr. Zappa. Ah, I'm very pleased to be here on behalf of the Administration 55.20
Thank you. Thank you. Thank you, thank you, thank you and thank you. 62.01
Thank you. Thank you very much. Thank you very, very, very much. I'd like to tell you a little bit about this here band 82.02
Thank you very much. We'll play another conglomerate item for you now 91.13
Thass right, folks! We talkin' de hypocritical Jeezis-jerknuh parodise dey call LAS VAGRUS NEVADRUH! 41.10
That is the sound of a very short cymbal  97.03
**That Ol' G Minor Thing Again** 50.13
**That Problem With Absolutely Free** 85.63
**That Would Be The End Of That** 63.39
**That's Not Really A Shuffle** 50.15
**That's Not Really Reggae** 50.07
That's religious superstition. 63.13
That's right, honey  99.02
That's right, "Muffin Man"! Girl, you thought he was a man but he was a muffin 71.12
That's the kind of guy 60.27
**The Adventures of Greggery Peccary** 24.01, 65.26, 82.06-09
The adventures of Greggery Peccary! 24.01, 65.26
**The Air** 6.20
The air escaping from your mouth 6.20
THE BEST BAND YOU NEVER HEARD IN YOUR LIFE 55
**The Birth of Captain Beefhear**t 68.07
**The Black Page #1** 23.10, 65.14
**The Black Page #2** 23.13, 37.03, 89.15, 95.20

**The Black Page Drum Solo** 23.10
**The Blackouts** 64.01
**The Booger Man** 56.26
**The Broadside (Pomona)** 68.14
**The Central Scrutinizer** 28.01, 93.28
**The Clap** 11.08
The clock upon the wall, has struck the midnight hour 13.15
**The Closer You Are** 40.01, 56.30
The closer you are 40.01, 56.30
The clouds are really cheap 18.06
The cosmos at large 36.04
**The Dangerous Kitchen** 36.06, 51.23
The dangerous kitchen, if it ain't one thing, it's another... 36.06, 51.23
**The Deathless Horsie** 32.05, 51.22
**The Downtown Talent Scout** 58.01
**The Duke Of Prunes** 2.02, 7.03
**The Duke Regains His Chops** 2.04
**The Ending Line** 73.05
**The Eric Dolphy Memorial Barbecue** 10.06, 55.27, 96.02
The essence of it is that, uhm, that if, if we get enough kids in America playing guitar all the same way 85.71
**The Evil Prince** 56.07
The first word in this song is "discorporate." It means "to leave your body." 4.09, 85.18, 85.39
**The Girl In The Magnesium Dress** 39.03, 62.07
**The Girl Wants To Fix Him Some Broth** 13.31
The girl wants to fix him some broth 13.31, 13.32
THE GRAND WAZOO   16
**The Grand Wazoo** 16.02, 64.22
**The Grand Wazoo (Think It Over)** 82.02
**The Groupie Routine** 51.09
**The Gumbo Variations** 8.05
The guy who came to see us, who was the staff producer at Verve, Tom Wilson, had other priorities 77.68
**The Handsome Cabin Boy** 64.17, 68.29, 72.07
The hotter the sound is, the more putrid it smells. 63.29
**The Idiot Bastard Son** 4.14, 7.05, 52.10, 85.23, 85.44
The idiot bastard son, the father's a Nazi in Congress today   4.14, 7.05, 52.10, 85.23, 85.44
**The Illinois Enema Bandit** 23.06, 59.24, 65.09, 70.11, 83.07, 84.02, 98.07
The Illinois enema bandit   59.24, 98.07
The kids are freaking out   58.01
**The Lad Searches the Night For His Newts** 13.30
The lad searches the night for his newts 13.30
**The Legend of the Golden Arches** 6.06
**The Legend of the Illinois Enema Bandit** 65.09
**The Little House I Used To Live In** 9.08
**The Little March** 58.09

**The M.O.I. American Pageant (2nd in a series of underground oratorios)** 2.10-15
**The Man From Utopia** 56.33
THE MAN FROM UTOPIA 36
**The Man From Utopia Meets Mary Lou** 36.07
The man with the woman head 21.08
The mating call of the adult male Mud Shark 91.34
**The Meek Shall Inherit Nothing** 34.14, 41.09, 80.04
THE MOFO PROJECT/OBJECT 77
THE MOFO PROJECT/OBJECT (fazedooh) 78
The Muffin Man is seated at the table 21.09
The mystery man came over, said "I'm out of sight" 18.05, 54.25, 55.03, 80.05, 81.10
The name of this song is "The Black Page #2" 95.20
The name of this song is "Bobby Brown Goes Down" 95.15
The name of this song is "Camarillo Brillo." 71.11
The name of this song is "Dupree's Paradise" 96.11
The name of this song is "San Bernardino" 95.27
The name of this song is "Stranded In The Jungle." 86.20
**The Nancy and Mary Music** 11.04
The next piece that we're going to play . . . Maybe I should tell you what we were doing 64.06
**The Orange County Lumber Truck** 10.10, 51.08, 57.06, 92.06
**The Orange County Lumber Truck (Part I)** 61.18
**The Orange County Lumber Truck (Part II)** 61.20
**The Original Group** 77.65
**The Perfect Stranger** 39.01
**The Phone Call/My Babe** 72.06
**The Pigs' Music** 63.26
The planet of my dreams 40.10
**The Purse** 75.06
**The Radio Is Broken** 36.04
The reason for this hearing is not to promote any legislation 44.09, 93.29
**The Rejected Mexican Pope Leaves The Stage** 61.07
The rejected Mexican pope leaves the stage 61.07
**The Return of the Son of Monster Magnet** 1.14, 77.14, 78.14
The Sanzini Brothers! 60.40
The ship is arriving too late, to save a drowning witch 54.09
**The $600 [six hundred dollar] Mud Shark Prelude** 91.33
The '60s [sixties] was really stupid 77.70, 78.24
The story of music of the Mothers is the story of a combination of what I knew about music 72.12
**The Story of Willie The Pimp** 68.31
**The Surgeon General, Doctor Koop** 53.07, 93.26
**The Torture Never Stops** 22.03, 23.14, 33.01, 51.16, 55.21, 55.24, 56.16, 70.13, 79.09, 79.13, 80.16, 86.07, 89.04
**The Torture Never Stops Original Version** 56.16
The tragic story of the three assholes 89.19
**The Uncle Meat Variations** 6.11

**The Way I See It, Barry** 3.01
The way I see it, Barry, this should be a very dynamite show 3.01, 85.29
**The Way The Air Smells**   95.08
The Whisky was the home base for Johnny Rivers 77.67
**The Wide Screen Erupts** 13.36
The word "beautiful" is used erroneously, but these are very beautiful people 77.43
**The World Will Be A Far Happier Place** 85.71
THE YELLOW SHARK 62
THEM OR US 40
**Them Or Us** 40.12
**Theme From "Bonanza"** 55.22
**Theme From Burnt Weeny Sandwich** 9.04
**Theme From Lumpy Gravy** 57.08, 85.59
**Theme From The 3rd Movement Of Sinister Footwear** 34.05
**Theme From The Bartok Piano Concerto #3** 57.19
Then we can sell them ladders 63.34
Then, from out of the corner from the stage, comes Roy Ralph Estrada 61.05
There are artists who do not write their own material 88.06
There is a ship arriving too late 80.08
**There Is No Heaven From Where Slogans Go To Die** 94.11
**There Is No Need** 77.71
There was a man 91.11
There will come a time when everybody who is lonely will be free to
sing and dance and love 4.16, 70.19, 84.05, 85.25, 85.46, 98.10
There's a big dilemma about my Big Leg Emma 23.11, 65.15
There's a bomb to blow your mommy up, a bomb for your daddy too 2.12
There's a green Chevy 51.15
There's a lady who's sure all that glitters is gold 55.28
There's a ship arriving too late to save a drowning witch 35.04
There's a story that, um, during one of your recording sessions 77.56
There's an ugly little weasel 'bout three-foot nine 53.17, 93.31
**There's No Lust In Jazz** 60.32
These executives have plooked the fuck out of me 29.06, 53.14, 56.19
They do know that we exist in Europe 77.59
They got lies so big 53.05
**They Made Me Eat It** 63.04
They were originally just called The Mothers 77.66
They're gonna clear out the studio 13.34, 59.36
They're really getting professional now in the dressing room... 58.22
THING-FISH 41
**Thing-Fish Intro** 93.27
**Things That Look Like Meat** 50.28
**Think It Over (some)/Think It Over (some more)** 73.08
**Thirteen** 59.25
**This Ain't CNN** 63.25
This album is not available to the public. 64.08

This girl is easy meat 30.02, 58.26, 71.04, 80.14, 81.06
This here song might offend you some, if it does it's because you're dumb 22.01, 59.14, 70.12, 86.05
This is a song, folks, about dental floss. 96.10
This is a song about the union, friends 36.08, 56.02
This is a song about vegetables. They keep you regular, they're real good for you. 2.05, 7.04, 91.09
This is a special request, hope you enjoy it 2.15, 7.11
This is a story, tell it quick as I can 70.15, 70.27
**This Is A Test** 69.02
This is a true story about a famous criminal from right around Chicago 23.06
**This Is All Wrong** 63.28
This is all wrong. 63.28
This is dedicated to the two guys in the crew who went to see the doctor today 54.14
**This Is Neat** 60.04
This is neat! 60.04
This is Paul Jackets, and tonight we're interviewing a very interesting guest 75.09
**This Is Phaze III** 63.01
This is Phaze III. 63.01
This is the CENTRAL SCRUTINIZER 28.01, 93.28
This is the CENTRAL SCRUTINIZER... again. Hi!...It's me again, the CENTRAL SCRUTINIZER. 28.09
**This Is the Show They Never See** 95.02
This is the story 'bout Bald-Headed John 29.04
This is underground psychedelic acid-rock freak-out music... 58.23
This is what I joined for. This I don't think is pertinent. 60.5
This little number is in thirteen... 59.25
**This Town Is A Sealed Tuna Sandwich (Prologue)** 13.04
**This Town Is A Sealed Tuna Sandwich (Reprise)** 13.07
This town we're in is just a Sealed Tuna Sandwich 13.04, 13.05, 13.07, 13.08
This, as you might have guessed, is the end of the movie 13.34
This, excuse me, the ending line 73.05
**Thou shalt have no other gods before Me** 88.03
**Thou shalt honor thy father and thy mother** 88.07
**Thou shalt keep holy the Sabbath day** 88.06
**Thou shalt not bear false witness against thy neighbor** 88.11
**Thou shalt not commit adultery** 88.09
**Thou shalt not covet the house of thy neighbor** 88.12
**Thou shalt not Kill** 88.08
**Thou shalt not make unto thee any graven image** 88.04
**Thou shalt not steal** 88.10
**Thou shalt not take the name of the Lord thy God in vain** 88.05
Three hundred years ago I thought I might get some sleep 17.05, 51.18, 55.07
**Tiger Roach** 64.08
**Time Is Money** 25.05, 65.30
Time is money … but space is a long, long time 25.05

**Times Beach II** 62.05
**Times Beach III** 62.13
**Tink Walks Amok** 36.03
TINSEL TOWN REBELLION 30
**Tinsel Town Rebellion** 30.11, 45.02, 67.12, 80.07, 93.30
**Tiny Sick Tears** 56.24
**Titties and Beer** 23.01, 37.02, 65.24, 67.07, 86.11, 89.13, 95.18
**Toads of the Short Forest** 10.04
TOKEN OF HIS EXTREME, A 97
**Token of My Extreme, A** 29.01, 52.01, 81.01, 97.11
**Tom Wilson** 77.69, 78.23
Tonight though I, I tell you one thing 37.01
Tonight we'd like to do a song about an important social problem: Disco. 71.15
Tonight you guys are going to try and figure out the pigs' music 63.26
**Too Ugly For Show Business** 50.25
**Torchum Never Stops** 41.05
**Torture Never Stops, The** 22.03, 23.14, 33.01, 51.16, 55.21, 55.24, 56.16, 70.13, 79.09, 79.13, 80.16, 86.07, 89.04
**Touring Can Make You Crazy** 13.10
**Tracy Is A Snob** 59.16
TRANCE-FUSION 79
**Trance-Fusion** 79.08
**Transylvania Boogie** 11.01, 61.13, 92.03
**Treacherous Cretins** 31.05
**Trouble Comin' Every Day** 1.12
**Trouble Every Day** 1.12, 45.03, 58.13, 77.12, 77.29, 77.52, 78.12, 78.15, 92.08, 93.09
**Truck Driver Divorce** 40.06, 56.22
Truck driver divorce, it's very sad 40.06, 56.22
**Trudgin' Across The Tundra** 83.04
**Tryin' To Grow A Chin** 26.13, 51.07, 59.32, 65.07, 86.06, 89.05
**Tuna Fish Promenade** 13.05
**Tunnel Into Muck, A** 63.33
Turn turn, turn turn, we're turning again 44.05, 59.28, 67.08, 93.11
**Tush Tush Tush** 52.01
**Twenty Small Cigars** 11.03
**25 [Twenty five] Hundred Signing Fee** 77.68
200 [Two hundred] MOTELS 13
**200** [Two hundred] **Motels Finale** 59.36, 91.17
**200** [Two hundred] **Years Old** 21.05, 93.18
**Two, Three, Four, One** 68.25
**Typical Sound Check** 60.03


**Ulterior Motive** 82.05
**Uncle Bernie's Farm** 2.12
**Uncle Frankie Show** 68.11, 75.11
UNCLE MEAT 6

**Uncle Meat** 52.17, 62.03, 81.04, 96.08, 97.01, 99.05
**Uncle Meat Film Excerpt Part I** 6.23
**Uncle Meat Film Excerpt Part II** 6.25
**Uncle Meat Variations, The** 6.11
**Uncle Meat: Main Title Theme** 6.01
**Uncle Remus** 18.08
**Uncle Rhebus** 94.07
**Undaunted, The Band Plays On** 61.08
**Underground Freak-Out Music** 58.23
**Underground oratorios** 2
UNDERSTANDING AMERICA 93
**Unfinished Ballet in Two Tableaux** 1.14, 77.14, 78.14
**Union Scale** 77.67
**Unit 2, Take 9** 85.54
Unit 2, take 9. The timp can play a little heavier out there 85.54
**Unit 3A, Take 3** 85.53
**Unit 9** 85.57
**Untouchables** 53.08
**Up and Down** 85.03


**Valarie/Valerie** 9.09, 87.18
**Valley Girl** 35.02, 67.13
Valley Girl, she's a Valley Girl 35.02, 67.13
**Variant I Processional March** 82.11
**Variations On Sinister #3** 50.18
**Variations On The Carlos Santana Secret Chord Progression** 32.01
**Venusian Time Bandits** 74.08
**Version Of Himself** 60.56
**Very Distraughtening** 3.13
**Very Nice Body, A** 63.06
**Village Inn** 68.04
**Village of the Sun** 19.04, 52.05, 96.14, 99.07
**Vicious Circle, A** 3.17
**Vito Rocks The Floor (Greek Out!)** 77.40
**Voice Of Cheese, The** 6.02


**Waffenspiel** 63.41
**Wait A Minute** 26.08
Wait a minute; we gotta get somethin' happenin' here 26.08
WAKA JAWAKA 15
**Waka/Jawaka** 15.04, 74.09
**Walking Zombie Music** 94.04
Watch me now, because the name of this song is "Conehead" 95.16
**Watermelon In Easter Hay** 29.09, 50.29, 66.06, 66.07, 89.24
**Watts Riot Demo / Fillmore Sequence** 78.29

WAZOO 82
We are . . . actually the same note, but . . . 63.24
**We Are Not Alone** 36.05
We are the other people 4.18, 7.02, 85.27, 85.48
We can get our strength up by making some music 63.39
**We Can Shoot You** 6.18
We could share a love 52.04
We got de talkin' shoes! We de MAMMY NUNS! 41.02
We gotta do two shows tonight? 60.36
We have now a special request, now you better leave the lights on onstage because we have to read this music, we've never played it before 52.14
We lived in a little room, man. 64.05
**We Made Our Reputation Doing It That Way** 72.12
We must say good-bye 34.02
We released a single from the album Ruben and The Jets 87.17
We will translate, as we go along, some of the more important facets of this particular piece 91.20
We would like to play for you "The Legend Of King Kong." 92.14
We'd like to perform for you now a tune known to the civilized world as "The Orange County Lumber Truck" 92.06
We'd like to play something from our new movie. 91.17
We'll play you our special number 92.13
We're gonna play another instrumental event for you 96.18
We're gonna put a little motor in 'em 63.35
WE'RE ONLY IN IT FOR THE MONEY 4
We're playin' in a tent, it's payin' the rent 40.02, 54.08, 67.04
We're shooting the uh, title sequence for Uncle Meat right now 6.23
**We're Turning Again** 44.05, 59.28, 67.08, 93.11
**We've Got To Get Into Something Real** 26.08
WEASELS RIPPED MY FLESH 10
**Weasels Ripped My Flesh** 10.11
**Wedding Dress Song** 64.16
**Wedding Dress Song/Handsome Cabin Boy** 68.29, 72.07
Weist scho i hab naufgeschaut und da ist's ganz dunkel 69.01
Welcome to the First Church of Appliantology! 29.01
**Welcome To The United States** 62.15
**Well** 60.22
Well . . . Ahem. In the dark Where all the fevers grow 97.05
Well I found out baby you told me a great big lie... 56.32
Well I'm about to get sick, from watchin' MTV 45.03
Well I'm about to get sick, from watchin' my TV 19.09, 55.25, 58.13, 77.29, 77.52, 78.15, 78.29, 92.08, 97.10
Well I'm about to get upset, from watching my TV 1.12, 77.12, 78.12, 93.09
Well it's contest time, ladies and gentlemen... 59.05
Well right about that time, people, a fur trapper 18.02
Well this is the story of a man who lived in Pistoria... 56.33

Well well well, now, dis de nasty sucker dat be respondable fo de enwhiffment o de origumal potium... 56.07
Well, operator? Hold for a minute, please 4.05, 85.14, 85.35
Well, Catholic girls, with the tiny little mustache... 59.3
Well, here we are in Boston, ladies and gentlemen 82.01
Well, I have been in you, baby 26.01
Well, I think what we're gonna do right now is make something up  96.13
Well, I'll give you the best example of why such a panel is a pure fiction and a pure fantasy 88.07
Well, I'm goin' to Chicago 72.08
Well, I'm lost in a whirlpool 64.02
Well, it's as simple as this: the PMRC goes to the record industry 88.04
Well, my dandruff is loose 17.04
Well, somebody called me anyway and I— Here I am 85.58
Well, the character I play is a great guy 60.53
Well, the next . . . Relax, ladies and gentlemen . . . I'll tell you what you're going to hear, that's "Billy The Mountain." 91.30
Well, this is the story of a man who lived in Utopia 36.07
Well, to the record industry it means a little bit more hope for their bill 88.11
Well, uh, my opinion is that it's probably the worst thing that has happened to songwriters 88.03
Well, yeah, well, oh yeah, she was a fine girl 30.01
Well, you see, at the time Freak Out! came out, there was no such thing as psychedelic music 77.54
Went on the road for a month touring 13.11
**Were We Ever Really Safe In San Antonio?** 50.12
What do you do? You join the Mothers and you end up working for Zappa! 60.57
What do you say we all go out and have a dinner  95.02
What do you think about the, uh, current state of rock and roll 77.58
What do you think's gonna be next, after psychedelic? 77.6
**What Ever Happened To All The Fun In The World** 26.06
What ever happened to all the fun in the world? 26.06
What is happenin' to me! 41.2
What key do you wanna do it in? 64.03
**What Kind Of Girl Do You Think We Are** 12.03, 86.18, 93.13
**What Kind Of Girl?** 53.16
**What The Fuck's Wrong With Her?** 85.60
What the? Heh heh heh 81.01
What was it like working with Tom Wilson? 77.69, 78.23
What wickedness id dis? 41.19, 56.06
**What Will This Evening Bring Me This Morning** 13.25
What will this evening bring me this morning 13.25
What will you do if we let you go home? 1.03, 7.08, 77.03, 77.62, 78.03, 91.18, 93.05
What you need is … Motherly love 72.02, 77.43
What, I'm supposed to kiss her?... 59.23
What's a girl like you, doin' in a place like this 12.03, 53.16, 86.18, 93.13
What's goin' on here? I thought we were gonna play a Rock and Roll concert. 68.24

**What's Happening Of The Universe** 85.70
What's it like when . . . when they play the piano? 63.04
**What's New In Baltimore?** 44.08, 45.06, 58.29
What's the thing that they's talkin' about everywhere? SEX 36.02, 67.06
What's the ugliest (OWW!) of your body? 70.20, 84.06
**What's The Ugliest Part Of Your Body?** 4.08, 4.17, 70.20, 84.06, 85.17, 85.26, 85.38, 85.47, 85.66
What's the ugliest part of your body? 4.08, 4.17, 85.17, 85.26, 85.38, 85.47
What's there to live for? Who needs the peace corps? 4.02, 55.05, 85.11, 85.32, 93.06
What's your name? I'm Martin Tickman 60.31
Whatcha need is Motherly love 77.43
Wheet! Wheet wheet! 68.08
When I won your love, I was very glad 1.06, 5.03, 68.17, 70.06, 72.11, 77.06, 78.06, 87.03
When I'm dancing with Deseri 5.04, 87.04
**When Irish Eyes Are Smiling** 55.18
When it feels natural 73.10
When it's perfect 73.01
**When No One Was No One** 50.08
**When The Lie's So Big** 53.05
When they first heard us, we were working at a club in Hollywood called the Whisky à Go-Go 77.55
**When Yuppies Go To Hell** 57.02
Where did they go? When did they come from? 16.01
**Where Is Johnny Velvet?** 58.11
**Where's Our Equipment?** 58.19
**Which One Is It?** 50.02
Whiff it, Boy! Whiff it good, now! 41.22
While I was down in W.D.C. 53.1
While the well-disciplined Ian Underwood plays selected fragments from Mozart's piano sonata in B-flat... 58.05
While we're at it, we have a sort of a cowboy song we'd like to do for ya 21.04
**While You Were Art II** 47.03
**While You Were Out** 31.04
While you WORK THE WALL 80.04
**Whipping [Whippin'] Post** 45.10, 40.14, 50.07, 50.21
**White Boy Troubles** 41.16
White juice on his beard, the booger man, get down... 56.26
**White Person** 59.10
**White Ugliness** 3.14
**Whitey (Prototype)** 69.10
**Who Are The Brain Police?** 1.03, 7.08, 77.03, 77.23, 77.31, 77.49, 77.62, 78.03, 78.16, 91.18, 93.05
Who came up with the name "Mothers of Invention"? 72.01
**Who Do You Think You Are?** 98.04
**Who Needs The Peace Corps?** 4.02, 55.05, 85.11, 85.32, 85.74, 93.06
Whoa, that's really great! Botulism on the hoof! 60.33

Whoever we are, wherever we're from 34.15, 51.24, 67.09, 93.25
**Why Does It Hurt When I Pee?** 28.07, 54.14
Why does it hurt when I pee? 28.07, 54.14
Why don't you -- see also Why don'tcha
**Why Don't You Like Me?** 53.09
Why don't you like me? 53.09
Why don't you sharpen it then    97.07
Why don't you strap on this here bunch of cardboard boxes, daddy-o 13.26
Why don't you take it down to C-sharp, Ernie? 26.11
**Why Don'tcha Do Me Right?**  2.09, 75.04
Why don'tcha do me right? 2.09, 75.04
**Why Johnny Can't Read** 33.04
Why not come over? 30.12, 80.10
**Why Not?** 63.34
**Wild Love** 26.17, 74.05, 79.02
**Willie The Pimp** 8.02, 12.06, 56.04
**Willie The Pimp, Story of** 68.31
**Wind Up Workin' In A Gas Station** 22.01, 59.14, 70.12, 86.05
**Winos Do Not March** 50.23
**Wistful Wit A Fist-Full** 41.20
Wo, are we movin' too slow? 18.08
Woaaaaaa-aaaaaah! SATAN? 57.03
**Wolf Harbor Movements I-V**   100.03-07
**Won Ton On** 41.22
**Wonderful Tattoo!** 69.13
**Wonderful Wino** 22.07, 60.18, 64.23, 91.27
Wooo! Looka-dat! A big ol' truck, 'n a box uh NODOZ 41.17
Work the wall, work the floor 34.14
**Working All The Live Long Day/ Chain Gang (Persuasions)** 91.02
**Worms From Hell** 90.04
**Worst Reviews** 60.55
Would ya b'lieve it 44.01, 93.21
**Would You Go All The Way?** 11.06, 86.16
**Would You Like A Snack?** 13.11
Would you like to come up here and sing with us? 58.11
**Wowie Zowie** 1.07, 77.07, 77.48, 78.07
Wowie zowie, your love's a treat 1.07, 77.07, 78.07
**WPLJ** 9.01, 45.08


**Xmas Values** 63.09

**Ya Hozna** 40.03
Yeah, I do have some last words 85.78
Years ago in Germany 10.01
Yes ... be hot ... and everybody workin' on it 10.05
Yes . . . I kind of miss him 63.06
Yes indeed, here we are! At Saint Alfonzo's Pancake Breakfast 18.03
Yes, ladies and gentlemen, coming to you direct from high atop the Konrad Adenauer Inn 60.06
Yes! I'm only fourteen, sickly 'n thin 65.07, 86.06
**Yo Cats** 44.07, 67.15
Yo cats, yo yo 44.07, 67.15
**Yo' Mama** 26.18
You always see the future by looking backwards, okay? 88.08
You are the girl 53.03
YOU ARE WHAT YOU IS 34
**You Are What You Is** 34.12, 41.07, 80.02
You are, are my desire 89.20
You are, you gotta tell me something 12.07
**You Call That Music?** 51.19, 56.11
You can be scared when it gets too real 73.04
YOU CAN'T DO THAT ON STAGE ANYMORE VOL. 1 51
YOU CAN'T DO THAT ON STAGE ANYMORE VOL. 2 52
YOU CAN'T DO THAT ON STAGE ANYMORE VOL. 3 54
YOU CAN'T DO THAT ON STAGE ANYMORE VOL. 4 56
YOU CAN'T DO THAT ON STAGE ANYMORE VOL. 5 58
YOU CAN'T DO THAT ON STAGE ANYMORE VOL. 6 59
**You Didn't Try To Call Me** 1.08, 5.09, 51.05, 77.08, 77.28, 77.44, 78.08, 78.18, 78.29, 86.09, 87.09
You didn't try to call me 1.08, 5.09, 51.05, 77.08, 77.44, 78.08, 86.09, 87.09
**You Got Your Armies** 60.34
You know as well as I do that cold light generation depends on your state of health and energy 63.37
You know how to do it? 98.05
You know I love you, baby, please don't go, well, well 60.22
You know, a lotsa people don't bother about their friends in the VEGETABLE KINGDOM 60.28
You know, sometimes in the middle of the night, you get to feeling uptight... 56.24
You know, today the church is in a terrible state... 56.17
You know, you know that reminds me of a real sad story 57.12
You know, you've heard those lines so many times 80.22
You know, your mama and your daddy 10.08, 56.03, 58.25
You-you-you-ooo, look like a dor-r-r-k 36.1
You may find me, baby 64.21
You might think my hat is funny, but I don't. 64.22
**You Never Know Who Your Friends Are** 94.06
You say there ain't no use in livin' 34.17, 51.26, 71.14
You surely must be trying to break this heart of mine 5.08, 87.08

**You There, With The Hard On!** 60.11
You thought he was a man, but he was a muffin  59.22
You took a chance, on Jumbo's love  34.19
You was a fool, oh Carol, you fool  54.11
You, you there with the hard-on!  60.11
You're a lonely little girl  4.15, 70.18, 84.04, 85.24, 85.45, 85.77
**You're Just Insultin' Me, Aren't You!** 63.36
You're just insulting me, aren't you?  63.36
**You're Probably Wondering Why I'm Here** 1.11, 7.07, 77.11, 77.21, 77.22, 78.11, 93.10
You're probably wondering why I'm here  1.11, 7.07, 77.11, 77.21, 78.11, 93.10
You're the old lady, from the society pages  34.06, 54.18
Your ethos, your pathos  30.10
**Your Mouth** 15.02
Your mouth is your religion  15.02
**Your Teeth and Your Shoulders and sometimes Your Foot Goes Like This**  96.11


**Zanti Serenade** 60.12
ZAPPA IN NEW YORK 23
Zappa is the best guitarist in the city  95.07
**Zeets** 71.08
**Zilofone** 78.30
**Zolar Czakl** 6.04
**Zomby Woof** 17.05, 51.18, 55.07
ZOOT ALLURES 22
**Zoot Allures** 22.08, 32.04, 40.06, 45.01, 50.05, 50.08, 54.17, 55.09, 66.03, 66.05, 70.22, 84.08


End of Title/First-Line Index

Transcription and Score Index

Numerical references are for the Zappa Family Trust numbered entries as used in the Catalogue section.

Individual song listings are for album number and track number. For example, the song "A Cold Dark Matter" will have the reference 79.04, which signifies album number 79 (Trance-Fusion) and track 4.

I. Published transcriptions authorized by Zappa or the Zappa Family Trust

a.

"DB [Down Beat] Music Workshop: Frank Zappa's 'Little House,'" *Down Beat* 36 no. 22 (30 October 1969): 30, 32-33.

from *Burnt Weeny Sandwich* (no. 9):

Manuscript source material for "The Little House I Used To Live In"      9.08

b.

*The Frank Zappa Songbook,* volume 1, arranged for piano by Ian Underwood. Los Angeles: Frank Zappa Music; Astoria NY: Big 3, 1973

| | | |
|---|---|---|
| pp. 11-29 | Brown Shoes Don't Make It | 2.14 / 7.01 |
| pp. 30-35 | Mother People | 4.18 / 7.02 |
| pp. 36-38 | Igor's Boogie | 9.02 |
| pp. 39-44 | Penis Dimension | 13.24 |
| pp. 45-51 | How Could I Be Should A Fool | 1.06 / 5.03 |
| pp. 52-56 | Let's Make The Water Turn Black | 4.13 |
| pp. 57-61 | Oh No | 10.09 |
| pp. 62-64 | America Drinks and Goes Home | 2.15 / 7.11 |
| pp. 65-68 | Son of Suzy Creamcheese | 2.13 |
| pp. 69-74 | Music for Electric Violin and Low-Budget Symphony Orchestra (two excerpts) | |
| pp. 75-83 | I'm Not Satisfied | 1.10 / 5.05 |
| pp. 84-89 | Mom and Dad | 4.04 |
| pp. 90-97 | Absolutely Free | 4.09 |
| pp. 98-102 | Uncle Meat | 6.01 |
| pp. 103-106 | The Idiot Bastard Son | 4.14 / 7.05 |
| pp. 107-112 | Little House I Used To Live in (piano introduction only) | 9.08 |

c.

*Frank Zappa Songbook,* arranged for piano by Ian Underwood. Cologne, West Germany: Amsco; Frankfurt: Melodie der Welt, 1982. (reprint of music previously published as *The Frank Zappa Songbook* [1973].)

| | | |
|---|---|---|
| pp. 7-23 | Brown Shoes Don't Make It | 2.14 / 7.01 |
| pp. 24-29 | Mother People | 4.18 / 7.02 |
| pp. 30-32 | Igor's Boogie | 9.02 |
| pp. 33-36 | Penis Dimension | 13.24 |
| pp. 37-43 | How Could I Be Should A Fool | 1.06 / 5.03 |
| pp. 44-48 | Let's Make The Water Turn Black | 4.13 |
| pp. 49-53 | Oh No | 10.09 |
| pp. 54-56 | America Drinks and Goes Home | 2.15 7.11 |
| pp. 57-62 | Son of Suzy Creamcheese | 2.13 |
| pp. 63-66 | Music for Electric Violin and Low-Budget Symphony Orchestra (two excerpts) | |
| pp. 67-73 | I'm Not Satisfied | 1.10 / 5.05 |
| pp. 74-79 | Mom and Dad | 4.04 |
| pp. 80-85 | Absolutely Free | 4.09 |
| pp. 86-88 | Uncle Meat | 6.01 |
| pp. 89-92 | The Idiot Bastard Son | 4.14 / 7.05 |
| pp. 93-97 | Little House I Used To Live in (piano introduction only) | 9.08 |

d.

Frank Zappa, *The Frank Zappa Guitar Book*, transcribed by Steve Vai. Los Angeles: Munchkin Music, distributed by Milwaukee, WI: Hal Leonard, 1982.

from *Shut Up 'n' Play Yer Guitar* (no. 31):

| | | |
|---|---|---|
| pp. 10-16 | five-five-FIVE | 31.01 |
| pp. 17-22 | Hog Heaven | 31.02 |
| pp. 23-43 | Shut Up 'N Play Yer Guitar | 31.03 |
| pp. 44-69 | While You Were Out | 31.04 |
| pp. 70-78 | Treacherous Cretins | 31.05 |
| pp. 79-89 | Heavy Duty Judy | 31.06 |
| pp. 90-105 | Soup 'N Old Clothes | 31.07 |

from *Shut Up 'n' Play Yer Guitar Some More* (no.32):

| | | |
|---|---|---|
| pp. 108-117 | Variations On The Carlos Santana Secret Chord Progression | 32.01 |

| | | |
|---|---|---|
| pp. 118-123 | Gee, I Like Your Pants | 32.02 |
| pp. 124-135 | The Deathless Horsie | 32.05 |
| pp. 136-152 | Shut Up 'N Play Yer Guitar Some More | 32.06 |
| pp. 153-158 | Pink Napkins | 32.07 |

from *Return of the Son of Shut Up 'n' Play Yer Guitar* (no.33):

| | | |
|---|---|---|
| pp.160-203 | Stucco Homes | 33.05 |

from *You Are What You Is* (no. 34):

| | | |
|---|---|---|
| pp. 206-212 | Theme From The 3rd Movement Of Sinister Footwear | 34.05 |

from Joe's Garage, Acts II and III (no. 29):

| | | |
|---|---|---|
| pp. 214-225 | Watermelon in Easter Hay | 29.09 |
| pp. 226-242 | Packard Goose | 29.08 |
| pp. 243-249 | Outside Now | 29.06 |
| pp. 250-268 | He Used To Cut The Grass | 29.07 |

from Sheik Yerbouti (no. 26):

| | | |
|---|---|---|
| pp. 270-274 | Sheik Yerbouti Tango | 26.11 |
| pp. 275-280 | Rat Tomago | 26.07 |
| pp. 281-290 | Mo' Mama (transcription of unreleased Zappa track) | |

from Zoot Allures (no. 22):

| | | |
|---|---|---|
| pp. 292-301 | Black Napkins | 22.02 |

e.

Mike Keneally, "Shut Up 'N' Learn This Lesson," Guitar Player 29, no. 10 (October 1995): 86-91

pp.88-89    Penguin in Bondage (guitar solo only)        19.01
[pp.90-91   Excerpts from "five-five-FIVE," "Hog Heaven," "Shut Up 'N' Play Yer Guitar," and "Heavy Duty Judy," all quoted from transcriptions previously published in The Frank Zappa Guitar Book (1982)]

f.

Frank Zappa, *Hot Rats*, transcribed by Andy Aledort. Milwaukee, WI: Hal Leonard, 2001.

| pp. 9-13 | Peaches En Regalia | 8.01 |
| pp. 14-29 | Willie The Pimp | 8.02 |
| pp. 30-42 | Son Of Mr. Green Genes | 8.03 |
| pp. 43-44 | Little Umbrellas | 8.04 |
| pp. 45-64 | The Gumbo Variations | 8.05 |
| pp. 65-71 | It Must Be A Camel | 8.06 |

g.

Frank Zappa, *Over-nite Sensation,* transcribed by Paul Pappas. Milwaukee, WI: Hal Leonard, 2010.

| pp. 6-16 | Camarillo Brillo | 17.01 |
| pp. 17-26 | I'm The Slime | 17.02 |
| pp. 27-37 | Dirty Love | 17.03 |
| pp. 38-52 | Fifty-Fifty | 17.04 |
| pp. 53-73 | Zomby Woof | 17.05 |
| pp. 74-85 | Dinah-Moe Humm | 17.06 |
| pp. 86-102 | Montana | 17.07 |

h.

Frank Zappa, *Apostrophe (')*, transcribed by Andy Aledort. Milwaukee, WI: Hal Leonard, 2003.

| pp. 7-10 | Don't Eat The Yellow Snow | 18.01 |
| pp. 11-22 | Nanook Rubs It | 18.02 |
| pp. 23-31 | St. Alfonzo's Pancake Breakfast | 18.03 |
| pp. 32-38 | Father O'Blivion | 18.04 |
| pp. 39-48 | Cosmik Debris | 18.05 |
| pp. 49-53 | Excentrifugal Forz | 18.06 |
| pp. 54-70 | Apostrophe' | 18.07 |
| pp. 71-77 | Uncle Remus | 18.08 |
| pp. 78-94 | Stink-Foot | 18.09 |

i.

Frank Zappa, *One Size Fits All*, transcribed by Addi Booth. Milwaukee, WI: Hal Leonard, 2011.

| pp. 6-39 | Inca Roads | 20.01 |
| pp. 40-49 | Can't Afford No Shoes | 20.02 |
| pp. 50-62 | Sofa No. 1 | 20.03 |
| pp. 63-95 | Po-Jama People | 20.04 |
| pp. 96-117 | Florentine Pogen | 20.05 |
| pp. 119-121 | Evelyn, A Modified Dog | 20.06 |
| pp. 122-142 | San Ber'dino | 20.07 |
| pp. 143-171 | Andy | 20.08 |
| pp. 172-180 | Sofa No. 2 | 20.09 |

II. Scores

a.

*Zappa!* (a special issue from the publishers of Keyboard and Guitar Player magazines, 1992)

pp. 66-72    The Girl in the Magnesium Dress (piano part only)    62.07

b.

Scores used on Zappa's albums (*Orchestral Favorites* (no. 27), *London Symphony Orchestra* volumes 1 and 2 (nos. 38 and 48) complete, *The Perfect Stranger* (no. 39, tracks 1, 2 and 4), *The Yellow Shark* (no. 62 tracks 4, 18 and 19) and *Lather* (no.65)) available for rental through Schott Music:

| Bob In Dacron | 48.02 |
| Bogus Pomp | 48.01 |
| | |
| Dupree's Paradise | 39.04 |
| Envelopes | 38.03 |
| Get Whitey | 62.18 |
| G-Spot Tornado | 62.19 |
| Mo 'N Herb's Vacation | 38.04-06 |
| Naval Aviation In Art? | 39.02 |

| | |
|---|---|
| Outrage at Valdez | 62.04 |
| Pedro's Dowry (chamber) | 27.02, 65.19 |
| Pedro's Dowry (orch.) | 38.02 |
| | |
| The Perfect Stranger | 39.01 |
| Sad Jane | 38.01 |
| Strictly Genteel | 48.03 |

Inquiries for additional scores and other notated materials (including the lead sheets for *Freak Out!* [no. 1] ) may be made in writing to Zappa's music publishing firm Munchkin Music at munchkinmusic@zappa.com.

Chronological Index

Date entries follow the format year/month/date (YYYYMMDD).

Numerical references are for the Zappa Family Trust numbered entries as used in the Catalogue section.

Individual date listings are for album number and track number. For example, the date 19650325 means March 25, 1965, and the references 68.10 and 75.08 are to track 10 of *Mystery Disc* (no. 68) and to track 8 of *Joe's XMASage* (no. 75)

As stated at length in the Introduction, this Chronological Index is something new and quite risky in the field of Zappa discography. Since 1967, recorded performances from the past have been bundled into collage-likecompositions and album collections. When the source recordings are rearranged in chronological order, what sort of historical or biographical survey emerges? Certainly, Zappa's evolution and growth as a composer will be suggested. But also, some concerts, at least in part, may be reconstructed from the various official Zappa releases (which offer superior sound, in contrast to the often grainy, even coarse-sounding audience recordings).

One caveat regarding the daes used in this index: dating historical performances was not one of Zappa's high priorities -- his correction of dates for *You Can't Do That On Stage Anymore* volume 1 in the booklet for *YCDTOSA* volume 2 is his tacit admission of that. To obtain many dates of concert recordings made and used by Zappa, I have had to use several collector/researcher sites, especially the Information Is Not Knowledge website on globalia.net. (as acknowledged in full in the Acknowledgements section). These efforts have been made mostly from private collections of concert audience recordings, documents, and ephemera. Yet few if any of these intrepid collectors/researchers have had opportunities to check their data to the documents and tapes maintained by the Zappa family. Therefore, the Chronological Index is approximate, but it may also shine some light. (For an alternate chronological index that covers every documented Zappa recording [including performances not released through the Zappa Family Trust], see the "chronology" tab-portion of the Information Is Not Knowledge website http://globalia.net/donlope/fz/chronology/index.html, accessed June 12, 2015)


19580000 (home recording): 64.01

19581200-19590100 (junior college recording): 64.02

19610000-19620000 (home recording): 64.03-05

19621200 (home recording): 75.01

19630000: 75.02, 75.06, 75.09

19630100 (studio recording): 68.13

19630300 (studio recording): 64.10

19630400 (studio recording): 87.21

19630519 (Mount St. Mary College college concert): 64.06

19630600 (studio recording): 75.03

19630700 (studio recording): 75.04

19640000 (Saints 'N Sinners club, Ontario, CA): 68.09, 75.05

19640000 (*Run Home Slow* soundtrack sessions): 64.09, 64.11, 64.13, 68.01-02

19640100 (studio recording) : 64.07

19640200-19641200 (studio recording): 64.14, 68.12, 85.59

19640801 (Studio Z recording): 68.03

19640900-19641200 (Studio Z recording): 64.08, 64.12, 68.06-08, 68.12

19641000 (Studio Z recording): 68.11, 75.11

19650000 (Village Inn club, Sun Village, CA): 68.04-05

19650000 (studio recording): 72.02-05

19650325 (studio recording): 68.10, 75.08

19650500 (The Broadside club, Pomona CA): 68.14-15, 72.06-08

1965 Fillmore West  see:  19660624-25

19650900 (studio recording): 78.29

19650000-19660000 (studio recording): 72.09-11

19660100 (rehearsal studio): 68.16-17

19660309-12 (*Freak Out!* sessions): 1 complete, 7.06-08, 7.10, 77.01-41, 77.48-53, 77.62-64, 78.01-22, 78.25-28, 78.30-31, 93.01, 93.04-05, 93.09-10

19660624 or 25 (Fillmore, San Francisco, CA): 58.01, 68.18-19

19660625 (Fillmore, San Francisco, CA): 77.43-47, 78.29

19661112-15 (*Absolutely Free* sessions): 2 (complete), 7.01, 7.03, 7.04, 7.09, 7.11, 93.02, 93.07

19670213, 19670314-16 (Capitol sessions for *Lumpy Gravy*): 3, 85

19670700 (WRVR radio interview, New York City): 77.56, 77.58-59, 77.61

19670721 (*Cruising With Ruben & the Jets* session): 87.18

19670724 (*Cruising With Ruben & the Jets* session): 87.16

19670800-19670900 (*We're Only In It For The Money* sessions): 4, 7.02, 7.05, 64.19, 72.01, 72.12, 85, 93.03, 93.06, 93.08, 94.08

19670923 (Royal Albert Hall, London, England) : 6.7

19671000 (studio sessions for *Lumpy Gravy*, *We're Only In It For The Money*, *Uncle Meat*, and *Civilization Phaze III*): 3, 4, 6, 63 (tracks 1,3, 4, 6, 8,10, 12-14, 16, 18, 20, 22, 24, 26, 29-37, 39), 85

19671001 (Copenhagen, Denmark): 6.16, 58.19

19671000-19680200 (studio sessions): 64.15-18, 85.60

19671100 (*Uncle Meat* studio sessions): 6

19671113 (Detroit interviews) : 77.54-55, 77.57, 77.60, 85.63

19671200 - 19680200 (studio sessions for *Cruising with Ruben & the Jets*, *Uncle Meat*, and *Weasels Ripped My Flesh*): 5, 6, 10.07, 10.09, 68.27, 68.29, 68.34, 87

19680419 (Fillmore East, NYC, NY): 68.20

19680518 (Miami [FL] Pop Festival): 6.31

19680723 (Whisky a Go-Go, Los Angeles, CA): 58.17

19680825 (Vancouver, BC, Canada): 92 complete

19680900 (studio session): 94.09

19681025 (Royal Festival Hall, London, England): 10.03, 10.10, 61 complete, 68.21-26, 68.28

19681127 (KPPC radio interview, Pasadena, CA): 87.20

19680000-19690000 (*Burnt Weeny Sandwich* studio sessions): 9.01-02, 9.04-05, 9.07-09

19690000 (general recordings): 64.20-22, 85.70

19690000 (Greyhound tour bus): 58.07, 58.15

19690131 (WMEX radio interview, Boston): 87.17

19690200: 94.06

19690207-08 (Thee Image, Miami, FL): 10.04, 58.06, 58.21, 58.23, 68.32

19690207-08 (Criteria Studios, Miami, FL) 58.10, 58.24, 68.33, 68.35

19690213 (FZ: The Bronx, NYC; NY GigList: New Haven, CT): 10.05, 51.15, 56.24, 58.11-13

19690214 (New York City, NY): 56.11, 58.02-03, 58.08-09, 58.14, 58.20, 94.11

19690216 (Stratford, CT): 68.30, 94.12

19690221 (lecture, The New School, New York City, NY) : 85.51, 87.17

19690300 (Providence, RI): 58.22

19690302 (Philadelphia, PA): 10.01

19690400: 51.08, 51.19-20

19690530 (Birmingham, England): 10.11

19690600 (A&R Studios, NYC, sessions including *Weasels Ripped My Flesh*): 10.06, 58.25

19690606 (Royal Albert Hall, London, England): 58.05, 94.01-04

19690700 (studio sessions used on *Hot Rats*, *Burnt Weeny Sandwich*, *Weasels Ripped My Flesh*, and *Chunga's Revenge*): 8, 9.03, 9.06, 10.02, 11.03

19690708 (Boston, MA): 58.04, 58.18, 94.07

19690800 (studio sessions originally towards *Hot Rats* and *Weasels Ripped My Flesh*) : 8, 10.04, 10.08, 18.06, 24.03, 64.28, 68.31

19690910 (photo shoot, Sunset Hollywood): 58.16

19700000 (undated tour tape): 51.21 (spoken quote only)

19700300 (sessions originally for *Chunga's Revenge*): 11.07, 18.09, 64.30

19700301 (Zappa home basement): 74.07

19700400 (tour tape): 51.01

19700705 (Minneapolis, MN): 11.04

19700828 (*Chunga's Revenge* sessions): 11.01-02, 11.05-06, 11.08-10, 93.12

19700900 (unspecified tour tapes): 60.03-04, 60.08-10, 60.27-33, 60.36

19700917 (Spokane, WA): 60.01, 60.05-06

19700900-19701000 (Jacksonville, FL): 59.01

19700919 (FZ: Edmonton, Alberta, Canada; Giglist: Vancouver): 60.02, 60.35

19700921 (probably Portland, OR): 60.07

19701009 (Tallahassee, FL): 60.21

19701023 (Buffalo NY): 60.11

19701105-07 (San Francisco, CA): 60.34, 60.49

19701129 (London, England): 60.38

19710100 (undated tour tape): 60.47

19710118 (Kensington Palace Hotel, England): 60.41, 60.46, 60.48

19710119 (Kensington Palace Hotel, England): 60.50

19710100-0300 (*200 Motels* filming): 13 complete, 60.51-57

19710521 (Chicago, IL): 94.05

19710605-06 (*Fillmore East June 1971* live album concerts): 12 complete, 59.13, 60.17, 60.37, 60.39-40, 60.42-43, 93.13

19710606 (Fillmore East, New York City, NY, second night): 60.22-26

19710807 (*Just Another Band From L.A.* live album concert, UCLA, Los Angeles, CA): 14 complete, 51.09, 59.35-36, 60.13

19711011 (Carnegie Hall, New York City, NY): 91 complete, 94.13

19711022 (KBEY-FM radio interview, Kansas City, MO): 77.42, 85.56

19711210 (Rainbow Theatre, London, England): 51.02-03, 54.24, 60.12, 60.14-16. 60.18-20

19720000 (undated recordings): 33.06, 94.10

19720300 (rehearsal recordings): 73 complete

19720400-0500 (*Waka/Jawaka* and *The Grand Wazoo* studio sessions): 15 complete, 16 complete, 18.08, 64.23, 74.09

19720900 (unspecified tape): 65.05

19720924 (Boston, MA): 82 complete

19721027 (Montreal, Quebec, Canada): 76.01, 76.04, 76.07

19721101 (Waterbury, CT): 76.06

19721107 (Electric Ladyland studio, New York City, NY): 18.07

19721110 (Philadelphia, PA): 76.02

19721111 (Washington, DC): 76.05, 83.04

19721202 (Kansas City, MO): 76.03

19730319 (studio session): 65.06

1973000-0500 (*Over-Nite Sensation* sessions): 17 complete, 67.11, 93.14, 93.16, 93.19

19730403 (studio session): 64.27

19730404 (studio session): 64.25

19730526 (*Apostrophe* session): 18.05

19730625 (Sydney, Australia): 59.07, 83.08

19730700-1200 (*Apostrophe* sessions): 18.01-04, 22.07

19730823 (Helsinki, Finland): (early show) 96.05-09, 96.13, 96.17, 96.19   (late show) 96.18

19730824 (Helsinki, Finland): 96.01-04, 96.10-12, 96.14-16, 96.24

19731207-12 (*Roxy and Elsewhere* live album concerts, Los Angeles, CA): 19.01-07, 19.10, 57.05, 99 complete

19731212 (Roxy, Los Angeles, CA): 51.12-13, 54.15

1973-1974 (undated studio session): 64.24

19740508 (Edinboro, PA): 19.08-09

19740511 (Chicago IL): 19.01

19740827 (KCET television taping, Los Angeles, CA): 81.01, 81.03-05, 83.07-11, 97 complete

19740922 (Helsinki, Finland): 53 complete

19740925 (Gothenburg, Sweden): 26.10

19740926 (Paris, France): 83.01

19741001 (Basel, Switzerland): 74.08

19741108 (Passaic, NJ): 51.10-11, 56.25-26, 83.02

19741200 (*Lather* sessions): 65.01, 65.12, 65.21, 65.27, 65.30

19741200-19750400 (*One Size Fits All* and *Lather* sessions): 20 complete, 24.04, 25.02, 25.03, 25.04, 25.05, 25.06, 40.10, 93.22

19750100-0200 (*Lather* sessions): 24.01, 24.02, 65.03

19750520-21 (*Bongo Fury* live album concerts, Austin TX): 21 complete, 56.16, 93.18

19750825 (rehearsal) 98.01-04, 98.07, 98.09-10, 98.13-14

19750900 (rehearsal) 98.05-06, 98.08, 98.11-12, 98.15

19750918-19 (Royce Hall, UCLA, Los Angeles CA): 24.01, 27 complete, 30.02 (middle section), 65.02, 65.11, 65.19, 65.22, 65.26, 74.01-03, 83.03, 83.09

19751026 (Hempstead NY): 22.06

19751101 (Williamsburg VA): 84 complete

19751103 (Philadelphia PA): 59.14

19760000 (*Lather* sessions): 65.10, 65.17, 65.25, 65.30

19760106 (pre-tour rehearsal): 70.27

19760120 (Sydney, Australia) : 70.01-26

19760203 (Osaka, Japan): 22.02, 22.08, 32.04, 54.16-17, 65.03, 74.06

19760205 (Tokyo, Japan): 70.06

19760229 (Copenhagen, Denmark): 59.11

19760500-0600 (*Zoot Allures* and *Lather* sessions): 22.01, 22.03-05, 22.09, 24.03, 25.01, 25.07, 41.05, 41.14, 65.23, 67.02, 93.15, 93.17

19761029 (Philadelphia PA): 86 complete

19761226-29 (*Lather* and *Zappa in New York* live album concerts, New York CIty, NY): 23 complete, 65.13, 65.16

19761227 (*Lather* live portions concert, New York CIty, NY): 65.20

19761228 (*Lather* live portions concert, New York CIty, NY): 65.14, 65.15, 65.18

19761229 (*Lather* live portions concert, New York CIty, NY): 59.27, 65.09, 65.24, 67.07

19770100-0200 (*Lather* session): 65.07

19770125 (Neunkirchen am Brand, near Nuremburg, West Germany): 59.10

19770216 (London, England): 65.08

19770217 (London, England): 32.07, 65.04, 65.28

19771028-31 (*Baby Snakes* filming, New York City, NY): 37.02, 37.06-07, 95 complete

19771028 (*Baby Snakes* filming, New York City, NY): 79.02

19771029 (early) (*Baby Snakes* filming, New York City, NY): 37.04,

19771030 (*Baby Snakes* filming, New York City, NY): 26.16, 37.05, 67.14

19771031 (*Baby Snakes* filming, New York City, NY): 26.05, 37.03, 59.02, 59.08, 59.32

19780000 (studio session): 64.26

19780100-0200 (*Sheik Yerbouti* sessions): 26.04, 26.09, 26.13, 26.14, 67.01

19780125 (London, England): 26.01, 26.02, 89.16-18, 89.28-29

19780126 (London, England): 89.09, 89.12-15, 89.19-22, 89.25-17

19780127 (London, England): 26.03, 89.01-02, 89.24

19780215 (Berlin, West Germany): 26.07, 26.11

19780224 (Eppelheim, West Germany): 83.06

19780225 (Neunkirchen am Brand, near Nuremburg, West Germany): 51.16

19780228 (London, England): 26.12, 37.01, 26.15, 26.17, 26.18, 74.05, 89.03-08, 89.10-11, 89.23

19780300 (studio session): 74.04

19780430 (studio session): 74.10

19781013 (Passaic NJ): 71.14

19781021 (*Saturday Night Live*, NBC television, New York City, NY): 71.15

19781027(early) (New York City, NY): 30.09, 34.05, 71.04-05, 71.10-12

19781028 (New York City, NY): 56.12, 71.07

19781030 (WPIX radio interview, New York City, NY): 71.16

19781031 (New York City, NY): 56.01, 59.17, 59.23, 59.25-26, 59.29, 59.33, 59.37, 71.01-06, 71.13

19790000 (unspecified live tapes): 31.04, 33.05

19790217 (London, England): 31.03, 31.05, 33.04

19790218 (early) (London, England): 30.15
19790218 (late) (London, England): 30.03, 30.14, 30.15, 32.02, 32.06, 51.06-07, 51.14, 57.23, 59.03

19790219 (London, England): 30.13, 32.03, 32.05, 33.02

19790321 (Eppelheim, West Germany): 79.06, 83.05

19790327 (Wiesbaden, West Germany): 50.26

19790331 (Munich, West Germany): 50.10

19790400-0600 (*Joe's Garage Acts I-III* sessions): 28 complete, 29 complete, 67.10, 93.28

19800200 (studio session): 64.29

19800429 (Upper Darby, PA): 30.02 (opening), 34.07, 34.19

19800508 (New York City, NY): 57.09

19800700-0900 (*You Are What You Is* sessions): 30.01, 34.01-05, 34.06, 34.08-18, 34.20, 67.03, 93.23, 93.25

19800703 (Munich, West Germany): 51.05

19801016 (Austin, TX): 36.06

19801017 (Dallas, TX): 30.12

19801018 (Tulsa, OK): 31.02

19801025 (Buffalo NY): 80 complete

19801030 (New York City, NY): 33.01

19801115 (Carbondale, IL): 30.08, 36.09

19801116 (Madison, WI): 59.05

19801203 (Salt Lake City): 59.16, 59.18

19801205 (early) (Berkeley, CA): 30.04, 30.10, 30.11, 30.12, 33.03

19801205 (late) (Berkeley, CA): 30.05, 30.06, 30.07, 30.10, 30.11, 30.12, 31.06, 41.04, 93.30

19801211 (Santa Monica, CA): 30.02 (closing), 30.10, 31.07, 32.01, 41.04, 59.04, 59.09, 59.12, 59.34

19810700-19820200 (*Ship Arriving Too Late To Save A Drowning Witch* and *Thing-Fish* sessions): 35.01-03, 35.05, 40.04, 41.07-09, 41.17, 67.13

19810900-19820700 (unspecified sessions): 44.01, 44.06, 93.21

19811031 (New York City, NY): 51.24-26, 54.18-21, 81.02, 81.06, 83.07

19811115 (Owings Mills, MD): 40.05, 44.08

19811117 (New York, NYC): 40.06, 40.07, 41.10

19811121 (Champaign, IL): 44.08

19811127 (Chicago, IL): 36.11

19811128 (Minneapolis MN): 40.07

19811207 (Salt Lake City, UT): 50.05, 50.28

19811210 (Berkeley, CA): 44.08, 50.25

19811211 (Santa Monica, CA): 35.04, 35.06, 40.14, 44.05, 67.08, 93.11

19811212 (San Diego, CA): 40.14, 50.01, 50.24

19820000 (*The Man From Utopia* sessions): 36.01-.5, 36.07-.08, 36.10, 67.06, 93.24

19820500-0700 (unspecified live tape): 40.06

19820511 (Copenhagen, Denmark): 50.15

19820521 (Cologne, West Germany): 50.08, 50.20

19820522 (Duesseldorf, West Germany): 50.31

19820528 (St. Etienne, France): 47.07

19820530 (Cap d'Agde, France): 54.17, 54.24

19820601 (Bordeaux, France): 50.11

19820611 (Frankfurt, West Germany): 40.08, 50.16, 58.26-37

19820619 (London, England): 40.09, 50.04

19820622 (Metz, France): 57.17

19820623 (Boeblingen, West Germany): 40.05

19820624 (Zurich, Switzerland): 50.13

19820626 (Munich, West Germany): 40.07, 50.02, 57.20-21, 58.26-37

19820701 (Geneva, Switzerland): 58.26-38

19820703 (Bolzano, Italy): 40.12, 54.09, 58.26-37

19820705 (Genoa, Italy): 41.02

19820707 (Milan, Italy): 50.27, 51: 17-18

19820708 (Pistoia, Italy): 50.32, 51.27-28, 57.08, 57.33-34

19820709 (Rome, Italy): 56.18

19820714 (Palermo, Italy): 51.04, 54:22-23

19830112-14 (*London Symphony Orchestra* sessions): 38 complete

19840000 (*Them Or Us* and *Thing-Fish* studio sessions): 40.01-.03, 40.11, 40.13, 41.01-.3, 41.06, 41.11-13, 41.15-16, 41.18-22, 67.04-05, 93.20, 93.27

19840000 (overdubbing studio sessions): 4, 5, 85

19840110-11 (*The Perfect Stranger* Paris studio sessions): 39.01-02, 39.04

19840200-0400 (Synclavier sessions for *The Perfect Stranger* and *Francesco Zappa*): 39.03, 39.05-07, 42 complete

19840811 (Madison, WI): 50.18

19840816 (Jones Beach Theatre, Wantagh, NY): 50.29

19840824 (Detroit): 56.29-32

19840825 (New York City, NY): 67.09, 79.05

19840826 (New York City, NY): 51.21-23, 54.07, 59.20, 67.12

19840924-25 (London, England): 56.07, 56.22

19840925 (London, England): 45.01, 45.03, 50.07

19841026 (Providence RI): 45.01, 79.10

19841028 (Amherst MA): 45.09, 56.10

19841110 (Upper Darby, PA): 45.06, 50.03, 56.19

19841123 (Chicago IL): 45.02, 50.22, 54.02-04, 54.08, 54.10-14, 54.22, 59.19, 59.21-22

19841125 (Atlanta GA): 50.06, 50.14, 50.21

19841130 (Sunrise FL): 50.17, 50.19

19841201 (St. Petersburg, FL): 45.03-04, 45.09, 56.29-32

19841204 (Memphis TN): 50.23, 79.03

19841210 (San Antonio TX): 50.12

19841217 (Seattle WA): 54.05-06, 54.09, 54.25, 79.12, 79.14

19841218 (Vancouver BC, Canada): 45.02, 45.04-05, 45.09, 50.30, 56.02, 56.13

19841220 (Portland OR): 50.09, 56.22, 56.27

19841223 (Universal City, CA): 45.06-10, 54.01, 54.03-06, 59.24

19850000 (*Frank Zappa Meets the Mothers of Prevention* sessions): 44.02-04, 44.07, 44.10, 67.15, 88.03-13

19850919 (U.S. Capitol, Washington DC, hearing): 44.09, 88.01, 93.29

19860000 (*Jazz From Hell* and *Feeding The Monkies At Ma Mansion* Synclavier sessions): 47.01-06, 47.08, 90 complete

19860000 (MTV television interview) 77.69-70, 78.23-24

19860214 (Maryland State Legislature, Annapolis MD): 88.02

19860308 (*Playboy* magazine interview, Utility Muffin Research Kitchen): 77.71

19880209 (Washington DC): 53.02-05, 53.17, 57.02-03, 93.31

19880210 (Washington DC): 57.20

19880212 (Upper Darby, PA): 57.14, 59.30

19880213 (Upper Darby, PA): 53.09, 53.13

19880214 (Upper Darby, PA): 55.20

19880220 (Boston MA): 57.01

19880223 (Poughkeepsie NY: 55.25-26

19880225 (Pittsburgh PA): 55.23, 57.18

19880226 (Royal Oak MI): 53.07, 53.12, 93.26

19880228 (Royal Oak MI): 55.27

19880301 (Muskegon MI): 53.10-11, 53.16

19880303 (Chicago IL): 53.12, 57.04-06

19880303-04 (Chicago IL): 59.31

19880312 (Burlington VT): 57.24

19880316 (Providence RI): 53.08

19880317 (Binghamton NY): 55.18-19

19880319 (Allentown PA): 55.07, 57.21, 79.04, 79.11

19880320 (Hackensack NJ): 55.24

19880323 (Towson MD): 59.06, 59.15, 59.28

19880416 (Brighton, England): 55.09, 79.07

19880418 (London, England): 57.11

19880419 (London, England): 53.14, 55.21, 55.22, 57.07, 79.01

19880422 (Wuerzburg, West Germany): 55.01-03, 55.05-06, 55.13

19880426 (Lund, Sweden): 57.23

19880501 (Stockholm, Sweden): 79.09

19880503 (Rotterdam, the Netherlands): 55.08, 57.08, 57.19

19880508 (Vienna, Austria): 53.15, 55.28, 57.10, 79.15

19880509 (Munich, West Germany): 53.06, 55.04, 79.16

19880513 (Bilbao, Spain): 57.14-15

19880515 (Seville, Spain): 57.25

19880518 (Montpelier, France): 55.17

19880523 (Strasbourg, France): 55.10-11

19880524 (Stuttgart, West Germany): 53.01, 55.14, 57.13, 57.15-16, 79.08

19880525 (Mannheim, West Germany): 57.22

19880528 (Linz, Austria): 55.15-16

19880605 (Modena, Italy): 57.17

19880607 (Rome, Italy): 57.09

19880609 (Genoa, Italy): 59.35, 79.13

19910000 (speaking studio sessions for *Civilization Phase III*): 63.25, 63.28-29, 63.35-37

19910700 (*Everything Is Healing Nicely* studio sessions): 69 complete

19910000-19930000 (*Dance Me This*): 100 complete

19920000 (music studio sessions for *Civilization Phase III*) : 63 (tracks 2, 5, 7, 9, 11, 15, 17, 19, 21, 23, 27, 38, 40, 41)

19920917-28 (*The Yellow Shark* live album concerts): 62 complete

19930300 (*BBC Late Show* interview with Nigel Leigh, Utility Muffin Research Kitchen, Los Angeles CA) : 77.65-68

END OF CHRONOLOGICAL INDEX

About the Librarian of the group:

Edward Komara is the Crane Librarian of Music at the State University of New York at Potsdam. Previously he was the Music Librarian/Blues Archivist at the University of Mississippi. His chief publications have been about the blues, most recently *100 Books Every Blues Fan Should Own* (with Greg Johnson; Rowman and Littlefield, 2014) and *The Road to Robert Johnson* (Hal Leonard Corporation, 2007). He has also published essays about jazz musician Charlie Parker, graphic novelist Dave Sim, and our hero Frank Zappa.

Scott Parker is an author and musician from Newtown, CT. His books include the acclaimed *Recordings Of Frank Zappa* series, as well as books chronicling the work of artists as diverse as The Who and The Monkees. He is also the host of ZappaCast, the world's premier Frank Zappa podcast. He lives n Connecticut with his wife and daughter.

14840971R00199

Printed in Great Britain
by Amazon.co.uk, Ltd.,
Marston Gate.